THE NÉMIROVSKY QUESTION

THE NÉMIROVSKY QUESTION

The Life, Death, and Legacy of a Jewish Writer
in Twentieth-Century France

SUSAN RUBIN SULEIMAN

Yale

UNIVERSITY PRESS

Yale University Press books may be purchased in quantity for
educational, business, or promotional use. For information,
please e-mail sales.press@yale.edu (U.S. office) or sales@yaleup.co.uk
(U.K. office).

Excerpts from Irène Némirovsky, *Le vin de solitude*, are quoted with
the permission of Albin Michel Publisher, Paris.

An earlier version of chapter 1 appeared in *Yale French Studies*,
no. 121 (2012).

Set in Janson Text type by Integrated Publishing Solutions.
Printed in the United States of America.

Library of Congress Control Number: 2016941798
ISBN 978-0-300-17196-9 (cloth : alk. paper)

A catalogue record for this book is available from the British Library.

This paper meets the requirements of ANSI/NISO Z39.48-1992
(Permanence of Paper).

10 9 8 7 6 5 4 3 2 1

To Emma, Pablo, Alexander, and Nessa

To ask oneself about Jewish identity is already to have lost it. But it is to hold on to it still, for otherwise one would not be asking. Between that *already* and that *still* is located the limit, stretched like a tightrope on which the Judaism of Western Jews ventures forth and takes its risks.

—EMMANUEL LEVINAS

What have I in common with the Jews? I don't even have anything in common with myself.

—FRANZ KAFKA

Admittedly, every man is other than himself, and in fact being human consists in that possibility of being outside and beyond one's self. . . . But the Jew is doubly absent from himself, and in that sense one could say that he is the human being par excellence.

—VLADIMIR JANKÉLÉVITCH

Contents

Note on Translations and Citations

UNLESS OTHERWISE STATED ALL translations from the French are mine. For Némirovsky's works I generally give page references to the French texts, citing the original in a note. A number of her novels have been ably translated by Sandra Smith, whose translations I have consulted in doing my own. The specific works by Némirovsky that I mention are listed in the bibliography, along with the titles of published English translations where available; the page references are to Némirovsky's *Oeuvres Complètes* in two volumes, edited by Olivier Philipponnat (abbreviated as *OC*).

In first citing the titles of Némirovsky's works, I give the original French title followed by English in parentheses (in italics if an English translation exists). After the first mention, I generally cite the title in English or French, not both.

THE NÉMIROVSKY QUESTION

Introduction

A Writer Reborn . . . and Debated

FALL IS THE SEASON for the big literary prizes in France. Winning one guarantees an author visibility and sales, sometimes even best-seller status. On a November afternoon in 2004 Denise Epstein-Dauplé had just turned on the radio in her kitchen when she heard the announcement: the Renaudot Prize, one of the top fiction prizes, had been awarded to *Suite Française* by Irène Némirovsky. Denise, who would be turning seventy-five the next day, sat down, feeling dizzy.[1] Irène Némirovsky was her mother, whom she had last seen more than sixty years earlier. Arrested by French police on July 13, 1942, in the village where the family had taken refuge at the outbreak of the Second World War, Irène was sent to the camp at Pithiviers where Jews were being assembled for deportation. Two days later she was put on a transport to Auschwitz, where she died a month after her arrival.

And now this prize. No such prize had ever been awarded to a dead author, let alone for a book written half a century earlier. *Suite Française* was the novel Némirovsky had been working on when she was arrested. Unfinished, it had never been published, but the manuscript had survived in a suitcase of papers and photographs, the only inheritance her daughters could claim of her. Among the papers in the suitcase was a notebook filled with Némirovsky's cramped handwriting, which they could not bear to read for years—they thought it was her diary. Sometime in the 1970s, Denise told me when I first met her in 2008, she finally read it and, realizing that it was an unpublished novel, spent months transcribing and typing up the manuscript.[2] She and her younger sister, Elisabeth, thought about showing it to a publisher—after all, their mother had been a well-known, much-lauded novelist before the war. But Elisabeth, who was making a career as a translator and a rising young editor in Paris, worried that the novel was unfinished and not quite good enough to publish: Némirovsky had written it quickly and had had no chance to revise or polish it.

Denise did not insist. It was not until many years later, after Elisabeth herself had died, that Denise went back to her earlier typescript, retyped it on her computer, and showed the text to an acquaintance, the writer Myriam Anissimov, who had published well-regarded biographies of Primo Levi and Romain Gary. Anissimov read it, loved it, and showed it to her editor, Olivier Rubinstein, who was editor in chief of the Denoël publishing firm. He called Denise immediately. Within a year Rubinstein had published the novel, with a preface by Anissimov and an appendix containing excerpts from Némirovsky's wartime journal and correspondence, which told the tragic story of her final years in Nazi-occupied France. Born in Kiev in 1903, Némirovsky had been living in France since she was a teenager and wrote all her works in French but had never obtained French citizenship. Under the Vichy regime she was classified as a foreign Jew, the most vulnerable kind of foreigner (and of Jew) at the time. Her husband, Michel Epstein, also an immigrant from Russia, suffered the same fate as Irène: arrested in October 1942, he was sent to the camp at Drancy on the outskirts of Paris and deported a few weeks later. Michel's younger brother Paul, his older sister Sophie, and his older brother Samuel and Samuel's wife were also deported from Drancy that year. None of them returned.

In a way the prize awarded to Némirovsky posthumously was also her daughter's, since without Denise Epstein's efforts the book would never have seen the light of day. I had the privilege of interviewing her several times before her death in April 2013 at the age of eighty-three. A devoted and much-loved mother and grandmother as well as something of a celebrity in her own right in the last decade of her life, Denise Epstein would still choke up on occasion when speaking about her parents. She was twelve years old when they disappeared from her life, and it was palpable that she never fully got over her loss. When she spoke about Némirovsky, whether in published interviews or in private conversation, she usually referred to her as Maman.

Was the awarding of the Renaudot Prize a compensatory gesture, a way to assuage France's continuing feelings of guilt about its wartime collaboration in the Nazi persecution of Jews? Or was *Suite Française* a brilliant novel miraculously saved from oblivion, the work of an important novelist whose untimely death put an end to what would have been a major postwar career and who now had a chance to become known again—to be reborn? Plausibly, both of those claims are true. The shameful treatment of Jews by the Vichy regime is still a sore point in France, which prides itself on being the homeland of the first Declaration of Human Rights (in 1789) as well as the first country in Europe to grant full citizenship to Jews (in 1791). And if the victim of persecution was a well-known writer in a country that still venerates its writers, the shame is redoubled. But *Suite Française* is a brilliant novel, well deserving of the honor it received, and it would not have become an international best seller, translated into dozens of languages, if it had not touched a deep chord in readers.

Suite Française was written in the last two years of Némirovsky's life, alongside dozens of short stories and three other books. She wrote during those final years as if the devil were at her heels or as if she knew she had very little time left. For today's reader this novel has the strange quality of a letter found in a bottle washed up on the seashore. Written almost simultaneously with the events it recounts, it tells a story of France under the first year of German occupation. Part 1, titled "Storm in June," is a tour de force, a description from multiple perspectives of what the French call the *exode*, the exodus of June 1940, when tens of thousands of civilians from Paris and the north took to the road in cars, on bicycles, on foot, carrying as much as they could of their household belongings, fleeing from the advancing Germans. Surprisingly few novelists have tried to describe the days of terror and confusion that followed the German invasion, before Marshal Philippe Pétain signed the armistice that initiated four years of German occupation with the collaboration of the French government at Vichy. Némirovsky tells this story by following the movements of a dozen or so characters from various walks of life, people who find themselves on the road as refugees. Her observations and insights are often stunning, delivered in a coolly objective or ironic tone. She is pitiless in relating the "hardships" suffered by some members of the privileged classes as they make their way in chauffeur-driven cars to country houses and luxury hotels; and she shows them back in Paris very soon after the armistice, ready to resume life as usual, even if it means accommodating themselves to the German occupants. The only characters for whom the author shows sympathy are a couple of poor but honest bank employees, the Michauds, who married for love many years earlier and whose only son is in the army. He is seriously wounded but he survives, and Némirovsky had grand plans for him, imagining him as a leader of the Resistance in subsequent volumes she did not live to write.

The novel's second part, "Dolce," set in a village during the first year of the Occupation, focuses on a much smaller cast of characters. Here Némirovsky's insights are even more impressive than in the exode chapters. She seems to have understood right away what would be among the most painful questions for ordinary French people during the years of occupation: How to behave with the enemy? How to behave with one's neighbors if they collaborated or, on the contrary, if they resisted? Némirovsky spent more than two years with her husband and daughters in an occupied village in Burgundy before being arrested, so she based the story on personal observation. She shows the gamut of human interactions that inevitably occur between the occupiers and the occupied, ranging from seething hatred to tender but impossible love. Describing the arrival of young, good-looking German soldiers in a town emptied of its able-bodied men, she writes, "The mothers of prisoners or soldiers killed in the war looked at them and begged God to curse them, but the young women just looked at them."[3] Although Némirovsky planned several more volumes (waiting to see what history would bring, she wrote in her journal), the novel in its current form does have an ending: the German soldiers in the village are ordered to depart "toward the East" on the day after Hitler's declaration of war on the Soviet Union, in June 1941.

It is strange to read this novel today, when we have the advantage of historical hindsight. Leo Tolstoy, one of Némirovsky's literary heroes, wrote *War and Peace* half a century after the events he recounts in fictional form. Némirovsky wrote her war novel when the war had just begun—and what makes it strange, almost uncanny, is that she writes about her present *as if* it were history. In other words, she looks at the life around her as if she were observing it from far away. Hers is the gaze of an outsider, one who knows the scene well but is not fully part of it and can therefore see it all the more clearly. Readers often ask why there are no Jews among the many French people Némirovsky depicts in this novel, on the road or in the occupied village, whose collective existence she details. Some see it as a sign of her troubled relation to Jewishness, which made her neglect—or refuse—to include Jews in her epic portrayal. But there is a Jew in this novel, and an omnipresent one at that, even though she is never named or otherwise identified. It is the narrator, whose steady gaze and judgment inform everything we are given to see. The narrator is the one who remarks on how appreciatively the young French women look at the German soldiers—she does not condemn them for it, but she takes note. Elsewhere, her observations are so cruelly precise that no explicit judgment is needed. The wealthy porcelain collector Charlie Langelet, for example, gets run over by a car after returning to Paris, having siphoned out the precious fuel from the gas tank of a young couple he tricked into befriending him on the road. The narrator observes at Charlie's death, "The car's fender had shattered his skull. Blood and brains spattered with such force that a few drops landed on the woman who was driving." There is no need to tell us that the loathsome Charlie gets what he deserves. While the narrator mostly lets readers draw their own conclusions (Némirovsky was an admirer of Gustave Flaubert, famous for his objectivity), she does occasionally express an ironic put-down of a character she dislikes. Thus the wife of the local aristocrat writes a patriotic article in the newspaper exhorting farmers to donate all their grain to "le Maréchal" (Pétain) instead of feeding it to their hens. But the narrator remarks that the lady "naturally" excluded her own farmyard from that injunction, "for she was very fond of her hens."

If *Suite Française* brought Némirovsky back from the dead, a first resuscitation had already been achieved a dozen years earlier, when Némirovsky's younger daughter, Elisabeth Gille, published a book about her mother titled *Le Mirador*. When *Le Mirador* came out in

1992 Gille was a senior editor at a major publishing house and had translated more than fifty books by well-known American and British writers. Unlike Denise, Elisabeth had very few personal memories of her parents, as she was only five years old when they were arrested. However, as a successful Parisian editor and translator, she had a professional as well as a personal interest in her mother's life and career. *Le Mirador* was Elisabeth Gille's first book, and it garnered many positive reviews. She was invited to participate in radio and television programs about the "once well known writer Irène Némirovsky."[4] A woman of great poise and authority used to speaking about and with intellectuals, Elisabeth in these interviews always referred to her mother by name, not as Maman. Her stance was more that of a dispassionate analyst than of a bereaved daughter; one did not have to dig very far, however, to realize that her involvement with Némirovsky was a deeply personal one.

Like a number of her colleagues in French publishing, Elisabeth had grown up as an assimilated Jew who never thought much about questions of Jewish identity. Her former colleagues don't recall her ever talking about it, despite the horrible loss she had suffered as a Jewish child during the war.[5] But starting in the late 1970s she became preoccupied with her own and her family's wartime history. This personal evolution coincided with the growing public memory of Jewish persecution under Vichy, which had been gaining momentum in France since the publication of Robert Paxton's groundbreaking book *Vichy France*, in 1972, and its translation into French the next year. Paxton's book, together with Marcel Ophuls's film *The Sorrow and the Pity*, released in 1971, inaugurated what the historian Henry Rousso has called the period of obsession in France with the memory of Vichy, which continues to this day. The publication, in 1978, of Serge Klarsfeld's monumental *Memorial of the Deportation of Jews from France*, which lists the date of every transport that left France "for the East" between 1941 and 1944, along with the names of all the deportees in each, allowed many French Jews who had survived the war to find out for the first time exactly when their loved ones had been deported. In the following decade the claims of "Jewish memory" became ever more pressing, even as renewed antisemitism and Holocaust denial flourished. The extradition of the former Nazi Klaus Barbie to France in 1983 and the four-year-long preparation of his trial kept the fate of the Jews under Vichy in the news.[6]

When Elisabeth decided to write about her mother she had all this in mind. But she was also aware that she would have to confront a problem: although Irène Némirovsky had died as a victim of the Holocaust, a persecuted Jew, her relation to Jews and Jewishness during her lifetime was fraught with ambivalence and self-contradiction. *David Golder* (1929), the novel about a Jewish financier that made Némirovsky famous at the age of twenty-six, was called antisemitic by some Jewish readers at the time (and later as well) because of the harsh way it portrayed its protagonist and other Jewish characters. Elisabeth herself was dismayed by what she called her mother's obliviousness (*inconscience*) to the growing dangers facing Jews, especially poor Jews who did not have access to the comforts she herself enjoyed as a successful writer during the 1930s. "She lived in a privileged world without understanding what was happening around her," Elisabeth told an interviewer in 1992.[7] The challenge for Elisabeth was to write a book about her mother that would be sympathetic, without overlooking the problem or pretending it didn't exist. If she was going to bring Némirovsky and her story back to life, she would, in a sense, have to reinvent her.

Le Mirador is in fact a reinvention. Elisabeth Gille called it "dreamed memoirs," her imagined sense of what her mother might have written in an autobiography. Like Gertrude Stein writing the "autobiography" of her lifelong partner, Alice, *The Autobiography of Alice B. Toklas*, Elisabeth projected herself into her mother's mind and voice. And the way she solved the problem of Némirovsky's "obliviousness" was by having Irène tell her story at two moments widely separated in time, 1929 and 1942. In Elisabeth's version, if Irène was oblivious to her own and other Jews' precarious status when she wrote about her childhood and youth, she had become painfully aware of it by the time she told the rest of her story. Introducing yet another layer in time and consciousness, Elisabeth inserted one-page reminiscences of her own between the chapters about her mother, and by an interesting turnabout she wrote these autobiographical fragments about "l'enfant" (the child) in the third person. A few years later she made a similar choice in her novel *Un paysage de cendres* (*Shadows of a Childhood*), which tells the bleak story

of a young Jewish orphan girl during the war and in the years following. The book received rave reviews, but unfortunately Elisabeth
Gille never lived to see them. She died of lung cancer in September
1996, the day before her novel appeared in bookstores.

It was through Gille's *Le Mirador* that I first became acquainted
with Irène Némirovsky. I was writing a book at the time which had
a long chapter on child survivors of the Holocaust who later became
outstanding writers, and I had read Gille's novel about her childhood. After that I read her "dreamed memoirs" about her mother,
whose story I found fascinating. But when I followed up by borrow-
ing *David Golder* from Widener Library at Harvard (the original
edition of 1929, its pages faded and brittle; most of Némirovsky's
books had long been out of print), I found the book disappointing.
The writing was good, I thought, but conventional, and the story it
told was conventional too. What did I care about the last days of a
self-made Jewish businessman who has troubles with his unloving
wife and his frivolous daughter? Truth to tell, I did not even finish
the book.

But that was before *Suite Française*. I read that novel soon after it
appeared and felt deeply moved by it, not only because of the author's tragic backstory detailed in the appendix but also because of
the message-in-a-bottle quality of the work itself. As a professor of
French literature with a long-standing interest in Vichy France, I
was astounded by how sharp and accurate Némirovsky's understanding of that first year of German occupation was and by her ironic
yet often sympathetic view of the French people whose lives she
observed. Just as I was telling myself that I had perhaps been too
hasty in my dismissal of her earlier work, her former French publishers started reissuing all her novels. I read them and, somewhat
to my surprise, became a fan. I still considered her writing style to
be conventional, typical of so-called quality writing by establishment authors of the 1930s. Personally, I was more interested in the
avant-garde. Many of her plots were repetitive, chiefly stories about
unhappy families, each one different in its own way, as Tolstoy said.
Most of the characters were recognizable bourgeois types, stereotypes even: philandering or indifferent husbands, faithless or long-
suffering wives, femmes fatales worried about growing old, children

who dislike their parents or even hate them, together with venal politicians and greedy businessmen—all well-known figures to any reader of French realist fiction. A few of her works were set in Russia, while several others featured Russian immigrants in France. A number of them had Jewish protagonists, always portrayed as outsiders, out of place in their surroundings in one way or another. One novel, *Les Biens de ce monde* (*All Our Worldly Goods*), uncharacteristic in its portrayal of a happy marriage rather than a miserable or merely resigned one, features a French couple who marry for love and remain devoted to each other as they face the hardships of the First World War and other crises, right up to the Second World War.

While the focus is always on individual lives, History with its collective catastrophes, whether war, revolution, a pogrom, or a stock market crash, is never far away, ever ready to assert its heavy hand. Sometimes a fleeting allusion is all it takes to evoke a whole collective history. In one of Némirovsky's very first published works, a novella about a Jewish boy poet from a dirt-poor family living in a Russian city that sounds like Odessa, the narrator tells us that the boy's grandfather had once been "a usurer and rich," until his house was burned down in a pogrom on Easter Sunday after the assassination of Tsar Alexander II. This detail is totally superfluous to the plot, but it's a touch that introduces a collective dimension into the family story, and it serves as well to alleviate the unflattering description of the grandfather as a usurer.[8]

Such touches are among the things that make Némirovsky's prose, and gaze, compelling even when she indulges in commonplace stereotypes. French has a lovely adjective to describe someone you find endearing or admirable despite their flaws: *attachant*, literally, someone to whom you get attached. To me and to many other readers I have met since I began working on Némirovsky, she is *une écrivaine attachante*, an "attaching writer," not only despite her flaws but also in some curious way because of them. If I notice her using a cliché, I slide over it, the way one overlooks a dear friend's occasional or even more than occasional lapses of taste; if I wince at some of her descriptions of Jewish characters, I excuse them as being of her time, not ours, and find other descriptions of Jewish existence that strike me as extraordinarily clear-sighted and true.

When the English translation of *Suite Française* was published in

2006, it garnered generally glowing reviews in England and the United States. Some reviewers called it a noble effort but not quite attaining greatness, while others found it brilliant, dazzling, and incomparable. All of them mentioned Némirovsky's personal story with great sympathy; a few in the United States remarked on the fact that Némirovsky did not include any Jewish characters among her large cast but did not condemn her for it. The book, in hardback and paperback editions, appeared for more than two years on the *New York Times* best-seller list. *Suite Française* was soon followed by translations of other works by Némirovsky, including *David Golder*, which appeared in 2007 in a volume with three other short works, accompanied by a thoughtful preface by the American novelist Claire Messud.[9]

Meanwhile, the Museum of Jewish Heritage in New York was preparing, in collaboration with the French archive that houses Némirovsky's papers, to mount a major exhibition devoted to her. The exhibit opened in the fall of 2008, with many luminaries in attendance, including the author of the best-known Holocaust memoir, *Night*, and winner of the Nobel Peace Prize Elie Wiesel, and the former French minister of culture Jack Lang. Denise Epstein, who was almost eighty years old at the time, was there, together with Némirovsky's British translator, Sandra Smith, as well as Olivier Philipponnat, who had published a thoroughly researched biography of Némirovsky with his collaborator Patrick Lienhardt in France the previous year. Philipponnat would go on to curate the expanded French version of the New York exhibit at the Mémorial de la Shoah in Paris and to edit Némirovsky's complete works in two scrupulously annotated volumes, which appeared in 2012. Philipponnat, who in addition to his writing is an editor at a French publishing house, devoted close to ten years of painstaking work to Némirovsky's oeuvre and became one of Denise Epstein's most trusted friends.

By the time of the New York exhibit, however, Némirovsky's image had become tarnished in the view of some readers. From a tragic heroine she had metamorphosed into something almost repellent. After the publication of *David Golder* in English, these readers had discovered what they perceived to be her antisemitic portrayals of Jews. A Jewish antisemite, a self-hating Jew—that is how they saw her, and they condemned her for it. The opening salvo had been

fired in England, where some readers noted that a sentence in Myriam
Anissimov's preface to *Suite Française*, in which she had referred to
Némirovsky as a self-hating Jew, had been removed from the English
translation. The preface itself, which paints Némirovsky in sympathetic terms, had been moved to the back of the book. The omission
of "self-hating Jew" was seen as a ploy by the British publisher, who
feared alienating Jewish readers. The full attack, however, came in
the United States, in the form of a long article in January 2008 in
the *New Republic* that laid out "the nasty truth about a new literary
heroine." The author, Ruth Franklin, a senior editor at the magazine, had done her homework, buttressing her reading of *David
Golder* with a biography of the author by the American scholar Jonathan Weiss, who had paid detailed attention to Némirovsky's portrayals of Jews. Weiss had emphasized Némirovsky's collaboration
with the right-wing paper *Gringoire*, where she had published many
of her stories and two of her novels in installments between 1934
and 1941. Weiss was quite harsh in his analyses of Némirovsky's
early works in which Jews appear, especially *David Golder*. But he
judged that she had become more sympathetic toward the Jewish
characters in her novel of 1939, *Les chiens et les loups* (*The Dogs and
the Wolves*), which offers her fullest, most subtle treatment of Jewish
"foreigners" in France. Franklin, however, would have none of that.
In her eyes Némirovsky was deplorable from beginning to end, "the
very definition of a self-hating Jew." *David Golder*, with its "crude
antisemitic stereotypes," was "an appalling book by any standard," a
"racist travesty of a novel." And worse still, "Némirovsky did it over
and over again," unwavering in her hostility toward Jews from novel
to novel. Indeed, the absence of Jews from *Suite Française* was itself,
according to Franklin, a sign of Némirovsky's antisemitism. While
no one could wish it on her, her deportation, Franklin concluded,
was a supreme irony "that could have come directly from her own
fiction," for she "would die alone in an eastern country, far from her
family, and leave behind a fortune in manuscripts."[10]

Franklin's passionate condemnation set the tone for others to
come. When *The Dogs and the Wolves* appeared in England in 2009,
the reviewer in the *Times Literary Supplement* found its portrayals of
the Jewish characters so repulsive that she claimed a "Nazi publishing house" intent on the "perpetuation of racial stereotypes" would

have been very happy with it.[11] Although other critics praised the book, as of January 2016 *The Dogs and the Wolves* had still not been published in the United States. In 2011, when *All Our Worldly Goods* was published in the United States, a long review in the widely read online journal *Jewish Ideas Daily* appeared under the headline "Portrait of the Artist as a Self-Hating Jew." Given the total absence of Jews in this novel, the label may seem startling. But the reviewer, who calls *All Our Worldly Goods* "a marvelous, decades-spanning love story," finds precisely that absence a cause for condemnation. Since the novel first appeared in 1941 (in serialized form under a pseudonym, Jewish authors having been banned by Vichy from publishing in the press), the reviewer finds it incredible that there is "not a single mention in the book of Jews, Jewry, or Judaism." And he asks, "Why might this be?" The answer follows immediately: "Here we come to the problem with Némirovsky: She was an anti-Semite." It does not occur to the reviewer that the only overt mentions of "Jews, Jewry, or Judaism" in the French press in 1941, when all opposition views had been silenced or gone underground, were necessarily hostile, ranging from simple slurs to vicious denunciations, so that Némirovsky's silence about Jews was, if anything, a sign of anxiety, not of antisemitism. On the contrary, the reviewer pursues his indictment: "There is no evidence that she was a fascist; but, as Ruth Franklin reports in her definitive 2008 essay in the *New Republic*, Némirovsky trafficked in 'the most sordid anti-Semitic stereotypes.'"[12]

To be sure, these accusations have not gone unchallenged. Smith and Philipponnat have both defended her, as have numerous ordinary readers. Others, also not surprisingly, have sided with the accusers. The result has been frustration on both sides, as the debate threatens to turn into a shouting match. I say this out of personal experience, having participated in a forum with Franklin at the Museum of Jewish Heritage in New York in December 2008. She reiterated there her earlier argument that Némirovsky's novels are antisemitic, while I countered that one had to be more generous in reading these works. Ultimately, it came down to *how to read* Némirovsky, both as a person and as a novelist. Perhaps the most surprising thing about that evening was the degree of heat, even anger, generated by that question. Why reasonable readers can argue with such passion about the alleged self-hatred (or not) of a Jewish writer who has been dead for almost three-quarters of a century is itself a subject worthy of discussion.

Is this debate a purely Anglo-American phenomenon? Is it a sign of historical shortsightedness, as readers today neglect to situate Némirovsky properly in the context of her time? The answer to both questions is yes and no. Yes, English and American readers have been the most indignant and outspoken, but they are not the only ones who have condemned Némirovsky as a self-hating Jew or who have read her fiction as trafficking in antisemitic stereotypes. In France similar views have been expressed in recent years, along with their opposite. As for history, it is true that perceptions of and attitudes toward antisemitism today are radically different from those of the 1930s and can lead to distorted judgments. But Némirovsky's portrayals of Jews provoked condemnations as well as defenses among Jewish readers even in the 1930s.

While it is neither restricted to the English-speaking world nor distortedly presentist, the controversy over Némirovsky's supposed antisemitism and self-hatred does seem to matter almost exclusively to Jews. Non-Jewish critics generally praise her work, or, if they have reservations, these don't bear on her portrayals of Jewish characters. The Nobel Prize–winning novelist J. M. Coetzee, for example, in a long article devoted to Némirovsky in the *New York Review of Books*, stated outright that he would not broach that issue.[13] The reason for the passion among Jewish readers, I think, is that the question of Némirovsky's attitude toward Jews and Judaism touches on something much broader. It concerns ambiguities and dilemmas of Jewish identity in modern times, both before and after the Holocaust, in the United States and in Europe. Today's responses to her life and work, which include her daughter's book about her, highlight the differences between pre-Holocaust and post-Holocaust perspectives on antisemitism and on Jewish identity.

A totally dispassionate critic would probably place Némirovsky among the interesting but not major writers of the interwar period, who nevertheless stood out as one of the rare women novelists to be taken seriously by critics at the time. Perhaps alone among women of her generation she was designated by reviewers not as a "lady nov-

elist," or *romancière*, but as a *romancier*, a novelist in the masculine
"universal." Today's dispassionate critic would also, no doubt, acknowledge that she wrote at least one great novel, *Suite Française*,
and that she could have become a truly major writer if she had lived
longer. Her writing was not experimental or avant-garde, even
though she lived in the capital of both the English and French literary avant-gardes in the interwar period; not for nothing was James
Joyce's *Ulysses* first published in Paris, along with French Surrealist
manifestos and poetry. Némirovsky's writing leaned toward the establishment, not toward those who contested established modes.
Stylistically, she can slip into clichés or formulas, and she often relies on stereotyped characters. Yet she has a way of looking at the
world that is striking in its lucidity and unsentimentality. She was
harsh toward almost all of her characters, including those that resembled her, and she was especially harsh toward Jews from poor
backgrounds who succeed in fighting their way to the top, the people she knew best. *David Golder*, the novel that established her as
a writer to be reckoned with, is the story of a Jewish businessman
born in Russia who leaves behind his wretchedly poor family and
works his way to wealth, emigrating to the United States before
settling in France; but his wealth brings him no happiness, and he
dies alone.

Novels by Jewish writers featuring poor Jews who become rich
by dint of cleverness and fierce ambition and who are often morally
compromised in the process are a familiar modern genre—think of
What Makes Sammy Run? and *The Apprenticeship of Duddy Kravitz*—
and they were already known when Némirovsky wrote *David Golder*.
In the United States, Abraham Cahan's *The Rise of David Levinsky*, a
popular success published in 1917, tells the story of another poor
Russian immigrant named David who makes his way to the top but
finds himself a lonely man despite his riches. It is unlikely that
Némirovsky had read Cahan, but she didn't need to: she had her
own father as a model. Léon, né Leonid, Némirovsky, born into a
poor Yiddish-speaking family near Odessa, had made a fortune, first
in various business ventures and then in banking, before the First
World War and was able to reap profits even during the early days
of the Russian Revolution. Irène was fascinated throughout her life

by the phenomenon of Jewish upward mobility, with all of its stresses and contradictions, not least among them the class differences between rich Jews and poor Jews, between, in Hannah Arendt's terminology, the assimilated parvenus and the ghetto pariahs. Within Némirovsky's own family, her father resembled the pariah who succeeds in escaping from the ghetto but remains a "little Jew" in the eyes of those with higher pretensions. Némirovsky's mother, Anna, or Fanny, as she was called, was one of the latter, the older daughter in a family in which French was the language of choice and Yiddish was looked down on. Anna's family lacked money, but she could still feel superior to her husband. Mismatched couples are legion in Némirovsky's fiction.

Irène loved her father and loathed her mother, who seems to have been singularly lacking in maternal feelings. She appears in photographs as a beautiful woman dressed to the nines, often accompanied by a younger man in addition to her husband; she made her daughter wear little-girl clothes as a teenager so that she herself would appear younger. Némirovsky's fiction is full of neglectful or vengeful mothers hated by their daughters. After the death of her father in 1932, she and her mother rarely saw each other, and by the time the war started they had not been on speaking terms for years. Anna survived the war in Nice with a fake passport, then returned to her Paris apartment. After the war Denise and Elisabeth knocked on her door one day, accompanied by the woman who had saved them after their parents were deported. Anna refused to let them in. "Orphans have their place in an orphanage," she said from behind the closed door.

Irène Némirovsky's troubled relation to her mother adds one more knot to the complications and ambivalences that defined her being in the world. A foreigner in France at a time when foreigners were looked on with suspicion, a woman in a literary field where men set the rules and standards, Némirovsky succeeded, for a short time, in creating a life and a career others might envy. She had talent, ambition, and a desire to fit in. But she was a Jew in a time and a place where, increasingly, Jewishness was perceived as a death sentence. Did one have to cease being Jewish in order to survive and thrive? Could one cease being Jewish, even if one tried? These and

similar questions about individual and group identity had preoccupied secularized Jews in Europe for over a century. Némirovsky's
way of dealing with them, and their reverberations among her descendants and among Jews today, are the subject of this book.

PART I

Irène

CHAPTER ONE

The "Jewish Question"

In a society on the whole hostile to the Jews . . . it is possible
to assimilate only by assimilating to anti-Semitism also. If one
wishes to be a normal person precisely like everybody else,
there is scarcely an alternative to exchanging old prejudices
for new ones.

—HANNAH ARENDT, *Rahel Varnhagen: The Life of a Jewess*

TOO OFTEN TODAY THE term self-hating Jew is used as a bludgeon,
usually by Jews against other Jews whose opinions, whether real or
imagined, they find objectionable. But in fact the concept of Jewish
self-hatred has a complicated history. Although the term itself was
not coined until relatively recently and was not widely used until
after the First World War, the idea that assimilated Jews might consider their Jewishness a burden or a shame goes back to the early
nineteenth century, when Jews in Europe had their first opportunity
to enter the Christian mainstream. The life of Rahel Varnhagen
(1771–1833), a German Jewish writer and salonnière, offers a perfect
illustration. The daughter of a wealthy businessman, Rahel married
a minor German aristocrat and converted to Christianity but never

lost the feeling of being an outsider in German society. Jewishness, as she famously stated on her deathbed, was at once the source of the greatest "shame and misery" in her existence and the thing she would on no account have wanted to miss.[1]

Self-Hatred or the "Jewish Question"

The German Jewish philosopher Theodor Lessing published a book in 1930 titled *Der jüdische Selbsthass* (Jewish self-hatred) in which he suggested that the sense of worthlessness many Jews felt about themselves and about other Jews was an understandable response to the suffering they had experienced as members of a despised minority in European history and culture. While he was addressing himself primarily to German Jews, his remarks also applied to Jews in other countries. Lessing saw self-hatred as a widespread human malady, and his book was meant to encourage Jews to affirm both their own worth and that of every human being. Lessing blamed narrow nationalisms for devaluing anyone who was not seen as belonging to the nation. He placed his faith in an internationalist movement that would make such chauvinism a thing of the past, and Jews, he intimated, could overcome their self-hatred by joining or even leading such a movement.[2] Paul Reitter, a scholar of German Jewish history who is the author of a recent book on this subject, likens Lessing's book to a "self-help book, where your sufferings give you opportunities for self-transcendence and improving the world."[3]

In more recent times the term *Jewish self-hatred* was put into circulation by Sander Gilman in 1986 in his book of that title. Gilman, a noted scholar of modern German literature and culture, analyzes what he calls the psychological "structure of self-hatred," which is not limited to Jews but can be observed in any group that is devalued in a given society, from women to foreigners to racial minorities. Self-hatred, as Gilman explains it, is a process in which the member of a devalued group internalizes the negative stereotypes by which the majority defines the group and seeks to distinguish himself or herself from those stereotypes as an exception. Thus, in Jewish self-hatred, Gilman writes, "Jews see the dominant society seeing them and . . . project their anxiety about this manner of being seen onto other Jews as a means of externalizing their own status anxiety."[4] This projection is a form of splitting: the self-hating Jew seeks to make himself into a "good" or exceptional Jew who is different from the stereotypical "bad" Jew. Hannah Arendt had already analyzed and condemned the phenomenon of "exceptional" Jews in her writings in the 1940s and later, but Gilman gave a systematic account of the psychological process it involved. While one can argue with him on specific issues, there is no doubt that he treats Jewish self-hatred as an analytic concept, not as a bludgeon. In ordinary discourse, however, and even in some critical writing, *self-hating Jew* usually functions as an accusation: the person accused of being a self-hating Jew is implicitly contrasted with the non-self-hating or self-loving Jew, among whom the one launching the accusation presumably counts herself. Curiously, this kind of splitting recreates the very same process that the concept of self-hatred seeks to analyze. It's as if the accuser were saying, "Némirovsky [or Franz Kafka, Gertrude Stein, Hannah Arendt, Philip Roth, Joseph Roth, or Isaac Babel, among great twentieth-century writers who have been called that] is a self-hating Jew, but I am not." Such splitting excludes the possibility of ambiguity and ambivalence, concepts I find more useful in discussing psychological attitudes toward Jewishness or any other minority group identity in relation to the mainstream.

Besides, since the term *self-hating Jew* can be and indeed has been applied to very many people, it becomes so broad as to be almost useless. What modern, urban, educated, secular Jew has not, at one time or another, felt a sense of shame, or merely uneasiness, at the look or manners or behavior of other Jews that he or she recognizes as being of the same ancestry or ethnicity yet also perceives as embarrassingly different from his or her own self or ideal? It would be dishonest to claim that one has never felt ambivalence about being Jewish, if one is a relatively assimilated or integrated Jew living among a non-Jewish majority. (Assimilation and integration are sometimes distinguished from each other, but for my purposes the two terms are pretty much interchangeable.) This is true even in the United States today, where multiculturalism and minority differences are celebrated, and it was certainly true of both Europe and the United States in the decades before the Second World War, when *difference* was a negative word and openly antisemitic discourses were widespread and almost casual. Even among non-antisemites or anti-antisemites, Jewish "difference" and stereotypical representations of Jews were often taken for granted, both before and after the war: witness Jean-Paul Sartre's well-meaning but stereotypical portrait of the Jew in his *Réflexions sur la question juive (Antisemite and Jew)*, published in 1946. It can hardly come as a surprise if many Jews at the time wished they could give up that privilege.

Rather than speak of Jewish self-hatred, it makes historical as well as philosophical sense to speak of the ambiguities and ambivalences regarding Jewish identity and self-definition during this period. The problem had to do with the relations not only between Jews and the wider culture in which they lived but also between and among Jews themselves. There exists a historically rich and complex term to designate this problem: the "Jewish question," *die Judenfrage, la question juive*. The appropriation of this term by the Nazis, who claimed to have found a "final solution" to it, has rightly discredited it from civilized usage, except in quotation marks. But it is salvageable—in quotation marks—and a useful alternative to *Jewish self-hatred* if one wants to think about dilemmas of Jewish identity in modern times.

According to historians who have studied the evolution of this term, it first became widespread in Germany in the nineteenth century. *Die Judenfrage* entered public discourse with the publication in 1843 of Bruno Bauer's book of that title (first published as a series of essays); a year later, Karl Marx responded with his own essay bearing the same title.[5] While Marx and Bauer disagreed on details, they agreed on one point, namely, that "the social and economic drive of the acculturated Jew was the real crux of the Jewish question."[6] In other words, this question could come about only after the political emancipation of Jews in Europe had opened the door to Jewish participation in national life. Even though Jews in Germany did not gain full citizenship rights until after the revolutions of 1848, by the early decades of the nineteenth century many had achieved economic and professional success as well as intellectual recognition. A considerable number had even converted to Christianity in order to try, mostly unsuccessfully, to gain full integration into German society. What the "Jewish question" put into question was precisely the trustworthiness of Jews as members of the nation. Bauer claimed that even acculturated Jews didn't really want to be fully absorbed into the Christian mainstream, clinging to their "illusory" Jewishness, while Marx claimed that Jews represented the essence of capitalism and were therefore inimical to a just society. Either way, as Jacob Toury noted in his historical-semantic study of the term, "the 'Jewish question' as a slogan did not take root until it had established itself as an anti-Jewish battle-cry." This is what enabled the virulent antisemitisms of the late nineteenth century to propagate and popularize the term, carrying it through the 1930s and beyond. The common denominator between earlier and later anti-Jewish uses of the term, Toury concludes, was "the insistence upon the *alien character of the Jews as a group*" in relation to the mainstream.[7]

The "Jewish question," then, in its antisemitic formulation, was not a question at all but a declaration. The historian Vicky Caron has summed it up well: "Jews, no matter how assimilated, can never be truly French."[8] Or German or Hungarian or Polish or, for that matter, American, for in the United States, too, Jews were seen as a problem by antisemites, who were not afraid to express their views. Father Charles Edward Coughlin, a Canadian Catholic priest based in the United States, had a popular following on his weekly radio program, during which he often spewed anti-Jewish rhetoric even as he denied being an antisemite. In the 1930s, as in the 1890s, radical nationalisms in Europe combined with economic crises to create an ideal climate for such formulations, as well as for schemes to find supposed solutions to the "Jewish question." Thus in April 1938 the rabidly antisemitic French weekly *Je suis partout* (I am everywhere) devoted a whole issue to "La Question Juive." The solution proposed in front-page articles by the two main editors, Robert Brasillach and Lucien Rebatet, both of them notorious antisemites, was to strip French Jews of their nationality. "It is impossible, as many liberals believe, to belong to two nations, the Jewish and the French," wrote Brasillach. "We demand that Jews be returned to their condition as Jews," wrote Rebatet, which to him meant "stripping Jews of French citizenship, and of all the rights that go with it."[9] Their words were accompanied by antisemitic cartoons that reinforced the message visually: Jews, with their hooked noses, fleshy lips, fat paunches, and grabbing hands, could not be true Frenchmen.

By an interesting twist, however, antisemites were not the only ones to refer to the "Jewish question" in their writings. The term was also used by Jews in a fairly wide variety of ways. Theodor Herzl, arguing for the necessity of a Jewish state in his book *Judenstaat* (1896), subtitled the book *Versuch einer modernen Lösung der Juden-frage* (Attempt at a modern solution of the Jewish question). Herzl reasoned that the only solution for Jews was to become a separate nation, so in a sense his assumption tallies with that of the antisem-ites who considered the Jews unassimilable in Europe. But for the many Jews who did not wish to leave their European homelands, the "Jewish question" was a different matter: they either denied its exis-tence altogether, dismissing it as an antisemitic invention ("There is no Jewish question, or at least there should not be one—Jews are loyal citizens, and their religious practice is their private affair"); or else it became for them a question of individual identity, often ex-perienced as a feeling of estrangement both from the non-Jewish mainstream and from other Jews, who themselves came in many varieties. The Jews of postrevolutionary Europe were a hugely di-verse and varied population, divided by class, language, degree of re-ligious practice, ideological and political allegiances, and many other factors. What is striking is how much writing there was, throughout the nineteenth century and well into the twentieth, on the "Jewish question" by Jewish writers and how much anguish they expressed. This was especially true in Germany and Austria, where the ques-tion, which was basically the question of assimilation, was felt most acutely.[10] But the question existed wherever Jews had or could dream of emancipation and full participation in civic life.

To vary the examples a bit, I will cite a Hungarian one.[11] In 1917, at a time when the so-called Golden Age of Hungarian Jewry was already drawing to a close, the distinguished scholarly journal *Huszadik Század* (Twentieth century), founded and edited by the secular Jewish historian Oszkár Jászi, ran a special issue titled "The Jewish Question in Hungary." It included a survey that asked, "Is there a Jewish question in Hungary, and if so, what is its essence? What is the cause of the Jewish question in Hungary? What do you see as the solution to the Jewish question in Hungary?" Of the sixty Jewish and non-Jewish intellectuals who responded, only a few stated that there was "no Jewish question." These were the staunchly op-timistic Jews who reaffirmed their belief in Enlightenment ideals.

"According to my experience there is no Jewish question in Hungary," wrote the director of the Budapest rabbinical seminary, Dr. Lajos Blau; "but supposing that there is, it is essentially a leftover of medieval feeling and thought in non-Jews who insist on a Jewish question."[12] The "leftover," Blau claimed, would disappear once people became enlightened. Alex Bein has noted in his book on the history of the "Jewish question" that to many Jewish leaders in Germany as well, "the Jewish question existed only in the imagination of or through the activities of Jew-baiters."[13]

The great majority of respondents to the Hungarian questionnaire in 1917, both Jews and non-Jews, stated that there was indeed a Jewish question. According to most Jewish respondents, its essence was antisemitism, itself a reaction to the problems and tensions of modernity. This response is not much different from that of the notables who claimed there was no Jewish question except in the minds of antisemites. Among the replies by non-Jews, the one by a university professor from Transylvania stands out for its tone as well as its content. Yes, there is a Jewish question, wrote the professor, and its essence is in some Jews' refusal to become Hungarian, in their stubborn clinging to a nationhood different from that of the Magyars: "It's that spoiled, Germanic-dialect-speaking, orthodox, strongly Oriental-looking Jewry that in ordinary parlance is called Galizianer [Yiddish-speaking Jews from Galicia, in Poland]." Such Jews, he stated, provoked the antipathy not only of Magyars like himself but also of "every other people brought up in a Christian civilization." He urged the Jews of Hungary to "exterminate" the characteristics of this group from their midst (the verb kiírtani in Hungarian has acquired the same sinister connotations after the Holocaust as the English).[14] One could hardly find a more graphic evocation of the divide between acculturated Jews and Yiddish-speaking Ostjuden that haunted so much of late nineteenth- and early twentieth-century Jewish thinking and writing about group identity than under the pen of this Christian Transylvanian scholar, whose own geographic marginality in relation to Hungary may have made him especially sensitive to issues of exclusion and inclusion. Jewish writers and intellectuals in Hungary as well as in Germany, France, and England were acutely and often painfully aware of the differences between themselves and the poor, orthodox shtetl Jews of Poland and

Russia, some of whom were their own grandparents.[15] Even within
Poland and Russia class divisions existed. Sholem Aleichem, the creator of the immortal Tevye the Dairyman, treated them in the comic
mode and in the very language of the shtetl. The bittersweet stories
that would become *Fiddler on the Roof,* like many of Sholem Aleichem's other works, all written in Yiddish, emphasize the disdain or
else the condescension with which "rich Jews from Yechupetz," his
name for Kiev or Odessa, approached or, more often, avoided poor
ones like Tevye. In western Europe a number of Jewish writers wrote
stories and novels about the psychological consequences of such divisions, affecting Jews on both sides. Among the best known of these
writers was the British novelist Israel Zangwill, whose works, for
example, *Children of the Ghetto* (1892), which thematized the split
between traditional and modern Jews in England, were widely translated. (Zangwill was the inventor of the term *melting pot,* to designate the integration of Jews and other minorities in the United States,
in his 1909 play of that title.) In Hungary, Károly Pap (1897–1945)
wrote some outstanding stories and novels about the inner contradictions of Jews caught between the old ways and the new, as did Isaac
Babel in Russia, Abraham Cahan in the United States, and Albert
Cohen in France. Némirovsky's name can be added to this list.

One of the most interesting responses to the Hungarian survey
was that of the poet and artist Anna Lesznai, who insisted on the
psychological aspect of the "Jewish problem." Lesznai belonged to
a wealthy Jewish landowning family and participated as a rare female member in the leading modernist literary journal in Hungary,
Nyugat (West). She was thus part of a successful, assimilated Jewish
elite, yet she wrote in her response, "The Jewish problem exists
even when a person of Jewish origin is sitting alone in his room. It
exists not only in the relations between a Jewish individual and
Hungarian society. The seriousness of the problem lies in that the
Jew feels like a 'Jew' for himself."[16] Forty years later, more than a
decade after the end of the Second World War, the French philosopher Vladimir Jankélévitch expressed a very similar idea when he
spoke at a gathering of Jewish intellectuals in Paris about "Jewishness, an internal problem." Jankélévitch wrote, "It is not enough to
convert in order to cease being Jewish. . . . [T]here is an essential
otherness that is characteristic of Jews." The complication of being

Jewish, which prevents Jews from ever being "one hundred percent French, or Russian, or even Israeli," was, according to Jankélévitch, both a kind of malady and a kind of privilege that defines the Jew's very being. While all human beings are in some way other than themselves, he concluded, Jews are doubly so, caught in an unresolved and unresolvable dialectic between the desire to be "just like everyone else," that is, assimilated, and the desire to affirm their difference.[17]

Are such observations manifestations of self-hatred? Perhaps. But in that case one would have to conclude that self-hatred has been the condition of the majority of educated, upwardly mobile Jews throughout Europe and beyond for almost two centuries. In *The Origins of Totalitarianism*, Arendt devoted many insightful pages to a historical analysis of this condition. She noted that in the course of the nineteenth century "the Jewish question became an involved personal problem for every individual Jew."[18] Arendt herself did not believe in individual solutions to the "Jewish question." All such attempts ended in failure, she argued again and again, including in her quite harsh essay on the celebrated Austrian Jewish novelist Stefan Zweig, written shortly after his suicide in 1943. Zweig's error, Arendt remarked somewhat cruelly, had been to believe that being part of the "international society of the successful" would grant him equal rights as a Jew; he ignored the political realities around him, and when he finally saw "a world in whose eyes it was and is a disgrace to be a Jew," all he could do was to kill himself. But, Arendt concludes, "from the 'disgrace' of being a Jew there is but one escape— to fight for the honor of the Jewish people as a whole."[19] Arendt here was expressing the Zionist view on the "Jewish question," which she had arrived at on the basis of her own experience in Nazi Germany. But she also had a very keen understanding of the existential dilemmas of those she called assimilationists, who lived the "Jewish question" as an individual rather than as a collective problem. In one of her essays from that time she referred to the "hopeless sadness of assimilationists," precisely because their hopes of assimilation had been so devastatingly crushed. The essay is titled "We Refugees," which implies that she includes herself, but since she claimed not to believe in individual solutions, she may have wanted to point up the difference between a Zionist like herself and individualists like

Zweig and others who had seen their illusions destroyed.[20] It may seem odd to refer to Arendt as a Zionist, given the harsh criticisms she received, along with accusations of being a Jewish antisemite and self-hating Jew, after publishing *Eichmann in Jerusalem*. In fact, she worked for several Zionist organizations in Germany and France in her youth, and, as she makes clear in her famous letter of 1963 to Gershom Scholem, she never became an anti-Zionist, even though she could be critical of Israel. About her own sense of Jewishness, she wrote to Scholem, "To be a Jew belongs for me to the indisputable facts of my life, and I have never had the wish to change or disclaim facts of this kind. . . . This attitude makes certain types of behavior impossible—indeed precisely those which you chose to read into my considerations [regarding Eichmann]."[21]

Whatever one may think of the collective solution, most Jewish writers in Europe in the first half of the twentieth century, and many Jewish writers in Europe and the United States today, grapple with issues of Jewish identity in existential and individual terms. If to antisemites the "Jewish question" was summed up as What shall we do with the Jews?, to individual Jews the question often appeared and continues to appear as a form of inner division and as a personal dilemma, most strikingly summed up in Kafka's famous question to himself, "What have I in common with the Jews? I have hardly anything in common with myself."[22] But Kafka's modernist formulation, which allowed him to envision existential estrangement in universal rather than in specifically Jewish terms in his fiction, was not the only way to formulate the existential dilemmas faced by Jews who were out of the ghetto. Among the more banal, everyday questions emancipated Jews in Europe could ask themselves in the early twentieth century were, What have I in common with the Jews? Do I have to marry a Jew? Must I feel solidarity with Jews who don't speak my language, don't dress like me, don't belong to my world, just because they're Jews? And what about my fellow-citizens, the non-Jews—will I ever belong to their world, really? Maybe I would belong if I converted, so should I convert? Some of the same questions continue to be asked even now, and not only in Europe. Today, we must add to them some version of What is my relation, as a Jew, to Israel and Israeli politics?, with its myriad contested, often painful replies.

The "Jewish Question" in Interwar France

Since France was the country of emancipatory rhetoric and political assimilation, French Jews for a long time idealized the Republic. "Happy as a Jew in France" was a widely shared dictum, one which spread beyond France's borders. French Jews were largely hostile to Zionism insofar as they thought of it as competing with assimilation to Frenchness. But they did not need to renounce their Jewishness in order to assimilate, for they could maintain the idea that Jewishness was a purely private, religious affair that in no way affected their loyalty to France. Many Jews rose to high positions in the service of the French state under the Third Republic, including the army, and yet kept close family and institutional ties with other Jews and observed endogamy, even if they stopped practicing Jewish religious rites.[23] Some historians have referred to the decades before the First World War, when Jews could aspire to high public office even while maintaining a serene identification as Jews, as the Golden Age of French Jewry.[24] However, Maurice Samuels has more recently shown that despite this happy moment of Franco-Jewish synthesis, the existential versions of the Jewish question were an intense and vexed subject of discussion by Jewish writers in France throughout the nineteenth century. Even for Eugénie Foa, who has the distinction of being both a successful woman writer at a time when women in the literary field were rare and the first French Jewish writer to treat Jewish themes in fiction (she published her "exotic" novel *Le Kidouschim* in 1830), Jewish identity was, Samuels writes, "a problem to be struggled with, a series of questions to be answered."[25] And the same was true, he argues, for Jewish writers who followed Foa, among them Marcel Proust's great-uncle Godchaux Weil and including Proust himself. Weil, writing under the pen name Ben-Lévi, published dozens of stories in the Jewish press in the mid-nineteenth century, probing the contradictions and tensions of Jewish assimilation to French culture and society.

The hoped-for harmony between French and Jewish identities came under stress by the influx of Jewish immigrants from eastern Europe starting in the early 1880s, a trend that continued in increasing numbers after the First World War. The arrival of these *Juifs de l'Est* (Jews from the East), most of them poor, Yiddish-speaking, and either much more religious or much more left-wing in their politics than French Jews, not only elicited waves of antisemitism in France but also created problems for established French Jews, most of whom sought to distance themselves from the new immigrants. The crisis of the Dreyfus Affair in the last decade of the nineteenth century exacerbated both antisemitism and questions of French Jewish identity. The career of Alfred Dreyfus, who had risen to the rank of captain in the French army before being falsely accused of treason, demonstrated France's political acceptance of Jews as full citizens. But the social and ideological reactions to his condemnation in 1894 and then to the affair itself a few years later demonstrated just how deeply divided the country was over the "Jewish question." Many middle- and upper-class Jews who had lived with the conviction that there was no problem about being both French and Jewish saw the Dreyfus Affair as a watershed—and not all Jews chose the side of Dreyfus. Even Bernard Lazare, who became the first hero of the affair when he published his defense of Dreyfus in 1895, *Une erreur judiciaire: la vérité sur l'affaire Dreyfus,* did not at first think to contest the condemnation of the Jewish captain for treason. It was only after Dreyfus's tireless defender, his brother Matthieu, met with Lazare and showed him that major improprieties had occurred at Dreyfus's trial that Lazare threw himself into the battle on the pro-Dreyfus side. Around the same time, he became interested in Zionism and wrote polemical articles against antisemitism in France. In his youth, Lazare, like most assimilated Jews of the time, had considered himself a citizen of the Republic equal to any other, and on occasion he even attacked Jews for their "separatism." In her often-quoted essay "The Jew as Pariah," written in 1944, Arendt placed Lazare, admiringly, among those Jewish writers who consciously chose the status of pariah rather than adopting the illusory hope of the parvenu who sought to join the national mainstream. In fact, Lazare's attitudes toward Jews and Jewish identity were sometimes hard to pin down and shifted considerably over time, but there is no doubt that his anarchist allegiances placed him on the side of poor Jews and the powerless, not those he identified as capitalist or bourgeois.[26]

Issues of political allegiance and social class came to the fore with even more intensity in the period between the two world wars, when France was flooded by Jewish immigrants fleeing Hitler's Germany and other parts of central and eastern Europe. Between 1920 and 1939 the Jewish population in France rose from roughly one hundred thousand to three times that number. Most of the immigrants were poor, Yiddish-speaking, and considered to be troublingly foreign by French Jews. Arendt has some wonderfully humorous remarks about the way she and other German Jews were received in France circa 1933: "French Jewry was absolutely convinced that all Jews coming from beyond the Rhine were what they called *Polaks*— what German Jewry called *Ostjuden*. But those Jews who really came from Eastern Europe could not agree with their French brethren and called us *Jaeckes*. The sons of these *Jaecke*-haters—the second generation born in France and already duly assimilated—shared the opinion of the French Jewish upper classes. Thus, in the very same family, you could be called *Jaecke* by the father and a *Polak* by the son."[27] *Jaecke* was the name given by poor Jews from the East to arrogant German Jews who looked down on them. Just how fraught these relations could be in the early years of the twentieth century, especially in Arendt's native country, has been amply documented by Steven Aschheim in his book whose title speaks volumes: *Brothers and Strangers: The East European Jew in German and German Jewish Consciousness*. But as Arendt points out, it all depends on who is doing the naming, for to some arrogant French Jews in the 1930s even a Jaecke could appear like a "little Jew" from Poland.

The ambiguities of naming were also apparent in the major linguistic and social divide of the period in France: the one between *Israélites* and *Juifs*. Long-established French Jews, most of whom were middle-class, usually referred to themselves as Israélites, while the more recent arrivals, wherever they came from, were Juifs. The question of how to name oneself or other Jews became the theme of quite a lot of writing during the interwar years. In 1930 Edmond Cahen, the editor of the Reform Jewish journal *Archives israélites*, published a novel titled *Juif, non! . . . Israélite*, whose title says it all, yet within the text assimilated middle-class Jews are occasionally referred to as Juifs, which shows how uncertain the division was. Today, Israélite is very rarely heard in French usage and appears slightly ridiculous, but both the opposition of the two terms and the uncertainty about their use continued into the postwar years. Thus in November and December 1945 the newly founded journal *Les Temps Modernes,* edited by Sartre, ran brief biographies of two "typical" Jews in France: "Vie d'un Juif" (Life of a Jew) told the story of a poor immigrant from Turkey who survived the war even though most of his family was deported, while "Vie d'un bourgeois français, magistrat israélite" (Life of a French bourgeois, an Israélite magistrate) told the story of a Jewish judge whose father had been an army officer. The magistrate's father staunchly believed that Captain Dreyfus was guilty. The magistrate himself, who was a young man during the affair, believed that Dreyfus was innocent, but he admits that he sometimes felt repulsed by others who shared his belief.[28]

Aside from the linguistic conundrum, the tension between Israélites and Juifs in the interwar period occasionally took on harsh political connotations when many Israélites sought to limit the number of Juifs in France. Emmanuel Berl, a well-known essayist and journalist from a distinguished Jewish family, wrote increasingly hostile editorials against immigrants in the 1930s and moved so far to the right in his desire to proclaim his patriotism that he became a speechwriter for Marshal Pétain for a few weeks in June and July 1940. Not long after that, the Vichy government's first anti-Jewish decree defined Berl as a member of the "Jewish race," making no distinction between him and the recent immigrants he had thundered against. Berl lived long enough to look back on his past, but he never repented his positions, though he did admit he had underestimated the virulence of Hitler's antisemitism and was shocked by Pétain's Jewish decrees of 1940 and 1941, which forbade writers like himself to publish.[29] While not many Israélites went as far as Berl in trying to affirm their Frenchness, they all considered the influx of foreign Jewish immigrants to France a problem, increasingly so as the political climate of the thirties became more polarized and more hostile to foreigners, especially to Jews. The historian Jérémy Guedj, who has studied in detail the attitudes of French Jews toward Jewish immigrants during the interwar period, concludes that the hostility of "*Israélites* toward their Jewish brethren can be seen as evidence of the lack of assurance on the part of French Jewry at the time."[30]

Indeed, the greatest fear of French Jews, as shown in the many articles devoted to the problem of immigration in Jewish journals from the mid-1920s on, was that other Jews who were obviously not

French would call unwanted attention to them and possibly question their own allegiance to France. The need for Jews to give up their foreign ways and become rapidly integrated into French society was one of the permanent themes in these discussions. "The world has its eyes on us," wrote a worried contributor to *L'Univers Israélite*, the journal of France's official Jewish community, the Consistoire, in October 1925. While French Jews should be sympathetic to the unfortunates who were forced to flee their homelands, the author argued, they must also demand that the immigrants make an effort to become French "as quickly as possible, in heart, in language, in customs"—otherwise, they were welcome to go to Palestine.[31] In the following decade the anxiety displayed in this article would be multiplied and produce some shocking results from today's point of view, for example, the founding in 1934 of a Patriotic Union of French Israelites, which was rabidly hostile to "foreign Jews."[32] But this was only one of a wide range of specific responses and attitudes: like Jews always and everywhere, those in France did not speak with a single voice.

Némirovsky's Israélite, Christian Rabinovitch

Némirovsky's place in the linguistic and sociological field of French Jewry was untypical though by no means unique. She was a "foreign Jew from the East" but not a Juif de l'Est, or Ostjude, in the usual sense since she was wealthy, well educated, and politically conservative (or at least nonleftist). Thus, while most Russian Jewish immigrants living in France in the interwar period clearly belonged among the Juifs in the Israélite/Juif dichotomy, she and her husband, Michel Epstein, whom she married in 1926, did not. Her choosing to marry someone like herself—the child of a wealthy banker, Russian, Jewish, not at all religious, wanting to live well and be assimilated in France—is significant, for it reinforced her status as a foreign Jew. It also confirmed her class allegiance: although her father, a self-made man, came from a poor Jewish family, her mother's family had middle-class pretensions, which explains why Irène had a French governess and apparently spoke only French with her mother as a child. As the many interviews and photographs of Némirovsky that appeared in the press after the success of *David Golder* and throughout the 1930s attest, she lived a life of bourgeois ease and comfort. Her aspiration, in literature as in life, was to be a respected member of the establishment, and her ideal was the Académie Française, not the avant-garde.[33]

Despite her class allegiance, however, which would normally have placed her among the Israélites—one of her close friends was the writer Jean-Jacques Bernard, son of the famous playwright Tristan Bernard and an Israélite of the highly assimilated kind—Némirovsky did not really belong in that category because she was a recent immigrant to France and not French. The lack of French nationality made her much more vulnerable during the war, but even before then it placed her in a somewhat ambiguous position. This in-between position lends particular acuity to her views of and on Jews. Most of her Jewish characters are recent arrivals in France, having made their fortune or trying to make it after a childhood of poverty in Odessa or some other city "in the East." They are at best newly rich, outsiders whose contacts with French people, including French Jews, are rare. One major exception is the short story "Fraternité," which stands out as the only one of Némirovsky's works that features an Israélite as its main character. It thus offers an excellent perspective on her view of the "Jewish question" in France. She made extended notes about this short text in her writing journal, even though normally she did not lavish so much attention on her short stories.[34] She wrote the story in less than a month, in October 1936, when she was pregnant with her second child and feeling anxious about lack of inspiration for a novel. It was published in February 1937 on the literary page of the politically right-wing weekly *Gringoire*.

"Fraternité" stages a brief but memorable encounter between an Israélite and a Juif on a train platform in the French countryside. The date is not mentioned, but various details indicate that it is the present, circa fall 1936. The character through whose eyes and mind we observe this encounter is the wealthy banker Christian Rabinovitch, whose name is almost too transparently indicative of his inner division—and it is also a false note in the text because Israélites at that time were never called Christian. They had French names that appear in the Christian calendar without carrying any religious connotation, names like Henri, Léon, and Alfred, or occasionally a biblical name such as Emmanuel, which could also be borne by non-Jews. Despite this false note, however, Némirovsky makes good use of her protagonist's name, which she does not reveal right away. Instead, she begins by describing him physically and emotionally: he is around fifty, a widower, thin and somewhat frail, sedentary in his ways, with a strong tendency to anxiety and worry, especially about his health and that of his grown children, and also about the future, which he feels is always capable of bringing misfortune when one least expects it. His Jewishness is alluded to quite early by means of a narrative cliché ("his lips, always dry, seemed withered by an ancient thirst, a fever transmitted from generation to generation") and a bit of internal monologue ("My nose, my mouth, the only specifically Jewish traits I still possess").[35] Only about a third of the way into the story do we learn his name. At that point it has an almost comic punch-line effect or else that of allegory: a man named Christian Rabinovitch cannot possibly be anything other than conflicted about his identity. Dressed in fine English wool and carrying a case with expensive hunting rifles, although we are told that he hates hunting, Christian is on his way to spend a country weekend at the home of an aristocratic friend. He has had a car accident, which is why he is reduced to taking the train and exposing himself to a chance encounter with a man he would normally never meet, a poor immigrant Jew who is sitting near him on the train platform hugging a child he later identifies as his grandson.

To Christian's shocked surprise, this poor Jew from Russia is named Rabinovitch. When Christian tells him that that is his name as well, the immigrant asks him when he arrived in France. Christian asserts stiffly that both he and his father were born in France, but the other man is not deterred: "So it must have been before your father," he tells him, because "all the Rabinovitches come from over there." At this point Christian recoils and asks himself the Kafka question, reported in free indirect discourse by the narrator: "What was there in common between this poor Jew and himself?"[36] This is the question posed by the story's title as well. Are Christian's brothers the wealthy bourgeois and aristocrats he frequents in his work and social life (he refers earlier to "the rich bourgeois, his brothers"), as is promised by the French slogan *Liberté, Égalité, Fraternité?* Or is his brother this poor foreign Jew with his "feverish" eyes that seem to "run from one object to another," looking "anxiously" for something he will never find?

Although the story is told from Christian's point of view, Némirovsky gives the immigrant Rabinovitch a long monologue in which he recounts his and his family's tale, and here we have in concentrated form a history of Jewish upward mobility and emigration from Russia in the first decades of the twentieth century, complete with the various choices Jews made. One son, refusing to be a humble tailor, went to university and ended up as a Zionist in Palestine, where he died of tuberculosis; another son became a photographer and settled in Berlin, while the father left Russia after the Revolution and settled in Paris. But when Hitler came to power, the Berlin son had to leave Germany. He came to France for a few years and now lives in Liverpool. It is this son's child who is with the immigrant Rabinovitch on the station platform. The monologue reaches its high point with the immigrant's reflection on exile: "Where doesn't God throw the Jew? Lord, if only we could be left in peace! But never, never are we left in peace! No sooner have we won, by the sweat of our brow, a piece of dry bread, four walls, a roof for our head, than comes a war, a revolution, a pogrom, what have you, and goodbye! 'Pick up your stuff, get out. Go live in another town, another country. Learn a new language—at your age, you aren't discouraged, right?' No, but we're tired."[37] Christian listens to all this without interrupting, then asks him about his profession, to which the other replies that he does a little bit of everything. And he makes a remark that creates extreme discomfort in Christian: "Happy are the ones who were born here. Just see, looking at you, how wealthy one can become! And doubtless your grandfather came from Odessa, or from Berditchev like me. He was a poor man . . . The fortunate ones, the rich ones, didn't leave, you can be sure of that! Yes, he was a poor man. And you . . . Maybe one day he too . . ."[38] He points to his grandson. That gesture, which suggests that only a couple of generations separate the wealthy Rabinovitch from the poor one, again highlights the question implicitly asked by the story: who are Christian's brothers?

The train's arrival spares Christian from having to respond to the man, but when he finds himself alone again in his first-class compartment, his earlier question about their relationship returns in a more virulent form: "Wretched creature! Was it possible that he himself was of the same blood as that man? Once again, he thought to himself: What is there in common between him and me? There's no more resemblance between that Jew and me than between Sestres [Christian's aristocratic friend] and the lackeys who serve him! The contrary is impossible, grotesque! An abyss, a chasm! He touches me because he's picturesque, someone from another age. Yes, that's how and why he touches me, because he's far, so far from me . . ."[39] It does not require much thought to conclude that Christian doth protest too much. Even as he denies any relation to "that Jew" and tries to explain away his being "touched" by him, the reader is invited to draw a different conclusion. In the only passage in the story where the narrator intervenes above the character's head, we see Christian swaying back and forth, unaware, the narrator notes, that he is replicating the swaying of his ancestors in prayer or work. But even without this intervention, the reader is aware that Christian and "that Jew" have a number of traits in common despite their enormous social distance: they are both beset by anxiety, and the narrator uses the word "inquiétude" in relation to both. Furthermore, they are both devoted fathers who worry about their children. The immigrant Rabinovitch worries about his son in Liverpool and about his grandson, while the French Rabinovitch worries about his son Jean-Claude, who plans to marry the daughter of the Catholic aristocrat. Will this mixed marriage work out? Christian Rabinovitch has his doubts, for they will probably never truly understand each other. Finally, he himself becomes convinced that the source of his disquiet is his Jewish heritage: "That's what ails me. . . . That's what I'm paying for in my body, my mind. Centuries of wretchedness, illness, oppression. . . . Thousands of poor bones, feeble and tired, created mine."[40]

When the train finally stops and his Catholic friends come to greet him, Christian abandons these bitter ruminations. But his body continues to mark his difference, as he shivers from the cold air while his host revels in it. And we can be sure he will have a terrible time at the hunt the next day. Hunting really is not his thing. The relation of Jews to hunting is a recurring motif in interwar literature and film: in Cahen's *Juif, non! . . . Israélite*, the Jewish protagonist's Frenchness is shown not only by his valor as a soldier in the First World War but also by his love of the land and especially of hunting. In Jean Renoir's *The Rules of the Game* the refined Jewish aristocrat who is the film's most sympathetic figure is an expert hunter. Characteristically, Némirovsky offers a less idealized portrayal. Christian Rabinovitch's dislike of hunting indicates his difficult assimilation into French society, despite his having been born there.

Is this story, which packs so much into a few pages, proof of Némirovsky's antisemitism and self-hatred? No, but it is possible to read it that way if one has a mind to. Némirovsky does not eschew stereotyping, both physical and psychological: the little Jewish boy has big ears and "bright, nervous" eyes like his grandfather, while Christian thinks of his mouth and nose as his "Jewish traits." On the psychological level, the anxiety and feeling of insecurity that even the wealthy Israélite experiences daily are attributed to his Jewishness. But was it a sign of antisemitism to suggest, in 1936, that Jews had reason to be anxious about their security in the European world? Némirovsky was particularly attuned, as a "foreign Jew from the East," to all the ways in which even the country of emancipation and equality for all could become a very cold place for Jews. In "Fraternité" she presents the painful self-questioning of an assimilated French Jew as he confronts what is for him a distant Jewish heritage.

The exact nature of this heritage is left somewhat vague in the story. Is it biological, racial even, or is it the heritage created by a shared history of "wretchedness, illness, oppression," as Christian puts it to himself? In her journal notes for the story Némirovsky seems to vacillate between those two views. In one entry she writes, "The rich one is (thinks he is) totally free of his religion, but the poor one is too. Their brotherhood does not reside in religion, but in race, oh Hitler, you're not wrong." This is immediately followed by, "J'ai des scrupules," which could mean something like "What have I just said? Maybe I'm wrong." But this in turn is followed by, "And yet, there is before and above all the inalienable right to truth." She knows she is skating on thin ice, but she maintains the thought. A few lines later, however, she implies that the brotherhood and the heritage reside above all in history, not biology. Commenting on the immigrant Rabinovitch's monologue as she plans to write it, she says, "The meaning of all these experiences is that things always end badly, in failure ... to start over, and then over again, to bend your back and start over. But the one who didn't have to do that, the rich one, still has *sickening fear* [in English], that heritage." Below that she writes, "In sum, what I demonstrate is inassimilability, what a word, oh Lord ... I know that it's true."[41]

Hers was not a happy view of Jewish existence. Her conclusion that the Jews are inassimilable may appear to tally with antisemitic views of the time, for antisemites also harped on this theme. But she didn't write that word in the text: the story is more ambiguous than what she writes in her notes. On the other hand, she also writes in her notes that when she submitted the story to the highly respectable *Revue des Deux Mondes*, which had recently published one of her other stories, its longtime editor, René Doumic (who was not Jewish), rejected it "as antisemitic"! She then submitted the story to *Gringoire*, which also had published some of her earlier work, and it appeared there on February 5, 1937. A few years later, during the war, Horace de Carbuccia, the paper's editor, would take risks in publishing her work under a pseudonym when she desperately needed the money. In February 1937, however, her turning to *Gringoire* was a decision fraught with problems. The paper had become more openly antisemitic after the elections of 1936, which had brought the Popular Front to power and the Socialist leader Léon Blum, an extraordinarily cultivated Israélite, to the position of prime minister. Némirovsky's French biographers, Olivier Philipponnat and Patrick Lienhardt, following the lead of her daughter Elisabeth Gille, suggest that the literary pages of the paper were quite separate from the political pages.[42] If one looks at the issue for February 5, 1937, however, one finds that the separation between literature and politics was not so clear-cut. The page following the one where Némirovsky's "Fraternité" appeared features a "historical narrative" by one Georges Oudard titled "A Communist Experiment. Kon, aka Bela Kun." An illustration shows a thick-lipped Kun dominating the Hungarian parliament in 1919, and the story purports to show how the Jews planned to take over Hungary! Béla Kun, from an assimilated Jewish family, was the head of the short-lived Communist government that ruled after Hungary's defeat in the First World War. "To be continued," says a note at the bottom of the page.[43]

It is impossible to know, today, how readers of *Gringoire* in February 1937 interpreted "Fraternité." One can surmise that, as always, individual interpretations varied widely. But even if many readers at the time saw in this portrayal of an Israélite a confirmation of their worst prejudices about Jews, that should not prevent us from seeing it differently today. In my view, Némirovsky's pessimism about Jewish "inassimilability" is a sign not of antisemitism but of anxiety and unease, and indeed Jewish writers living in other hostile environments during that period were arriving at the same conclusion. The Hungarian novelist and short story writer Károly Pap, who called himself a "writer of the Jewish people" and who perished at Bergen Belsen, expressed similarly despairing views about assimilation in his stories of the late 1930s. Pap too was accused by some members of the Jewish community of being a self-hating Jew.[44]

Antisemites claimed that inassimilability was due largely to the Jews' refusal to assimilate, their clannishness in sticking together, whence the paranoid theories of worldwide Jewish conspiracy. To racial antisemites there was the added element of blood or race, which would prevent Jews from properly mixing with the French. A sympathetic reading of Némirovsky points out, by contrast, that in her view the determining factor of Jewish inassimilability is neither sociology nor biology but history: centuries of persecution and exclusion have had their effect, even among Jews who are now privileged. In her notes for the story she mentions "Loewel" as a possible real-life counterpart to Christian Rabinovitch. The reference is no doubt to Pierre Loewel, a politically conservative Israélite lawyer and essayist who had reviewed *David Golder* glowingly when it appeared and who continued to review Némirovsky's works throughout the 1930s, always very favorably. Loewel generally published in the right-wing press, but that did not prevent him from voicing his admiration for the defenders of Captain Dreyfus. In 1929 he published a lavishly illustrated book on "figures of the Palace of Justice" in which he sang the praises of Dreyfus's defense lawyers, men of principle who were willing to sacrifice their careers to defend an innocent man wrongly accused.[45] In her notes, Némirovsky eventually decides that Rabinovitch should be even more *mondain*, at a higher level socially and less acute intellectually than Loewel was. She expresses quite a bit of sympathy for her Israélite, even as she notes that his typically "Jewish traits" are sickliness, anxiety about money and the future, and love of his children, in that order. Rabinovitch, as she notes in her journal, is a Jewish father who worries about "the humiliation of being rejected, for example by a French family. The son's engagement maybe . . ."[46]

The view that emerges from Némirovsky's fiction is that successful Jewish assimilation is impossible, not only because Jews are ultimately unable to transcend their origins, whether one calls them racial or historical, but also because French xenophobia and class snobbism get in the way. Although this view is expressed in the preparatory notes, it is not apparent in the published text of "Fraternité," where the assimilated Rabinovitch seems to have only solicitous, unprejudiced Christian friends. But it is emphasized in the last novel Némirovsky published in book form during her lifetime, *The Dogs and the Wolves*, her most sustained effort to examine the "Jewish question" and the last of her works in which Jewish characters appear. In one of the most dramatic moments in the novel, two Jews from Kiev, one poor and one rich, one apparently assimilated, the other not, confront each other. The poor one, who in this case is a blood relation of the rich one, his first cousin, cries out, "You who look at us from on high, who scorn us, who want nothing do with the Jewish riffraff, just wait a bit! Wait! You'll soon be mixed up with them again. And you'll be part of them, you who had left them behind, you who thought you had escaped."[47] One can hardly think of a more pessimistic—or more prescient—view that the same fate awaited all Jews in Europe, even those who thought they had put the ghetto behind them. This realization adds one more irony to the title of "Fraternité," for if the promise of the revolutionary slogan turned out to be false, then Jews could not be part of the French brotherhood. The historian Todd Endelman, who has written a book about the attempts of European Jews to become fully assimilated, in some cases to the point of conversion to Christianity, notes that even in countries where progressive change occurred, "it failed to uproot well-entrenched views about Jewish otherness, neither erasing the stigma of Jewishness nor ushering in an era of unconditional social acceptance. Jews became 'less Jewish' (in language, dress, manners, etc.) but opposition to their full acceptance persisted."[48]

In the end "Fraternité" is best seen as an exploration of the "Jewish question" *from an individual Jewish point of view*, by which I mean that Némirovsky was writing about her Jewish characters from the inside, sometimes observing them harshly and even unfairly but always from a position that can accommodate our seeing her gaze as that of a Jew. Not a member of the Jewish community or the Jewish people defined in collective terms, but a Jew nevertheless, one who struggled precisely with those issues of Jewish identity and Jewish belonging that defined the "Jewish question" for Jews, not for antisemites. Her anxious, conflicted Israélite Christian Rabinovitch may not be to everyone's liking. But the questions his story raises continue to resonate.

Reading "Fraternité" as a brief but profound meditation on the "Jewish question" allows us to answer another question, one which many readers have asked about Némirovsky's posthumous novel, *Suite Française:* Why is there no mention of Jews or Jewish persecution in a work that purports to deal with the French defeat of 1940 and the first year of Nazi occupation, when Vichy laws started to openly discriminate against Jews?

Readers who like to see in Némirovsky an example of Jewish self-hatred attribute this absence to her lack of sympathy for or identification with Jews. She and her husband converted to Catholicism in 1939, which confirms her lack of identification, but nothing allows us to say she had no sympathy for either persecuted Jews or any other persecuted group. One of the short stories she published shortly after the outbreak of the war, in December 1939, featured a wealthy South American aesthete, unmarried and childless, who finds himself in Paris on the day war is declared in September. He feels sympathy for the French but remains a mere spectator to human suffering (the title of the story is "Le Spectateur") until he himself is caught up in it. The ship he is traveling on to escape from Europe is torpedoed, and he suddenly understands that "it was his turn now. It was no longer a Chinese child, a Spanish woman, a Jew from Central Europe or those poor charming French who were suffering, it was he, Hugo Grayer!"[49] Earlier he had noticed that among the panicked passengers crowding the decks no distinction was made between the wealthy ladies in furs and those who traveled in third class, like the "little German Jewish children that a charity wanted to resettle in an orphanage in Uruguay." During his final moments as he awaits his death, wounded and freezing, Hugo holds the hand of a woman, a total stranger, who comforts him.

Fleeting evocations of historical catastrophes in Europe and elsewhere, as well as of the victims they created, occur in many of the stories Némirovsky wrote around this time. They indicate that she was starting to think about the major theme of *Suite Française* well before she actually began writing the novel.[50] The question she explores there, variously and brilliantly, is how individuals respond to a collective crisis. Her focus in *Suite Française*, as in the stories that precede it, is on specific lives but always with the awareness of how History dominates and transforms private life in a time of catastrophe, bringing out the worst in many people but the best in at least a few. The character Hugo Grayer is an early, more positive version of the self-centered art collector Charlie Langelet in *Suite Française*. Hugo finally feels true kinship with those who suffer, while Langelet remains blindly egotistical right up to his absurd death. In "M. Rose," a story published in August 1940, the title character, another wealthy loner, discovers a similar sense of solidarity among the refugees fleeing Paris in June 1940; this collective flight would become the subject of part 1 of *Suite Française*.

Being the writer she was, however, Némirovsky made sure to temper any edifying conclusions one might be tempted to draw from conversions in extremis like Monsieur Rose's and Hugo Grayer's. She ends "Le Spectateur" with a cruel image, as Hugo foresees the compassionate but ultimately indifferent reaction of moviegoers, still other spectators, to the newsreels that would announce the sinking of his ship on the high seas: "Those crowds were like chickens who let their mothers and sisters be slaughtered while they go on clucking and picking at grains, without understanding that the same passivity and inner consent would end up delivering them, when their turn came, to a strong, pitiless hand."[51] The notion of barnyard fowl letting their kin be slaughtered is a bit odd, as if they had agency and choice, but the thought it conveys about human indifference and even stupidity in the face of other people's suffering is of a piece with the disenchanted vision that would dominate *Suite Française*. Indeed, even Némirovsky's presumed lack of Jewish identification came up against the harsh fact that in the late spring of 1942, while she was most intensely working on the novel, she walked around the village of Issy-l'Évêque wearing a yellow star. Whether she liked it or not, she was identified as a Jew, and she made no effort to escape it. That is another of her life choices that many readers puzzle over: why did she not attempt to leave France or at least the Occupied Zone, as most Jews in her situation did?

One plausible explanation for the absence of Jews in *Suite Française* is that, since this novel is wholly focused on the way "ordinary French people" responded to the first year of German occupation, there was no real call to focus on Jews. One could say that by *not* showing any of her French characters as being aware of the Vichy statutes that excluded Jews from public life, or of the roundups of Jews that began as early as March 1941, Némirovsky was realistically depicting their indifference to the distress of fellow citizens—not to mention the distress of foreign Jews like herself. But this explanation overlooks a somewhat important question: if Némirovsky wanted to depict the responses of ordinary French people, why could she not imagine at least one ordinary French person of the Jewish faith as part of that category? Here one could go into some minute historical analysis, starting with the fact that in June 1940 the Jews were not yet being persecuted in France, so there was no point in singling them out among others on the road fleeing the German army.[52] And when the second part of the novel takes place, between October 1940 and June 1941, the setting is a tiny French village that could be plausibly represented as having no Jewish inhabitants. But still, this explanation seems a bit weak, especially as Némirovsky herself was such an inhabitant in such a village. She and her family were the only Jews there, it's true.

A stronger explanation becomes possible if one admits that by the time she started working on *Suite Française* Némirovsky had arrived at the hopeless conclusion that Jews would never feel or be fully accepted by the French. Her journals from 1940 to 1942 indicate a great deal of bitterness, which is reflected in the sarcasm of the novel's narrator toward most of the characters. This could have resulted in the impossibility of her representing Jews together with the French, as if she could not see them in the same viewfinder—or in the same story and history. If so, then that would be the most pessimistic conclusion of all, consonant with the despair and anger she felt, for good reason, as she was writing what would turn out to be her posthumous masterpiece.

CHAPTER TWO

Némirovsky's Choices,

1920–1939

[As a child] you believe with all your heart that life is full of monsters. Later, life will not succeed in dissuading you. It will often do its utmost, will reward you with all the riches in the world, honors, true affections even. You will see it 'til your dying day with your childhood eyes: a horrible mess.

—NÉMIROVSKY, Notes for "Le Charlatan," 1938

"IN MY ADOLESCENCE, I blamed her for being so oblivious politically. She hadn't saved herself, even though she had every possibility for doing so, and she had put us, my sister and me, in danger. We were arrested and logically we should have ended up, like her and my father, in Auschwitz. Her blindness was criminal. During the 1930s, even in her work, she was not at all concerned by what was happening to the little Jews who lived in the poor neighborhoods of Paris." So said Némirovsky's daughter Elisabeth Gille in an interview in 1992 after the publication of *Le Mirador*, her book about her mother's life. But she immediately qualified this harsh judgment:

"My mother, however, was not a right-winger: she thought the Russian revolution was justified. But she lived in a privileged world without understanding what was happening around her."[1] Gille expresses here, in a strikingly concise way, a problem that is familiar to anyone who looks back on a life, whether their own or someone else's: If I had known then what I know now.... The point is that nobody could have known then what they know now, and Gille implicitly admits as much: her adult view is not the same as that of the adolescent who lashed out at her mother's "blindness." But she also recognizes that some aspects of her mother's life are hard to understand or to accept when looked at from a later perspective.

Irène Némirovsky, like most people, lived her life by making choices, some after much deliberation, some on a sudden impulse, and some without thinking at all, as if they were inevitable. Some of her choices in the 1930s may appear to us, viewing them today, as extremely troubling. The challenge is to examine them without adopting the position of a judge, who is called on to condemn or to exonerate. Némirovsky is not on trial. The choices she made determined her life, for better or worse, but life is not a judicial proceeding, even when it unfolds in tumultuous or frightening times.

Behind all this lies a thorny philosophical question: Do one's choices constitute a system or logic that becomes impossible to break out of, so that the chain of choices acts like a determinism: once you are launched there is no turning back or shifting direction? Or does every new day offer the chance to make a new choice, independently of what went before? This opposition is too stark, however, for neither of these alternatives is realizable in practice. Every choice we make restricts the possibilities for making other choices (the road not taken will not present itself again in the same way), but that does not mean we are prisoners of our past. The influential sociologist and theorist Pierre Bourdieu, who died in 2002, is associated with the first position, although he protested whenever critics accused him of determinism. Perhaps the best known exponent of the second position is Sartre, whose concept of freedom allows even last-minute changes of direction, with every choice potentially a new beginning.

In examining Némirovsky's choices, one would do well to try to balance these two approaches, for if the first allows too little freedom to the individual subject, the second, no doubt, allows too much. One way to achieve this is to situate a person's choices in the larger field of possibilities available at a given time, comparing them to those of others who found themselves in a similar situation. Such comparison is not at all the same thing as judging in hindsight or projecting on the past what we know now as if we should have known it then. In his book *Foregone Conclusions* (1994), the literary theorist Michel André Bernstein called this kind of projection backshadowing, a form of distorted perspective that is the symmetrical opposite of foreshadowing. In foreshadowing, a storyteller who knows the ending prepares the reader or listener by insinuating the outcome before it happens; in backshadowing, we who know the ending act as if those who lived in the past should have known it too. Bernstein proposed instead the concept of sideshadowing, which he defined as the attempt to perceive, from a historical vantage point, the alternative possibilities that may have presented themselves to individuals in a past situation, possibilities they either did not see or did not choose. Sideshadowing does not suggest that they *should* have seen or chosen differently, only that they could have done so. What choices, then, led Némirovsky to her astonishing success in the 1930s, on the way to her tragic end in 1942?

"Young Guys and Girls, All Russians"

Irène and her parents left Russia in January 1918, when she was about to turn fifteen. They spent time in a village in Finland with other Russian exiles before moving to Stockholm and then Paris; they arrived there in June 1919, just as the Russian emigration was gathering speed. While thousands of Russian Jews had started fleeing poverty and pogroms in the late nineteenth century, the emigrés who left after the Revolution of 1917 were more numerous and more diverse. In the early 1920s the emigration reached floodlike proportions: according to one specialist, four hundred thousand Russian emigrants lived in France during those years, most of them in Paris.[2] In addition to writers and intellectuals, many of them left-wing, who were opposed to the Bolsheviks, thousands of nobles, bankers, and businessmen found themselves as exiles in the French capital. Some were ruined, reduced to driving the mythologized Russian taxi, while others continued to live in high style. A few Soviet writers, like Ilya Ehrenbourg and Vladimir Mayakovsky, also spent time in Paris, but they didn't count as emigrés since they could travel back and forth. The Némirovskys were among the fortunate ones, for Léon Némirovsky was able to continue his banking and business career in Paris until his death in 1932. The family rented apartments in the elegant 16th *arrondissement* and vacationed in Nice and Biarritz and at spas frequented by other wealthy Russians as well as by the French upper classes. Photos from that period show them elegantly attired, Léon wearing white gloves and spats, his wife in pearls and broad-brimmed hat, or else both in evening clothes seated at a table near other diners in a fancy restaurant, with a champagne bucket and flowers on the starched tablecloth. One photo of Irène, taken in Nice in 1920, shows the seventeen-year-old dressed in a white linen chemise dress in the latest fashion, with black buttons as decoration and a black cloche hat, smiling and striding down the Promenade des Anglais as if she owned it. At this time she had an English governess and chaperone, who remained with her even after she started attending the Sorbonne a year later. One grudgingly admiring journalist who interviewed her in 1930, after the success of *David Golder* had made her famous, wrote, after describing her as "small, slender, dark-haired, typically Jewish [in] appearance, without beauty," that she had "manners of effortless elegance, the fruit of an impeccable upbringing."[3]

Given her background and gender, it was not taken for granted that Irène would attend university. In 1920 very few women in France obtained university degrees, and most of these were young women preparing for a teaching career who for one reason or another could not count on marrying well. Simone de Beauvoir, born in 1908 and just a few years younger than Némirovsky, recounts in her autobiography that when she was a teenager her father told her that since she was poor and had no dowry she had better prepare to earn a living. Beauvoir's family, while of the minor aristocracy, had lost its fortune years earlier.[4] Némirovsky, on the other hand, was in no such need, and when she enrolled at the Sorbonne in the fall of 1920 it was not with financial security in mind. Unlike those bound for an academic career she never stood for the highly competitive *agrégation* examination, which guaranteed a good teaching position for life. Beauvoir and her contemporary Simone Weil became *agrégées* in philosophy, the most rigorous academic field at the time. Némirovsky earned a *Certificat* in Russian literature in 1922 and another in comparative literature in 1924. The following year, her last at the university, she earned a Certificat in Russian philology in March 1925.[5] She would have needed four Certificats to be awarded a *licence*, the equivalent of a bachelor of arts.

Némirovsky's choosing to study mainly Russian and other non-French writers (in comparative literature) at university may seem odd, given her literary ambitions in French. But the position of being between languages and cultures seems to have been one she cultivated. In Paris she discovered the two great Russian writers who became most important to her in her own work, Tolstoy and Anton Chekhov. As a child in Russia she had read some of the French classics under the tutelage of her French governess, and in her auto-biographical novel *Le Vin de solitude* (*The Wine of Solitude*), published in 1935, she shows the young protagonist writing her first "literary text" in French in St. Petersburg. Némirovsky's own first literary attempts, however, were in Russian: her youthful notebooks contain several poems in Russian, written during the family's travels on their way to France.[6] Had she been a few years older when she arrived in Paris she might well have started writing fiction in Russian, like her contemporary Nina Berberova (1901–1993), who left the Soviet Union when she was twenty-one and ended up in Paris four years later. Berberova lived in Paris for twenty-five years and wrote half a dozen books there, all of them in Russian. After moving to the United States in 1950 she taught Russian at Yale University and continued to write in her native language.[7] Vladimir Nabokov, another near-contemporary, is a perfect counterexample, for he switched languages as a writer more than once, moving from Russian to French to English.

After her first attempts at poetry, Némirovsky wrote exclusively in French, and she sought publication while she was still a teenager. In the summer of 1921 she sent a satirical dialogue featuring a scatterbrained young Parisian girl of "easy virtue," a familiar stereotype of boulevard comedy and the popular press, to the humor magazine *Fantasio*, which printed it with no changes. The author was eighteen, still chaperoned, and signed her text Topsy.[8] She wrote several

more dialogues featuring the sweetly dumb "Nonoche," but they
remained unpublished until the recent edition of her complete
works. Her next published story appeared under her real name in
the respectable daily *Le Matin* in May 1924, on a literary page directed by none other than Colette. Titled "La Niania," it was a story
about an elderly Russian nanny, the Niania of the title, who accompanies the family of aristocratic emigrés she has served for many
years to Paris after the Revolution but finds herself unable to adapt
to life there. Némirovsky would later expand this story into her novella of 1931 *Les Mouches d'automne (Snow in Autumn)*, in which she
draws a contrast between the old servant and the young people in
the emigré family, who adapt quickly to their new environment. The
daughter, Natacha, attends the Sorbonne.

At the Sorbonne, Irène herself had the opportunity to meet
French students, but the subjects she studied attracted many Russians and other foreigners as well. Her French friend at that time
was a young Catholic student from a solid provincial family, René
Avot, whose family owned a paper manufacturing business in the
northern industrial town of Lumbres, not far from the Belgian border. René invited her to visit his home and introduced her to his
slightly older sister, Madeleine. The two young women became
friends, or at least pen pals, for Madeleine continued to live with her
family in Lumbres. Irène's letters to her are particularly precious
because they are among the few pieces of her personal correspondence that have survived; they had been kept by the Avot family and
given to Némirovsky's daughters after the war. Most of the other
letters by her that have come to light so far are professional, addressed to her publishers and to a few French writers with whom
she was on a fairly formal footing.

The letters to Madeleine, dating from 1920 to 1925, offer the
image of a lively, carefree young woman who loves to dance and flirt
(the word she uses), staying out during a good part of the night at
the luxury resorts where she vacations with her parents. But she still
had her English governess and chaperone watching over her, as be-
fitted a proper young lady of her class. In one long letter sent from
Paris in July 1922 she describes with some humor the week she has
just spent at the spa in Vittel, perhaps to celebrate her first Certificat
in Russian literature. She hung around with what she calls a band of

three girls and three boys, including her "flirt," who went by the very French name of Henry La Rochelle. As a result of staying out so late, she caught a bad cold. The moral of the story, she tells Madeleine, is, "When you go out to flirt in the park, be sure to dress warmly."[9] Irène was constructing a frivolous image of herself in these letters, one whose relation to the reality of her life was at best approximate. In at least one letter she mentions that she is grappling with a "black melancholy" but then immediately makes light of it: "The reason? I have no idea. Sorrow in love or indigestion due to lobster, I'm not sure."[10]

Némirovsky's American biographer, Jonathan Weiss, sees in the letters to Madeleine Avot a sign of Némirovsky's lifelong "profound desire to become something she was not. Her fascination with Madeleine and the entire Avot family, far from being a transitory whim of adolescence, would have a lasting effect on her values and her literary sensibility."[11] It is true that the Avots represented a kind of established French bourgeoisie that Irène found fascinating and that she portrayed with a great deal of sympathy in her late novel *Les Biens de ce monde (All Our Worldly Goods)*. The novel, published in installments in 1941 and as a book, posthumously, in 1947, spans the period from before the First World War to the outbreak of the Second World War and tells the story of a prosperous, patriotic, generally good-hearted family of northern industrialists over two generations. This is one of Némirovsky's rare works to display un-ironic affection for the main characters, a couple who marry for love over the objections of the wealthy young man's parents and who remain devoted to each other for decades. A similar couple, the Michauds, appears in *Suite Française*, which Némirovsky was starting to write around the same time. The Michauds stand out for the sympathetic treatment accorded to them by the often caustic narrator of that novel.

But if the Avot family represented for Irène a kind of Frenchness she admired, her admiration was by no means blind or naïve, nor did she desire to be exactly like them. Some of her letters to Madeleine gently tease her about her provincial propriety in contrast to Irène's foreignness. In March 1922, for example, she writes that she is working seriously on preparing for her exams and dances "a little, just so I don't lose the habit. Yesterday I invited some friends, Russians,

among them little Tania and a few gigolos." Irène uses this word
frequently and rather loosely to designate young men she has met
at dances who normally earned their living as paid dance partners.
They were not of her social class but evidently acceptable to have at
parties. She adds, "It was fun and I would have liked to have you
there, just to scandalize you a little bit," then goes on to say why she
hasn't seen René lately: "I'm so busy, and I don't dare to invite him
to my Russian parties for fear of shocking him or perverting him.
Absolutely."[12] In an undated letter from around the same time she
apologizes for not writing for a while, her excuse being the Sorbonne, where she has never been as assiduous as she is these days.
But she is enjoying it since there are friends to study with: "We work
a lot, and we're not too bored—we're a likeable band, young guys
and girls, all Russians."[13]

In sum, Irène was both fascinated by the Avots and just a little
bit ironic toward them, exactly like someone who finds herself in
between and likes it that way. She did not always try to keep her two
worlds separate, for she introduced Madeleine to the Russian friends
she saw most often, notably Alexandre "Choura" Lissianski, a young
Russian Jewish exile who was part of the band and remained a lifelong friend. Another close friend at that time was Emilie "Mila"
Gordon, also from a Jewish family, who was exactly Irène's age and
had arrived in Paris with her parents and younger sister just a few
months after the Némirovskys, in January 1920. Like the Némirovskys, the Gordons rented a large apartment on the posh Avenue
d'Iéna in the 16th arrondissement. Mila's father, Boris Gordon, had
owned a tobacco factory as well as a newspaper and a theater in
Rostov-on-Don. The Gordons, wealthy Jews, belonged to a higher
social class than the Némirovskys, who never forgot Léon's extremely
modest origins. Perhaps because he had felt sufficiently comfortable
in his integration into Russian life, or at least as comfortable as any
Jew in Russia could, Boris Gordon maintained a degree of Jewish
religious practice that the Némirovskys shunned. He observed the
holidays and the Sabbath, although his daughters did not follow him.[14]
In *The Wine of Solitude* Némirovsky comments sharply on the class
differences among wealthy Jews in Russia and draws a contrast between the nouveaux riches, who abandon all religious identification
in their drive to assimilate, and the "Jews from good families," who

"followed with a prideful humility the rites of their religion."[15] She placed her own family among the nouveaux riches, while the Gordons seem to have belonged to the "good families."

Irène took pleasure in telling her friend Madeleine, shortly after she had spent a few days in Paris and met some of Irène's band, that she had "wreaked havoc in many Russian hearts, no doubt about it."[16] A year or so later, in April 1924, Madeleine became engaged to a proper Frenchman named Cabour, and Irène wrote to congratulate her. After that, except for a few letters and New Year's cards, their correspondence would not be renewed until December 1940, under very different circumstances.

"The Short, Brown-Haired Fellow"

Irène met Michel Epstein after a party on New Year's Eve 1924, when they shared a taxi with Madeleine and Choura in the small hours of the morning. A few weeks later she wrote to Madeleine that "the short, brown-haired fellow with a dark complexion" who had sat between them in the taxi was courting her, "and I must say, I find him to my taste." So much so that she was not planning to leave Paris for a while as "the romance is quite heated at the moment."[17] A year and a half later, on July 31, 1926, Irène and Michel were married in a synagogue, according to the wishes of Michel's parents. The religious ceremony was followed by the civil one, at the *mairie*, or town hall, of the 16th arrondissement. Irène was twenty-three, and Michel, born in October 1896, was twenty-nine. Although she described him as being short, he was quite a bit taller than Irène, as one can see from a photo of the two of them taken around that time. They could not have looked more proper, she in a wool plaid dress and wearing elegant but sensible shoes, he in pin-striped trousers and black vest and jacket topped by a stiff white collar, wide tie, and a white handkerchief in his breast pocket.

The Epsteins were a respected banking family from Moscow and St. Petersburg. Michel's father, Efim Moisevitch Epstein, held a teaching position at a university-level School of Economics in Moscow and St. Petersburg and a directorial post at the Azov-Don Commercial Bank. During the Revolution he managed the bank's affairs in St. Petersburg after a number of other executives had em-

igrated. He and his family left the country in the fall of 1919, settling in Paris a few months later. They too lived in a fashionable part
of town, near the Champs-Elysées.[18] In 1925 Efim Epstein published a quite scholarly book in French on the history of commercial
banks in Russia, which, he argued, played an important role not
only in that country but also in the European economy as a whole.
He considered their nationalization by the Bolsheviks a catastrophe
and proposed the American Federal Reserve System, which had been
created only a few years earlier, as a model for the "post-Bolshevik"
government.[19] The Azov-Don bank was a major stockholder in the
French Banque des Pays du Nord, where Michel obtained a middling
position that he kept until the summer of 1940. His younger brother,
Paul, worked at the bank of Lazard Frères, and his older brother
Samuel was in the film business.[20] Like the parents of Irène's friend
Mila Gordon, the older Epsteins were observant Jews. Michel and
his siblings were not, but the fact that he agreed to a synagogue
wedding (in France the most common way of getting married was to
go to the mairie with two witnesses) suggests he was on warm filial
terms with them. One photo, taken with his mother around the time
of his marriage, shows him standing close to her. She is an elderly
lady with an ample bosom and no makeup, wearing a black, ankle-
length dress with a bow fastened by a large brooch, a maternal figure quite far from that of Irène's glittering mom. Michel was also
close to his older sister Sophia, nicknamed Mavlik, and to his two
brothers, especially Paul, who was unmarried. Némirovsky's daughter Denise Epstein recalled that her parents socialized a great deal
with the Epstein siblings, along with other Russian friends. According to her, their most intimate, comfortable friendships were with
Russian Jews.[21]

Némirovsky's choice of Michel Epstein as a husband made excellent sense, in addition to satisfying her "taste" for him. He was
attractive, belonged to a distinguished, close-knit family unlike her
own very small, mismatched one, and fit in well with her circle of
young, well-off Russian emigrés and their French friends. By all indications he was a cultivated man, spoke and wrote excellent German in addition to French and Russian, and shared Irène's desire to
succeed and be accepted in French society. He became a devoted
husband and father, one who, as Elisabeth Gille recalled years later,

played whimsical word games with his daughters and admired and abetted his wife's literary success. During the war, when Irène became the family's sole breadwinner, he typed all her manuscripts. Given the similarities between herself and Michel, psychologists might characterize Irène's choice of a spouse as a narcissistic object choice—certainly not a self-hating one. What seems certain is that by marrying Michel Epstein, Némirovsky confirmed her preference for the between position she had already manifested in her studies and friendships. Just as she could have studied French literature at the Sorbonne, she could have sought out a French man to marry, if not a Catholic, then an *Israélite* more established in France than she or Michel. Mila Gordon's younger sister, Hélène, who was born in Rostov in 1909 and became famous after the Second World War as the founding editor of the women's magazine *Elle*, married her first husband, a non-Jewish Frenchman, a year after Némirovsky married Michel Epstein. A few years later, after divorcing, she married Pierre Lazareff, who was to become one of France's most powerful newspaper editors both before and after the war. Lazareff came from a Russian immigrant family, but he was born and raised in Paris.[22] Nathalie Tcherniak, who after the Second World War became known as one of France's most respected writers under her married name, Nathalie Sarraute, was born in Russia in 1900 and spent years of her childhood shuttling between her divorced parents and between the two countries. She studied law at the Sorbonne during the same years Némirovsky was there and married Raymond Sarraute, a French Catholic (whose mother was Jewish, however) in 1925, one year before Irène married Michel.[23]

In fact, in the 1920s many young Jewish women from wealthy or once-wealthy immigrant families that had lived in France for no more than a generation married Frenchmen from Catholic families, many of them intellectuals or writers who were in a rebellious relation to their backgrounds. Thus Clara Goldschmidt, whose parents had immigrated from Germany in the 1880s (Clara was born in Paris in 1897 and was bilingual in German and French), married the brilliant young modernist poet André Malraux in 1921, then embarked with him on an adventure in Cambodia that would form the basis of his first novel, *Les Conquérants* (1927), before he went on to worldwide fame as the author of *Man's Fate* and *Man's Hope* among many other works. The couple divorced some years later, and Clara herself became a writer.[24] A surprising number of young men in and around the Surrealist group, all of them slated for fame, married Jewish women in the 1920s: André Breton married Simone Kahn, born in Peru into a prosperous Jewish family of Alsatian origin, while Raymond Queneau married her younger sister Janine.[25] The four Maklès sisters, whose family was from Romania, all married writers or artists associated with the Surrealists. The best-known one, Sylvia, who had a brief but remarkable career as a film actress, married Georges Bataille in 1928, and after their divorce in 1946 she married the psychoanalyst Jacques Lacan.[26] Elsa Triolet, who was born Ella Kagan in Moscow and married her first husband, André Triolet, in Paris in 1919, became the lover of the Surrealist poet Louis Aragon in 1928 and married him ten years later, by which time he had become the iconic writer of the French Communist Party. Triolet and Aragon went on to become one of the French literary world's most famous couples, both of them writing prizewinning novels after the war. Their collected works, published in tandem, run to more than twenty-five volumes.[27]

While all of the Surrealists had middle-class backgrounds, they thought of themselves as left-wing revolutionaries. But they did not have an exclusivity on love or marriage with Jewish immigrant women. Henri Massis, a right-wing Catholic intellectual who de-nounced the influence of Orientals on Western values and called for the "defense of the Occident," had a long extramarital love affair, starting in the 1920s, with the much younger Dominique Arban, the daughter of a Russian Jewish family of emigrés who had settled in France shortly before the First World War. He felt guilty about the affair, Arban recounts in her autobiography, but did not break it off. He abandoned her in 1940, however, when she most needed his support.[28] All of these women were from thoroughly secular Jewish families, though in many cases their grandparents or even their parents were practicing Jews. The rapid process of secularization, whereby the children and grandchildren of Yiddish-speaking ortho-dox Jews became totally distanced from any form of religious prac-tice, even as they rose in the world socially and economically, was a phenomenon that fascinated Némirovsky and that she treated in various ways in many of her books. It was also a phenomenon that preoccupied other Jewish writers of the time, including Walter Benjamin and Hannah Arendt, who devoted insightful pages to it in a number of her works. The subject also fascinated Kafka, who was painfully aware of the disconnections and fractured identities that resulted from the process. As he wrote to his friend Max Brod, in an often-quoted letter of 1921 describing his situation and that of other Jewish intellectuals of his generation, "With their hind legs they were still stuck to the Judaism of their fathers, and with their uncertain forelegs they found no new ground."[29]

Némirovsky's choosing to marry Michel Epstein, whose parents still kept a kosher home despite their high socioeconomic status, becomes all the more interesting in light of these comparisons. For someone who aspired to assimilate to French bourgeois society, her choice does not appear to have been the most strategic one: whatever positive attributes Michel possessed, he lacked a French passport. Being older, he had completed his education in Russia before emigrating. Like Irène, he loved France, but he seems to have felt most at home in the company of other emigrés, including his own brothers and sister. And yet in many ways he was the perfect choice for her. Unlike the women who married brilliant young French writers, many of whom became the first wives of these famous men, Irène could be sure that her own literary career was the one that mattered in their household. Michel was a helpmate and supporter, never a rival for the limelight. Just as, in the years that followed, she would end up earning the bulk of the family's income, as Michel's ill health and perhaps lack of ambition kept him from rising to a high position at the Banque des Pays du Nord, she clearly enjoyed being the center of attention. By all indications she loved Michel dearly and evidently meant it when she told Madeleine she found him to her taste. But that may have been partly due to the fact that in the steering of their life together, she stood at the helm.

"Cher Maître": The Literary Establishment

To put it as an understatement, it was not easy to be a respected woman writer and to earn a living as one in France between the two world wars. Those years did see the rise of professional women writers able to earn a living from their work, and many women published poetry and fiction without having to worry about income. But women who could claim both the respect of the literary world and the comfort of solid earnings from their work were extremely rare, more so than in other European countries or the United States, where some women managed to combine recognition and good earnings and a few were even awarded the Nobel Prize for Literature.[30] The fact that French women did not receive the vote until after the Second World War may be indicative in this regard. While French publishers were always on the lookout for new talent and were starting to exploit the publicity methods familiar today, including interviews in the press and on radio, promotion for literary prizes, and gossip columns where possible, their eye for such promotion almost never fell on a woman. The Académie Française, founded in 1635, continued to be the highest, if stuffiest, mark of recognition. But its forty Immortals, elected for life, did not include a woman until 1980, when Marguerite Yourcenar was chosen to fill the seat left vacant by the death of the poet and essayist Roger Caillois. Currently, the Académie has five women members, four of whom were elected after 2000.

The big exception, to be sure, was Colette. In April 1939 a professional writers' weekly, *Toute l'édition*, asked twenty Académiciens to respond to the question, Are you in favor of a woman entering the Académie Française? Most said no but a few said maybe and mentioned Colette as the only possible candidate.[31] She never made it to the academy, but in 1945 she was elected to the smaller Académie Goncourt, which awards the highly desired Prix Goncourt every year. She was seventy-three years old.

This was the world into which Irène Némirovsky made her extraordinary entrance at the age of twenty-six, when the Éditions Bernard Grasset, one of France's premier publishing houses, published *David Golder*. Bernard Grasset had started his firm in 1907, a few years before his closest rival of those years, Gaston Gallimard, launched his. Grasset prided himself on discovering and cultivating new authors. In 1913, after every other major publisher had rejected Marcel Proust's *Swann's Way*, Grasset published it—at the author's expense, but it was still a daring step. Gallimard, Proust's first choice, took over the other volumes a few years later, to Grasset's chagrin.

A brilliant publicist who sought commercial profit even as he pro-
moted quality writing, Grasset went on to publish some of the most
successful and respected writers of the period, including André Maurois, François Mauriac, Jean Giraudoux, Henri de Montherlant, Paul
Morand, Raymond Radiguet, Jean Cocteau, Jacques Chardonne,
Colette; of the above, more than half ended up in the Académie
Française. Their politics varied, though none were on the left; most
did not treat overtly political themes in their fiction. However, Grasset also published novels by André Malraux, Louis Guilloux, and
Paul Nizan, who were engaged left-wing writers: Nizan was a member of the French Communist Party, and Malraux and Guilloux
were close to it.[32]

In 1929 Grasset started a series he called "Pour mon plaisir"
(For my pleasure), in which he placed his personal favorites, books
he had fallen in love with at first reading. *David Golder* was among
the first to appear in the series, along with Cocteau's *Les Enfants
terribles*. Cocteau was already a famous, much published poet, novelist, and playwright, while Némirovsky was totally unknown. She
had published a few stories and short novels, some under a pseudonym, but most of these had appeared in a literary monthly, *Les
Oeuvres Libres*, that printed several works in each issue. *David Golder*
was her first real book. She had sent the manuscript to Grasset in
the proverbial brown paper wrapper under the name M. Epstein,
"in case it was refused," she later explained. She didn't even include
her address, and it was only after Grasset had placed an ad in the
newspapers looking for "the author who sent a manuscript to the
éditions Grasset under the name Epstein" that she finally appeared
at his office.[33] Meanwhile, on November 9, 1929, she had given birth
to her and Michel's first daughter: they called her Denise France.

David Golder was an astonishing critical success, reviewed and
praised in all the major newspapers. It remained throughout Némirovsky's life her best-selling book and was the one work by her that
stayed in print even during the decades when her name was almost
completely forgotten. It made her, virtually overnight, into a famous
writer as well as a highly respected one, placing her on a level that
no woman except Colette, who was thirty years her senior, attained
during those years. One sign of her new status was the long interview

that the editor in chief of the weekly *Les Nouvelles Littéraires*, Frédéric Lefèvre, published in his regular column, "Une heure avec . . ." (An hour with . . .) in January 1930, just a few weeks after the publication of *David Golder*. To be interviewed by Lefèvre was "incontestable proof of the celebrity of a writer," as the biographer of another highly successful novelist of the period, Joseph Kessel, whom Lefèvre had interviewed in 1925, has noted.[34] As it happens, Kessel too was a Russian Jewish, anti-Bolshevik immigrant to France who had acquired fame and fortune with his first novel, published in 1923 when he was twenty-five years old. A prolific journalist as well as novelist, Kessel would go on to become a member of the Académie Française after the Second World War. He was one of the founders, in 1928, and for a while the literary editor of the political and literary weekly *Gringoire*, where Némirovsky would publish many of her stories and serialize several of her novels.

The interview with Lefèvre demonstrates the full measure of Némirovsky's ambition as well as her ability to forge what we would today call a brand for herself as a writer. Lefèvre, as is his habit, begins by describing the writer physically: petite, fashionably dressed, with short, jet-black hair and black eyes, looking even younger than her young years, Madame Némirovsky struck him as a "beau type d'Israélite" (a fine example of an Israelite). The ink portrait in profile that accompanies the article is anything but flattering, accentuating Némirovsky's prominent nose, but Lefèvre evidently intended no insult because he goes on to say, somewhat condescendingly, that she seems to him a "perfect and rare mixture of the Slavic intellectual familiar to the habitués of the Sorbonne and the woman of the world." She received him in a large salon that doubled as her study but contained no writing desk. In fact, she explained, she usually wrote stretched out on the sofa, with a big notebook on her lap. "I am not a woman of letters," she told him: writing, to her, was a pleasure, not an obligation. And who knows, maybe after *David Golder* she wouldn't write anything for several years. Why does she write? Lefèvre asks. Because she is bored, she replies.

This was pure invention, of course, a pose concocted for the occasion. Némirovsky wrote constantly and wanted to be well paid for her work. She rode the wave of *David Golder*'s success by publishing two more novellas with Grasset, *Le Bal* and *Les Mouches d'automne*, before the end of the following year and a longer novel in the "Pour mon plaisir" series, *L'Affaire Courilof*, in 1933. But she needed an image. If young men like Kessel and Malraux could present themselves as reckless adventurers and hard drinkers, she would pose as a young woman brought up in luxury who had lived through exciting times in the Russian Revolution and the emigration that followed. She told Lefèvre the story of how she had spent days with her family shut up in their apartment in Moscow in 1918 while bombs were exploding in the street, and of how she had found relief by curling up and reading Guy de Maupassant, Oscar Wilde, and Plato's *Symposium*. Grasset had told the press she was even younger than she was, lopping two years off her real age, as if a twenty-six-year-old woman author was not young enough, so she made sure to mention her (false) birth date to Lefèvre since he "liked precise facts," she told him. The birth date she mentioned, February 11, 1905, would have made her thirteen when she was reading Plato in the middle of the Revolution! As it was, reading him at fifteen was precocious.

Némirovsky's ambition to be a respected writer in France was all to her credit, and it certainly shows through in this interview. After the preliminary flimflam, she and Lefèvre got down to a serious discussion of her work. Lefèvre had read not only *David Golder*, praising it as a "firm, virile, brutal book, like the passions it puts into play," but also the two earlier works Némirovsky had published under her own name in *Les Oeuvres Libres* in 1926 and 1927: *Le Malentendu* (The misunderstanding), her first novel, about a love affair that goes awry because of the differences in wealth and social status between the lovers, and *L'enfant génial* (The Child Prodigy), a novella about a young Jewish poet in czarist Russia. Lefèvre praises both works, especially *Le Malentendu*, which, he says, "joins the objectivity of a clinician to the tenderness of a nurse watching over a sickbed" as it analyzes the painful but eternal problem of social differences. But he reserves his most detailed discussion for *David Golder* and its main character, the only character in the novel for whom he feels a certain "tendresse." Némirovsky expresses pleasure that he finds her protagonist Golder "sympathique" and pulls out a quote from a review by a critic in another Paris newspaper who had made a similar comment. Clearly, the critical reception of *David Golder* mattered to her a great deal, and she followed it closely, not at all like a woman of leisure who writes out of boredom but as a writer intent on success.

And success was what she enjoyed, throughout the decade that followed. While none of her subsequent novels attained the commercial success of *David Golder*, which was adapted into a critically acclaimed film and a play, they were all bountifully reviewed in the French press, and she was interviewed often by journalists after that first piece by Lefèvre. Her name appeared regularly in *Les Nouvelles Littéraires* and in the professional writers' weekly *Toute l'édition*, next to those of well-known male writers. In fact, between 1936 and 1939 she was mentioned in the professional weekly more often than Colette, who nevertheless was the only woman that the Académiciens who responded to the survey about women in the Académie could imagine as a maybe for admission. Furthermore, like Colette, Kessel, and other quality writers who were able to earn a living from their work, Némirovsky discovered the advantage of serializing a novel in a newspaper before issuing it in book form. Almost all of the novels she wrote after *David Golder* first appeared in serialized form in the weekly press, allowing her to earn two sets of payments. This kind of marketing was shunned by the literary avant-garde but sought by writers who wanted to gain commercial as well as professional success. Very few of them were women.

The pinnacle of Némirovsky's success was marked by the article devoted to her work in November 1936 in the venerable *Revue des Deux Mondes*, which was known to many as the "antechamber to the Académie." The *Revue*, a literary and political bimonthly founded in 1829, had been shaped by the long tenures of its editors. Under the editorship of René Doumic, who was only its fourth editor and held the position from 1916 until his death in 1937, the journal sought to maintain a moderately conservative position in both its politics and its literary choices. While strongly antisocialist and anticommunist, it also condemned Nazism. It was a genteel publication, and its contributors included some of the most famous, most established writers of the interwar period. Many of them were, by the 1930s, of a certain age, and few are still read today, but at the time, the names of Henry Bordeaux, Henri de Régnier, Georges Duhamel, Jacques de Lacretelle, Pierre Benoît, the Tharaud brothers Jérôme and Jean,

Paul Morand, Francis Carco, and Henri de Montherlant were guar-antees of quality. In November 1936 Némirovsky was discussed as a member of the "new team" (la nouvelle équipe), a term designating young, up-and-coming writers to whom the *Revue* devoted occa-sional articles.[35] Némirovsky was the only woman writer to receive that honor and one of the rare French women writers whose work was published in the magazine during the 1930s. The *Revue* did pub-lish fiction by English and American women writers, however: Edith Wharton, Virginia Woolf, Pearl Buck, and Daphne du Maurier all appeared there during those years.[36] Némirovsky published her first story in the *Revue* in April 1935, followed by a longer, two-part story a year later and two more over the next four years, but as we saw in the previous chapter, Doumic turned down her story "Fraternité" just around the time that the admiring "new team" piece about her appeared.

Perhaps nothing indicates more clearly Némirovsky's ambition to be part of the literary establishment than the twenty-six letters she wrote between 1930 and 1936 to a prolific, well-connected, but now totally forgotten writer, Gaston Chérau (1872–1937), whom she addressed unfailingly with the honorific "cher Maître" (dear Mas-ter), usually reserved for members of the Académie Française. These letters, discovered in a Paris library by Némirovsky's biographer Olivier Philipponnat only after the publication of the biography, are important because of their coherence and number and for what they show about her professional conduct.[37] Chérau was the author of provincial novels set in and around his native province of Berry in the center of France as well as of some nonfiction works in which he expressed moderate conservative political views. Although not a mem-ber of the Académie Française, he was a member of the Académie Goncourt, composed of ten prominent writers who awarded the prestigious Prix Goncourt every year. He thus played an influential role in designating the writers who merited attention, and Némi-rovsky treated him accordingly. Her first letter to him is dated May 3, 1930, and she encloses with it a copy of *David Golder* as well as what she refers to as "the copy annotated by you" of *Le Malentendu*, her early novel that was about to be reissued separately as a result of *Golder*'s success. Chéreau had apparently read the early version and sent her suggestions for changes in the new edition. She thanks him effusively for this "magnificent lesson in literature"—she has examined and reflected on every one of his pencil strokes, she says. She then reminds him that he had promised to help her obtain membership in the Société des Gens de Lettres, the professional writers' association. Could he tell her to whom she should address her request for admission, and would he be willing to act as her sponsor? A month later, on June 10, not having heard from him, she writes to him again to ask whether he received her letter, and two weeks after that she thanks him for his generous offer of help. Chérau had apparently not forgotten his promise and had even found another sponsor for her, one of his colleagues at the Académie Goncourt, Roland Dorgelès, the author of a well-known antiwar novel. Némirovsky's candidacy for the Société des Gens de Lettres sailed through without difficulty.

The support of an older, established figure who could smooth the way with introductions, recommendations, and the well-placed article in the press was and no doubt still is essential to any young writer aiming to enter the high-end literary market—all the more so for a woman. Over the next four years Némirovsky wrote to Chérau frequently, inviting him to dinner on occasion and mentioning vacations and family news as well as professional matters. She sent him the manuscripts or page proofs of three more novels, expressing gratitude each time for his precious annotations. In October 1933 Chérau published an admiring article about her in the large-circulation daily *L'Intransigeant,* in which he echoed a theme that had already been touched on by the first reviewers of *David Golder* and that became practically a leitmotif in the critical reception of her works: although very feminine in appearance and lifestyle, she was not a "woman writer." As Chérau put it, "Némirovsky, so womanly in life, is formally masculine." By that he meant that, like all "real novelists" (he wrote *romancier,* the masculine form, not the feminine *romancière*), she had a "native competence in organizing the action" of her novels, to the point of allowing the story to take on a life of its own rather than sticking to a predetermined plan. Her characters were forcefully drawn, but she let readers discover them through suggestions and imagination, the surest way to make a reader feel interested in a character. Chérau mentioned all of her works to date and concluded with an extraordinary compliment: "One can find five hundred authors of novels; but there is not always a novelist among them."[38]

Némirovsky, in sum, was that rarity, a woman, a mother, and a true (male) novelist. As if to illustrate the point, Chérau's article was accompanied by a photo, furnished by Irène, showing her with Denise, not yet three years old, posed in front of a wall full of books. The day after the article appeared, *L'Intransigeant* began publication of Némirovsky's novel *Le Pion sur l'échiquier* (The pawn on the chessboard), which ran every day for several weeks and, after being duly annotated by Chérau, was published as a book the following spring. By then Némirovsky had switched publishers, following Chérau's advice. She had signed on with the firm of Albin Michel, bigger and even more prestigious than Grasset, the publisher of the Nobel laureate Romain Rolland among other literary giants. Némirovsky would remain with Albin Michel until the end of her life, and beyond, for her posthumous works before *Suite Française* were all published by that press.

By the time she wrote *Le Vin de solitude*, the novel that followed *Le Pion sur l'échiquier*, she apparently felt she could do without Chérau's editing. She mentions the book to him in February 1935 as a work soon to be published (it appeared in August, after being serialized) but does not send him the manuscript. She continues to write to him, however, albeit more rarely, always in the most flattering terms, praising his works and commenting on them to show that she had read them. She assures him that her husband too finds his writing irresistible. Chérau died in April 1937 in Boston while on an American lecture tour. Némirovsky's last letter to him is from April 1936. She apologizes for not writing sooner to thank him for his latest book and announces the sad news that her mother-in-law has died, a "charming woman" to whom she and her husband felt very close. She expresses regret at seeing him so rarely these days, for "I could well use the advice you were kind enough to give me in the past. I have gotten older, but I need it just as much."

In fact, Némirovsky was still a young writer, thirty-three years old, when she wrote those words. One sometimes forgets, considering how much work she produced, that she was not yet forty when she died. In a sense her whole career consisted of early years. As she did with Chérau, she took care to cultivate the goodwill of older establishment writers she met throughout the 1930s. When Henri de Régnier, a famous poet and novelist who was a member of the Académie Française, reviewed *David Golder* in *Le Figaro*, the newspaper of record at the time, she wrote to him immediately to thank him, expressing her joy and astonishment that "the great writer I admired from afar could not only read a work by me but speak about it with such benevolence." Four years later, when he reviewed *Le Pion sur l'échiquier*, she wrote to the "cher Maître" again: "I admire you so very much. Every word of praise from you fills me with a profound and very delicious pride." Charmingly, in that same letter she reminded him that a dozen years earlier, during her student days, she had lived in an apartment in the same building as he and disturbed his peace with her "detestable girlish" ways.[39] At his death in 1936 she sent a handwritten telegram to his wife (also a writer, the daughter of a famous nineteenth-century poet, José-Maria de Hérédia) to express her heartfelt condolences.[40] Born in 1864, Henri de Régnier was almost old enough to be Némirovsky's grandfather. Her faith in the benevolence of kindly old Frenchmen would not be broken until a few years later.

Gringoire

As a writer Némirovsky was attracted neither to the radical, left-wing avant-garde represented by the Surrealists, who scorned realist fiction, nor to the international modernist circles in Paris associated with the names of James Joyce and Gertrude Stein, a group which included a number of women writers besides Stein: Djuna Barnes, Kay Boyle, Anaïs Nin, and the poet H.D., among others. She was not drawn even to the group of relatively young writers at the highly elitist *Nouvelle Revue Française*, the journal founded by André Gide and published by Gaston Gallimard. The writers of the "NRF," all of them men, prided themselves on being modern without engaging in the perceived excesses or the revolutionary rhetoric of the Surrealists—who, despite their radical politics, considered the women in the group during those years mostly as wives and girlfriends, even when they produced art. Némirovsky's choice of Grasset as her first publisher reflected a sense of innovation but also a desire for a large readership and for recognition by writers who were in line for a place at the Académie Française, if they were not already members of it. By temperament as well as stylistic affinity, she sought the approbation of quality mainstream authors and their public, who best represented the characteristics she associated with Frenchness: moderation, a sense of adventure "within reasonable bounds," respect for family, property, propriety. Her own values were not necessarily identical, for she was capable of looking at this Frenchness with an ironic eye, seeing its pettiness and stultifying narrowness as well as its virtues. Yet she undoubtedly wanted the approval of authors and readers who, in her mind, represented it.

Unfortunately, those authors and readers became increasingly conservative and xenophobic as the decade of the thirties moved toward its disastrous close. If Némirovsky was to maintain her place among the writers whose approval she sought—not only much older figures like Chérau and Régnier but also the successful bourgeois novelists, fifteen or twenty years her senior, with whom she shared space in the literary field, such as Paul Morand, Jacques de Lacretelle, Jacques Chardonne, all highly successful and all participating, with various degrees of gentility, in the ambient antisemitism and xenophobia—she would have to close her eyes to the fact that what they wrote about foreigners and Jews was often detestable and might also have something to do with her. These writers were not right-wing ideologues, nor did they become rabid antisemites like Robert Brasillach and Lucien Rebatet and Louis-Ferdinand Céline, who were all closer in age to Némirovsky. They were, rather, well to do Frenchmen with increasingly ugly prejudices, like many of their countrymen. The economic and political crises of the 1930s, which led to increasing waves of immigrants arriving in France from Germany and eastern Europe, contributed to the rise in xenophobia and to the general move toward the right among large swaths of the population in the years leading up to the Second World War. This prewar trend explains at least in part why the Vichy regime was relatively popular among the majority of the French during its first two years.

Némirovsky did close her eyes, and her daughter Elisabeth reproached her for it in the interview she gave after the publication of *Le Mirador*. In the book itself Elisabeth sought to soften this harsh judgment by recalling that Némirovsky was not alone in this blindness, which was shared by many conservative Israélites such as Jean-

Jacques Bernard and Emmanuel Berl, whom Némirovsky frequented socially and professionally. Bernard and Berl were quite distant from Jewish institutions and Jewish practice, and Bernard eventually converted to Catholicism, but even some Jews who were members of the Consistoire and contributed to its journal, *L'Univers Israélite*, expressed concern over the number of Jewish immigrants who were arriving in France and who risked arousing antisemitism with their unassimilated ways. "The immigrants must learn to fit in" was a recurrent theme in articles and editorials appearing in *L'Univers Israélite* throughout the 1930s and as early as the 1920s.[41]

Many Israélites even sought to distance themselves from other assimilated French Jews who attracted the fury of the establishment. First among the latter was Léon Blum, who inspired fear and loathing in many members of the French bourgeoisie, both Jews and non-Jews, despite his pedigree as a member of the intellectual elite. Born in 1872 into a Parisian lower-middle-class Jewish family, Blum was a product of "l'école républicaine," the school system famous for promoting talent based on merit. He rose to the highest position in public service as a member of the Conseil d'État, the closest French equivalent to the United States Supreme Court, and also pursued a career as a literary critic and essayist. After the First World War he entered politics, becoming the head of the Socialist Party and a leader of the Popular Front, the alliance of parties on the Left that had been formed as a response to right-wing agitation. When the elections of 1936 brought the Popular Front to power and Blum was in line to become prime minister, a delegation from the Consistoire tried to dissuade him from taking the post, for fear of attracting hatred against Jews.[42] In order to prove how genuinely French they were, these Israélites advocated discretion, which meant keeping their heads low in the face of attacks from the extreme Right. Their call for discretion demonstrated their sense of insecurity and vulnerability, although one must suppose that many also genuinely espoused conservative political ideas and were critical of Blum for that reason. Némirovsky must have felt even more insecure than they, as a stateless immigrant in France who had childhood memories of fear and exposure to danger during the Russian Revolution.

The political and literary weekly *Gringoire*, founded in 1928 by the well-connected journalist Horace de Carbuccia, was among the most widely read Parisian papers when Némirovsky published her first story there, in December 1933.[43] Carbuccia had recruited a number of successful young writers, most of them his close friends, to be founding editors. Joseph Kessel's best-selling novel *Belle de jour* appeared first in installments in *Gringoire* and helped its inaugural issue attain a circulation of over 150,000. By 1937 the paper had a circulation of 650,000, more than any other weekly.[44] *Gringoire* was known for paying its authors handsomely. Each week it devoted about half of its six or eight large-format pages to literature. Individual short stories, serialized novels, or historical vignettes took up a whole page, some by famous authors like Cocteau, Colette, and Maurois, some by hacks who were already unknowns at the time and remained so, and some by up-and-coming writers like Némirovsky or even by total beginners like Romain Gary. (Gary recounts in his autobiography how excited he was to see his first story published there in 1935.)[45] Kessel, a drinking buddy of Carbuccia's, edited the literary pages for a year but resigned the position in 1929, disliking the obligations the job involved. For almost a decade longer, however, he continued to publish in the paper, contributing *grands reportages* on travel and politics in far-off places as well as works of fiction.

Critics who know or know of *Gringoire* as the virulently anti-semitic collaborationist paper it became in its later years never fail to reproach Némirovsky for publishing there. Indeed, her participation in *Gringoire* is a trump card in any argument about her supposed Jewish self-hatred. It is quite astonishing to learn, therefore, that in the early years after its founding *Gringoire*'s political line was defined by Carbuccia as Left, although strongly opposed to the Communists and the Socialists, who were considered the extreme Left. Kessel's biographer reports that Carbuccia's dictum for the paper in the beginning was "to tell the truth and maintain a politics of the left."[46] The moderate left party at the time were the Radical Socialists, who were in truth neither radical nor socialist but who dominated the political scene for most of the interwar years. When she started publishing in *Gringoire*, Némirovsky found herself in respectable company, and her embrace by the paper confirmed her position in the mainstream quality area of the literary field.

What is difficult to grapple with, from our perspective, is her continuing to publish in *Gringoire* even at a time when the political coloration of the paper had become overtly xenophobic and anti-semitic. The first major change in its politics can be dated fairly precisely: it was in early 1934, when the novelist and journalist Henri Béraud, who had been one of the paper's founding editors and had written only literary essays for it until then, began to publish vitriolic front-page political commentaries. The rotund Béraud had won the Prix Goncourt in 1922 for a novel about the suffering of a fat man, *Le Martyre de l'obèse*. According to the memoir Carbuccia published many years later, it was he who had asked Béraud to switch to political commentary.[47] Writing decades after the Second World War, Carbuccia manifested no regrets, continuing to blame the influx of foreigners and especially of "unscrupulous" foreign Jews for France's troubles during the 1930s, if not for the war itself. Béraud did not need to be asked twice, however: if Carbuccia wanted hard-hitting polemics, Béraud would deliver. His first political article, dated January 12, 1934, was a response to what soon became known as the Stavisky Affair. Alexandre Stavisky, a Russian Jewish immigrant born in Kiev who went by the name of Serge Alexandre, had lived the high life as a financial speculator, befriending politicians in high places as well as some writers, Kessel among them. Stavisky was a handsome, seductive man, but he turned out to be a crook. His schemes collapsed, and in January 1934 he committed suicide in his mountain chalet, though some claimed he was murdered to keep him quiet. The great filmmaker Alain Resnais devoted a film to Stavisky in 1974 starring Jean-Paul Belmondo as the charming scoundrel. Stavisky had implicated a great many politicians in his shady dealings, recalling earlier scandals, notably the Panama Scandal of 1897, which almost brought down the then young parliamentary regime because of the number of deputies who had accepted bribes. In 1934 as well the financial scandal gave opponents of the regime a perfect opportunity to rail against corrupt politicians. In fact, members of various right-wing groups tried to topple the regime in February 1934 during a day of clashes with police that produced several deaths. The failed coup of the "6th of February," as the event is known in history books, led to the formation of the Popular Front later that year and eventually to the election of Blum as prime minister.

Stavisky's Russian Jewish origins were fodder for right-wing commentators. Béraud devoted more than half of his first political column in *Gringoire* to denouncing the large number of foreigners in France, who not only corrupted the country but also besmirched its good reputation among nations.[48] The corruption of politicians in power and the danger represented by foreigners, first among them the Jews, became two of Béraud's favorite themes. And he did not attack only foreigners. When Blum, a refined Parisian intellectual and Israélite, became prime minister in June 1936, Béraud launched a vicious campaign against him. He was not the only right-wing journalist to do so, but his articles were particularly scurrilous, portraying Blum as an "Oriental," not truly French. The Prime Hebrew, as Béraud called him, was endangering France by stuffing his government with "circumcised ones" like himself. On Christmas Day 1936 Béraud published an article titled "Midnight, Christians," in which he listed all the Jews in Blum's cabinet and in other government posts. Although Jews constituted only 2 percent of the population, they were deciding the fate of the nation. Not that he was an antisemite, Béraud added. Some Jews had brought glory to France, and he listed several names, including that of Kessel. But on the whole, Béraud declared himself to be appalled at the "Jewification" (from *enjuiver*, a very ugly verb) that Blum was bringing on France.[49]

A few weeks later, on February 5, 1937, Béraud's front-page article consisted of his long response to a letter to the editor Carbuccia had received from Kessel. Kessel's letter was brief, and Béraud quoted it in full in his article. Kessel thanked him for the honor of being praised by him as one of France's good Jews, but he felt obliged to make one thing clear: "I don't feel that I am a special kind of Jew. And I want to be considered, by those who establish categories of different kinds of Frenchmen, in the same category as all the Jews of France." He then noted that he couldn't help detecting in Béraud's Christmas article "a very clearly antisemitic tone." Béraud responded to his "friend" Kessel that many other Israélites had written to him to affirm their respect and understanding of his position. He reiterated his earlier argument against Blum and drew up a list of other left-wing historical figures with Jewish-sounding names (all of whom had as their master Karl Marx, he remarked) who had brought disaster on Europe, from Alexander Kerensky to Rosa Luxemburg to Béla Kun of Hungary.[50] After this, Kessel stopped contributing to *Gringoire*.

By a truly striking coincidence Némirovsky's short story "Fraternité" appeared in the same issue as this article by Béraud. She continued to contribute to *Gringoire* until February 1942, publishing short stories and serialized novels, none of which ever referred to Jews again. It must be counted to Carbuccia's credit that he bought her work when she most needed the money, after the Vichy decrees of October 1940 and June 1941 forbade Jewish authors to publish in newspapers. Her name could not appear, so he allowed her to use pseudonyms. The serialized version of *All Our Worldly Goods*, which appeared between April and June 1941, was signed simply "By a young woman." However, in the spring of 1942 Carbuccia stopped accepting her work, thus depriving her of a financial lifeline. In a letter to her trusted editor at Albin Michel, André Sabatier, dated 17 May, 1942, she speaks of the "state of bitterness, fatigue and disgust" in which Carbuccia's refusal had left her.[51]

By that time *Gringoire* was publishing more and more vile articles against Jews and foreigners on its political pages. Béraud, continuing in the vein he had mined before the war, still blamed Blum for France's troubles, even though he had been out of office since April 1938: "Wretched Blum, a foreign Jew."[52] Other, equally hateful voices joined in, notably that of Philippe Henriot, the "voice of Vichy" on the radio, who would later be named minister of information by Pétain. On April 10, 1941, the day the first installment of Némirovsky's *Les Biens de ce monde* ("By a young woman") appeared on page 6, page 2 carried an item by Henriot applauding the "cleanup" of the French movie industry, which had been dominated until then by Jews.[53] Michel Epstein's brother Samuel, as I noted earlier, was a movie producer. In June 1944 Henriot was assassinated by the Resistance. Béraud was arrested a few months later, after the Liberation, and condemned to death in December 1944 for intelligence with the enemy, the formal designation for treason. Charles de Gaulle commuted Béraud's sentence to life imprisonment, and he was released in 1950 on grounds of illness. He had time to write a book of self-justification before dying in 1958.[54] As for Carbuccia, he fled to Switzerland after being sentenced to jail in

1944 but returned a few years later and was exonerated by a military tribunal, which dropped all charges against him.[55]

The wartime, however, requires a separate discussion. What is more troubling is that Némirovsky chose to stay with *Gringoire* earlier, at a time when she had more freedom to maneuver. If Kessel had severed his ties with the paper after years of friendship with Carbuccia and Béraud, why did she not do the same? One possible explanation is that she was indifferent to politics, caring only for the literary company she kept. After all, in addition to *Gringoire* and another conservative weekly, *Candide*, she also published stories in the women's magazine *Marie Claire* and in the center-left weekly *Marianne*, whose editor was Berl. This is what Elisabeth Gille as well as Némirovsky's biographers suggested when they said that *Gringoire's* political pages were separate from its literary pages, but the separation was not quite as airtight as they thought, for Némirovsky's "Fraternité" appeared just a page away from an antisemitic piece of supposedly historical fiction about Jews and Communism in Hungary.[56] Besides, it is almost insulting to Némirovsky's intelligence to think she would not have read the front pages of a paper she contributed to, especially when it carried frequent ugly caricatures of Jews as well as blaring headlines about them.

Another, more plausible explanation for her ongoing connection to *Gringoire* after 1937 is that it paid very well and she needed the money. Unlike Kessel, who had a steady income from his best-selling books and his journalism, she and Michel seem to have lived almost from hand to mouth, that is, from story to story and book to book. Both the Némirovsky and the Epstein families had lost their fortunes in the crash of 1929, and after Irène's father died of a heart attack in 1932 she had no one to rely on for extra help. In many journal entries around 1936 and later, including the notes for "Fraternité," she expresses her distress over financial worries. Michel, although earning a good salary at the bank where he worked, spent twice as much as he earned, she noted in one entry in 1938. Ten days later, in the same journal, she noted bitterly that they didn't have enough money to go to the movies, despite the fact that she was "the author of D.G. [*David Golder*], the young woman full of talent."[57] The family's lifestyle, with the huge apartment near the Invalides, several servants, and vacations by the sea, required a large budget. She was receiving a monthly stipend from Albin Michel, but she needed the additional payments that serialization and newspaper publication brought in.

Angela Kershaw, the author of a fine book on Némirovsky, adopts an approach close to Pierre Bourdieu's in discussing Némirovsky's career choices, including her choice to continue publishing in *Gringoire*.[58] According to this view, once Némirovsky had established her position in the literary field, among the respectable bourgeois novelists, most of whom had no trouble sharing space with antisemites even if they did not themselves express extremist views, there was no turning back or switching course. This argument, invoking the logic of the literary field independently of individual choice, possesses a certain attractiveness, but I think it is too deterministic: it cuts off the possibility of "enormous changes at the last minute," to echo the title of one of Grace Paley's best short stories. Actually, quite a few intellectuals in the interwar years switched their ideological allegiances, though most of them did so from Left to Right, not vice versa. Jacques Doriot, who became a leader of a French fascist party, started out as a communist. Némirovsky was not engaged in politics, but she feared communism after her adolescent experience of the Revolution, and she obviously felt most at home with members of the privileged classes. When it came to *Gringoire*, did she feel helpless, unable to see any alternatives to the paths she had already taken?

There is another possible explanation for Némirovsky's continued participation in *Gringoire*, namely, that she agreed with the vicious views about foreigners and Jews spewed on the paper's political pages. This thought no doubt lies behind the most indignant accusations of Jewish self-hatred one sometimes finds expressed about her. She had so thoroughly adopted the views of the most extreme Jew-haters about Jews, the accusation goes, that she felt no compunction about seeing her work appear next to theirs. Worse still, she totally disassociated herself from the fate of the Jews, in a quasi-pathological attempt to disavow her origins and assimilate to what she misguidedly considered as true Frenchness. There were, after all, less hateful ways of being French.

This explanation has some truth in it—but only some. One proof of it, discovered only in 2015 by Olivier Philipponnat, is the three-part article Némirovsky published in another right-wing weekly, *Le Magazine d'aujourd'hui*, a few months after the Stavisky scandal. The journal, founded in 1933 by Massis, the theorist of Occidentalism, lasted only about a year or two, and copies of it exist today in just one library in France.[59] Némirovsky's contribution, appearing from May 16 to May 30, 1934, was titled "Rois d'une heure" (Kings for an hour), a play on kings for a day but also on kings of the world (*rois du monde*), a commonly used expression to designate the powerful financiers and industrialists who supposedly ruled the world. Némirovsky began her article by evoking that term and citing some of the names that exemplified it: "Basil Zaharoff, Ford, Bata, sir Deterding, etc." As it happened, none of those magnates was Jewish, but they were not the object of Némirovsky's scrutiny. Her article described a much less imposing figure: the shady, restless foreigner who might rise to the top for a while but would inevitably fall, dragging others with him. She called this figure the *macher*, the Yiddish name for a clever, if not totally trustworthy, businessman. But she was careful to point out that not only Jews fit the description; to think so was unfair, she wrote, harmful to a "whole people." Not only Jews but all the "races of the Orient" were represented by the macher: "Armenians, Greeks, Romanians, Poles, Russians, Jews, etc." Still, she added, Jews were often identified with this type, and that was because the macher's outstanding characteristics are his homelessness and statelessness (*apatride* is the adjective in French, though she uses the German *heimatlos* here) and his "chaotic, feverish" existence as he wanders all over the world "without leaving a trace." Then comes the crux: "For an exiled person . . . who lives in France and earns his bread honestly, through hard work, the 'macher' is a torment [une plaie]: he brings discredit and shame on him [that is, on the honest exile]."[60] The rest of the article is a long, analytical portrait of this figure, who obviously fascinated Némirovsky and repelled her in equal measure. David Golder, her creation, is a macher and her own father, Léon, was not far from being one, as were some of the other memorable characters she created in her fiction, most notably one of the protagonists of her late novel *The Dogs and the Wolves*, Ben Sinner. But in her fictional works the macher can be a surprisingly rounded, even sympathetic, figure. In this article, which may have received some editing at the hands of Massis, the macher is presented as an occasionally amusing but mostly dangerous foreigner "from the East" that good, honest Frenchmen must avoid like the plague.

"Rois d'une heure" appears to have been Némirovsky's only foray into political journalism, and it is not a piece that does her credit. Was she feeling especially vulnerable on the heels of the Stavisky affair, since she shared not only the nationality but even the native city of the charming scoundrel? Or was she responding to a more general anxiety about the fate of Jews in Europe? At almost the same time as this article, in March 1934 she wrote a very interesting theater review, one of several she published that year, about the French adaptation of a German anti-Nazi play, *Les Races*. While she found the play too didactic to be fully successful as a work of art, she considered it important and wrote about it at length: "It poses anguishing questions to every one of us, to the extent that the personal fate of every individual depends on the fate of his race and his nation. This play provokes thought and stirs up the soul." The play, she wrote, provided a disquieting vision of the "war against the Jews in Germany" and "revealed a state of mind that is terribly troubling for the neighbors of a nation where sadism, pride and cruelty are glorified to such a degree." It's true, she concluded, almost as if to reassure herself as well as her readers, that "France is too profoundly imbued with civilization to even imagine such excesses."[61]

There is no doubt that Némirovsky sought to distance herself from "shady Jews" who might bring discredit on honest, hardworking foreigners like herself. Her private journals show that she suffered from periods of debilitating depression and that she was prone to a striking degree of anxiety and fear for the future, despite her extraordinary professional success. Much of this feeling of insecurity had to do with money and with the evolving political situation in Europe, but it probably went deeper than that. She made light of her depressions when she mentioned them to friends, if she mentioned them at all, as she had done with Madeleine Avot. But her journals speak more darkly of her "black moods," and she allowed herself outbursts of feeling and language there that she would not utter or write in public.

The trouble with all explanations that isolate a single factor in accounting for human motivations is that they are too simple. We must allow for all of the above possibilities and for others we may not even be aware of in trying to understand Némirovsky's choices during the 1930s. Ascribing responsibility to her for her choices is unavoidable if we want to recognize her as a human subject, but that does not mean we can fully account for them. She probably made choices the way we all do—not knowing how they will turn out, sometimes barely aware of them *as* choices, simply following the current and hoping for the best.

"My Country . . . My Homeland. It Is a Great Thing"

One question that often comes up in discussions of Némirovsky's life is, Why did she wait so long to apply for French citizenship? Why did she and Michel not request naturalization in the 1920s, when it was relatively easy to obtain, waiting instead until the political mood of the country and the increasing wave of immigrants crowding into France made it much harder? In their biography of 2007 Philipponnat and Lienhardt gave November 1935 as the date Michel and Irène filed their first request for naturalization. Subsequently, after discovering her letters to Chérau, Philipponnat revised the date to earlier: in his introduction to Némirovsky's complete works he quotes from a letter to Chérau that seems to imply she had applied in 1930.[62] But the story turns out to be more complicated.

The immigration and naturalization laws in France, as in other countries, have varied with political and economic circumstances, both local and international. In times of relative stability and economic well-being countries often welcome foreign workers and make room for their naturalization, but in times of political crisis or economic downturn immigrants become a target of resentment, especially if they are seen as "stealing" jobs from the native population or profiting from social services that should be reserved for citizens only. After the First World War, France saw a decade of prosperity and had reason to encourage the growth of its population, which had been severely affected by the loss of young men during the war. Starting in the mid-1920s naturalization laws were relaxed, and in 1927 the National Assembly passed a new law that reduced the requirements for citizenship. Its main novelty was that a foreign resident no longer had to wait ten years before applying for naturalization but could apply after three years of residence in France. This led to a doubling of naturalizations before the end of the decade, although the numbers were still quite modest by current standards: 22,500 in 1928 and 1929. The total number of foreigners in France at the time was more than 2 million, roughly 6 percent of the population.[63]

The financial crash of 1929 and the worldwide depression that followed did not change the law, but it changed the climate of opinion about foreigners in France. As in the case of *Gringoire*, which was just one of many right-wing papers, the attitude toward immigrants became more and more hostile as the decade advanced, but as early as 1930 a paper founded two years before by the right-wing perfume manufacturer René Coty, *L'Ami du Peuple*, was spewing xenophobic rhetoric in its pages. "Around Paris, too many *heimatlos*, too many exotics spread a zone of physiological and moral infection," stated one article.[64] Starting in 1932 talk began about denaturalizing undesirable citizens, and some naturalizations were indeed revoked in the following years, in the case of criminals, for example. A decade later the Vichy regime would act on it in earnest.[65] Although xenophobia in this period is often thought of as another word for antisemitism, in fact only 7 percent of immigrants to France in the 1930s were Jewish. The proportion of Jewish immigrants was much greater in Paris, but non-Jewish foreigners seeking work, from Italy, Poland, Spain, Germany, Hungary, and other European countries, far outnumbered Jews.[66]

Acquiring citizenship was an extremely complicated process, even after the liberalized law of 1927. One had to create a dossier at the local town hall (*mairie*) containing a letter that explained why one sought to become French, accompanied by a number of documents, including letters of recommendation about one's character. If the dossier was found satisfactory at the local level, it was forwarded to the Préfecture, reviewed again, and if all went well, forwarded to a bureau at the Ministry of Justice. The process took about a year. If the ministry's decision was favorable, and the large majority were, given the selection process at every step, the newly declared citizen's name was published in the *Journal Officiel*. In 1931 only about 5 percent of requests were rejected outright, while 17 percent were adjourned, which meant the applicant could try again later.[67]

It now seems certain that Michel Epstein filed his first request for naturalization in 1932. Irène, as his wife, was included in the application. A very helpful archivist at the Archives Nationales, with whom a historian of immigration put me in touch in the summer of 2013, succeeded in finding the number of the dossier: 3012X 32. She explained that 32 referred to the year in which the initial request was made; any subsequent requests were simply added to the dossier, the number remaining unchanged. To my dismay she informed me a few days later, after she had tried to obtain the dossier, that it was missing, with no "phantom" left behind. A phantom is what French archivists call the blank sheet that is inserted whenever a file is taken out, showing the name of the person who borrowed it and the date. In this case there is no such sheet in place, and it is therefore impossible to know why, when, and under what circumstances the Michel Epstein dossier went missing. From here on it becomes a matter of piecing together fragments of information.

We know that Michel and Irène submitted a request for naturalization at least twice more, in 1935 and 1938. Some documents relating to the 1938 date are among the Némirovsky papers at the Institut Mémoires de l'Édition Contemporaine (IMEC), an archive in Caen that houses materials from writers and publishers, where I consulted them in 2009 and again in 2015. In addition to official certificates and Michel's letter of application of November 1938 there are three recommendations for him from colleagues at the Banque des Pays du Nord, including the bank's director. Irène's recommenders were even more stellar: Jean Vignaud, the president of the Société des Gens de Lettres, and André Chaumeix, a member of the Académie Française who had been editor in chief of the daily *Le Figaro* from 1926 to 1930 and who succeeded Doumic as the editor of the *Revue des Deux Mondes* in 1937. One indication of the importance accorded to this dossier was the letters addressed to the bank director and to Vignaud by the Garde des Sceaux, the official in charge of naturalizations at the Ministry of Justice, in December 1938. The Garde assures both of them that he will pay particular attention to this dossier, given the support of such distinguished people. But close to a year later, in September 1939, nothing had happened. On the fateful date of September 1, when Germany invaded Poland and provoked the declaration of war, Vignaud wrote another recommendation to the Garde des Sceaux, mentioning that "no doubt the circumstances have retarded the decision on this request, which was favorably received."[68] Unfortunately, the "circumstances" only got worse in the months that followed. The Epsteins never did receive the citizenship they sought, which just might have saved their lives.

The story turns out to have another twist, however. Némirovsky's letters to Chérau indicate that she and Michel were indeed planning to apply for citizenship in 1930 but changed their mind at the last minute. The reason they did so is quite astonishing. Apparently, Chérau, who was a member of the Académie Goncourt, was planning to nominate Némirovsky's *David Golder* for the Prix Goncourt that year, which would have been quite a coup since no woman had ever won the prize. But one of the stipulations at the time was that the author had to be French (today, it is enough to write in French and be published by a French publisher, without regard for nationality). Chérau must have suggested that she apply for citizenship, for she wrote to him on June 23, 1930: "As concerns naturalization, since we had no idea whom to contact, my husband and I thought it would be better to put it off until the fall, as we will be away from Paris until the 10th or 15th of September. What do you think?" We don't know what he replied, and her next letter to him, in August, does not mention the subject. The one after that, however, dated October 22, 1930, indicates that she was replying to a suggestion he had made once again. Read today, this letter feels like a bombshell: "I am certain that you will approve when I tell you that it is precisely because naturalization can facilitate my receiving the Prix Goncourt that I have decided to put off applying. It is my dearest wish to become French . . . , able to say proudly: my country . . . my homeland. It is a great thing. But precisely because I value it [French nationality] so highly, I would like it to be absolutely disinterested on my part, so that the moral and material benefit of the Prize should in no way influence a gift as I understand it. I am sure you will pardon me for not acceding to your wishes, and I dare hope that you will approve." As for the prize, she continues, she would have been very happy to have it, "but since it's impossible . . ." As it is, his judgment that she deserves the prize is enough for her: "I am perfectly satisfied, I swear it."[69]

Talk about a noble gesture. One can only marvel at the ease with which she was able to renounce the coveted Prix Goncourt. At the same time, this is one of those occasions where today's reader feels the full weight of what in theater parlance is called tragic irony: If only she had known! If only she had been content to appear less noble in the eyes of her mentor. It is striking that she takes full responsibility for the decision—"I have decided to put off applying"— even though in her earlier letter she had said "my husband and I" when referring to their application.

Did she perhaps foresee and try to fend off the attacks that would be aimed at her if by chance she did win the prize? In fact, a few weeks later, on November 22, a venomous unsigned note appeared in *Les Nouvelles Littéraires* under the heading "Two questions." The questions explicitly targeted Némirovsky's *David Golder.* One, had the Goncourt judges decided about the admissibility of women to this famous competition? And, two, did naturalization give a foreigner the right to receive the Prix Goncourt?[70] In the end it was another foreign Jew, albeit a French citizen by virtue of her marriage to a Frenchman, who became the first woman to receive the Prix Goncourt: Elsa Triolet, the wife of the poet and novelist Louis Aragon, was awarded the prize in 1945 for *Le premier accroc coûte deux cents francs* (The first infraction costs two hundred francs), a book of linked stories about France during the Occupation.

If Irène had not changed her mind and if they had applied in 1930, would the Epsteins have been granted citizenship? And if so, would that have saved them from deportation and death? We will never know the answers to those questions, but we cannot help dreaming about them.

"Only Believe, Zaïre"

Why did Némirovsky convert to Catholicism? She and Michel and their daughters were baptized in February 1939, and that date may suggest a simple answer: she was trying to protect herself and her family from what she sensed was going to be a catastrophe for Jews, not realizing that the protection afforded by baptism was an illusion. But the reality is more complicated.

In modern France the conversion of Jews to Catholicism has

always been a private matter, not a job requirement. While Germany and Hungary, two other European countries where Jews enjoyed great opportunities for advancement starting in the nineteenth century, imposed strict limits on civil service and academic or professional careers for non-Christians, no such limits existed in France, at least not officially. The career of Alfred Dreyfus, who rose to the rank of captain in the French army in the 1880s even while remaining Jewish, would have been unthinkable east of the Rhine, where even conversion would not have gained him entry into the officers' ranks.[71] To be sure, Dreyfus's condemnation as a traitor to France on the basis of the most flimsy evidence, much of it forged for the occasion, would not have occurred if he had not been Jewish. The Dreyfus Affair was a wake-up call for many French Jews at the time, who had basked too easily in the promises of French republicanism. On the other hand, by finally exonerating Dreyfus the Republic lived up to its ideals, according to many. Dreyfus himself, reintegrated into the army after more than a dozen years of suffering and struggle to clear his name, considered the outcome of the affair to be a triumph for the French Republic and its principles.[72]

The decades around the turn of the twentieth century saw several famous conversions to Catholicism by writers and intellectuals, most of whom had been born Catholic but had strayed from the faith. Paul Claudel, who became one of France's great poets and playwrights, was among the first to return to his Catholic origins. After a spiritual crisis he experienced in 1886, at the age of eighteen, he was baptized and remained a devout, even dogmatic Catholic for the rest of his long life (he died in 1955). Many other writers followed, some of them older and already well known at the time of their conversion. The former Naturalist and Decadent novelist Joris-Karl Huysmans returned to Catholicism in 1897, the influential literary critic Ferdinand Brunetière in 1900, the society novelist Paul Bourget in 1901. The biggest wave of these conversions occurred in the decade preceding the First World War. The philosopher Jacques Maritain, brought up as a progressive Protestant, was baptized Catholic in 1906, together with his wife and lifelong intellectual partner, Raïssa, who had been born into a Russian Jewish family that immigrated into France when she was ten years old. The poet and publicist Charles Péguy, famous as a defender of Dreyfus, announced his return to Catholicism in 1907; Jacques Rivière, a founder of the *Nouvelle Revue Française*, returned to his Catholic roots in 1913, the same year as Ernest Psichari, a poet and the grandson of the nineteenth-century positivist Ernest Renan, whose works had been condemned by the Catholic Church. Such "return" conversions continued through the 1920s and 1930s and included well-known figures like Jean Cocteau, who was baptized in 1925, Erik Satie also in 1925, and François Mauriac in 1928. Conversions often occurred among friends and relatives who influenced each other, and some were the result of active proselytizing by other converts. Jacques and Raïssa Maritain were known for their persistent, often successful attempts to persuade both Christian and Jewish friends of the necessity of Catholic faith. They succeeded even in having Raïssa's father, a Jewish tailor from Rostov-on-Don, baptized on his deathbed.[73]

Jewish converts to Catholicism, Raïssa Maritain being a major example, were fewer during those years but Jews came in as the second largest group to undergo conversion, after those born Catholic. In absolute terms the numbers were small though not insignificant. The historian Frédéric Gugelot, the author of a book on the subject, cites a total of 769 Jewish conversions registered in Paris, where most of them occurred, between 1915 and 1934, when the Jewish population in the city numbered around 150,000. Forty-nine percent of these were by foreign Jews. The estimate given by a Jewish leader in 1937 was 1,000 conversions in the country as a whole between 1910 and 1930 out of a total Jewish population of 250,000.[74] The Jewish converts of those years included a few who were or later became well-known figures in the Parisian literary and intellectual world, among them the poets Max Jacob, baptized in 1915, and René Schwob in 1926 and the philosopher Gabriel Marcel in 1929.

A number of converts among writers and intellectuals, both Jews and non-Jews, subsequently wrote accounts of their conversion. The "récit de conversion," whether book-length or shorter, became a particular genre of autobiography, focusing on the author's spiritual development. These accounts played a role as a kind of advertisement for the Catholic Church and were often written at the request of a priest, who also undertook to publish them.[75] Understandably, many writers were reluctant to relate an experience as personal and powerful as a conversion and had to be prodded. The Latin etymology of the word *convertere*, "to turn around," indicates that conversion involves a radical transformation of the individual. Whether it is the result of a gradual process of reflection or of a sudden illumination, conversion always implies a before and after and carries with it a dramatic element of irreversibility. To outside observers, and sometimes even to the person undergoing it, it may appear incomprehensible. At the same time, a conversion usually involves a public element, a declaration to the world. The philosopher Catherine Chalier, who has written very thoughtfully about modern conversions, argues that even while the process itself must in some ways remain secret, unavailable to clear explanation, an effective conversion always implies a witness: "Every conversion is necessarily a testifying before an other."[76] This is one reason, she suggests, why some conversions, even though they are desired and intended, are never carried out: the would-be convert realizes that it is impossible, under the circumstances, to take the step over the line between before and after.

The example of the celebrated philosopher Henri Bergson is often invoked in this regard. Bergson, who was totally ignorant of Jewish tradition and learning despite his wide erudition, sought spirituality in Catholic thought and faith. He was convinced, along with many other secular Jews of his time, that Judaism had no spiritual sustenance to offer, and he was ready to take the final step of baptism. But as he explained in his testament, written in 1937, four years before his death, he realized that the Jews of Europe were threatened with terrible persecution and felt therefore that he could not abandon them at that time. As Chalier points out, this decision, admirable as it was, was made on moral and political grounds, not religious ones. Bergson's negative and, she adds, uninformed opinion of Judaism had not changed. In the same testament he requested that at his funeral a Catholic priest be asked to say the prayer, and if that proved impossible, then a rabbi. In the end there was neither a priest nor a rabbi. Bergson died on January 4, 1941, and was buried two days later. The poet Paul Valéry gave a speech in his honor at the Académie Française on January 9 in which he described the intimate gathering of mourners at Bergson's home, after which the casket was transported to the cemetery unaccompanied: "No funeral [ceremony], no speeches."[77] The previous fall, when the German victors decreed, with Vichy's cooperation, that all Jews in occupied France, even those from families that had lived in the country for generations, had to register with the police, Bergson had followed the order.[78] Irène and Michel also obeyed the order, registering their children as well. According to the racist definition of Jewishness that Vichy went by, which was even more stringent than the Nazi Nürnberg laws of 1935, conversion meant nothing.

Why did Némirovsky convert? Denise Epstein maintained, whenever the question came up, that the decision was purely expedient, a sign of her parents' anxiety and sense of insecurity as foreign Jews in France. Elisabeth Gille, in *Le Mirador*, imagines her mother looking back on her conversion in 1942 and expressing remorse over it, but she too implies that worry over security was uppermost in Némirovsky's mind. She imagines her mother writing, "If, perhaps in a cowardly way, I wanted to cut my last ties with a people whose strange identity had always seemed incomprehensible to me, it was in order to take the final step toward the nationality of my choice and to protect my children."[79] Gille, writing decades later, is aware that Némirovsky could be accused of abandoning her people in a time of danger, precisely what Bergson had refused to do. Bergson was a venerated figure—a member of the Académie Française and a laureate of the Nobel Prize for Literature among other honors—whose nationality was never in doubt, while the Epsteins had reason to be worried. Still, taking the step of conversion was not something one did lightly. The Archives of the Catholic Archdiocese in Paris have kept records of all the baptism certificates of those years, including those of the Epsteins. Reading them today, one can be shocked at the standard wording of these texts, which stated that the baptized person had "renounced the blindness of the Jews and recognized Our Lord Jesus Christ as the Messiah promised by the Holy Scriptures of the Old Testament."[80] Contemporary conversion documents no longer put it this way, but to sign such a document in 1939 took determination, a willingness to make a truly radical break. Little wonder that Jewish institutions as well as individual Jews who may have been quite assimilated were extremely critical of those they considered to be apostates.[81]

It's true that many Jews obtained baptism certificates in extremis during the war, aided by priests willing to help. Némirovsky, how-

ever, took the first steps toward conversion in 1938, a year before
the outbreak of the war, and nothing about the process allows one to
conclude that she didn't really mean it. Even some conversions that
appeared purely expedient became genuine, as in the case of Aaron
Lustiger, who was converted as a teenager in 1940 and remained a
Catholic, rising as Jean-Marie Lustiger to become the archbishop of
Paris. While Némirovsky, unlike some other converts, never wrote
a récit de conversion, a few notations in her journals show that she
was meditating on Christian themes at the time. In June 1938, as she
was beginning to work on a novel she planned to call "Le Charlatan
ou Enfants de la nuit" (The charlatan or children of the night—it
eventually became *Les Échelles du Levant [The Ports of the Orient]*,
appearing in installments in *Gringoire* in 1939 and as a book only in
2005, under the title *Le maître des âmes [The Master of Souls]*), she
wrote,

> I mix up with all this, I don't know why, an idea of Grace. A
> novel should always be mostly dark, sordid, full of human
> interests and passions, but it should also allow us to glimpse
> into souls.
>   Jesus is a man like us; that is to say, he is a God. These
> words: "You don't think about the things of Heaven; you love
> only the things of the earth." Humanly, humbly, reasonably,
> we can, and must, strive to describe only those [people].

On the back of the same page, below the title "Les Enfants de la
nuit," she writes a possible epigraph, lifted and slightly misquoted
from the Gospel of John: "The word of Jesus: 'You, be children of
light.' "[82] She is struggling to reconcile the Christian notions of grace
and of the divinity of Jesus with her own disenchanted view of the
world. Yes, grace exists, but the novelist's task is still "mostly" to
probe the passions of those who, careless of heaven, love only the
things of the earth. Jesus is a God, but that's the same as saying he is
"a man like us." These views may not be the most orthodox from the
point of view of Catholic theology, but neither are they the ruminations of someone who is contemplating conversion only as an expedient. In an entry dated June 17, two days after writing the above,
she goes further: "Saw C. yesterday. It went better than I had hoped,

thank God. And, parallel to this, a kind of peace. If one could be free of desire, and above all of fear. No, not to desire is impossible. But not to be afraid, and at the same time to smile, to resign oneself, to efface oneself, how easy life would be! There is a word I cannot tire of repeating: Do not fear, Zaïre, only believe ... [Ne crains pas, Zaïre, crois seulement]."[83] Némirovsky knew at least two important men in 1938 whose name began with *C*: Horace de Carbuccia and André Chaumeix. But neither name fits this context, which seems to call for a philosopher or a person associated with religion, not with the literary marketplace. "Ne crains pas, crois seulement": a Google search of these words produces dozens of French Christian websites with homilies citing chapter 5 from the Gospel of Mark, which re-counts some of Christ's miracles. When the distraught father of a girl who has just died appears in the crowd surrounding him, Jesus tells the man, who is the "ruler of the synagogue" in the King James version, "Do not fear, only believe" (Mark 5:36), and proceeds to revive the dead girl. Similarly today, say the homilies, faith in Jesus will come to the aid of the distressed.

Here again Némirovsky's version is unorthodox, but it is ex-tremely revealing, for in the middle of the biblical verse she inserts the name of Zaïre, the heroine of a tragedy by Voltaire. Voltaire, whose name was synonymous with Enlightenment skepticism and anticlericalism, was the author of several works that remained on the Catholic Church's Index of Forbidden Books from the moment he published them until the index itself was abolished in the 1960s. *Zaïre*, first performed in Paris in 1732, was not among the con-demned works, although its attitude toward Christianity is quite ambiguous. It is a story of larger-than-life passions and inner con-flicts set in the time of the Crusades. Zaïre, a beautiful slave woman who was captured as a child by the sultan Orosmane when he de-feated the French crusaders, explains to her confidante that despite her Christian origins she feels closer to Islam, the religion in which she was brought up. What's more, the sultan, a noble and generous soul, loves her and wants to marry her, and she loves him too. Enter a Christian soldier who turns out to be her long-lost brother, and from there the story takes an operatic turn. Torn by conflicting loyalties, as her brother and her father enjoin her to return to her Christian faith and give up her love, Zaïre pours out her heart in a monologue that contains the following line: "Alas! Am I in fact a Frenchwoman, or a Muslim? [Hélas! Suis-je en effet Française, ou Musulmane?]"[84] The story ends badly, with both the heroine and the noble sultan dead. The play contains a lot of speeches by Christians exhorting Zaïre to return to her faith, but it does not contain the line "Ne crains pas, Zaïre, crois seulement." That was Némirovsky's invention.

Apparently, she found some resonance between her situation and the tragic heroine's, even though Voltaire's Zaïre does not express the kind of fear that would need to be assuaged by a leap of faith. But the young heroine does express a dilemma about split loyalties, one Némirovsky could identify with. Was she a Frenchwoman or a Jew? Where did her true loyalties lie? Zaïre feels an obligation toward her Christian origins and family, but her love and her deepest memories go toward Islam. Which, then, is the stand-in for Judaism in Némirovsky's algebra, Christianity or Islam? Némirovsky's origins and family were Jewish, as were her deepest memories, but the Frenchness she aspired to and the France she loved implied Christianity, not Jewishness. This is what psychologists call the double bind: whichever she chose, she would be betraying the other. The ending could only be tragic.

Six months after writing these journal entries, on December 21, 1938, Némirovsky wrote her first letter to Monsignor Vladimir Ghika, a Romanian prelate whose father was related to the Romanian royal family. Monsignor Ghika, who was sixty-five years old at the time, was himself a convert to Catholicism, having been baptized at birth into the Russian Orthodox Church. He appears to have been a man of great cultivation and spirituality as well as a tireless traveler and activist for the Catholic Church. In Paris he ran a charity for poor children in addition to conducting his priestly duties, but he also moved easily in Parisian literary and social circles, including that of the novelist Paul Morand and his wife, Hélène Soutzo, who had been married to a Romanian prince before marrying Morand.[85] Némirovsky knew the Morands and treated them with great respect. Paul Morand was a diplomat and an author in vogue, known for his cosmopolitanism, which in his case did not include a fondness for Jews. A few years earlier he had published a nasty satire against Jews in the film business, who he said were ruining France. He called the book *Doulce France*, a traditional phrase meaning beloved, sweet country of France, a title clearly meant as a satirical barb against Jews who thought they could take over the country.

It was not the Morands, however, who put Némirovsky in touch with Monsignor Ghika. He had been recommended to her by the abbé Bréchard, a priest in the village of Besse-en-Chandon in central France, where Némirovsky had spent a few vacations with her family. The abbé, she reminded Monsignor Ghika in her letter, had already been in touch with him about the matter at hand: "My great desire, and that of my husband, [is] to receive Holy Baptism for us and for our two children."[86] She hoped he would agree to meet with her and was entirely at his disposal as to the date and time. Evidently Monsignor Ghika responded promptly and positively, for when she next wrote to him a few weeks later, on January 16, 1939, it was to apologize for not being able to go and see him as she had planned due to a case of mumps in the family. But, she added, if the date of 2 February for the conversion was still possible, as they had discussed, that would be perfect. Ten days later, on the twenty-seventh, she apologizes once again: she cannot keep her appointment with him as she has a bad cold and is afraid of the cold air in the church, especially with the baptism approaching. She managed to be present for the baptism on 2 February. Two days later she writes to say she won't be able to go to see him, on doctor's orders, because she has the mumps. But she and her family are so happy to have been baptized on Thursday.

Némirovsky's French biographers point out that the apologies and broken appointments referred to in these letters and in still others that followed point to a certain ambivalence on her part.[87] One wonders as well just how much instruction in the faith she could have received with all the missed appointments. The quick turnaround time, less than two months, between her first letter to Monsignor Ghika and the baptism, suggests a quasi-unseemly haste, although it is possible that she thought of this as the culmination of a gradual, much longer process and that Monsignor Ghika was persuaded of it too. She continued to write to him fairly regularly until early July and arranged for him to officiate at Denise's first communion on July 2. The communion may not have taken place, however,

for Denise is inscribed among the children receiving first communion in June 1941 in the village where the family lived during the
Occupation. Monsignor Ghika appears to have asked for Némirovsky's help in finding a publisher for the work of a friend of his,
and she put him in touch with her editor at Albin Michel. After that,
he was in Romania, where the declaration of war caught him on
September 3. She corresponded with him until April 1940 and tried
to get in touch with him again in early 1942 but received no reply.
In fact, he did reply in March 1942, but his postcard must not have
arrived until much later, perhaps even after Irène's arrest in July.[88]
Monsignor Ghika remained in Romania throughout the war, admin-
istering to prisoners and civilian victims. After the war he decided to
continue with his work despite the Communist regime's hostility to
the Church. He was arrested by the authorities in 1952 and died in
prison two years later. On August 31, 2013, he was beatified by the
Catholic Church.[89]

A desire for security and a hoped-for protection from persecution doubtless played an important role in Némirovsky's decision to
convert, as Denise Epstein surmised. But we should not discount
a genuine spiritual longing for which she found no satisfaction in a
Judaism her family had abandoned long before and about which she
knew very little. Her experience of Jewishness consisted largely of
observing her father's business associates and her family's acquaintances in social settings, and the portraits she drew of them in some
of her novels are notoriously caustic. It is possible that, like a number of Jews who converted during those years, she had concluded
that Judaism led by a kind of spiritual logic to Christianity. This was
the opinion of her friend Jean-Jacques Bernard, who seems to have
been the Israélite she frequented most. He wrote the preface to her
posthumous biography of Chekhov in 1946 and remained in touch
with her daughters after the war. Bernard, a prolific if minor writer,
was the son of a well-known playwright and humorist, Tristan Bernard, whom Némirovsky also knew. Bernard converted to Catholicism in 1943.[90] In 1946 he published an article in *Le Figaro* titled
"Judaism and Christianity" in which he explained that the two religions, far from being opposed, were linked like mother and child.
This image would probably not have appealed to Némirovsky, whose
feelings about her mother were extremely negative. But Bernard

went on to say that to Jews who had grown up totally alienated from Judaism and any form of religious practice but who later "came to Christ with a sincere heart," conversion not only opened the door of the Church but also made them discover their lost Jewishness. He concluded that "the water of baptism made them into Jews at the same time."[91] Some years later, in a book he wrote about his father, who, for his part, remained unconverted as well as irreligious, Bernard reinforced this idea: "My entry into the Catholic Church brought me closer to Jews who had remained faithful to the mother-religion than to those who converted only out of expediency, or to Christians who betrayed the spirit of Christianity."[92]

Bernard offers yet another possible clue to Némirovsky's motivation. In 1941–1942, not long before his conversion, he spent several months in a detention camp in Compiègne, near Paris, along with a group of other distinguished Israélites who had been arrested in December 1941 in reprisal for attacks on German officers. Among the group of lawyers, magistrates, engineers, bankers, and professors was Léon Blum's younger brother René, one of the founders of the Ballets Russes de Monte Carlo, who was subsequently deported and died in Auschwitz. After returning from Compiègne in March 1942, Bernard wrote a book about it, Le camp de la mort lente (The camp of slow death), published in 1944 and perhaps the only work of his for which he is still remembered. He recounts in compelling detail the daily routines and privations as well as the occasional pleasures of the camp, such as good conversations and evening lectures by the renowned inmates. He also reports on the ongoing debates about Jewish identity and Jewishness between the Israélites and the foreign Jews with whom they shared space in the camp. According to Bernard, the Israélites almost without exception rejected being identified primarily as Jews and even refused to think of themselves as Jewish victims: "We felt persecuted as Frenchmen, not as Jews, or if you like, we were persecuted for what we were not." Were he to die there, he told his friends, "I would be dying for France; I don't want to be claimed as a victim by Judaism."[93] Things were different, however, for the foreign Jews, according to Bernard: these so-called stateless (apatrides) immigrants from central Europe "kept in the depths of their heart the feeling of a Jewish community. That feeling was generally unknown and even rejected by most of the Frenchmen who had been arrested with me." The "national reflex" (sursaut national), he concluded, was almost unanimous among "these men born and raised in the French climate, a climate imbued with Latin and even Christian tradition."[94] While the Israélites felt equal to the foreigners in their suffering as human beings, he emphasized, they were also keenly aware of their difference in the matter of identity.

It was apparently while he was writing this book that Bernard converted to Catholicism. His remarks about the "national reflex" suggest that he viewed his conversion not only as a spiritual matter but as an affirmation of national identity: to be fully French meant to be Catholic. Could Némirovsky have had something similar in mind (or in the back of her mind) when she undertook her baptism, as if to become more French by espousing the "Christian tradition"? Possibly. But if we recall her slightly amused attitude toward Madeleine Avot and her brother René, those "very French" friends who she thought might be shocked by the goings-on of her fellow Russians, and if we recall also her attraction to the between status of a foreigner in France, we may well decide to qualify that hypothesis.

Némirovsky's American biographer, Jonathan Weiss, has pointed out that, paradoxically, it was around the time of her conversion that Némirovsky started writing her longest and most complex exploration of Jewish identity in Europe. Her last novel with a Jewish theme, *Les chiens et les loups* (*The Dogs and the Wolves*), appeared in April 1940, a few weeks before the Nazi invasion of France. "Even as she found herself spiritually a Christian, she seemed to become particularly sensitive to her Jewish roots," Weiss remarks.[95] Writing that novel when she did was not the least of the contradictions in Némirovsky's choices of the 1930s.

CHAPTER THREE

Choices and Choicelessness,

1939–1942

His life should have gone on, long and productive, but it's
as if someone had pronounced the sentence so often heard
by Chekhov: "The work must be finished by such and such
a date. . . ." On the page, someone is already tracing the
word: end.

—NÉMIROVSKY, *La Vie de Tchekhov*

PEOPLE WHO KNOW NÉMIROVSKY'S story often ask, Why did she
and Michel not try to hide or leave France or at least leave the zone
occupied by the Germans in June 1940? Why did they register as
Jews in October, when the first statutes relating to members of the
"Jewish race" made it clear that the Vichy government was no friend
of the Jews, especially foreign ones? And why did they continue
scrupulously observing the law, even when the law itself had become
unlawful? Could they have saved themselves if they had made better choices? As we have seen, the adolescent Elisabeth blamed her
mother for "being so oblivious politically. She hadn't saved herself,

even though she had every possibility to do so, and she had put us, my sister and me, in danger."[1] But did she in fact have "every possibility" to save herself? Was she really blind to what was happening around her?

These questions seem inevitable, but here more than ever we must resist the temptation to judge by hindsight. While Némirovsky was responsible for her choices, she was not responsible for the fate that befell her. That responsibility lies with the iniquity of the Vichy regime and of the German occupiers of France. Recent historical studies, together with a huge number of personal testimonies published over the past several decades, have shown that survival was unpredictable, often a matter of sheer luck, and that Jews who survived did so in many ways. There was no right way to decide on what to do, since similar decisions could produce strikingly different results. Many Jews who lived in Paris were deported, but many were not; many who fled to the Unoccupied Zone survived, but many did not. The only sure way to escape deportation was to leave the country, but leaving the country was extremely difficult, especially for those who had no valid passports, and even those with documents were often stymied. Walter Benjamin, detained at the Spanish border with a group of refugees and despairing of ever being able to reach Palestine even though he had valid entry documents, took his own life in September 1940; not long after that, all those who had been with him were allowed to cross over.[2]

On the whole, Jews in France fared much better than those in other occupied countries. Whereas 75 percent of Jews in Holland and 60 percent in Belgium were deported or murdered, "only" 25 percent of Jews in France, roughly 80,000 people, suffered that fate.[3] Being a foreign Jew, however, made one's chances much worse: of the approximately 130,000 people in France who were classified in that category in 1940, 56,500 had been deported by the time the last transport left for Auschwitz in August 1944, a proportion of more than 2 out of 5. Jews who possessed French citizenship, whether of established or of recent vintage, fared better, as long as their citizenship had not been revoked in one of Vichy's denaturalization projects. Out of an estimated total of 200,000 in 1940, 25,500 were deported, a proportion of 1 out of 8. In other words, if you were a foreign Jew your chances of being deported were almost four times as high as those of a Jew classified as French. Pierre Laval, who was prime minister during the worst period of persecution, between 1942 and 1944, derived some pride from the fact that Vichy targeted foreign Jews before French ones, as if that did him honor—but then, Laval also insisted on arresting and deporting children, since they should not be separated from their parents.[4]

"Thrown from One Life into Another"

When war was declared on September 3, 1939, most French families were just returning from their vacations. Irène and Michel had spent the summer with their children, as usual, in the southwestern seaside town of Hendaye, near the Spanish border. In a short story published a few weeks later, one of several she wrote on this theme, Némirovsky describes the general state of shock and disarray that followed. The opening paragraph offers several clues to her own state of mind at that moment: "It was the first night of the war. In wars and revolutions, nothing is more dumbfounding than those first moments when you are thrown from one life into another, breathless, the way one might fall fully clothed from a high bridge into a deep river, without understanding what is happening to you, your heart still harboring an absurd hope."[5] Feeling as if one had fallen off a bridge and was drowning yet retaining an "absurd hope": these were familiar emotions to Némirovsky, as her brief allusion to revolution makes clear. By a striking coincidence Benjamin, in a letter to his friend Theodor Adorno, used a similar image a few months later to describe the situation of refugees seeking to flee France: "I have seen a number of lives not just sink from bourgeois existence, but *plunge headlong* from it almost overnight."[6] Némirovsky had no doubt experienced similar feelings during the flight from Russia as an adolescent. Psychologists have noted that one trauma often awakes memories of another, and terror of more to come. With an intuition that can strike one as premonitory, she sets this story, titled "La nuit en wagon" (The night in the wagon), in a crowded train compartment. In our days the train has become an emblem for the persecution of Jews during the Holocaust, owing in part to the brilliant use that Claude Lanzmann made of trains in his celebrated film *Shoah* (1985). But trains are excellent symbols for the collective experience of civilians during the Second World War in general given that so many people were displaced for various reasons during that time. The train in Némirovsky's story is heading from the southwest to Paris, and the narrator, an unidentified woman who could be a stand-in for the author, engages in conversation with a young woman who is going to meet her fiancé to spend a last day with him before he joins his regiment. Other people tell their stories as well, establishing an unusual degree of solidarity among strangers. But as the train pulls in to the Gare d'Austerlitz in Paris the solidarity evaporates and everyone is alone: "Suddenly, people seemed not to know one another. . . . The travelers had gone their separate ways without a word."[7] The narrator does not tell us anything about her own situation but acts as a clear-eyed observer of others. Readers of *Suite Française* will recognize here the stance of the anonymous narrator in that novel, who weaves together the various stories of people heading south in panic nine months later as the German troops overrun the country.

Disconcertingly, the first months of the war were uneventful in France, so much so that the French call them the *drôle de guerre*, the phony (or even funny) war. The men were at the front but in fact there was no front, only a line drawn at the eastern border, the Maginot Line, heavily guarded, where the expected German invasion never came. Sartre, drafted into the army and stationed in a village in Alsace, had enough leisure time to fill hundreds of pages of notebooks between September 1939 and March 1940, in which he mixed daily observations of life in the barracks with weighty considerations about authenticity and ethics. They would lead a couple of years later to his massive existentialist opus *Being and Nothingness*.[8] At the same time, in Paris, his lover and soulmate, Simone de Beauvoir, kept her own diary, in which she described her days spent writing in cafés in Montparnasse. She was working on her first novel, *L'Invitée* (*She Came to Stay*), which would be published in 1943, the same year as *Being and Nothingness*.[9]

In short, even though the world was transformed, life went on almost as before. Némirovsky published eight new short stories between October and May, most of them in *Gringoire* and a few in the women's weekly *Marie-Claire*, which evidently also paid well. Her novel *The Dogs and the Wolves*, which she had completed earlier that year, started appearing in serial form in the weekly *Candide*—known for its nationalist and anticommunist views, though not as much for antisemitism as *Gringoire*—in October 1939; it was published in book form in late April 1940. Still, Irène and Michel had been sufficiently alarmed at the outbreak of the war to send the children away from Paris. In *Le Mirador* Elisabeth Gille reports in her mother's voice that while they were still in Hendaye, on September 3, Irène called the girls' nanny, Cécile Michaud, and asked her to come and take them to Issy-l'Évêque, her native village, located in a corner of Burgundy near the foothills of the Morvan.[10] The girls spent the next eight months in the home of Michaud's mother and evidently enjoyed their initiation into country life. Denise recalled many years later that despite the hardships of an underheated house and outdoor latrines she felt happy and well cared for and had a wonderful time playing with the kids of a local shopkeeper.[11] Elisabeth, who was only two and a half years old, must have felt more disoriented, suddenly finding herself without her parents. Irène and Michel made regular visits from Paris.

Némirovsky's journals contain no indication of why she sent the children away at a time when no obvious danger threatened them. However, other children were also evacuated from the capital as soon as war broke out, and some families decided to stay in their summer homes instead of returning to Paris.[12] Possibly, anticipating the worst, Irène and Michel wanted to prepare a place where they could go if they too had to leave at a later time. Indeed, by the time the German army surged into France from Belgium, in the middle of May 1940, Irène was living with the girls in Issy, having left Paris at the beginning of the month. They were joined in early June by Michel, who had been ill. The bank where he worked, the Banque des Pays du Nord, seems to have seized the opportunity to fire him, and none of his attempts to be rehired had any effect.[13] Irène had thus become, now and for the foreseeable future, the family's sole breadwinner. On June 6 she wrote in her journal, "I realize it would be necessary to write one or two stories, while one can still—maybe—find a place to publish them. But . . . uncertainty, worry, anxiety all over: the war, Michel, the little one, the little ones, money, the future. The novel, the momentum of the novel cut short."[14] The novel in question was *Les Biens de ce monde*, which she did manage to continue that summer and which started appearing in serial form in *Gringoire* the following April. By then, it had to be published under a pseudonym, as the Vichy government had barred Jews from the press.

In Némirovsky's mind her writing and her immediate material problems, including her responsibility for her family's livelihood, were inseparable: she had to write to live. More than most writers of her class and social position, she relied exclusively on her publishing income and she had no backups, no country house to retire to, no inheritance. Despite her professional success and acquaintances there were very few people she could count on for support, moral and practical if not material. The ones she felt closest to, Michel's brothers and sister, who had remained in Paris, were as much in need of help as she was.

After that, things moved very quickly. On June 10, as the German army was approaching Paris, the French government and National Assembly headed south, in their own version of the exode. Many deputies were opposed to negotiating an armistice with the Germans, preferring to fight on or at least to form a government in exile, as had been done by Belgium and the Netherlands. But others, most of them conservatives who had opposed the leftward move of the Third Republic in the years immediately preceding the war, argued for an armistice, and they prevailed. On June 16 Prime Minister Paul Reynaud resigned, clearing the way for Marshal Philippe Pétain, whom he had appointed as a minister a few weeks earlier, to form a new government. Thus Pétain, the revered hero of the First World War, became, at the age of eighty-three, the prime minister of France, or, as he stated in his famous radio broadcast of June 17, he "bestowed on France the gift of [his] person." Five days later he signed an armistice with Germany, according to which France was divided into an Occupied Zone in the north and an Unoccupied Zone in the south, except for the coastal southern area, including Bordeaux, which was occupied. A demarcation line, which would soon be heavily guarded, separated the two zones. Issy-l'Évêque, where the Epsteins were living, was less than fifty miles north of the line. The Epsteins were thus in occupied territory, under the control of both French and German authorities and police. After November 11, 1942, when the Germans occupied all of France, the strict division no longer held, but some differences still existed between what were now called the northern and southern zones.[15]

Pétain bestowed more than his person on France. He also bestowed on it a National Revolution that turned the country from a parliamentary democracy into an authoritarian state. Beneath the mask of the kindly old war hero with clear blue eyes, who established his offices in a resort hotel, the Hôtel du Parc, in the spa town of Vichy, was an archconservative leader who blamed France's humiliating defeat on the moral and political decadence of the Third Republic, dominated by leftists, Jews, and Freemasons. "I hate the lies that did you so much harm," he thundered in a radio broadcast on June 25, 1940. By an ironic twist this famous sentence was written for Pétain by none other than Emmanuel Berl, who realized a few weeks later that Vichy was not a welcoming place for Jews and who, in spite of his privileged status, spent the rest of the war making himself inconspicuous. He lived from then on in a couple of small villages in the south and even went into hiding for several months in 1944.[16]

Pétain sought to create a "regenerated" France that would take its place alongside Germany in the new European order. Most French men and women were willing to support him, at least in the early weeks and months before the full extent of his National Revolution had made itself felt. On July 10, 1940, by an overwhelming vote of 569 to 80, including many Socialist and center-left deputies, the National Assembly voted him full powers to revise the constitution, which enabled his regime to claim full legality. But what followed can be compared to a coup d'état. Pétain's first step was to suspend Parliament indefinitely, thus de facto abolishing the Republic, and to appoint himself as head of state, answerable to no one and governing by decree. While some commentators who later sought to whitewash him claimed he was senile and manipulated by the conservatives who surrounded him, contemporary historians—starting with Robert Paxton, whose 1972 study on Vichy France inaugurated a whole new historiography of the Occupation years—have documented that this claim was false. Pétain knew what he was doing, and the men around him were following him as well as coming up with new ideas. An exhibition at the National Archives in Paris in the fall of 2014 documented in great detail the ideology as well as the activities of Pétain's government, including Pétain himself, in the persecution of Jews. Among the most damning documents was the typewritten draft of an anti-Jewish decree from 1940 that Pétain had annotated by hand, adding provisions that made the decree even harsher.[17]

Among the new ideas in the summer of 1940 were a series of decrees whose cumulative intent was to rid France of "undesirable" foreigners generally and to exclude Jews in particular from participation in public life. On July 22 Pétain's justice minister set up a commission to reexamine all naturalizations that had been issued since 1927, an act which ended up stripping 15,154 people of citizenship, among them 6,307 Jews.[18] In August and September new laws restricted membership in the medical and legal professions to those born of a French father, thus eliminating first-generation immigrants. Although Jews were not mentioned in these decrees, they were clearly targeted.[19] And they were most definitely mentioned and targeted in the decree of October 3, 1940. Known as the Statut des Juifs, this decree stripped Jews in France, regardless of whether they were native or foreign, living above or below the demarcation line, of basic civil rights. (This was the document annotated by Pétain that appeared in the exhibit of 2014.) The full text of the Statut des Juifs is available on several websites, and reading it today is a chilling experience. Article 1 defines who is a Jew: "Any person descended from three grandparents of the Jewish race, or two grandparents of that race if his or her spouse is also Jewish."[20] The matter-of-fact use of "race" to designate Jews did away with considerations of religion: converts who had three Jewish grandparents were Jews, whether they liked it or not. This article, like the rest of the statute, contravened every principle of the long French tradition of republicanism, according to which all citizens are equal before the law. Jews were henceforth forbidden to hold positions in the government, ministries, the police, the armed forces, the magistrature, including judges at all levels, and the teaching corps, from elementary school through university. And they could no longer work in publishing, journalism, radio, film, or theater, these being "professions that influence public opinion."[21]

The day after publishing the Statut des Juifs, on October 4, Vichy issued another decree, this time focusing on "foreigners of the

Jewish race." Such foreigners, the decree stated, could be interned in "special camps by decision of the Prefect of their *département* of residence" or else assigned to forced residence by the prefect. Each of France's ninety départements had a prefect appointed by the central government, and the Vichy regime instituted additional regional prefects, who were in charge of more than one département. Thus the Saône-et-Loire, where Issy-l'Évêque is situated, not only had a prefect and a subprefect but also fell under the jurisdiction, with several neighboring départements, of the regional prefect in Dijon. In the Occupied Zone, prefects reported both to Vichy and to the Germans, who regularly asked for reports on Jewish residents. A number of départements, among them the Saône-et-Loire, were cut in two by the demarcation line and therefore had an even more complicated administrative structure. The prefect of Saône-et-Loire, whose office was in the city of Mâcon in the Unoccupied Zone, reported to Vichy, but the subprefect, stationed in the next largest city, Autun, which was in the Occupied Zone, "fulfilled the role of Prefect," as was stated on all his correspondence, in relation to the "Authorities of Occupation." Thus the subprefect in occupied Autun sent reports to the German Sicherheitspolizei in occupied Chalon-sur-Saône, to the prefect in unoccupied Mâcon, and to the regional prefect in occupied Dijon, among others. Many of these reports survive in regional archives, some more carefully preserved than others. The Saône-et-Loire archives, located in Mâcon, are unfortunately among the less complete ones, but they still contain some revealing information. Among these is a report dated October 21, 1942, submitted by the subprefect in Autun to the Sicherheitspolizei at Chalon, listing Jews currently living in the area as well as those arrested since January 1942. The entire Epstein family figures on these lists: Michel and Irène appear among those arrested, and Denise and Elisabeth among those still living there. Presumably, their turn could come later.[22]

Several more Vichy decrees followed the Statut des Juifs, in 1941 and 1942, each one adding more restrictions. Historians have stressed that these decrees were not forced on Vichy by the Germans, as many people thought at the time and as some asserted for years afterward. They were the brainchild of Pétain's entourage, and Pétain himself oversaw them and signed them.[23] The Germans, how-

France, June 1940–November 1942, with detail of the department of Saône-et-Loire showing demarcation line.

ever, were busy issuing ordinances as well. On September 27, 1940, a few days before Vichy issued its Statut des Juifs, the Germans decreed that all Jews living in the Occupied Zone must register at their local police station or at the *sous-préfecture* of their department. The penalties for failing to do so would be, the German ordinance assured, harsh. Since the registrations didn't start until October, after the Statut des Juifs had been published, and since they were handled by French police, public memory associates the order to register with Vichy. In fact, French and German authorities worked in tandem to ensure that the identity cards of Jews in the Occupied Zone would henceforth bear the word *Juif* or *Juive* stamped on them.[24] Less than a year later, on June 2, 1941, Vichy extended the registration to Jews in the Unoccupied Zone, with similarly harsh penalties for noncompliance. In May 1942 the Germans issued yet another ordinance: starting in June, all Jews residing in the Occupied Zone were to wear a yellow star sewn on their clothing. They could pick up their stars at their local police station or sous-préfecture, with the usual sanctions if they failed to do so. In this, at least, Vichy did not follow the Germans' lead, and Jews in the Unoccupied Zone never wore the yellow star. But in both zones every Jew who registered became part of a huge surveillance system. In the Paris area individual Jews became part of a card file, or *fichier*, each person's *fiche* listing his or her name, address, profession, and place and date of birth. A person could have several fiches, coordinated with each other. Many people's itineraries, including those of Michel Epstein's brothers and sister, can now be followed right through from their first registration to their arrest and internment in the transit camp at Drancy near Paris to the date of their deportation from France. In the provinces things were often less well organized, and instead of card files the bureaucracy kept lists. The main thing was that the system as a whole was extremely efficient, allowing for roundups of Jews in both Paris and elsewhere. In this regard the French bureaucracy could compete in efficiency with the German.

One can imagine the dismay, disbelief, outrage, and panic the decrees provoked among the Jews of France. While the feelings were shared by all, the actions that accompanied them varied, and the outcomes varied too. Historians as well as survivors have recounted hundreds of individual stories, each of them compelling, but as far as chances for survival went, only vague generalizations can be drawn from them. It was better to have money, better to have good friends who were willing to help, better to be a French citizen, better to be in the Unoccupied Zone, and, best of all, to be in Switzerland or England or the United States if one could get there. Time was of the essence, for what was possible in June 1940 was no longer so in October and even less so the following year. Being inventive, seizing opportunities, daring to break the law if necessary—"se débrouiller" is the French term for it—were essential, but even that was no guarantee. Not all who could hide or escape tried to do so, some who tried, failed, while others who did nothing nevertheless survived—and so on, in a fascinating yet familiar litany. Much of the most interesting current work by historians of the Occupation years focuses on individual stories in all their variety or on in-depth studies of Jews in a single town or community. For example, Nicolas Mariot and Claire Zalc have studied in detail the Jewish responses to persecution in the northern mining town of Lens, basing their research on individual documents and official correspondence as well as on statistical data. Their work confirms that while generalizations are possible, individual stories often prove them wrong.[25]

One thing is certain: the overwhelming majority of Jews in France, both native and foreign, followed the orders to register. And once they had done so, as the historian Jacques Semelin notes, they became official victims of laws whose "purpose was to make them into pariahs."[26] Historians have speculated on the reasons for this massive obedience and generally agree on at least three: among foreigners, fear of being on the wrong side of the law was an ingrained habit, so registering was just one more bureaucratic rule they followed; among the French Israélites, their long-standing respect for legality and their confidence in the Republic, even if accompanied by indignation and defiance, led to similar results; finally, some in both groups felt a moral obligation to declare their solidarity with persecuted Jews. Bergson is often mentioned in this last regard, but other, less illustrious people felt similarly compelled. At the same time, some established French Jews sought to take advantage of exemptions that even the Vichy laws accorded to those who had "rendered exceptional service to France," as the decrees stated. But no exemptions were ever guaranteed. While in the eyes of Vichy some

Jews were less undesirable than others, in the end they were all members of the "Jewish race," and their differences could become, as the occasion required, negligible.

One of the more shocking stories Semelin tells illustrates just how unpredictable and arbitrary the fate of individuals was. The Lyon-Caen family, who traced their presence in France to the eighteenth century, prided themselves on a distinguished record of service to their country. Pierre Masse, a member of the family who had earned several decorations for valor in the First World War, had served for years as an elected member of the National Assembly and was a senator when he went to register and get the "Juif" stamp on his identity card in October 1940. Masse knew Maréchal Pétain personally and had been among the parliamentarians who had voted to give him full powers in July of that year. This was not all that unusual, as many other Israélites supported Pétain at first, and, as we have seen, Berl even wrote some of his first speeches. For a brief period the celebrated writer and war hero Joseph Kessel also supported the régime, before joining the Resistance and eventually fleeing to London, where he played an active role in the circles around de Gaulle.[27] After the publication of the Statut des Juifs, Pierre Masse wrote Pétain a letter dripping with pained sarcasm. Did the decree dismissing Jews from the army, he asked, mean he should tear off the insignia from members of his family who had died on the front in 1916 and 1940?[28] The letter received no response. In August 1941 Masse was arrested in Paris and taken to the transit camp at Drancy. After several more transfers and failed attempts by friends to have him released, he was deported to Auschwitz on September 30, 1942, and died there the following month. He had been advised earlier to leave Paris and seek refuge in his country home in the Unoccupied Zone but had refused to do it. The distinguished jurist Robert Badinter, who recently wrote an homage to Masse, speculates that he may have been secretly counting on the personal protection of Pétain.[29] Another member of the Lyon-Caen family, François Lyon-Caen, also counted on personal protection when he requested permission from the Vichy minister of justice to continue practicing as a lawyer at the Appellate Court in Paris. Permission was granted, but in August 1941 he too was arrested and taken to Drancy. He was deported to Auschwitz on September 2, 1943, and died there.[30]

At the opposite end of the social spectrum one finds similar arbitrariness. One family of poor Polish immigrants in Paris was saved after the husband had already fled south because the policemen who came to arrest him in July 1942 gave the wife and children a couple of hours to prepare for their own arrest—during which time the neighbors came and hid them, and afterward they too fled south. In another, very similar family during that same roundup the father was away working as a farm laborer for the Germans, but the mother and two daughters were arrested without being given a chance to prepare. The mother was deported, while the daughters were let go after a few months, and they and their father survived.[31]

Stories such as these, aside from their intrinsic interest, can help us understand more clearly Némirovsky's situation during the two years that followed the Nazi invasion of June 1940. As her journal entry of June 6, which I quoted earlier, shows, she was not at all oblivious, to use Elisabeth's word about her, to the realities and dangers that confronted her. Indeed, she monitored events closely, for she was planning her next novel, which she referred to in her journals as her "story about the French." Although this sounds like *Suite Française*, it was actually *Les Biens de ce monde*, for which Némirovsky started writing notes in the spring of 1940 but which she didn't finish until the next year. The novel traces the history of a salt of the earth type of French family of industrialists (no doubt inspired by Némirovsky's friends from university days, the Avots), from shortly before the First World War until the outbreak of the Second World War. Given the heavy presence of war in the novel, her notes for it sometimes overlap with what would become *Suite Française*. They include details about the bombings and troop movements of June 1940 as well as accounts of the *exode* that she may have heard from refugees or followed through the newspapers, for she herself was already in Issy-l'Évêque in June. Tucked away among voluminous notes for the novel and miscellaneous ideas for stories are brief observations about her everyday life in the village. On April 24, 1941, when she and the family were still living in the local hotel along with a number of occupying German soldiers, she writes, "Today, rain, cold, yesterday snow. A room full of smoke. 6 or 7 silent men, polite and mild-mannered, are drinking beer and smiling at 'Elissabeth.' [This pronunciation of her daughter's name indicates that the "mild-mannered" men in the room were Germans.] This morning, 2 prisoners taken away by 2 men with rifles. They gave them a quarter of an hour to get ready. French radio—idiotic ditties. I suppose French radio is meant for the amusement of children."[32] This last comment is Némirovsky at her most sardonic, a mood and a tone that alternate with anxiety and despair in these pages.

A Letter to the Maréchal

What did she do, faced with the dangers she was all too aware of? It may not come as much of a surprise, knowing what we know about her trust in the goodwill of elderly French men toward her and her writing, that among her first gestures upon learning of the anti-foreigner measures of Pétain's government in July and August 1940 was to write to the Maréchal himself. After all, weren't they both contributors to the *Revue des Deux Mondes*, shareholders in the company of French letters? Pétain, a member of the Académie Française since 1929, had contributed some articles of political analysis to the *Revue* in the 1930s. Némirovsky's letter to him, dated September 13, 1940, could not have been more polite or more distinguished. Invoking as a start their common acquaintance with André Chaumeix, the editor in chief of the *Revue des Deux Mondes*, she quickly gets to the point: she is worried because she has learned that "your government had decided to take measures against stateless people [les apatrides]," and she and her family fall into that category—but, she adds, "Our children are French. We have lived in France for twenty years, without ever having left the country." Monsieur Chaumeix will vouch for her, as will Monsieur René Doumic, the *Revue*'s previous editor, and his wife. The widow of another Académicien, Henri de Régnier, will do likewise. (Henri and Marie de Régnier were regular contributors to the *Revue*.) She goes on, "I have never been involved with politics, having written only works of pure literature." And in all her works, published in France or abroad, she has sought to "make people know and love France." Then comes the crux: "I cannot believe, Monsieur le Maréchal, that no distinction should be made between the undesirables and the honorable foreigners who, if they have received from France a royal hospitality, are aware of having done everything in their power to deserve it. I therefore request from your great benevolence that my family and I be included in this second category of persons, that we be allowed to reside freely in France and that I be allowed to exercise my profession of novelist."[33]

Elisabeth Gille, who reproduces this letter in full in *Le Mirador*, presents it as having been written at Michel's insistence, but it seems fully of a piece with Némirovsky's behavior toward powerful men— and women, to the extent they existed—throughout the preceding decade. In seeking to distinguish herself and her family from the "undesirables," she was reaffirming her sense of belonging to the class of respected establishment writers, a class in which she had actively and successfully sought membership. She was also anticipating what, unbeknownst to her, even the Statut des Juifs that would appear less than a month later would recognize, that exemptions could be given to Jews who had rendered "exceptional service to France." Arendt, in articles she wrote around that time as well as later in *The Origins of Totalitarianism*, had cruel things to say about "exceptional Jews" who tried to evade the status of pariah that the world assigned to members of their religion. But it would take a peculiar self-righteousness to condemn Némirovsky for trying to save herself and her family by claiming exceptional status, in this instance not as a Jew but as a foreigner. The Vichy laws of that summer had made no mention of Jews, only of foreigners deemed undesirable, a legal category at the time. Némirovsky was insisting, quite rightly, that the label did not apply to her.

What is obvious today but was much less so in September 1940 is that all the rules she had successfully lived by for more than twenty years were changing, indeed, had already changed. The well-known names she invoked to remind Pétain that she and he were members of the same intellectual and cultural world no longer had purchase. A few weeks before her letter, on August 15, 1940, the *Revue des Deux Mondes* had published the text of a speech by Pétain on education, in which he made clear the new values that Vichy represented: "Work, family, fatherland" (Travail, famille, patrie), with an emphasis on "rootedness" (enracinement) and a refusal of "nomadism." This text explicitly rewrote the slogan that had defined France since the Revolution: liberty would henceforth have to be "compatible with authority," equality with hierarchy, and fraternity would be national.[34]

A month later, on September 15, two days after Némirovsky posted her letter to him, Pétain published another article in the *Revue des Deux Mondes*, in which he elaborated on this transformation. The new values espoused by his government were, he said, "purely and profoundly French," while the others were "foreign imports."[35]

It hardly needs to be said that Némirovsky's letter received no reply from the Maréchal.

Meanwhile, her chief worry continued to be over work and money. Her surviving correspondence shows detailed exchanges that summer with the office of Albin Michel, which was being run by his son-in-law Robert Esménard in his absence. Esménard had written to her at the end of August 1939, just a few days before war broke out, offering to help in case she ran into trouble during these "anxious times that risk becoming tragic from one day to the next. You are Russian and *israélite*."[36] He would be pleased to attest, he wrote, that she was a writer of great talent, the author of critically acclaimed works, and that he had the highest personal esteem for her and her husband, in addition to his role as her publisher. One wonders, reading his letter today, whether he was trying to warn her or perhaps even to hint that she should look for ways to leave France, in which case she might need letters of recommendation for obtaining visas. This is sheer speculation, but it is striking how Esménard immediately zeroed in on her vulnerability: "Russian and *israélite*." Curiously, Némirovsky the novelist was aware of this too, for in the novel she had just finished, *The Dogs and the Wolves*, the Russian Jewish heroine Ada, an artist, is expelled from France as an undesirable foreigner, a category already in effect under the Republic before the laws of 1940. But Némirovsky the individual person apparently did not see herself in that description. Even a year later, in August and September 1940, her letters to Esménard are only about the practicalities of living in Issy-l'Évêque: would the monthly stipends that Albin Michel owed her continue to arrive? On September 8 she writes to his secretary, "Some persistent rumors around here make me think that one of these days we may be part of the free zone, and then how would I continue to receive my stipends?"[37] It is quite astonishing to see her worried that Issy might pass into the Unoccupied Zone, since many Jews were fleeing over the demarcation line precisely because of their desire to leave the Occupied Zone behind.

But mail between the zones was uncertain, and she was obviously panicked at the thought of being left without an income. She and Esménard exchanged several letters that month. He writes on September 13 that *The Dogs and the Wolves* had not sold as well as expected, and he is therefore not planning to send any more money before his father-in-law returns. She replies very firmly, insisting on her verbal agreement with Albin Michel, according to which she would receive monthly payments of three thousand francs at least through January 1941. Esménard asks for more details on this agreement, and after she provides them he writes to her on October 2, "In view of the details you have furnished, I yield." He would continue to send the stipends through December, he noted.[38]

The next day, October 3, the Statut des Juifs was published, less than a week after the German decree ordering Jews in the Occupied Zone to register. Irène and Michel obeyed the decree, even though they were Jews only by Vichy's and the Nazis' definition. Their identity cards probably perished with them, and there is no surviving fichier in the Saône-et-Loire departmental archives. We know they registered, however, not only by deduction—since they were deported they must have been classified as Jews—but also because from then on their names appeared on bureaucratic lists, some of which have been found. Since they were foreigners as well as Jews their residence now depended entirely on the German and French authorities. They were no longer free to move about at will, even inside the Occupied Zone. On October 29, 1940, Irène wrote in her diary, "At times, an unbearable anguish. Feeling of nightmare. Don't believe in reality." This is immediately followed by: "Absurd, fragile [? unreadable] hope. If I could just find a way to pull myself out of this [me tirer d'affaire], and my loved ones with me. Impossible to believe that Paris is lost for me. Impossible. The only way out seems to me to be the 'straw man,' but I have no illusion about the crazy difficulties that plan involves. And yet, I must."[39] Her idea of "pulling herself out of this" seems to have concerned the possibility of working, not of fleeing. The "straw man" solution, not spelled out, evidently consisted in finding someone who would be willing to act as the author of her works, so that she could publish and get paid. The journal entry continues with ideas for stories and reflections on the writer's craft: "What was Poe's manner? Absolute realism plus mystery." She wants to write a story that will be a combination of Prosper Mérimée, the author of *Carmen*, and Edgar Allan Poe, she says.[40]

In December 1940, to her great relief, Horace de Carbuccia agreed to publish her work under a pseudonym. In his editor's notes to her complete works, Philipponnat writes that before *Gringoire* she tried a Pétainist paper in Paris, *Aujourd'hui*, which refused the story she sent them. He quotes the letter she wrote to Carbuccia in which she asks for his help. The passage he quotes is from a later letter, but the fact is that Carbuccia did publish her work even after the exclusionary laws of October 1940.[41] During the next year and a half, until February 1942, eight new stories by Némirovsky and all of *Les Biens de ce monde*, in installments, appeared in *Gringoire*, some signed as Pierre Nérey, her very first pseudonym from when she was twenty, and some simply as A Young Woman. Reading these on a microfilm of the newspaper is a sobering experience, for every issue of *Gringoire* in which her work appears—in fact, every issue of *Gringoire* at this time—contains vituperative articles against Jews, by Henri Béraud and others, as well as scurrilous antisemitic cartoons. Foreign Jews get the worst of it, but then Léon Blum, according to Béraud, is a "foreign Jew, the cause of France's misfortune" (May 1, 1941). On May 9, 1941, the installment of Némirovsky's *Les Biens de ce monde* is accompanied, on the same page, by a large advertisement for *Signal*, the Nazi weekly published in Paris.

Even more sobering, however, is to realize that *Gringoire* was by no means the worst as far as antisemitic journalism went in those days. It was far outflanked in viciousness and hate speech by doctrinal collaborationist papers like *La Gerbe, Au pilori, Je suis partout*, and others. In their study of antisemitic writing during the Occupation years, *L'Antisémitisme de plume*, Pierre-André Taguieff and his colleagues don't even mention Béraud. Compared to the murderous rants of ideologues like Brasillach, Rebatet, Céline, Henri Coston, and Pierre-Antoine Cousteau, Béraud's vituperations were perhaps merely ordinary.[42] The sad truth is that in the France of the early 1940s no newspaper that expressed any disapproval of Vichy decrees or of its institutionalized antisemitism could be published. This is not surprising, given that even juridical experts and the Conseil d'État, the country's highest court, analyzed the anti-Jewish laws in learned detail, without a word of dissent about their legitimacy.

But the fact that Vichy's exclusionary antisemitism eventually over-lapped with the genocidal variety of the Nazis shouldn't prevent us from distinguishing them, as Taguieff argues.[43]

In December 1940 Némirovsky's editor at Albin Michel, André Sabatier, who was the senior literary editor (directeur littéraire) at the firm, returned to Paris after his military service, and they resumed a regular, friendly correspondence. From then on, perhaps due to Sabatier's influence but mainly because Albin Michel himself agreed to it, Robert Esménard no longer bothered her about her monthly stipends. He even advanced a lump sum of 24,000 francs, or eight months' worth, when she asked him for that favor in May 1941. The latest round of anti-Jewish measures worried her, she explained, and she asked him to send the money to her brother-in-law Paul Epstein in Paris, in his name.[44] Esménard did so, and he continued sending the stipends even when her account was far over-drawn: in March 1942 he wrote her that as of the past December her account showed a debit of 117,500 francs, or close to four years' worth of payments. Despite this, he wrote two months later to say that, as she had requested, he was increasing the monthly stipend to 5,000 francs.[45] As many commentators have noted, the publisher's support of Némirovsky and, after her deportation, of her daughters, deserves great praise.

One thing Esménard would not or could not do, however, no matter how much she pleaded with him, was to publish her new works. She had written a novelized biography of Chekhov in 1940–1941, using Russian sources and enlisting Michel as her research assistant, plus, as she reminded both Esménard and Sabatier, *Les Biens de ce monde* was ready as well. She had even received a fan letter addressed to the anonymous young woman author from a reader of *Gringoire*, which proved that "you don't need a well-known name" in order to be read.[46] This was obviously a hint about a straw man. In fact, she had found a "straw woman" in the person of Julienne ("Julie") Dumot, who had worked for her father and, before that, for the family of her friend Jean-Jacques Bernard. Dumot, who was then in her fifties—she was born in 1885—had had some schooling: her surviving letters show that she could write fairly correct French, and she was familiar with the ways of the upper classes that employed her. Her status as "dame de compagnie" was above that of a maid but below that of a secretary, a kind of general assistant and companion who could occasionally double as a nurse. In June 1941 the Epsteins invited her to live with them in Issy-l'Évêque, and she joined them a few weeks later. When Némirovsky wrote to Esménard in October, she named her "friend Julie Dumot" as the "author of the novel *Les Biens de ce monde*, of which M. Sabatier has the manuscript." She added that Julie, being "indisputably aryan," could also receive the monthly stipends, for Esménard had written that a recent German ordinance required all payments to "Israélite authors" to be deposited into a blocked account. A blocked account was of no use to her, she wrote him; therefore the moneys should be sent to her friend Julie, who would support her.[47] Esménard agreed to this as well and exchanged some letters with Julie as the author of Némirovsky's manuscripts.[48] Nevertheless, and despite promises from Sabatier, neither the Chekhov biography nor the novel appeared in Némirovsky's lifetime. (The biography was published in 1946 and the novel in 1947.) In September 1940 the Germans had published a list of forbidden works that must be withdrawn from circulation by their French publishers. Known as the Liste Otto, the list was named for the German ambassador in Paris, Otto Abetz. A quite haphazard collection of authors and titles, the Liste Otto was aimed at Jewish writers and at non-Jews who were considered hostile to Nazism. It was a hit-and-miss affair. Many Jewish authors, including Némirovsky, did not appear on it, and even among those that did, only some of their works were banned. This allowed Albin Michel to keep her already published works in print, and they sent her a detailed report on sales of various titles in April 1942.[49] On July 8, 1942, the Germans published a second list, and this time they were more systematic. The list of authors and titles was almost as haphazard as the earlier one and Némirovsky's name still did not appear on it, but it was preceded by a Notice that stated unequivocally: all works by or about Jewish writers in French, except for scientific works, were to be withdrawn from circulation. Presumably publishers knew who their Jewish authors were and were expected to comply, list or no list.[50] It is not clear whether Albin Michel withdrew any of her previously published works at that time, but they may have hesitated to publish new work by her even before then, even with her straw woman as an alibi.

Aside from work and money Némirovsky's big worry after settling in Issy was finding a place to live. The family lived in the town's only hotel, the Hôtel des Voyageurs, for more than a year before finding an acceptable house to rent. During some of that time they shared space with German officers who were billeted at the hotel. It was around then, in December 1940, that Némirovsky renewed her correspondence with her old friend Madeleine Avot, now Madeleine Cabour. "My dear Madeleine, you will perhaps be surprised to see my signature," she begins her letter of December 5, for "we have 'lost contact,' as the saying goes, for a long time." It must be "four or five years, or longer" since Madeleine's last visit to her in Paris, she adds. In the archives, the last written exchange between them dates to New Year's 1931. She inquires after Madeleine's family and mentions her own family's stay in Issy, where they are "for now quite content from the point of view of food and heat," although they miss Paris. Not a word about the Jewish decrees and how they have affected her. This was obviously an exploratory letter, to see whether Madeleine would respond despite their long silence. Tellingly, she signs it, and all the subsequent letters as well, with her full name, Irène Némirovsky or Irène Némirovsky-Epstein, not just Irène, as she had done twenty years earlier.[51]

Madeleine Cabour evidently responded very quickly, for on December 20 Némirovsky writes her a longer letter and thanks her. Madeleine must have described the family's flight south from Lille during the exode. Némirovsky expresses her sympathy and writes about the exode as well: she was already in Issy in June, but Michel had spent three days on the road for a trip that normally takes a few hours. Their life in Issy is boring but offers the advantage of food and heat; her daughter Elisabeth, who is only three and a half years old, doesn't know about running water or elevators but is no worse off for that. The older daughter, who is eleven, attends the village school, which is all right for now, but "the situation had better not stretch out, otherwise she'll be good for nothing but herding cows, and as I unfortunately have no cows . . ." The tone is playful, of wry humor in the face of minor annoyances. It is hard to believe that the person writing this is the same one who in her diary speaks of worry, anxiety, and despair and who in her letter to Pétain expresses outrage at being excluded from the world of French letters.

Némirovsky apparently found her former tone of lighthearted amusement the one most suitable for her old friend. She wrote Madeleine four more letters, between March and September 1941. She asked whether Madeleine knew of a place to rent where she and her family were staying, also in the Occupied Zone, as the accommodations at the hotel in Issy were very uncomfortable. Madeleine evidently replied, proposing a house for rent (her part of this correspondence is lost), and Irène then sent her a whole series of questions: was there plenty of food, a good doctor, someone to cook and clean and take care of Elisabeth as needed? And how did one get there with a lot of baggage?[52] Given what we know about the restrictions on foreign Jews, who needed permission to live anywhere and to travel, this seems like a strange exchange. Némirovsky behaves here as if she were free to live where she wanted and even writes in one letter, on March 17, 1941, that after two recent trips there she had decided Paris was impossible to return to with the children—as if she had a choice. Soon, however, the question of moving became moot, for, as she wrote to Madeleine in September 1941, she had finally found the house she wanted: it was comfortable, with a large garden, and they would be moving in in November.[53]

As far as travel was concerned, it seems she and Michel did both spend at least a few days in Paris in February and March 1941, although there is no trace of any official request or permission to do so. A letter dated 5 February from her to an unnamed person at her publisher, probably Esménard, whom she addressed as "cher Monsieur," bears the indication Paris and mentions that she will be returning the next day to Issy. On March 27 she writes to Sabatier, "cher ami" (dear friend), her standard way of addressing him, and mentions Michel's earlier meeting with him in Paris. Possibly things were still in flux in those early months of the Occupation, or perhaps they had obtained permission to travel from a sympathetic bureaucrat in Autun, where the personnel kept shifting: there were three different sous-préfets in Autun between fall 1940 and summer 1942. By late November 1941, however, she was explaining to Sabatier that in order to get to Paris she had to have the permission of the German authorities, asking him for his help and advice. If she wrote to the Kreiskommandantur in Autun to request permission, would that risk drawing their attention to her "humble person," she wonders?[54]

At this point, one might be tempted to agree with Elisabeth Gille's adolescent view of her mother's blindness. Surely by the end of 1941 she should have realized that to try and save themselves the family ought to flee or at least to hide. She chose not to leave Issy, thought Elisabeth, "even though she had every opportunity to do so." But that is obviously too simple, for Némirovsky's opportunities were limited, and, as we have seen, no individual choice guaranteed safety. To flee, one had to cross the demarcation line, and that carried its own dangers for those without the right papers. Dozens of people, including many non-Jews, were arrested in the Saône-et-Loire each week while attempting to cross. The archives in Mâcon contain regular reports on this, with every name duly noted.[55] As for hiding, which could also be more easily done in the Unoccupied Zone, the usual way was to obtain forged identity papers and rationing cards, not an easy thing for an entire family. Némirovsky's letters to Madeleine indicate a state of denial—"I can live where I want"—but that may have been largely a matter of posturing to her friend. What does seem clear is that she and presumably Michel had made the decision to stay put come what may.

On one level she was hopeful, urging Albin Michel to publish her work, making arrangements for the "straw woman" and signing a lease for the house, but on another level she was ready for the worst. On June 22, 1941, the very day Hitler invaded the Soviet Union and declared war on his former ally, she wrote a long letter to Dumot, "Ma petite Julie," stating in its opening sentence, "Learning that Russia and Germany were at war, we immediately feared the concentration camp." In fact, that was why she had asked Dumot to join the family in Issy, she told her.[56] The letter was meant to be given to Dumot at the Hôtel des Voyageurs in case Irène and Michel were "no longer here" when she arrived. The Epsteins had been living in the hotel for over a year: "It's a modest little inn, but the owners are totally trustworthy. We are leaving with them a box containing a few pieces of jewelry. . . . The box will also contain around 25,000 Francs in cash." Undoubtedly, Irène assumed the two girls would remain there even if she and Michel were taken away and that Julie would care for them. Her letter contains detailed instructions about the household on matters ranging from the girls' doctors' appointments and vaccinations to the purchase of wood for the fireplace of the house they had rented starting in November: "The house is not furnished, but we have made arrangements with Monsieur Billand, the carpenter, and with Maître Vernet [the *notaire*] to rent the necessary furniture. So you'll just need to get in touch with them." Julie should also be sure to find someone to tend to the garden, which would produce a lot of vegetables and fruit, and if she ran out of money she should sell the jewelry but "start by selling the furs you will find in our suitcases, and which you'll certainly recognize." Julie would recognize them because the furs belonged to Irène's mother.[57]

In short, the letter was a last will and testament. In the same mood, around this time Némirovsky deposited most of her manuscripts and writing journals, including those for *David Golder* and other early works, with the notary in Issy-l'Évêque for safekeeping. At the end of the year, hoping to get to Paris, she took them back, and they eventually found their way to a storage room at Albin Michel, where they were discovered more than seventy years later, in 2005, when the publishing house deposited its archives at the Institut Mémoires de l'Édition Contemporaine. These writing journals, added to the documents that Némirovsky's daughters deposited in 1995, now form a crucial part of the Némirovsky papers at the IMEC archive.

Némirovsky's letter of June 1941 to Dumot is important not only as a last will and testament but in another way as well. In it Némirovsky mentions for the first time that she has written a new novel she "[may] not have time to finish" titled "Storm in June." She will leave it with the owners of the hotel, and Julie may be able to use it "in the last extremity" if she runs out of money. Irène writes that she has been in touch with the Editions de France, the publishers of *Gringoire*, to ask whether they were interested in publishing it. If so, they would write to Julie and pay a large sum for it, but otherwise her publisher Albin Michel would probably want it. This mention helps us to date the writing of *Suite Française*. It shows that by the end of June 1941 Némirovsky had completed at least the first part of the novel, the one titled "Storm in June," and had possibly started on the second part as well. There is no trace of her letter to the Editions de France or to Carbuccia, who owned the press in addition to *Gringoire*. If Carbuccia had responded positively to her inquiry, we can be almost certain that the gripping story of the publication of *Suite Française* and all that followed from it would never have happened.

As it turned out, Irène's and Michel's worry about the "concentration camp" was premature, although only by about a year. To complicate things further, it appears possible that despite their detailed preparations for remaining in Issy-l'Évêque they may have attempted to leave France around the same time. This is suggested by a postcard preserved among Némirovsky's papers, sent by a relative of Michel's from New York in October 1944. Raïssa Adler, the widow of the celebrated psychoanalyst Alfred Adler (she and her husband had emigrated from Vienna to New York in the early 1930s), was related to Michel's father and had visited the family more than once in Paris. Now she wrote to Irène and Michel, both of whom were long dead, "The last time I heard from you was through the 'Red Cross' in October 1941. . . . How much I wanted you to come to this country, but unfortunately I could not do anything about it."[58] Did Michel and Irène try to obtain an affidavit for emigration in October 1941? Maybe. Or perhaps they had simply written to her as a first step, for the International Red Cross had a service, still in existence, that put family members in touch across borders. I have not succeeded in finding any trace of the correspondence Raïssa Adler refers to. It seems certain, however, that Michel and Irène knew the president of the French Red Cross at the time, Dr. Louis Bazy, for after Irène's arrest Michel wrote to him and also mentioned him to Sabatier as a person who might help to get her freed.[59] But, according to the archivist at the offices of the French Red Cross in Paris, all of the correspondence files of Bazy and the other presidents of the organization from that period were destroyed in a fire, and only the minutes of the board of directors, recorded in bound notebooks, remain. The minutes contain their own drama, for even in their bureaucratic way they show the Red Cross's efforts to maintain its independence in the face of German pressures. However, no individual cases are mentioned at these meetings.[60]

If Irène and Michel did make an attempt, no matter how tentative, to obtain emigration papers in October 1941, that would be an important piece in our puzzle, one more clue to the contradictory pressures that must have accompanied every decision they made at that time.

"I Suppose They Will Be Posthumous Works"

Unfortunately, other decisions were also being made, in Paris and Vichy and in Berlin, which would render all individual choices inconsequential. On May 13, 1941, over 6,000 foreign Jewish men living in Paris received polite convocations to present themselves at their local police stations, a development made possible by the massive registrations of October 1940. Those who showed up, about 60 percent (the others had evidently realized it was time to stop following orders), were immediately shipped off to the newly established internment camps in Pithiviers and Beaune-la-Rolande in the Loiret region, not far from the historic city of Orléans and about 150 miles northwest of Issy-l'Évêque. Pithiviers had served as a camp set up by the Germans for French prisoners of war in 1940 and was now repurposed by the Vichy government to house foreign Jews. Beaune-la-Rolande, less than 15 miles from Pithiviers, was newly built. For about a year the prisoners were kept there, many of them put to work in adjoining farms and factories, which were shorthanded because French laborers were being sent to work in Germany. The prisoners established a kind of social life, with lectures, concerts, and theatrical performances, and they also set up various clandestine groups, hoping to organize resistance.[61] But in the spring of 1942 all that changed. Over the course of a day's meeting on January 20 in a leafy suburb of Berlin, fifteen Nazi officials convened by Himmler's right-hand man Reinhard Heydrich had decided to implement the "Final Solution of the Jewish Question." Two months after the now-infamous Wannsee conference, on March 27, 1942, the first of more than seventy trains bound for Auschwitz left France from the station at Compiègne, with 1,112 men on board; 23 of them survived the war.[62]

Two months later, on May 28, 1942, the Germans published an ordinance that obliged all Jews appearing in public in the Occupied Zone to wear a "special insignia," the yellow star, sewn on their clothing. Vichy obliged by sending out orders to all the Préfets in the Occupied Zone, who in turn sent out orders that all Jews in their jurisdictions who had registered in October 1940 were to be given yellow stars, the material for which was deducted from their textile rations.[63] The following month, on June 25, the first of six transports from Pithiviers and the fourth to leave from France as a whole, with 999 men on board, left the train station, which was a five-minute walk from the camp. Three days later the first of two transports from Beaune-la-Rolande left with 1,038 people on board, this time including 34 women among the deportees. From then on women would make up a sizable number of all the transports. A report from the SS in Orléans to the SS in Paris explains that there were not enough male prisoners in Beaune-la-Rolande to make up the desired count of 1,000 per trainload, so they had arrested 104 Jews locally, among them the 34 women. Many of these people were French, not foreigners, and according to the report the local Préfet had tried to have them taken off the transport list, but his request was refused as per instructions from Paris. The author of the report noted that the "attitude" of this Préfet would be reported on in detail separately.[64]

Why this flurry of activity in late June 1942? Because the Germans and the French police were planning their biggest roundup yet of foreign Jews in Paris, this time including women and children. To make space for them before they were deported, the two camps in the Loiret had to be emptied of their longer-term occupants. The big roundup, notorious today as the Rafle du Vél d'Hiv, took place over two days, July 16 and 17. Altogether, 12,884 Jewish men, women, and children were arrested, and more than 8,000 of them, including 4,000 children, were taken to the huge cycling arena in Paris, the Vélodrome d'Hiver, where they lived for several days under horrifying conditions. No visual record of the interior of the Vél d'Hiv during those terrible days exists, but some testimonies by survivors have been published. The film *La Rafle* (*The Roundup*) (2010), directed by Roselyne Bosch, attempts to give a visual approximation of what this place was like, with no sanitary facilities and one doctor on the premises. After that, the detainees with families were transferred to Pithiviers and Beaune-la-Rolande and from there to the transit camp at Drancy, a suburb north of Paris. Single prisoners were sent directly to Drancy. With few exceptions they all died in Auschwitz.

Meanwhile, in Issy-l'Évêque life went on almost as usual. The Epsteins and Julie Dumot moved into their new house in November 1941. Némirovsky had hopes that Albin Michel would soon publish *All Our Worldly Goods*, with Dumot's name on the cover. She had started another novel that would span a French family's fortunes from one war to the other, *Les Feux de l'automne* (Autumn fires). It was a hasty job, mashing together themes she had treated earlier in *All Our Worldly Goods* and in the two novels immediately preceding it, *The Dogs and the Wolves*, published in April 1940, and *Les Échelles du Levant*, serialized in *Gringoire* in 1939. *Les Feux de l'automne* repeats the chronology of *All Our Worldly Goods*, roughly 1910 to 1940, but its main protagonist is closer to the main characters in the two earlier works: young men who, even in the absence of war, experience the world as a battlefield where only the strong—the wolves, in Némirovsky's recurrent metaphor—survive. One difference is that in the two earlier works the wolf characters are foreigners and are either explicitly or implicitly designated as Jews. In *Les Feux de l'automne* the protagonist, Bernard, is a Frenchman with no foreign ancestry. And for good measure Némirovsky added several dashes of Pétainist rhetoric to the mix. Thus Bernard realizes, after tragedy strikes his family, that the real causes of this terrible war were the "disorder" (a term used by some Pétainists to characterize the period before the National Revolution) and profiteering that had followed the last war, corrupting the souls of honest Frenchmen. Némirovsky was evidently hoping for a quick publication, preferably in a newspaper that would pay well, and we can surmise that the Pétainist touches were meant to please her presumed publishers. Her real feelings about the Vichy government are evident in *Suite Française*, where the narrator makes several sarcastic comments relating to it. In fact, *Les Feux de l'automne* did not appear until 1957, in the version she had in mind circa 1942. An Italian scholar, Teresa Lussone, has recently shown that Némirovsky deleted the most obvious echoes of Vichy themes before she died, and the latest version in her complete works respects those deletions.[65]

In January 1942 school resumed after the Christmas break. Elisabeth, now almost five, was enrolled for the first time. Her name appears in the school registry, which also indicates that Denise had earned her first diploma, the Certificat d'Études Primaires, the previous year. Irène, for her part, was hoping to be allowed to spend a few weeks in Paris. On February 11, 1942, she sends a letter, in perfect German and no doubt written by Michel, who was fluent in the language, to the Kreiskommandantur in Autun: "I am Catholic, but my parents were Jewish." Her books have been authorized to be published in Paris, she explains, and she needs to see her publisher. Also, her daughter must see the eye doctor there.[66] The following day, she writes to Hélène Morand, the wife of Paul Morand, in Paris, thanking her for sending her Monsignor Ghika's address in Romania. But mainly she wants to ask Madame Morand for a favor: she really must go to Paris to deal with her landlord and her publisher and to see her oculist, but the current regulations forbid her to leave her residence. Would Madame Morand know someone who might intervene on her behalf with the German authorities, so that they would grant her a travel permit for one month? It may be useful for Madame Morand to know, she adds, that the authorities have granted her publisher permission to keep her works in print and to publish her new ones. Her *Life of Chekhov* is to appear soon.[67]

The Kreiskommandantur refused her request for permission to travel. Hélène Morand evidently replied, suggesting that Némirovsky ask Bernard Grasset for his help. Némirovsky wrote to thank her on February 25. She hadn't contacted Grasset, she explained, because, as was well known, he was willing only to receive favors, not to do them. "If I succeed in escaping from Issy-l'Évêque, it will be a great pleasure for me to go and see you [in Paris]. My husband kisses your hand. Please give my best to Monsieur Paul Morand."[68] In the end Némirovsky sent Julie (who, being "aryan," could travel freely within the Occupied Zone) to Paris in April with a list of errands, accompanied by Denise. Denise's letters to her parents from that trip have survived along with a few Némirovsky sent to her. Denise wrote that she had a wonderful time in the big city with her uncle Paul.[69]

One wonders what Némirovsky had in mind, exactly, in asking Hélène Morand for help. She evidently knew, or imagined, that the Morands were in the good graces of the Germans, as participants in the Parisian salons where German officers regularly gathered with French writers and artists.[70] In *Storm in June*, the first part of *Suite Française*, which she had finished by this time, Némirovsky heaps scorn on the bourgeoisie that found its way back to Paris with nary a qualm in the summer and fall of 1940. But in her life she was clearly willing to appeal to members of the same bourgeoisie to use their influence. She overestimated what they could do, however, and underestimated the single-minded ferocity of the Germans where Jews were concerned. Even Colette, who was part of the Franco-German salons in Paris, had no illusions about what to do to protect her third husband, Maurice Goudeket, who was Jewish. She succeeded in getting him freed after he had been taken to Compiègne in December 1941, on the same roundup as Jean-Jacques Bernard and other notables, but it took two months of maneuvering to do so, and after that she realized it was best not to ask for special favors from the "occupying authorities." Goudeket wore the yellow star in Paris in June 1942, but not long after that he escaped to the Unoccupied Zone with false papers. He returned to the capital after the Germans occupied the whole country in November 1942 and spent the remaining twenty months of the war hiding every night in case the Gestapo came for him.[71] Némirovsky, for her part, takes pleasure in informing Madame Morand that the Germans have allowed her to continue publishing even her new works, but she neglects to mention that those new works have been signed for by a third party and will not appear under her name. One of Némirovsky's favorite books was Oscar Wilde's *The Picture of Dorian Gray*. The phenomenon of a double self, which that novel explores, seems pertinent here: one part of her knew things that the other part could not or would not admit.

Or perhaps she was still relying, like a reflex and despite many signs to the contrary, on the goodwill of people she perceived as powerful, who had done her favors in the past. On February 20, 1942, thus probably before she heard back from Hélène Morand, she sent a long letter to Carbuccia in Paris, a draft of which survives among her papers, with many crossings-out that show her hesitations. As she had done with Morand, she begins by reminding the editor of *Gringoire* of his kindness to her in the past and then launches into a heartrending cry for help. She starts a sentence but crosses it out in the middle of a word: "Je suis seule et désem" (I am alone and lost at). The incomplete word is "désemparée," which translates literally as "lost at sea." Then she starts again: her husband, who once held an important job with a Parisian bank, is now out of work, so they live entirely on her income. But the "recent laws" forbid her to publish in journals and weekly newspapers, and yet the German authorities have allowed her to publish her new works, and the *Life of Chekhov* will appear very soon. However, from a material point of view this will benefit above all the publisher, who has already given her significant advances. Thus, only new publications in the press will allow her to make ends meet. Then she returns to a theme she had already touched on with Maréchal Pétain almost two years earlier: certain Jews, among lawyers and doctors for example, are exempted from the regulations for "professional merit," and does she not deserve to be among them? She has always refrained from politics, writing works of pure literature, and has even refused honors proposed to her. She says she turned down an offer to be awarded the Légion d'Honneur. But now she needs help. "You alone, dear Monsieur de Carbuccia, with the influence you possess and the position that has always been yours, can, if you wish to do so, intervene on my behalf with the government." The government in question here is Vichy, not the Germans. If the government granted her the authorization, and "made it public," then the editors of newspapers that had published her in previous years would certainly accept to publish her again, either under her name or under a pseudonym. And then, the ultimate plea: "You know me, you know that I have never asked for anything, happy to live simply from my work, but frankly I don't know where to turn anymore: all the exits in sight seem to be blocked. It's so cruel and unjust that I can't help believing it will be understood and I will be offered help."[72]

Carbuccia replied, in a typed letter on formal stationery, on March 17: "In the Unoccupied Zone, a ministerial decree forbids weekly papers to solicit the collaboration of Israélites, but the fact that the German authorities have authorized your publisher Albin Michel to publish and reissue your works will allow me to submit your personal case to the French authorities in Vichy. As soon as I have a reply, I will not fail to write to you."[73] No other letters from Carbuccia are to be found among Némirovsky's papers, but he may have written to her bearing bad news, for two months later, on May 17, she writes to André Sabatier about "the state of bitterness, fatigue and disgust that I find myself in, and that the response of H. de Carbuccia only exacerbates, as you can imagine." After February 1942 *Gringoire* no longer published her work, and it appears she didn't even try to send them anything.

Rereading her letter to Carbuccia, in which she again emphasizes the injustice of not being recognized as exceptional, I am suddenly reminded of a scene in the Hungarian director István Szabó's powerful film *Sunshine* (1999). The protagonist, an Olympic fencing champion from a Jewish family who had converted to Catholicism as a young man in order to be allowed to join the army officers' fencing league, finds himself with other Jews in a forced labor camp during the war. He is wearing his officer's jacket, and when a Hungarian gendarme guarding the group sees this he barks an order at him: "Take it off, Jew." Instead, the prisoner states his name and qualifications: "I am Iván Sors, Olympic fencing champion and officer in the Hungarian Army." This so infuriates the gendarme that he strips Sors naked and strings him up by the arms on a tree in freezing rain, ordering him to identify himself as "Jew." Sors continues to repeat his name and his status as a Hungarian officer, until he is turned into a block of ice. His teenage son, paralyzed by fear and horror, watches from below.

This scene does not, in my view, condemn Iván Sors for his refusal to call himself a Jew. Rather, it suggests that for a man like Sors, who has worked all his life to bring honor to himself as well as to a country he considers his homeland, to be stripped of his name and titles is worse than death itself. What he refuses is not to call himself a Jew but to define himself as *nothing but a Jew*, a Jew reduced to anonymity as part of a mass. I believe that Némirovsky's continued insistence that she deserved to be recognized as exceptional for her achievements and her service to France had a similar basis.

There was also the fact that technically she was no longer Jewish, but that is secondary. She had registered as a Jew in October 1940 since that was how Vichy defined her. But she wanted to be recognized as more than that: as Irène Némirovsky, a celebrated novelist. And if the authorities wouldn't do that, she would still continue to write, not for money but for the honor of her name. This explains the tenor of her last letters to Sabatier, written between May and July 1942. He had come to visit her in Issy for two days in March, a sign of his devotion, for the trip by train from Paris was quite long and involved several changes, which she detailed to him in a letter on March 23. It was on that occasion, very likely, that she gave Sabatier all the manuscripts she had repossessed from the notary and that now constitute the bulk of her surviving papers. On May 4 she writes to him that soon Julie will send him a story he can submit to a journal that had shown interest in her work, which should be published under a pseudonym. But there is also the matter of the novel they had talked about. If the project is still on, then Julie will work on it, but she has to be certain that "it will be published soon, and well paid." This may be a reference to *Chaleur du sang (Fire in the Blood)*, a short novel that was discovered and published only in 2005. Then she goes on, "For otherwise, she prefers to continue with what she has been working on for the past two years, a novel in several volumes that she considers to be the most important work of her life [l'œuvre principale de sa vie]. And that one, I assure you, will be published only in circumstances and conditions she judges to be favorable."

This "most important work of her life" was, of course, *Suite Française*. One can only be dumbfounded to realize that in addition to all the other works she had written over the previous two years, more than fifteen stories, three novels, and a biography, she was writing her private "War and Peace," as she referred to it in her journals. I am convinced that by this time she had made or perhaps confirmed a conscious choice: she would continue to write, even (or especially) in the absence of publication, for writing was what made her *who she was*. In some of her letters she expresses worry only about the present, pleading with Sabatier to persuade Albin Michel to provide her with higher monthly payments, for she cannot support her family on what he currently gives her. Sabatier succeeded, and she wrote to him on June 1 to thank him, as he and Albin Michel had given her "a bit of tranquility." At other times her immediate concerns are overtaken by a sense of fatality. Now that all doors are closed to her, she writes to him on May 17, she has "given all that up to think only about the future." By future, Némirovsky meant her posterity as a writer. On July 11, two days before she was arrested and taken to Pithiviers, she wrote to Sabatier, "Here life continues as you saw it: monotonous . . . fortunately. Think of me if you publish some interesting books. Reading is the only possible distraction. I've written a lot recently. I suppose they will be posthumous works, but it makes the time go by."

Choicelessness

On June 16, 1942, the sous-préfet at Autun reported to the Regional Head of the Police for Jewish Questions in Dijon that "Jewish stars" had been distributed to the Jews residing in occupied Saône-et-Loire. Among the 127 names that appear on his list are Michel and Irène Epstein (no mention of her maiden name), the only ones living in Issy-l'Évêque. Although children above the age of six were also required to wear the star, Denise's name does not appear on the list. Elisabeth, who was only five, was exempted. But Denise apparently wore the star, for Elisabeth includes a mention of it in *Le Mirador*, and Madeleine and Denise Jobert, sisters now in their eighties who have lived all their life in Issy-l'Évêque and who went to school with Denise, recall her wearing it as well. She tried to hide the star, they told me in June 2014, but that just made them want to see it all the more.[74]

After that, there were no more choices. On Monday morning, July 13, a gendarme presented himself at the door, looking for Irène Epstein. Denise and Elisabeth were home from school, as the summer vacation had started. Nobody cried, Denise recalled many years later, but the family held hands and stood silent for a minute, according to the Russian custom when a family member leaves loved ones behind. Later that day Irène was able to write Michel a penciled note from the *gendarmerie* in the neighboring town of Toulon-sur-Arroux. "Above all, be calm," she told him. She was sure this was only temporary, and he should try to contact people for help. She sent kisses to her beloved daughters and to him. Two days later, on Wednesday, she writes from Pithiviers: she has arrived there and finds the food surprisingly good. The next day, Thursday, July 16, she has time for only a very short note: "My dear love, my adored little ones, I think we leave today. Courage and hope. You are in my heart, my darlings. May God help us all."[75] In fact, the transport from Pithiviers left early the following morning, on Friday, July 17, but the train was loaded the night before. According to her camp registration card, Irène had arrived in Pithiviers that very day, the sixteenth, but her note dated Wednesday proves she was there on the fifteenth, and in fact her name does not appear on the transport list of women who arrived on the sixteenth; it appears on the general list of women in the transport.[76] The sixteenth was the day she was turned over to the occupying authorities, or A.O., *autorités d'occupation*, according to the shorthand notation on the back of her card. On the front, the first line contains the numbers 9-96, indicating that she was assigned to Barrack 9 and received the identification number 96.[77] This too indicates that she arrived before the sixteenth, for she would most likely not have needed to stay in a barrack before being loaded onto the train the same day.

Many people believe Némirovsky was denounced to the police—otherwise, how could she have been arrested? But the truth seems to be more banal, and all the more troubling for that: Pithiviers did not have enough prisoners to fill a train, so others had to be arrested. The same thing had happened with the transport of June 25 from Beaune-la-Rolande, but at that time only Jews residing in the region of Orléans were taken. This time the gendarmes had to go further afield: in addition to 52 people sent by the SS in Orléans, this transport carried 193 men and women sent by the SS in Dijon, whose jurisdiction included the Saône-et-Loire and six other departments.[78] Here one sees just how closely the Vichy police worked with the Germans, for the arrests were made by French gendarmes, but the lists sent to Pithiviers were attributed to the German security police, the Sipo-SD, a division of the SS. In fact, it was the French regional prefect in Dijon who, upon orders from the Germans, sent a telegram to the subprefect in Autun on July 11, instructing him that all foreign Jews between the ages of sixteen and forty-five residing in the region were to be arrested over the next two days and transferred to Pithiviers, to arrive there no later than 8 p.m. on July 15. This is one more indication that Irène must have arrived in Pithiviers before the sixteenth. The prefect's telegram ended on a threatening note: Any policeman or gendarme who failed to execute these orders as given would be fired immediately.[79]

All in all, 90 people living in the occupied part of the Saône-et-Loire were arrested during those two days in July and sent to Pithiviers; 33 of them, including Irène Némirovsky, were put on the transport of July 17.[80] The order to arrest only those between the ages of sixteen and forty-five was observed, with a few exceptions. That probably explains why Irène was taken but not Michel, as he had turned forty-five the previous October; she was thirty-nine. By the time he was arrested, on October 9, the age limit no longer existed. But that is a story we will pick up later, along with the stories of Denise and Elisabeth.

Michel's frantic attempts to marshal help for Irène's release are detailed in the telegrams and letters he sent in the days and weeks after her arrest to Sabatier and Esménard, to the Red Cross, to Madeleine Cabour, even to Ambassador Abetz. Sabatier got very involved too, writing to Hélène Morand and other influential people he knew. For a while he was in almost daily contact with Michel.[81] But all of this was in vain, for transport #6 had left the station at Pithiviers on the morning of July 17, 1942, at 6:15 a.m., bound for Auschwitz. It was comprised of 918 people, including 119 women, among them Irène Irma Epstein, née Nemiriawlsky, born in Kiew and exercising the profession of woman of letters, according to her registration card. They massacred the spelling of her name, but they got the profession right. The identification "femme de lettres" appears again on the final list of transport #6, the one that was transmitted to Eichmann and to the commander of Auschwitz.[82] Irène Némirovsky arrived in Auschwitz on July 19, 1942, and, according to official records, died there exactly a month later, on August 19.

Her works survived.

Left, Irène at the age of seven, dressed in a sailor suit, Russia, ca. 1910. Courtesy of the Némirovsky papers, IMEC Archive. Right, Irène and her father, Léon Némirovsky, n.d. (ca. 1918). Courtesy of the Némirovsky papers, IMEC Archive.

Irène and her mother, Fanny Némirovsky, n.d. (ca. 1916). Courtesy of the Némirovsky papers, IMEC Archive.

*Irène and her parents and maternal grandparents, Jonas and Bella Margoulis,
in the south of France, 1922. Courtesy of the Némirovsky papers,
IMEC Archive.*

*Left, Irène on the Promenade des Anglais, Nice, 1920. Private collection, courtesy
of Olivier Philipponnat. Right, Michel Epstein on the Lac d'Annecy, 1923.
Courtesy of the Némirovsky papers, IMEC Archive.*

Left, Irène and Michel around the time of their marriage, Paris, 1926. Courtesy of the Némirovsky papers, IMEC Archive. Right, Michel Epstein and his mother, n.d. (1920s). Courtesy of the Némirovsky papers, IMEC Archive.

Irène, Michel, and their daughter Denise on the beach at Hendaye, 1932. Courtesy of the Némirovsky papers, IMEC Archive.

Irène posing for a formal author photo, Paris, 1938. Photo Roger-Viollet, the Roger-Viollet Archive.

Left, Irène, Michel, and their daughters in Hendaye, summer 1939. Courtesy of the Némirovsky papers, IMEC Archive. Right, Irène in the early days of the Second World War, 1940. Courtesy of the Némirovsky papers, IMEC Archive.

*Left, Denise and Elisabeth Epstein at the time they were hiding, July 1943.
Courtesy of the Némirovsky papers, IMEC Archive. Right, Denise Epstein,
1950. Courtesy of the Némirovsky papers, IMEC Archive.*

*Left, Elisabeth Epstein, early 1950s. Courtesy of the Némirovsky papers, IMEC
Archive. Right, Elisabeth (Epstein) Gille, author photo for* Le Mirador, *Paris,
November 1991. Photo Ulf Andersen, Ulf Andersen Photo Shelter.*

Top, street sign, Place Irène Némirovsky, Issy-l'Évêque, June 2014. Photo by author. Center, Place Irène Némirovsky, formerly Place du Monument, with First World War and Second World War Memorial. In the background is the house where the Epstein family lived in 1941–42. Photo by author. Bottom, Denise Epstein with her daughter Irène Dauplé and granddaughter Julie Dauplé, Toulouse, June 2011. Photo by author.

Left, Némirovsky's granddaughter Marianne (Gille) Féraud, Aix-en-Provence, July 2010. Photo by author. Right, Némirovsky's grandson Nicolas Dauplé, Volnaveys-le-Bas, June 2014. Photo by author.

Left, Némirovsky's great-granddaughter Léa Dauplé, West Tisbury, Massachusetts, August 2014. Photo by author. Right, Némirovsky's great-granddaughter Nina Denat, Lille, January 2016. Photo by author.

Némirovsky's grandson Emmanuel Dauplé at his mother Denise's apartment, Toulouse, June 2013. Photo by author.

Family tombstone, Cimetière de Belleville, Paris, June 2013. The inscriptions on the tombstone include the names of Irène Némirovsky and Michel Epstein with the notation "Died in Auschwitz." Photo by author.

PART II

Fictions

CHAPTER FOUR

Foreigners and Strangers

Némirovsky's Jewish Protagonists

What will people think? Or, to be exact: What will the goyim think?

—PHILIP ROTH, "Writing about Jews"

What matters to me most: the Jew.

—NÉMIROVSKY, journal entry, 1938

AFTER SHARING A COPIOUS Thanksgiving meal with their Russian Jewish immigrant family in Queens, New York, in the fall of 2011, the up-and-coming young writer Gary Shteyngart and his father, Semyon, found themselves sitting together on the couch in the living room. On the television an ethnic cable station was showing a Russian soap opera set in the Stalin years, the years of Semyon's first memories. He had been a young child during the siege of Leningrad in the Second World War. Gary too was born in Leningrad, in 1972—his name had been Igor. Suddenly, Semyon leaned over to his son and said, "Don't mention the names of my relatives in the book you're writing." Gary assured him that he wouldn't; then Semyon added in a whisper, "Just don't write like a self-hating Jew."[1]

This anecdote, recounted by Shteyngart with his characteristic mixture of humor and sorrow in his memoir *Little Failure* (2014), illustrates just how long-standing and deep-seated is the anxiety, among a minority that feels persecuted or misunderstood, about the way they are portrayed by writers and artists, especially by a member of their own group. I say minority rather than Jews because the same phenomenon exists among African Americans, Hispanic Americans, and other ethnic groups that have experienced prejudice. When the film *Precious*, directed by the African American director Lee Daniels and based on the novel by Sapphire, was released in 2009, the well-known African American novelist Ishmael Reed published an op-ed essay in the *New York Times* denouncing the film and its director. *Precious*, which won Academy Awards that year for best supporting actress and best screenplay, tells the story of a black adolescent girl in Harlem, circa 1987, who becomes the teenage mother of two children after being sexually abused over several years by her father. Despite its grim subject, the film has a somewhat upbeat ending, for the young woman is helped by an African American teacher who inspires self-confidence in her and teaches her to read and write. Reed, however, wrote that he and other black men and women felt "widespread revulsion" at the film, which pandered to white audiences' most negative stereotypes about the black family. He quoted another writer, Jill Nelson, whose view he shared: "I don't eat at the table of self-hatred," she had written, nor did she embrace the "overwrought, dishonest and black-people-hating pseudo-analysis too often passing as post-racial cold hard truths."

Reed himself maintained that this film "cast collective shame upon an entire community" and that "such stereotyping has led to calamities being visited on minority communities."[2] The anxiety expressed here is based on a widely shared assumption, namely, that an unflattering portrayal of a member of a persecuted minority or even of a minority that is merely other in relation to the mainstream will bring shame and possibly harm on the community as a whole. This assumption accounts for the powerful feeling of indignation, or, as in Reed's case, of revulsion, that a reader or viewer may feel when she perceives negative stereotypes about her own group in a fictional work. Such perception is all the more distressing, and the resulting feeling on the part of a reader all the more heartfelt, if the author of a portrait deemed to be harmful is a member of the same group, sitting at the "table of self-hatred."

American Jews today do not perceive themselves as others in American culture, if we are to believe the detailed studies published by the Pew Research Center in its Religion and Public Life series.[3] But Shteyngart's anecdote suggests that his father, a relative new-comer to these shores, is not yet comfortable enough in his Ameri-canness to consider himself a full member of the pluralist majority, whence his plea to his son that he should not "write like a self-hating Jew." If we look back over the past century we find that even Jews born and raised in this country have at times felt very uncomfortable, outraged even, at what they perceived to be negative portrayals of Jews by Jewish writers. In 1959, when Philip Roth published his first story in the *New Yorker*, the magazine received numerous letters from Jewish readers, including several rabbis, who protested that Roth's story was antisemitic. One reader wrote to the Anti-Defamation League to denounce him.[4] The story, titled "Defender of the Faith," features two Jewish GIs during the Second World War, one of whom tries to manipulate the other into granting him special favors be-cause of their shared Jewishness. The title turns out to be ironic, for faith is very far from the concerns of these soldiers: self-interest and a sheer desire to survive are uppermost in their minds. There are no positive characters in this brilliant, thought-provoking tale. At the end, the reader is left to ponder what, if anything, Jews have in com-mon with each other and what they might owe each other.

The indignation among Jewish readers spread even wider a few months later, when *Goodbye, Columbus* appeared. In addition to the title novella, the book included "Defender of the Faith" and several other stories about American Jews. While it made Roth famous and was admired by many readers, Jewish and non-Jewish, others were convinced that Roth's work endorsed and even spread harmful ste-reotypes about Jews in American society. Roth himself was taken aback by the passions his book aroused and wrote several essays in response, defending the writer's duty to tell the truth as he sees it, even if it is a painful one. As far as stereotypes went, he noted that sometimes what comes across as a negative stereotype is also a fact:

"If people of bad intention or weak judgment have converted certain facts of Jewish life into a stereotype of The Jew, that does not mean that such facts are no longer important in our lives, or that they are taboo for the writer of fiction."[5] By "our lives" Roth meant the lives of Jews, among whom he obviously counted himself. In fact, the article appeared in the Jewish journal *Commentary*. But he may also have meant human beings in general, who might recognize aspects of themselves in some of his Jewish characters.

As I read the stories in *Goodbye, Columbus* I don't feel that Roth sees Jews as others, whether positively or negatively, but rather as people he knows intimately, who evoke in him the complicated feelings that often come with intimate knowledge. For example, there is the story about Epstein, a middle-aged New Jersey businessman whose humdrum existence is briefly transformed by his affair with his younger next-door neighbor, before a heart attack puts an end to his neoadolescent yearnings and restores him to the bosom of his wife. "Epstein" struck some readers of *Goodbye, Columbus* as hateful and potentially harmful to Jews, Roth recalled in his essay "Writing about Jews." But the protagonist's pathetic romance and his reunion with his scolding, devoted wife could also elicit a smile of recognition and sympathy, from Jewish readers as well as non-Jews. Jewish readers who don't feel offended by the story may, in turn, be accused by some others of being self-hating Jews like the author himself! There is no rulebook where readers' emotions are concerned.

Roth was not alone in attracting the ire of some Jewish readers. Almost a half century earlier, in 1913, the editor of the Yiddish-language newspaper the *Jewish Daily Forward*, Abraham Cahan, who had been among the first wave of Jewish immigrants from Russia in the 1880s, published his novel *The Rise of David Levinsky* in installments in the mainstream magazine *McClure's*. Many Jewish readers were appalled by it. The novel, which Cahan expanded considerably for its publication in book form in 1917 and which is now considered his major achievement as a writer, tells the story of a poor, yeshiva-educated Jew from Russia who arrives in New York as a penniless teenager, wearing sidelocks (*peyes*) and speaking only Yiddish, and who, by dint of cleverness and hard-driving, even ruthless, business practices, becomes a millionaire clothing manufacturer. An unhappy one at that, for Cahan had lifelong socialist sympathies that made him less than fully sympathetic to millionaires.

McClure's was not known for being sympathetic to Jews, and even less to Jewish immigrants, especially if they came from the "East," as opposed to Germany or Austria. The month before Cahan's first installment appeared, an associate editor at the magazine, Burton J. Hendrick, published a long article titled "The Jewish Invasion of America," in which he argued that Jews were taking over every aspect of American business, from the clothing trades to real estate, theater, even the railroads. At the end of his article Hendrick announced the forthcoming publication: "Mr. Cahan will show, by concrete example, the minute working of that wonderful machine, the Jewish brain."[6] The author of the introduction to the current edition of the novel, Jules Chametzky, notes that some years later Hendrick published a book titled *The Jews in America*, in which he sought "to demonstrate that the Russian-Polish Jews are a different race and civilization from previous Jewish immigrants and should be prevented from entering the United States."[7] Chametzky points out that *McClure's* framing of the book, accompanying it with illustrations that emphasized Levinsky's "Jewish traits," slanted its interpretation in a way that Cahan could not have foreseen. But he also notes that the novel continued to receive contradictory evaluations well beyond its first publication in *McClure's*. While some distinguished American critics like Harold Rosenberg and Leslie Fiedler have praised it, others have found it "undistinguished, a libel upon Jews, the central character repellent, an apology for predatory capitalism, or simply unsavory."[8]

Between Cahan and Roth, other North American Jewish writers came in for similar condemnations. Mordecai Richler's *The Apprenticeship of Duddy Kravitz* (1959), Budd Schulberg's *What Makes Sammy Run?* (1941), Jerome Weidman's *I Can Get It for You Wholesale* (1937), and Ben Hecht's *A Jew in Love* (1931), all of them featuring unscrupulous Jews scrambling to get rich, encountered outraged rejections before becoming, in some cases, literary classics (not all: I find *A Jew in Love* unreadable). The eminent French Yiddishist Rachel Ertel, in her book on the American Jewish novel, devotes an extended discussion to writers of the 1930s who found disfavor with the Jewish establishment because of what was perceived as their unsympathetic portrayals of Jewish characters. She notes the "existential malaise" of Jewish novelists of that time, on both sides of the Atlantic, who had to negotiate a position between their Jewishness and their belonging to the national literary tradition. The British critic Eric Homberger has called such writers "uncomfortable," opposing them to those who have "piously sought to present favorable 'role models' of Jewishness."[9]

A Jewish Antisemite?

Némirovsky too, as we have seen, has been tarred with the label of Jewish antisemite, in our time and in hers. Her breakout novel, *David Golder*, continues to provoke debates, especially among Jewish readers. The critics who first reviewed the book in the French press, however, were almost unanimously positive. They praised Némirovsky's "rigor" and other "virile" qualities, and her "pitiless" way of exposing "the soul" of her characters. Just about all of them noted that the novel did not present a happy view of human existence, but many found that the author demonstrated sympathy and compassion for her main character. In her career-making interview with Frédéric Lefèvre shortly after the book appeared, Némirovsky expressed pleasure that he found her portrayal of Golder sympathetic. While most reviewers noted that Golder was Jewish, many said his story was universal and tragic. If they saw him as a type, it was not of the Jew but of the self-sacrificing father or the modern capitalist, neither of which they identified exclusively with Jews. Some compared him to Honoré de Balzac's Père Goriot, who sacrifices his own well-being in order to enrich his daughters. The critic for the *New York Times*, reviewing the English translation in November 1930, compared Golder to King Lear because of his solitary death and his attachment to his daughter.

Surprisingly, one of the most detailed and sympathetic early reviews was by the twenty-year-old Robert Brasillach, who would go on to his notorious career as an antisemite but who at this point was just a young movie buff and aesthete, although on the right of the political spectrum, to be sure. Reviewing the book in the right-wing

L'Action Française under his nom de guerre Robert le Diable, a bad-boy hero of medieval legend, Brasillach wrote, "The need to make money is an instinct common to all the great capitalists," but "the disdain of that money . . . is less widespread . . . and is perhaps characteristic of Jews. Others disdain honor or glory."[10] That last sentence could be read as a sly dig at Jews, implying that they possess no honor or glory to begin with and thus have nothing to disdain in that regard. But if dig it is, it's a very indirect one, especially coming from the pen of Brasillach.

Jewish responses in the French press were more mixed, as could be expected. The independent Jewish monthly of Strasbourg, *La Tribune Juive*, defended Némirovsky against charges of antisemitism: "She has dealt not with a Jewish subject but with a universal one," wrote the reviewer. But the French Zionist paper of Tunis, *Le Réveil Juif*, was severe: yes, the book had literary qualities, but this paled before the fact that it presented a "modern Shylock" who would please antisemites and that the author had described only "odious Jews and Jewesses."[11] Among ordinary readers, as opposed to professional critics, the responses varied as well. Denise Weill, a psychoanalyst I interviewed in Paris who actually remembered seeing *David Golder* on her parents' bookshelf when she was a child in the 1930s, told me that in her family's milieu of liberal secular Russian Jews, Némirovsky was admired as a "local girl who made good," and her novel was considered to be a critique of high finance in general, not of Jews in particular.[12] On the opposing side, Némirovsky herself made public a letter she had received after the publication of *David Golder* from an anonymous Jewish reader in Italy: "You are a renegade and the daughter of a renegade," stated the letter, whose author judged that Némirovsky had provided ammunition to "our enemies," spreading hatred of her own people. The letter was signed "A wounded Jewish soul."[13]

L'Univers Israélite, the weekly journal of the Consistoire, the official representative body of the French Jewish community (Orthodox in its orientation), did not review *David Golder*, but it did report, in a "Talk of the Town"–type column at the end of January 1930, that the book was being much discussed and that Lefèvre, in his interview with the young woman author, had expressed special interest in the scene in the kosher restaurant on the rue des Rosiers. This had led, the journal noted with some irony, to visits to the street by a lot of men in broad-brimmed hats, obviously writers![14] A month later the weekly dispatched a journalist named Nina Gourfinkel to talk with Némirovsky, running the interview as the lead story in its issue of February 28. Gourfinkel, herself a Russian emigrée to France and a few years older than Némirovsky, published several books on literary topics after the Second World War along with two volumes of memoirs (they made no mention of Némirovsky). In her introduction to the interview Gourfinkel explains that she wanted to air with the author a question that has bothered many Jewish readers: Should David Golder, that unhappy businessman who discovers the uselessness of his lifelong struggle to become rich, be considered as a "type representative of the Jewish race"?[15]

Gourfinkel writes that she was apprehensive before meeting Némirovsky, as the novel had left her with a painful impression despite its undeniable literary qualities. She was expecting to see a stern-looking woman, but to her delighted surprise the person who greeted her was petite and very feminine, "with a kind and open face." Gourfinkel launches right into her subject: "Your novel depicts a Jewish milieu that is so repulsive, it has upset a lot of people. And . . ." Némirovsky completes the sentence: "And they accuse me of antisemitism! But that's absurd! Since I am Jewish myself and say so to anyone who wants to hear it!" Gourfinkel persists, however: None of the Jewish characters in the book elicit the reader's sympathy. Is there really nothing good about them? Némirovsky protests again: "I don't find them so unsympathetic. And some critics share my view." But does she know, Gourfinkel asks, that "our enemies" are using her portrayals of Jewish characters to buttress their very unpleasant arguments against Jews? Némirovsky replies, "And yet, that is how I saw them." Besides, she adds, the non-Jewish characters in the novel are not any better. Right, says Gourfinkel, but that may just go to show that Jews gather the "dregs" of non-Jewish society around them. She mentions a new novel by Jacques de Lacretelle, a sequel to his earlier success *Silbermann*, as a positive counterexample to *David Golder*, one that offers a very different version of "the Jewish soul." Némirovsky agrees that Lacretelle is a fine writer, but he writes about a different milieu, she says, and besides, he doesn't know Jews very well.

Clearly, neither party will win this debate: the journalist thrusts, the author parries. A reader today who knows Lacretelle's *Silbermann*, a novel published in 1922 that had gained a solid reputation for being sympathetic to Jews, and its sequel, *Le Retour de Silbermann* (1929), will find Gourfinkel's admiration for the portrayal of Jews in these works quite odd, for they are both redolent of the genteel antisemitism of the period. In both of these novels the Jewish protagonist is portrayed as an incurably alien figure in French culture. Silbermann, a French Jewish adolescent, is described at some length in the first book as being physically ugly, even repulsive. Although he is extremely brilliant, his arrogance and his difference from the other boys elicit a deep revulsion in the French Protestant narrator, who nevertheless becomes his friend before abandoning him. In the sequel, the narrator meets Silbermann again years later, when Silbermann returns to Paris after spending several years in New York. He is still brilliant but sick in both body and soul, literally consumed by his own feverish intelligence as well as by his growing awareness that he will never achieve the literary greatness he had aspired to when he was a schoolboy. Lacretelle even puts into Silbermann's mouth one of the most noxious antisemitic myths, made popular by Richard Wagner in his essay on Jews and music and a staple of anti-Jewish discourse in the 1930s: the myth of Jews' incapacity for artistic creation. Looking at his old school prizes, Silbermann bitterly remarks that he had been like a "little rabbi," able to recite the Torah, or, in his case, masterpieces of French poetry, by heart but unable to create anything of his own, unlike his former classmate, "the Christian," as he calls the narrator, who lacked his intelligence but had written a fine book.[16]

The dichotomy of "us versus them," French Christians versus Jews, dominates both of these novels by Lacretelle, creating a system of meaning that relegates the "Jewish soul" to the status of an exotic, in some ways fascinating but artistically sterile and ultimately repellent, object. Gourfinkel was right, if not in her appreciation of Lacretelle's "philosemitism," at least in contrasting his view of Jews with Némirovsky's. In Némirovsky's world the Jewish other is contrasted not with the French same but with other Jewish others: rich versus poor, assimilated versus "ethnic," dog versus wolf. Personally, I am more disturbed by Lacretelle's portrayal of Silbermann than by Némirovsky's Jews, just as I am disturbed by Sartre's portrayal of the Jew in his *Antisemite and Jew* (*Réflexions sur la question juive*, published in 1946), a book that certainly had no antisemitic intent. On the contrary, Sartre thought of himself and was perceived by many grateful Jewish readers as a defender of Jews. Yet he too reproduces in his book the us versus them opposition, Jews versus Frenchmen.[17] By now, however, it should be evident that in this particular area of interpretation there are no right answers, only more or less persuasive ones depending on who is judging.

Gourfinkel concluded her article with a curious remark: Irène Némirovsky was certainly not an antisemite, but neither was she Jewish! "Antisémite, certes, Irène Némirovsky ne l'est pas. Aussi peu que juive" translates literally as "An antisemite, certainly, Irène Némirovsky is not. No more than she is Jewish." Gourfinkel adds, "For just as one cannot judge the French based on a few Parisian neighborhoods that have been arranged to the taste of 'foreigners,' so one cannot judge a race based on a few individuals lacking in all moral sense, and whose true homeland is a fashionable resort where the dregs of every nation mingle." Is Gourfinkel suggesting that a Jewish novelist, in order to be truly Jewish, must present a complete sociological panoply of Jewish types, and that, having failed to do so, Némirovsky cannot be considered Jewish? Or is she merely saying that Némirovsky's Jewish characters don't represent all Jews, a statement Némirovsky would assuredly agree with? Whatever the case, Gourfinkel ends her article by expressing the hope that this outstanding young novelist, who has provided such a "pitiless image of a certain world," will soon produce a work that shows a different view of "the race": "less painful and more human."[18]

In July 1935, after Némirovsky had published two more novels and a dozen stories, none of which featured Jewish characters, *L'Univers Israélite* sent another journalist, Janine Auscher, to interview her. Auscher, an unabashed admirer of Némirovsky's work, had published two earlier interviews with her in the center-Left weekly *Marianne* and had already asked her about the "disenchanted," generally dark vision of her works—her latest novel, for example (*Le*

Pion sur l'échiquier), had ended with the self-inflicted death of its hero. Némirovsky had replied that her joyless childhood in Russia in the "declining years of the czarist regime," filled with lessons and tutors and no "distractions," might account for the pessimism of her works.[19] There was no mention of Jewishness in the *Marianne* interviews, but Jewishness was the principal theme for *L'Univers Israélite*. In fact, it was on this occasion that Némirovsky produced the letter she had received from the "wounded Jewish soul" in Italy after the publication of *David Golder*, authorizing Auscher to reproduce it in full.

Once again, the purpose of the interview was to air Némirovsky's response to accusations of antisemitism. Auscher makes clear from the start that she herself considers them to be based on a misunderstanding (malentendu). Still, she asks Némirovsky to defend herself, especially because, according to rumors, her next novel, *Le Vin de solitude* (*The Wine of Solitude*), would once again "provide arguments for our adversaries." In response Némirovsky smiles somewhat "mischievously," without "managing to adopt the contrite attitude that more severe questioners would doubtless demand," writes the journalist. Instead, Némirovsky asks a question of her own: What would François Mauriac (a celebrated Catholic novelist, whose depictions of French bourgeois Catholics are dark in the extreme) say if all the bourgeois of the Bordeaux region where his novels are set suddenly rose against him and blamed him for having painted them in such violent colors? Indeed, Auscher replies, Mauriac is not kind to his characters, but in their case the "question of race does not intervene." True, says Némirovsky, but she too paints only a certain type of Jew, not all Jews, and especially not the "French *Israélites* who have been established in their country for generations." She paints the "rich, cosmopolitan" Jews for whom the "love of money has taken the place of all other feelings" and has "gradually destroyed all love of traditions and of the family." She knows these Jews very well from her own experience, she adds "melancholically."[20]

Auscher, ever sympathetic, evokes an earlier occasion on which Némirovsky had told her about her unhappy childhood: it may be the source of "the harsh and disenchanted talent of the author of *David Golder*." Then, giving an unexpected twist to the Jewish antisemite label, Auscher adds, "The profound pessimism and occasionally cruel lucidity that mark Némirovsky's work" endow it with an "undeniably Jewish character." In other words, Némirovsky's particular cruelty toward her Jewish protagonists is the hallmark of her Jewishness! A similar opinion about Jewishness, paradoxical as it may sound, has been echoed by many a contemporary commentator and was perhaps best expressed by Isaac Deutscher in his often-quoted essay "The 'Non-Jewish' Jew." In Deutscher's view, renegade Jews like Freud, Marx, Einstein, and Spinoza, a list to which one could add Kafka, Proust, and many others, are profoundly Jewish in their very critique or renunciation of Jewishness.[21] Jacques Derrida expressed a similar view in a paper he delivered at the colloquium of French-speaking Jewish intellectuals in Paris in 1998, where he suggested that the inability to "live together" with other Jews, as well as with himself, defined his own ineluctable sense of being a Jew.[22] Némirovsky, as if to confirm Auscher's judgment, insists to her that she has never tried to hide her Jewishness, that she has in fact proclaimed it at every opportunity: "I am much too proud of being Jewish to deny it."[23]

This conversation took place in July 1935, two and half years after Adolf Hitler had become chancellor and then führer of Germany, where Jews of all "types" had become outcasts. Auscher therefore asked a question that rings with a terrible irony to anyone who knows what happened only a few years later to Jews in France, including the securely established Israélites that Némirovsky considered to be outside her purview: "May one suppose that, under a less humane regime than the one in our country, where Israélites are treated like other citizens, you would not have provided antisemites with the arguments that people reproach you for?" Némirovsky's reply is instructive: "It's certain that if Hitler had already been there [in 1929], I would have made *David Golder* a lot less harsh [j'eusse grandement adouci *David Golder*]." But she adds, echoing her earlier comment to Gourfinkel ("That is how I saw them") and resonating with Roth's later statement that a writer must be true to his vision no matter what "the goyim think": "And yet, I would have been wrong, it would have been a weakness unworthy of a genuine writer!" Auscher agrees with her and concludes her article with a vigorous defense of a novelist's right to artistic freedom. Anticlimactically, she also defends Némirovsky's cruel portraits of family life by emphasizing that in her real life she is an extraordinarily tender and attentive mother.

What's in a Stereotype? Reading Antisemitism in Fiction

There exists a vast critical literature on antisemitic stereotypes in the representation of Jews in modern times, in literature and film and in public discourse generally.[24] Our question here relates not to the representations themselves but to their perception: By what process of reasoning or, more likely, of instantaneous, nonreflective judgment does a reader or viewer decide that a novel or poem or film or play is antisemitic? The process involves, before all else, the reader's or viewer's perception that the work promotes harmful stereotypes about Jews. To be sure, at issue here are works on which readers' interpretations differ. Works that are unambiguously propagandistic, such as the Nazi film by Veit Harlan, *Jew Süss*, pose no interpretive conflict, at least not when it comes to the fact that the film portrays Jews as negative others who constitute a threat to virtuous Christians. (Some viewers may have considered the portrayal to be truthful, but that's a different matter!) In fact, *Jew Süss* is often invoked as an incontestable reference point when a reader or critic wants to label a work as antisemitic. Most works of fiction, however, and even many nonfictional works that lay claim to literary or artistic merit are not so clear-cut. The conflicts of interpretation that some works inspire show just how intricate and how deeply personal the act of responding to a work of fiction can be.

Professional critics are trained to explain and justify their responses to a work of fiction, with an eye to persuading others of their rightness. But every reader or viewer, no matter how ordinary, is able (and likely) to express a judgment when it comes to works that represent members of their group, and all the more so if they judge that representation to be unfairly negative or prejudicial. Think of how much ink has been spilled over Shakespeare's depiction of Shylock. The British lawyer and literary scholar Anthony Julius has devoted a book to explaining why he considers certain of T. S. Eliot's poems antisemitic. His detailed account of his response to Eliot's early poem "Gerontion" (1920) offers a rare and valuable glimpse into the process of perceiving antisemitism in a work of literature. His account begins with an unequivocal statement:

> No Jew reading the following is likely to doubt its anti-Semitism:

> "And the jew squats on the window-sill, the owner,
> Spawned in some estaminet in Antwerp,
> Blistered in Brussels, patched and peeled in London."

> These lines . . . sting like an insult. Purportedly referring to one Jew alone, they implicate all Jews in their scorn. . . . The poem, so to speak, does not want Jewish readers.[25]

The trigger that sets the process in motion is the reader's feeling of insult and offense, which appears immediate and visceral. Eliot's lines "sting" him, and, what is more, they exclude him and others like him. Julius takes it as a given that every Jewish reader will respond in the same way, as "no Jew . . . is likely to doubt its antisemitism." This assumption turns out to be somewhat problematic, for, as he notes in a long postscript to the book's second edition, a number of critics who disagreed with his interpretation were Jewish. In his opinion, however, to fail to see the antisemitism of "Gerontion" and some of Eliot's other early poems is to practice the worst kind of denial; it is "a refusal to acknowledge the self-evidently anti-Semitic nature of Eliot's text" (335). Julius does not specify whether *all* readers of goodwill must see the antisemitism in the text, on pain of being dishonest with themselves since the truth is self-evident, or only Jews. Rhetorically and in terms of logic, a self-evident truth requires universal recognition. What Julius does make clear at the outset is his own feeling of outrage and exclusion, as a Jew, from the poem and *by* the poem.

Later, he provides a more detailed interpretation of the verses in question: "The 'jew' is on the window-sill both because he has been denied any more secure resting place and because he himself may thus deny his tenant peaceable possession of his house. He crouches because he is weak. . . . The faulty posture of Jews, and in particular their weak feet, is an anti-Semitic theme. . . . This squatting Jew, in his inability to find any permanent place of rest, is also Eliot's gesture toward that most fatigued of cultural clichés, the Wandering Jew" (47–48). Later still, he summarizes his earlier arguments: "['Gerontion'] is anti-Semitic because it uses anti-Semitic language and because its tendency is to encourage readers to think badly of Jews" (306).

Following upon his first subjective response, Julius concludes that Eliot's poem is hostile and potentially harmful to Jews in general. The reason for this, he argues, is that the work reproduces and endorses and thereby propagates traditionally negative stereotypes and clichés about Jews: the homeless Jew, the physically weak or misshapen Jew, the deceitful Jew who preys on Christians. Julius also sees in the poem an evocation of the ancient figure of the Wandering Jew, who, according to Christian legend, was punished for his refusal to believe in Jesus Christ. This is an extrapolation on Julius's part, for Eliot makes no mention of this legendary figure. Thus far, then, we have two major criteria that seem to determine a reader's judgment that a work is antisemitic: the presence of hostile stereotypes that implicate and are potentially harmful to all Jews, and correlatively a structure of exclusion whereby the Jewish reader, but possibly any reader who has a distaste for antisemitism, feels that the work is not addressed to him or even that the work positively rejects and insults people like him.

Stereotypes, according to the definitions offered by social scientists, are commonly held beliefs in a given society that refer to the personal characteristics of a whole group of people, such that any individual member of the group is perceived in terms of the stereotype. A stereotype is a generalization, a schematized and simplified image with little relation to reality. While it may apply to some members of a group (some Jews really are good at making money, and some Frenchmen really are great lovers), it can never function as a reliable guide to all or even most of the group's members. Nevertheless, those who study how stereotypes work emphasize that they are extremely powerful and widespread and that their functions vary: they are not always negative or harmful. For example, they can serve as a positive self-identification for a group: "We Americans are hard-working, God-fearing, tolerant of others"; or "We women are more sensitive and nurturing than men"; or "We Jews are clever, always managing to survive despite hardships and persecution." Even when a stereotype is invoked to define a member of another group, one different from us, it is not necessarily accompanied by negative feelings, also known as prejudice, or by discriminatory actions. One example given by Ruth Amossy and Anne Herschberg Pierrot in their book on stereotypes and clichés is that one can share the stereotyped belief that Scotsmen are stingy without necessarily disliking them (prejudice) and without excluding them from one's neighborhood or workplace (discrimination). One might even invoke the stinginess of Scotsmen as a positive trait that the rest of us should learn from.[26] I am told that a number of books have been published in the past few years in China praising the ability of Jews to make money and exhorting the Chinese to follow their example.[27] In a different field, the nineteenth-century star of Parisian theater, Rachel, was often praised for her Oriental Jewish beauty. The stereotyped image of "la belle Juive," the beautiful Jewess, as opposed to the unattractive Jewish male, goes back at least as far as Shakespeare's Jessica in *The Merchant of Venice*.[28]

Obviously, a reader who judges a work to be antisemitic has in mind a different kind of stereotype: not a harmless, if false, generalization about Jews but a dangerous misconception whose ultimate aim is to do harm. Julius expresses this view in defending what he calls his adversarial reading of Eliot's early poems: "Anti-Semitism is . . . a stockroom of commonplaces and clichés about Jews, discovered and adopted anew by each generation of anti-Semites. . . . It has a two-part logic: this is what Jews are, and so this is what must be done with/to them. . . . It is a discourse, then, that leans towards harm" (303). As we saw earlier, Ishmael Reed suggested a similar effect, if not outright intent, to harm in his analysis of the negative stereotypes about African Americans in *Precious*. It is not clear, in Julius's formulation, whether "leans towards" implies conscious intention to harm on the part of the speaker or whether it designates only the effect of the discourse, independently of the speaker's intention. Generally, it is assumed that a work judged to be antisemitic was intended as such, but even if we leave the question of intention open for now, we can see why the perception of antisemitism in a literary work may arouse extremely strong emotions in a reader. In such a situation it makes no difference if the work in question is fiction or poetry with some claim to artistic merit rather than an outright screed. On the contrary, the reader may argue that fictional works can do all the more harm when they do not offer outright propositions about Jews as a group but work by way of connotation and implicit generalizations, what discourse analysts call topoi. A topos is a general proposition that is not explicitly stated or argued but that forms the logical basis for an assertion. "Pierre is rich, he won't offer to help," for example, is a statement based on the topos that rich people lack empathy.[29] Or consider an utterance like "Pierre is a Jew, he can afford to buy this house," which assumes that all Jews have money.

Interpreting stereotypes as a discourse of harm also explains why those who perceive them in this way are confident that their reading is the correct one. Julius maintains that a Jewish reader who disagrees with his assessment of "Gerontion" is in denial: "There is a small history to be written of Jewish critics' insensibility to the anti-Semitism of anti-Semitic works of literature" (49). Understandably, some Jewish readers may consider such assurance exaggerated, perhaps even paranoid. But Julius's rejoinder is hard to counter: "The uninsulted should not be too quick to give lessons to the insulted. . . . Nor should the uninsulted claim the right to determine whether an insult has been delivered" (312). In the domain of reading, subjectivity rules, which does not mean that no rational thought is involved in one's judgment. On the contrary, readers who perceive the presence of harmful stereotypes in a work of fiction tend to see them as part of a coherent system in which the stereotype is not a random effect but an essential part of the work. According to such a reading, an antisemitic work presents all Jews in a negative light, whether by themselves or in contrast to non-Jews or occasionally to "exceptional" Jews, who are positive. In other words, such a reading constructs the work as a redundant system in which identical meanings recur and reinforce each other. In Anthony Julius's reading of "Gerontion" "the jew" is presented by Eliot as unnatural or animal-like ("spawned"), deformed physically ("squats"), a moneygrubber ("the owner") as well as a modern embodiment of the accursed Wandering Jew.

The work interpreted as being antisemitic appears not only redundant but Manichean, setting up contrasting poles between Jews, who are presented as uniformly negative, and non-Jews or not "real" Jews, who are seen as positive: us versus them. The reader interprets the negative Jewish characters as stand-ins for Jews in the real world, whence the notion of harm and the subjective feeling of outrage as the reader experiences in a personal way the relegation of Jews to the negative side of a bipolar universe. Julius writes, "The distinction between Jew and Gentile [is what] most matters to anti-Semites" (xiii).

In my first book, *Authoritarian Fictions*, I spent a lot of time studying the mechanisms of the *roman à thèse*, the thesis novel or ideological novel, a genre that, I argued, is founded on a Manichean structure where a positive doctrine is contrasted with a negative one: Fascists are bad, Communists are good or vice versa. I sought to show, by means of complicated formulas (it was the heyday of structuralism), that this Manichean structure is created chiefly by redundancies: a character's actions, words, physique, and personality traits all reinforce his or her ideological position in the work, on the positive or negative side. The result is an airtight system of meaning with no major contradictory elements to disturb its coherence. It now occurs to me that reading a work as antisemitic is a way of reading it as *à thèse*, that is, as an ideologically coherent system governed by a unified vision that the reader attributes to the author or to the text or work as a whole. The author here is technically the implied author created by the text, who is not to be confused with the biographical writer. To be sure, the implied author and the real writer often share similar ideological views, especially where antisemitism is concerned, and readers tend to conflate the two, but the implied author is an *interpretive construct* formed by the reader in the course of reading. Like all large-scale interpretive constructs, as opposed to the construction of the meaning of individual sentences, the implied author emerges as the result of a circular process: the reader, continuously making deductions and associations in the course of reading, constructs the author's meaning gradually but in such a way that once an initial interpretation has been made, the others tend to confirm it. Philosophers call this the hermeneutic circle. After the first "sting" produced by an antisemitic stereotype, everything that follows falls into place. The interpretation reinforces itself both retrospectively, integrating earlier details that may have escaped notice on first reading, and prospectively, building up expectations for details to come. It then becomes possible to overlook aspects of the work that do not fit into the interpretive schema and to castigate readers who don't see what one sees.

In Anthony Julius's reading of "Gerontion" the sting occurs soon after the beginning of the poem, in verses 8–10 out of a total of 76. Although "the jew" is never mentioned again, those three jolting lines suffice to make Julius read the whole poem as an indication of Eliot's antisemitism. He later suggests that "Gerontion" is too negative about the whole world to propound a "thoroughgoing anti-Semitism" but nevertheless insists it is an "anti-Semitic poem, not just a poem about an anti-Semite."[30]

In the case of literary works it is likely that a reader comes to the work with certain expectations based on what she knows or may have heard about the author. If I open a book by Louis-Ferdinand Céline, for example, I expect to be stung. I may even be surprised to note that not all of his novels feature hateful portrayals of Jews. Céline was a brilliant stylist, a writer who cultivated the literary possibilities of slang and dark comedy. I cannot help but admire his linguistic exploits and his burlesque imagination, but many passages in his later novels sting me, confirming my worst expectations and turning me furiously against him, even without counting his so-called pamphlets, which go on for hundreds of pages ranting against "rich Jews."[31] By contrast, when I read a story about a poor Jewish dairyman in czarist Russia who is often insulted and made to feel inferior by rich Jews, even in his own family, and who exclaims, "There's no knowing what goes on in the mind of a rich Jew, of a Brodsky in Yehupetz, for example, or of a Rothschild in Paris," I don't interpret that as a sign of the work's or the author's or, for that matter, the dairyman's anti-Semitism. Nor do I feel any sting except that of the pleasure of reading Sholem Aleichem, even in translation.[32] One reason is that I know Aleichem was a Jew writing in Yiddish, designating his first readers as Jews and intending no harm. Like the Jewish teller of a Jewish joke to another Jew, he pulls me in to laugh with him. But let a Céline tell a Jewish joke, and I am very likely to feel insulted.

One could spend many lively hours comparing notes on antisemitic works of film or literature with like-minded or, better still, different-minded friends. The British independent film *An Education* (2009), based on a memoir by Lynn Barber and with a screenplay by the prolific Nick Hornby, generally earned critical praise and was nominated for three Academy Awards, including Best Picture. It is a coming-of-age story set in the 1960s and features a young girl who is seduced by an unscrupulous older man named David, a charmer who is not even handsome—and who is a Jew, revealed at the end to have a very Jewish-looking wife and child. When I saw the film I didn't fail to note the emphasis on David's Jewishness and the stereotyped looks of his wife and child, but I did not feel offended, perhaps because the most unpleasant character in the film, the headmistress of the heroine's school, makes overtly antisemitic remarks that the film obviously condemns. In other words, I did not consider the film itself as antisemitic. The reviewer for the Los Angeles *Jewish Journal*, by contrast, found it disturbingly so: "The more I watched, the more the character of David Goldman resembled the parasitical Jew of "Der Ewige Juden" [*sic*]—one of the infamous 1930s Nazi propaganda films I had studied . . . at UCLA," she wrote.[33] *Der Ewige Jude* ("The Eternal Jew"), which has a well-deserved reputation as the most scurrilous of Nazi propaganda films, was a so-called documentary released in November 1940 as a companion piece to the equally repulsive fiction film *Jew Süss*, which had been released two months earlier.

The fact that a viewer in 2009 could seriously compare a new British comedy to "The Eternal Jew" may seem astonishing, but it actually confirms the three criteria I have proposed for how one reads antisemitism in fiction. The reviewer reports that she noticed a whole slew of antisemitic stereotypes in the portrayal of the Jewish character: he is pudgy and effete as well as an adulterer and a small-time crook; she judges that these stereotypes are harmful to all Jews, and she evokes a Nazi film as the ultimate historical reference (this corresponds to Julius's evocation of the Wandering Jew as a historical reference in "Gerontion"); finally, she considers that the mutually reinforcing stereotypes form a coherent ideological system that can only be called antisemitism. It is highly unlikely that any argument to the contrary would persuade this viewer that her reading is wrong. In fact, she notes it is she who persuaded her husband and friends, who at first had not seen the film's antisemitism.

Lest the reader think I am always among the simple souls who fail to perceive an insult when it is given, let me briefly cite a counterexample. When I first read a novel titled *Gilles*, published in 1939 by the French writer Pierre Drieu La Rochelle, I gradually arrived at the conviction that it was a horribly antisemitic work. Drieu, who had been close to the Surrealists and to left-wing politics in his youth, had by 1939 become a militant fascist, and in 1945 he committed suicide rather than have to face a trial for collaboration with the Nazis. While not as original a writer as Céline, he was a good novelist, and *Gilles* is without a doubt his most important work. Not too many people read Drieu these days, but among scholars his reputation as a writer is quite high, even among those who are not at all sympathetic to his ideology. The story told in *Gilles* resembles Drieu's own: the hero, Gilles, fights in the First World War, returns to Paris feeling at loose ends, marries a rich "Jewess," then divorces her: she is too "rationalistic," and he soon finds her physically repulsive. He eventually ends up as a committed fascist intellectual who goes to Spain to fight on the side of Francisco Franco (Drieu himself did not go to Spain).

My reading of *Gilles* was not so much influenced by Drieu's history, however, as by the novel itself. The decisive moment came around the middle, when a minor Jewish character named Rebecca Simonovitch makes her appearance. Rebecca is ugly, has a shrill, high-pitched voice, is a foreigner from Russia, espouses both Marxism and psychoanalysis, and exerts such a nefarious influence on the gullible son of a government minister that the young man commits suicide, precipitating a political scandal. I became so outraged at Drieu's portrayal of Rebecca that I ended up writing an article, one of my very first publications, detailing just why I found this novel so loathsome, using the character of Rebecca as my point of reference.[34] Although I considered my argument incontrovertible, I am sorry but not truly surprised to report that a number of my students and colleagues with whom I have discussed this novel over the past twenty years don't find it as reprehensible as I do. They barely even noticed Rebecca Simonovitch, and besides, they often add, Drieu was a good writer.

All this helps to explain, I think, why even today some readers and critics feel like "wounded Jewish souls" when they read Némirovsky's Jewish fiction and condemn her for it, while others, with equally strong conviction, find her Jewish characters compelling. Neither side will win this debate because, as I have tried to show, the debate is not winnable. In the matter of emotional response to a work of fiction, subjectivity really does rule.

Still, one can try to probe a response: Why do I count myself among Némirovsky's defenders rather than among her attackers when it comes to her portrayals of Jews? Do I never wince when I read in one of her novels a description of Jews that sounds like a negative stereotype? Yes, I do wince at some moments. But hearkening back to my analysis of reading antisemitism in fiction, I would say that I shrug these moments off. I do not construct them as parts of a coherent system of meaning that seeks to discredit Jews—in other words, I do not read her fiction as *fiction à thèse*. In my reading, Némirovsky's novels that feature Jewish protagonists are not meant to prove an idea or an ideology, either about Jews or about anyone else. More important, they do not pit Jews against non-Jews as the negative or harmful other against the positive same. On a spectrum that places Sholem Aleichem at one end and Céline on the other, I situate her closer to Aleichem (though not too close!). Was it pure coincidence that Aleichem's real name, Rabinowitz, was the one Némirovsky chose for the two Jewish figures who meet on a train platform in her short story "Fraternité"? If so, it was a happy one: "Two Jews meet in a train" is one of Sholem Aleichem's favorite ways of starting a story.

Étrangers

Only about a quarter of Némirovsky's stories and novels feature Jewish protagonists, but they are among her strongest works, and they span virtually her whole career. Starting with her early novellas, *L'enfant génial* (1927) and *Le Bal* (1929), through *David Golder* (1929), then two more novels, *Le Vin de solitude* (*The Wine of Solitude*, 1935) and *Les chiens et les loups* (*The Dogs and the Wolves*, 1940), as well as the short story "Fraternité" (1937), she depicted in ever more detailed and explicit ways the existential choices and dilemmas Jews faced as they negotiated questions of identity and belonging in relation to the non-Jewish world. To these works we can add *Le maître des âmes* (The master of souls), which was published in book form in 2005 but had been serialized under the title *Les Échelles du Levant* in *Gringoire* in 1939. The protagonist of that novel is an impoverished foreigner in France, a doctor who starts out very poor but succeeds in becoming a psychiatric guru for wealthy neurotics in Nice and Paris. Némirovsky originally envisaged this character as a Frenchman and only gradually gave him his foreign background. In the process his name changed from Gabriel Dario to Dario Asfar, which has a more Oriental ring. The allusions to his past as a poor boy growing up in a slum in a "city in the East" recall the early lives of David Golder and Ben Sinner of *The Dogs and the Wolves*, and designate him implicitly as a Jew even though he is not labeled as such. The central issue in *Le maître des âmes* concerns the protagonist's simultaneous feelings of longing and hatred, love and scorn, for the French society that rejects him at first and then flocks to him. This is identical to the themes Némirovsky treats in her overtly "Jewish" works.

Indirection is often Némirovsky's preferred approach to the Jewish theme, even with characters who are explicitly identified as Jews. The protagonist of *David Golder*, which for many years was her best-known work, never asks, What does it mean for me to be a Jew?, let alone, What does it mean to be a Jew in modern Europe? But the reader is prompted to do so, and Némirovsky's cruel or despairing views on that question are one reason some readers condemn her as a self-hating Jew or a Jewish antisemite. Similarly, in *The Wine of Solitude*, her most autobiographical novel, the Jewishness of the Karol family, who flee Russia after the Revolution, is only alluded to or mentioned in passing rather than openly discussed, but it nevertheless forms a significant subtext, especially since Némirovsky emphasizes social differences within the Jewish family itself. The novella *Le Bal*, written around the same time as *David Golder*, is most often described as a mother–daughter tragicomedy focusing on the rage of an adolescent girl who feels unloved by her egotistical, social-climbing mother. Enmity, even hatred, between mothers and daughters is a quasi-obsessive theme in Némirovsky's fiction and is not necessarily linked to Jewishness. Indeed, in the film version of *Le Bal* (1931), which introduced the teenage Danielle Darrieux as the vengeful daughter, Jewishness is neither mentioned nor implied. But the work gains an extra dimension if we give full weight to the fact, duly emphasized by the narrator in the novella, that the father in the unhappy Kampf family is a newly wealthy "little Jew" who made a killing on the financial markets and whose marriage to a vulgar, uneducated Frenchwoman turns out to be a mismatch of sought-after assimilations: the husband seeking non-Jewish Frenchness and the wife aspiring to wealth.[35] Of all these works, *The Dogs and the Wolves* offers the most extended, explicit exploration of Jewish identities in Christian France, but, significantly, it deals with various members of a family of immigrants from Russia, thus linking the Jewish theme once again to foreignness.

The word for "foreigner" in French, *étranger*, is also the word for "stranger." The two meanings overlap but are not synonymous, for one can be a stranger to a community or group without being a foreigner; conversely, some foreigners are not strangers to a particular individual or group, for many people have foreign friends. But both words carry connotations of difference and possibly exclusion from the majority group or the nation. The foreigner does not have the right passport, if he has one at all, or the right accent or way of dressing or behaving, while the stranger does not quite fit in, even if she looks and speaks like others and tries hard to be one of them; occasionally, the stranger will not try to integrate, preferring instead to cultivate his feeling of difference. In all their varieties, foreigners and strangers are outsiders, perceived as such by others and in most instances by themselves as well.

Foreigners and strangers, both Jews and non-Jews, proliferate in Némirovsky's work. The foreigners are mostly Russian emigrés, as in a number of her short stories and novellas, including *Les Mouches d'automne* (*Snow in Autumn*, 1931) and *L'Affaire Courilof* (*The Courilof Affair*, 1933). The former tells the story of an aristocratic Russian family that flees Russia after the Revolution, taking along their aged servant, who is unable to make the transition to Paris and eventually drowns herself in the Seine; the latter is a story of intrigue and political assassination in czarist Russia, told by the aged former plotter and would-be assassin, living in exile in Nice. Némirovsky also wrote several novels and many stories that focus exclusively on French people at home, especially in her last years, the best known being *Suite Française*. But when she tried to explain, in 1934 in a radio interview, what her work was about, she put the emphasis on "dislocated" people who were far from their origins: "I continue to depict the society I know best, which is made up of dislocated people [des désaxés] who have left behind the milieu where they would normally have lived and whose adaptation to a new life is not without shocks and suffering."[36] The emphasis here seems to be on foreigners who actually move from one country to another, but her formulation applies equally well to anyone who feels out of place in relation to the milieu they find themselves in. At the time of this interview she had just published *Le Pion sur l'échiquier* (The pawn on the chessboard, 1934), which is about an exclusively French milieu in Paris in the early 1930s. The main character, Christophe Bohun, is an ordinary Frenchman (his father, however, was a businessman and speculator born in Greece) who feels totally estranged from his very proper bourgeois wife and son, so much so that in a moment of depression he attempts to slit his throat and ends up dying of blood poisoning. Suicide, or at least a desire for the restfulness of death, is a recurrent motif in Némirovsky's fiction. Emile Durkheim, in his classic work on suicide, associated it with what he called anomie, an absence of stabilizing social norms that are traditionally found first of all in the family.[37]

Historically, Jews have been the quintessential *étrangers* in European culture, in both senses of the word. Very often they were foreigners, given their frequent displacements across national borders as they fled pogroms, poverty, and revolutions in eastern Europe in the nineteenth century, followed by more of the same after the two World Wars. For much of that time, certainly until the Second World War and perhaps beyond, they were also seen as strangers, even when they stayed in place and despite their attempts to become integrated into the national culture. This was true even in countries where they were promised and indeed granted full status and equal rights as citizens, as happened in France after the Revolution and in England, Germany, and the Habsburg Empire after the series of emancipation bills enacted in the late nineteenth century. In her fiction Némirovsky emphasizes the difficulties and contradictions of Jewish existence, not only in repressive Russia but also in the more liberal West. She shows that France itself, which to many Jews appeared like a haven of tolerance, was not a place where they could feel totally at home. Her most searing insights, like those of many other Jewish writers of her time and place, dwelled on the obstacles, both internal and external, to Jewish attempts at assimilation. Her Jewish characters, who are generally divorced from religious practice, manifest both a strong desire to belong to the non-Jewish world and an equally strong sense of estrangement, the causes of which are to be found both in their own psyche and in the antisemitism that surrounds them. What Némirovsky emphasizes again and again is that they are estranged not only from the majority culture but also from other Jews who remind them of their Jewish roots by exhibiting "Jewish traits" they feel ashamed of. It is this estrangement experienced by Jews themselves from other Jews that some people call self-hatred or Jewish antisemitism. But the fact is that it existed and continues to exist, not only among Jews but also among other devalued minorities, and not only in Europe. It was the African American theorist W. E. B. Dubois who coined the phrase "double consciousness" to describe the split subjectivity that occurs in members of such a minority as they interact with their own group and with the privileged majority.[38]

Némirovsky was painfully aware of this phenomenon, becoming what one might call the chronicler of Jewish self-hatred *from the inside*. In this she was similar to Proust, who has also been accused of antisemitism, and Kafka, among other modern writers. Kafka, who once wrote to his non-Jewish lover Milena, in what Louis Begley calls an outburst, that he would like to "stuff the Jews," including himself, into a drawer and suffocate them. But at the same time, he toyed with the idea of learning Yiddish and moving to Palestine![39] What was involved here was an acute, debilitating ambivalence and conflicted identity that went hand in hand with a pessimistic response to the "Jewish question." Would Jews ever be considered full members of their non-Jewish national communities?

Némirovsky's answer to that question was no, and all the more so as the 1930s moved toward their disastrous close. Instead of tarring her with the label of self-hater or antisemite, we do best to consider her as a Jew who knew exactly where to pour salt on the deepest wounds of Jewishness—in other words, who was intimately familiar with the feelings of anxiety and existential unease, often coexisting with equally strong feelings of pride, ambition, and irony toward non-Jews as well as toward oneself, that she depicted and analyzed variously in her Jewish characters. These inner contradictions are nowhere clearer than in the protagonist of "Fraternité," Christian Rabinovitch, whose name says it all. But we also see it in the three main protagonists of *The Dogs and the Wolves*, who are members of the same family yet make widely divergent choices in relation to Jewishness, and in the protagonist of *Le maître des âmes*, Dario Asfar, who is a Jew in all but name. It comes down, finally, to this: no matter how hard a Jew tries or desires to be neither a foreigner nor a stranger in the country where she lives, she will never succeed completely or for long. The reason is both *internal* (the long history of Jewish persecution, the heritage of fear and anxiety that is the psychological lot of every Jew) and *external* (the refusal of the majority to fully accept the Jew).

Confronted with this situation, the Jews in Némirovsky's fiction, like Jews in real life, make existential choices, which may not even be perceived *as* choices by the one who makes them. David Golder and his friend Soifer prefer isolation or the company of other Jews, even as they feel estranged from them; Ben Sinner in *The Dogs and the Wolves*, Boris Karol in *The Wine of Solitude*, and for that matter David Golder in his youth seek above all to escape the poverty of the ghetto and become rich, at whatever price. Dario Asfar also fits this description, but he has the additional dream of being loved by a virtuous French woman whom he idealizes. Others, like Ben's cousin Harry, the "dog" in *The Dogs and the Wolves*, and Christian Rabinovitch of "Fraternité," already benefit from the wealth and privilege acquired by their parents or grandparents but nevertheless continue to feel insecure and anxious, heirs to a history they cannot shake. Finally, there are the artists and poets: the budding writer Hélène Karol in *The Wine of Solitude* and the painter Ada Sinner in *The Dogs and the Wolves*, introspective souls who take an ironic pride in not truly belonging anywhere. The fact that these artist figures are young women adds yet another element of difference to their self-perception as well as their perception by others. Women writers and artists, whether Jewish or not, were an exception in the 1930s, often considered as *bêtes curieuses*, "odd beasts," as Beauvoir wrote in her memoirs.[40] The child poet Ishmael Baruch in *L'enfant génial* belongs to the artist group as well, but he dies too young to fill out the role.

In all these cases Némirovsky emphasizes that the unease of Jews is experienced not only, or not even primarily, in relation to the mainstream culture but also in relation to other Jews. Poor Jews simultaneously admire and envy rich Jews, while rich Jews seek to distance themselves from the "ghetto Jews," who evoke memories of the wretchedness and poverty they or their parents have succeeded in escaping. In addition, Jews who have acquired refined taste and manners in the process of assimilation may look down on the "vulgarity" of the newly rich as well as on the "outdated" rituals of religious Jews. David Golder feels totally estranged from the wealthy but vulgar Jews who gather for the funeral of his former business partner Marcus—and he is positively revulsed by the rich Jew Fischl, who appears to him like a "cruel caricature" of a little Jew.

The sole passage in the novel in which Fischl appears in person is often cited as evidence of Némirovsky's antisemitism and is therefore worth a close look. Fischl is introduced as one of the guests at a party in the Golders' house in Biarritz, where Golder's wife and daughter live and Golder himself feels like a visitor. He has just arrived from Paris and is not well. During the previous night in the train he felt frighteningly ill, suffering what would later turn out to have been his first heart attack. Now, as the party is about to start, he muses on the vanity of these get-togethers, where "dukes and counts and maharadjahs," whom he calls filth (de la boue), come to feast at his table. They used to amuse him once, but now he is tired: "The older he got, and sick, the more he felt tired of people, of the racket they made, of his family, of life."[41]

Immediately after this, Golder sees Fischl, who calls out to him, "Bonjour, Golder!" Golder turns to him without responding: "Why did Gloria have to invite that man? Golder looked at him with a kind of hatred, as at a cruel caricature. He was standing by the door, a fat little Jew, red-haired and rosy, comical-looking, vulgar, slightly sinister, his eyes full of intelligence shining behind thin gold-rimmed glasses, with his big belly, his weak legs, short and crooked, his hands of an assassin calmly holding a porcelain box full of fresh caviar next to his heart."[42] Any reader sensitive to negative stereotypes of Jews is sure to wince at this description of Fischl. One of Némirovsky's severest critics, Ruth Franklin, points to it as a major piece of evidence when she calls *David Golder* "an appalling book by any standard."[43] But the passage becomes much more interesting if we read it as Golder's jaundiced view of a man who is not all that different from him: like Golder, Fischl is apparently a successful businessman who wins and loses millions with his dealings. If Golder has amassed a fortune by being ruthless in business (the novel's opening word, "Non," as Golder refuses to bail out his business partner, aroused the critics' admiration and earned Némirovsky her reputation as a "masculine" writer), Fischl is downright dishonest and unapologetic about it. He has been to jail in three countries, he tells Golder offhandedly, but is none the worse off for it. Talking with him, Golder feels almost guilty at his revulsion, for Fischl "had never done him any harm. 'I can't stand him, it's really odd,' he said to himself." Fischl, apparently unaware of Golder's disdain, sprinkles Yiddish into their conversation, as if to remind him of their shared identity and their common past as poor Jews. But Golder remains hostile: "'He must have made millions again, the pig,' thought Golder" ("'Il doit être riche à millions, de nouveau, le cochon,' pensa Golder").

Fischl as seen by Golder becomes a kind of distorted mirror image. If Golder can't stand him even though Fischl has never done him any harm, it is because Fischl looks and acts and talks too much "like a Jew" as seen by antisemites, and his presence threatens to contaminate Golder by association. Golder's revulsion to him is like the revulsion of Christian Rabinovitch toward the poor immigrant Jew whose name he shares: "What is there in common between him and me?" As I mentioned about "Fraternité," Némirovsky often stages this kind of confrontation between Jewish characters, in which one figure is the disturbing double of the other. These scenes pack a lot of meaning into a brief space and are highly effective dramatically. In the encounter between Fischl and Golder, for example, our attention is focused on Golder's view of Fischl, which tells us more about Golder than about Fischl. This is achieved by Némirovsky's use of free indirect discourse: the description of Fischl, although given in the third person, actually reports Golder's view of him. Free indirect discourse, perfected by Flaubert and carried to new levels of intricacy by Henry James, is an extremely supple narrative technique, and Némirovsky appears to be using it almost intuitively here. In later years, when she was reading theoretical works on the "craft of fiction," she used it more self-consciously, reminding herself in her journals that everything should be seen "from the point of view of the characters." The very suppleness of the technique, however, means that it can elicit conflicting interpretations, depending on whether one attributes a description or an opinion to the author or to a character. If I interpret Golder's view of Fischl as an indication of his own troubled relation to "looking like a Jew," I feel I have gained an important insight into both Golder and the broader phenomenon of group self-hatred. If I attribute the view of Fischl to Némirovsky herself, that may prompt me to condemn her as an antisemitic author.

In the film version of *David Golder* (1931) by Julien Duvivier the contrast as well as the similarity between Golder and Fischl is emphasized: Golder, played by the great actor Harry Baur, is a portly, well-dressed man who bears himself with dignity, with a look that commands respect. Fischl, by contrast, looks vulgar, even in a tuxedo, and his attempts to flirt with Golder's beautiful young daughter make him look at once abject and pathetic. In visual representation, the fruitful ambiguity of free indirect discourse disappears: since the character is embodied by an actor, who is costumed and made up to look a certain way, there is no ambiguity about who is seeing him that way. The camera's eye is objective—at least that is the illusion created by cinema. Interestingly, Duvivier's Fischl, played by an actor of the Comédie Française, Jean Coquelin, does not "look Jewish" in an obvious way nor does he address Golder in Yiddish, but he is still a negative character, and his name is emphasized as Jewish.

The other Jewish character that hostile critics invoke in their indictment of the novel is Golder's old acquaintance Soifer, who, like Fischl, is described in exaggeratedly stereotypical terms—and he is played that way in Duvivier's film, almost too much so. But in this case, even in the novel the description appears to be coming more from the narrator than from Golder. Soifer, we are told, was an "old German Jew" whom Golder had first met many years earlier in Silesia, which would mark him as being "from the East," and who has lost and gained several fortunes in his lifetime. These days he is immensely rich, but he "has walked on tiptoes all his life to make his shoes last longer," and he eats only soft foods because, having lost all his teeth, he wants "to save the expense of dentures." Soifer, the narrator tells us, would later "die alone, like a dog, without a friend, without a wreath on his tomb, buried in the cheapest cemetery in Paris, by his family who hated him and whom he had hated, but to whom he left a fortune of more than 30 million, thus fulfilling till the end the incomprehensible destiny of every good Jew on this earth."[44] This last remark is one place, I believe, where Némirovsky loses control of the narration by allowing her own conflicted feelings to be expressed without adornment or indirection. If the destiny of "every good Jew" is to die alone, even while affirming his bond to a family he hates and that hates him, what does that suggest about Jewish existence?

Golder too will die alone, leaving a fortune to his flighty daughter, whom he loves with no illusions about her supposed love for him and who is probably not even his biological child, as his wife, Gloria, spitefully informs him in one of their fights. We don't see Soifer's interactions with his family, but Golder's scenes with Gloria certainly bear out Némirovsky's jaundiced view of family life, a view which applies to both Jews and non-Jews in her fiction. Gloria, a child of the ghetto like Golder (her name used to be Havke) who seeks only to get hold of Golder's money after a heart attack leaves him an invalid, belongs in the gallery of selfish, grasping, unfaithful wives and mothers who populate Némirovsky's oeuvre and whose most complete embodiment is the mother in *The Wine of Solitude*. Significantly, all of these mothers have daughters, not sons. Jewish critics who interviewed her often asked Némirovsky why her painting of Jewish family life was so grim, given that Jews prized family so highly. Her usual reply, obviously based on her experience with her mother, Fanny, was, "That is how I saw them."

Soifer, like Fischl, is a kind of twin to Golder, but unlike Fischl, who disgusts Golder, Soifer amuses him, and the narrator tells us that it's because Soifer "had a kind of dark humor that was similar to Golder's own, and that made them like each other's company."[45] After Golder breaks with his family and gives up his business affairs (temporarily, it turns out), Soifer visits him each day in his huge, almost empty Paris apartment and the two play cards together. Although Soifer is a minor character not essential to the plot, Némirovsky is sufficiently taken with him to devote two whole chapters to him. One of these recounts a visit by the two friends to the Jewish slum, the rue des Rosiers, where Soifer knows of a restaurant that makes the best gefilte fish in Paris. He calls the dish "brochet farci," stuffed pike, but even under that fancy French name Golder turns up his nose at it. Nevertheless, Soifer persuades him to accompany him to the restaurant and even to pick up the tab! (Duvivier left this whole episode out of his film.) When they first enter the street, with its dark shops that smell of "dust, fish, and rotten straw," Soifer breathes it all in and turns to Golder: "'What a bunch of dirty Jews, eh?' he said tenderly. 'What does it remind you of?' 'Nothing good,' said Golder darkly."[46] Soifer's ironic nostalgia for the wretched conditions in which both he and Golder grew up is rendered here with beautiful economy by the "eh?" and the adverb "tenderly" that accompany his remark about the "dirty Jews." The remark thus functions like a Jewish joke told by one Jew to another and is obviously part of the "dark humor" Golder likes about his friend. Golder himself has no such nostalgia. However, once they are seated in the restaurant and he looks out the window as night is falling, watching two bearded Jewish men whose gestures seem totally familiar to him, he is suddenly transported to an earlier time, to the "shop where he was born," on a "street in the snow and wind that he sometimes saw in dreams." Like Soifer but with less self-irony, Golder experiences a moment of nostalgia: "'It's a long road,' he said out loud. 'Yes,' said old Soifer, 'long, hard and useless.'"[47]

At the end of the novel Golder actually returns to Russia, now the Soviet Union, to complete his last and biggest deal, after which, already dying, he finds himself in the port city on the Black Sea (evidently Odessa) from which he had set out many years earlier to make his fortune. Before boarding the ship that will carry him back to Europe, he revisits the neighborhood where he had lived as a young man and muses about how his life would have turned out if he had stayed—another brief moment of introspection and nostalgia on his part. He dies on board the ship, but before that happens he encounters yet another double of himself, a poor young Jew who is setting out in the world just as Golder had done. With this young man Golder speaks Yiddish, thus reconnecting with the language of his childhood. Whereas Fischl's use of Yiddish had simply increased

Golder's disdain for him, the Yiddish spoken by this young man makes Golder feel less alone on the ship, among the Russian boatmen and the "schouroum-bouroum," defined earlier by the narrator as Oriental carpet merchants. I find this whole scene extremely moving, but some critics find it racist, as if Némirovsky had "sent Golder back to where he came from, where he belongs," implying a racial determinism.[48] It's true that Némirovsky thought of Jewishness in terms of heredity, which she saw as both historical and biological: Jewish history, like Jewish blood, she often suggests, cannot be escaped. While this view may be interpreted as racist, once again, it depends on how you see it, for many Orthodox Jews also think in terms of bloodlines, whence their insistence that only a person born of a Jewish mother can be considered Jewish. On the other hand, they are not opposed to conversion, as long as it is to the Orthodox brand of Judaism, which implies that biological heredity is not the most important thing after all. Nothing is simple.

In *The Dogs and the Wolves*, the refined, assimilated Jew Harry Sinner marries a beautiful French bourgeois Catholic woman who loves him, but the "call of his blood" overcomes his desire for Frenchness and he falls madly in love with his cousin, the poor Russian emigrée artist Ada, to the point he is willing to leave his wife for her. Some critics have called this novel racist as well, and one particularly hostile review of the recent English translation compared it to a page out of some Nazi manual.[49] But to my mind, reading it that way is a form of what Sidra Ezrahi has called, in a different context, "dead-minded literalism."[50] Ezrahi was defending the use of humor or parody in Holocaust literature and film against critics who cannot abide anything other than solemnity in such works. One can expand her notion to include critics who cannot abide anything in a work of fiction that makes Jews "look bad."

As a final example of how different readers can arrive at widely divergent interpretations, I want to consider in detail one of Némirovsky's earliest works, *L'Enfant génial (The child prodigy)*, the first in which she portrayed a Jewish protagonist. *L'Enfant génial* appeared in 1927, two years before *David Golder*, in the serial *Les Oeuvres Libres*, which published several full-length novellas or short novels in each issue. Never reprinted during Némirovsky's lifetime, the novella was reissued in 1992 as a slim children's book under the title

Un Enfant prodige (A child prodigy), with a preface by Elisabeth Gille, who made a few minor cuts in the text. It tells the story of Ismael Baruch, the youngest child of dirt-poor Odessa Jews, who reveals a great natural talent as a poet at a very early age. He appears to be on his way to being a true prodigy, but the story ends badly. When Ismael reaches adolescence he finds himself no longer capable of writing poetry, and, with no one to guide him toward the hope that this too will pass, he commits suicide. This is the work of a twenty-three-year-old writer with a dark imagination, and it's full of literary clichés and stereotypes about both Jews and non-Jews. One wonders what Elisabeth Gille had in mind in considering it appropriate for children. Perhaps she thought it would interest young readers as a kind of folktale since it features gypsies, music, exotic settings, and colorful characters. Weiss reads it as a parable, though not a particularly childish one. According to him, it reveals Némirovsky's view that "Judaism . . . is detrimental to literary creation. To become an author, Irène would try to put a distance between herself and her Jewish heritage."[51]

The opening pages situate the Baruch family in Odessa's Jewish slum, and some of Némirovsky's stereotyped phrases here sound very offensive to contemporary ears. She could have found such phrases in the writings of the Tharaud brothers, Jérôme and Jean, for whom she often expressed admiration in interviews. Today the Tharauds are largely forgotten, but in their lifetime they were considered literary giants, and both ended up in the Académie Française. They wrote more than fifty books together, most of them published in the 1920s and 1930s, inspired by their travels in eastern Europe, Spain, and the Middle East. A number of their books feature the Jews in those regions, and for quite a long time the Tharauds had the reputation of being philosemites, even among Jewish readers. To anyone reading them today, however, they appear horribly antisemitic. One of their best-known novels, *Quand Israel est roi* (When Israel is king), published in 1921, is a fictionalized travelogue about the Jews of Budapest and Vienna, as observed by a young Frenchman who is both fascinated by their "exotic" ways and repelled by them. But he also fears them. The book's title feeds into the old, powerful antisemitic fantasy that Jews, if left unchecked, will take over the world. Mysteriously, many Jews in France found this book to their liking, even after the Second World War. A French friend from a Jewish family gave me a dog-eared copy in the 1970s (the book was long out of print by then), asking whether I thought it was antisemitic. He himself found it to be so, he said, but older members of his family thought very highly of it. I agreed with him, however, and so do contemporary critics who write about the Tharauds.[52]

On a quick reading, Némirovsky's opening description of Ismael Baruch's family seems to echo the Tharauds' combination of exoticism, disdain, and fear toward Jews, and in fact she borrows some of their imagery and vocabulary. Ismael's mother, with her curly black wig, looks like "a Negress washed by the snows," and his grandfather, now wretchedly poor, used to be a rich "usurer," a word Elisabeth Gille deleted in her reprint. But the narrator immediately adds a bit of information that qualifies the image of the powerful Jew and that one is not likely to find in the work of antisemites: the grandfather's current poverty, the narrator remarks, was caused by the pogrom that burned down his house on the Easter Sunday following the assassination of Czar Alexander II (1881). Then come two comparisons that are certain to shock anyone who knows about the Nazi propaganda of the 1930s that identified Jews with rats, though of course Némirovsky could not have anticipated that when she wrote the novella. The Jewish slum is full of scruffy children, the narrator tells us: "Babies were born in the Jewish neighborhood, multiplying like vermin [comme pullule la vermine]." Ismael and his siblings, who scrounge for money around the port by helping the stevedores, selling stolen watermelons and begging, "prospered like the rats that ran around on the beach, among the old boats."[53] Elisabeth Gille left in the comparison with rats but deleted the word "vermin." In her version the Jewish children simply "multiply." I counted only five cuts made by Gille, two of which are the word "usurer" to refer to the grandfather, but these tell us which words had become unpronounceable in the post-Holocaust era. They are indeed highly offensive to a contemporary ear and are often cited by critics who tax Némirovsky for antisemitism.

After these two pages that set the stage, Némirovsky abandons the verbal stereotyping, at least of Jews. She uses lots of narrative clichés, however: the dives in the port are full of drunken sailors, prostitutes, and the occasional slummer; just outside of town is a gypsy settlement with gaudy women and musicians, often visited by an "imperious woman" and her lover. Despite such clichés, the story of Ismael takes an interesting turn. At the age of ten he begins to frequent the cabaret in the port and to sing songs of his invention that the drunkards find consoling, so much so that they begin to look forward to his performances and give him money. "The boy never planned in advance what he would say; the words awoke in him like mysterious birds he merely had to let loose, and the right melody accompanied them in a natural way."[54] Ismael is a bit like a Surrealist child-poet, producing automatic poetry by simply opening his mouth and letting it all pour out. One night a well-dressed man shows up and is impressed by the boy's singing. Some time later this "Barine," who turns out to be a poet gone to seed, returns with his lover, the "imperious woman," who takes a fancy to the child genius and invites him to live with her and be educated. She makes a deal with his parents, who are very happy at this turn of events and drive a hard bargain to let Ismael go.

Alas, the fine education he receives at the home of the Princess does not do Ismael much good. While he soon gets used to luxury and refined food and manners, he wastes away with passion and longing for his beautiful benefactress (by now he is a teenager). One day, after she kisses Ismael "imperiously" on the mouth, he falls into a delirium with brain fever and is expected to die. He survives, but the lady seems to lose interest in him and goes off to Europe, sending him alone to her country house to recover. He stays there for over a year and recovers fully, becoming a strapping adolescent. The only problem is, he loses his genius in the process. "Nothing remained of the child genius, but a handsome fellow grew in his place," notes the narrator. Aside from spending long hours roaming the countryside, Ismael reads many books in the Princess's library, but the more he reads, the more hopeless he becomes about his own writing. The great poets awe him, and he judges his own early productions as "barbaric." One day his father arrives, clean shaven and dressed like a gentleman—earlier he had been described as a poor Jew with sidelocks (*peyes*, which the narrator writes as *peiss* and defines as "short curly locks on each side of his brow") wearing a caftan. While the father himself has been transformed by the Princess's money, he is not happy at the physical transformation in his son and makes him return to the city. Ismael must continue to be the soulful child-poet, for the Princess has become less generous, and the father needs money after a bad financial speculation.

The boy tries his hardest, but no words come, and this lack of inspiration makes him feel desperate. When his father takes him to see the lady again, he is tongue-tied: "Once, he had been a child genius; now, he was nothing but an awkward, stupid boy like the others. . . . The Princess looked at him with her cold eyes."[55] The fascinating thing here is that Ismael's family is as much in despair as he is: they *want* him to be a prodigy. But there is nothing to be done, his genius is gone. They then mock him, calling him Wunderkind and child prodigy. Finally, the Princess tells his parents to put him into an apprenticeship, which she will pay for. Reluctantly, they place him with a tailor. After that, he hangs himself.

There is a wonderful story by the great Russian Jewish writer Isaac Babel, written around the same time as *L'enfant génial*, about a Jewish boy in Odessa whose parents want him to become a violin prodigy. Indeed, every Jewish family in their poor neighborhood wants the same thing and for the same reason: "Our fathers, seeing no other escape from their lot, had thought up a lottery, building it on the bones of little children." The local violin teacher "ran a factory of infant prodigies, a factory of Jewish dwarfs in lace collars and patent-leather pumps. He hunted them out in the slums of the Moldavanka, in the evil-smelling courtyards of the Old Market." Babel's first-person narrator, who turns out to have no talent for the violin, fares a lot better than Némirovsky's Ismael, as he simply stops going to lessons and spends his days down by the port trying to learn how to swim. Babel derives great comic effect from the scandal that erupts when the boy's father finds out about his truancy. And Babel too indulges in some stereotyping of Jews: after announcing that he was unable to learn how to swim, the narrator adds, "The hydrophobia of my ancestors—Spanish rabbis and Frankfurt money-changers— dragged me to the bottom."[56] The boy in this story survived the scandal and maybe even learned to swim, thanks to his loving grandmother and to a kindly old Ukrainian journalist who took him under his wing. Némirovsky's tale, working with a similar paradigm, opts for the tragic mode.

In Jonathan Weiss's view, the reason for Ismael's failure must be sought in his Jewish family. Although the Russian bohemian poet "encourages Ismael's imagination, the boy's parents and the Jewish community keep him from composing his verse, preferring to have him work in their grimy shops."[57] This interpretation is somewhat surprising, for Némirovsky's text emphasizes precisely the opposite: the family is desperate to have Ismael produce poetry, and they become furiously mocking when he is unable to do it. It is not the "dark and dank" Jewish household in Odessa that is responsible for Ismael's poetic dry spell, but rather the luxuriant Russian countryside, whose discovery coincides with his burgeoning sexuality. The more robust and less soulfully Jewish (huge dark eyes, pale face, etc.) Ismael becomes, the less of a poet he is. This would suggest that Ismael's poetic genius and his wretchedness as a poor Jew are not at odds but, on the contrary, are linked. The authorial voice, however, makes clear that this interpretation is too simple as well. Trying to plumb the mystery of the child's sudden loss of inspiration, the narrator comes up with an explanation based on child development:

> Why had they fallen silent, the songs that earlier had come spontaneously to his lips? . . . Had his genius been a kind of morbid flower, blooming only because his life had been violent, excessive, unhealthy? . . . Alas! It was simply that he was entering the difficult period of adolescence. . . . But nobody told him that; nobody gave him the hope that his wonderful native talent would come back to him later, when he was a man. . . . Nobody was there to whisper to him: "Wait, hope. . . ." They were all bent over him, around him, hanging on to him, like people who with their sacrilegious fingers want to force open a flower.[58]

Ismael's problem is not that his Jewish family refuses to encourage his poetic activity, preferring him to "work in their grimy shops." Rather, as the concluding metaphor above indicates, the family tries to force the budding poet into flower before he is ready. True, the family's "sacrilegious" forcing of the boy can be seen as caused by their love of money, the Jewish avidity for riches being one of the stereotypes maintained throughout the tale. (One wonders whether it is altogether wrong to imagine poor Jews wanting to become rich.)

But in fact, the family's attitude toward the boy and toward poetry is not marked as specifically Jewish. The Princess does nothing to understand or encourage the young poet either, and it is she who finally directs his father to find him a trade.

Ismael, it would seem, is a confused adolescent, having no one to turn to as he faces the storms of puberty. He is not unlike the teenage writer of Némirovsky's most autobiographical novel, *Le Vin de solitude*, who feels totally misunderstood by her parents. (Yes, the parents are social-climbing Jews!) The author of *L'enfant génial* was herself barely out of her teens when she wrote that novella. Whatever else this supposed parable is about, it certainly expresses a young person's anxiety over the possible loss of poetic talent. Notably, the incident that precipitates Ismael's suicide is unrelated to his Jewish family. One day he returns to the cabaret by the port, where he meets the Barine who discovered him and who is no longer the Princess's lover. This aging drunkard and onetime poet bewails his own loss of inspiration, in terms that recall the narrator's earlier characterization of Ismael's poetic gift as "mysterious birds" that rise in his chest. The older man tells Ismael, "Listen, I'm going to tell you. Don't repeat this to anyone. Maybe . . . maybe they're dead, my marvelous birds."[59] It is after talking with the adult poet who lost his genius long ago that Ismael, as if foreseeing his own future, commits suicide.

If it is read without imposing the grid of Jewish antisemitism on it, *L'enfant génial* becomes a quite interesting work. Even in this early and often clumsy story Némirovsky makes some astute observations about the difficulties of Jewish existence in a non-Jewish world as well as about the challenges of assimilation. Like so many of her later Jewish protagonists, Ismael is a divided being, and, as in the case of Christian Rabinovitch, his inner division is hinted at by his name: *Ismael* alludes to the biblical outcast and non-Jew, while *Baruch* is the Hebrew word for "blessed."[60] When Ismael first goes to live with the Princess, he discovers the refined tastes and manners of a society to which he is a stranger and learns to emulate them; the narrator observes his attempts with sympathy. But what about those nasty descriptions of the Jewish ghetto that open the novella, which any contemporary reader will flinch at? The figure of the ghetto Jew, impoverished, smelly, living in crowded quarters, is a topos of late nineteenth- and early twentieth-century fiction by Jewish as well as non-Jewish writers, in France and elsewhere. Némirovsky's version is quite distasteful, since she compares the large number of Jewish babies to vermin and the children running around the port to rats. But it does not get us very far to point out indignantly, as some of her critics have done, that Hitler too considered Jews as vermin. To Hitler and his followers, the Jews' status as "vermin" meant they were infecting the "healthy" body of non-Jewish society and had to be exterminated. To Némirovsky, the image had no such implication, and the narrator points out that the wretched condition of Jews in turn-of-the-century Russia is at least partly the result of pogroms.

Negative stereotypes must be examined not in isolation but in terms of their function in the work as a whole. This means not only comparing Némirovsky's portrayals of Jews to those of others, ranging from Jewish writers to ideological antisemites, but also giving her works the careful reading they deserve.

CHAPTER FIVE

Portraits of the Artist as a Young Jewish Woman

Blessing: my writing stems from two languages, at least. In my tongue it is the "foreign" languages that are my sources, my agitations.

—HÉLÈNE CIXOUS, "Coming to Writing"

It seemed to her sometimes that, by a mysterious power in her soul, she could feel or guess the thoughts of others.

—NÉMIROVSKY, *The Wine of Solitude*

"THE SUBJECT IS NOT the confession of a solitary drunkard, although that could actually be quite amusing to take on, don't you think? No, by this title I want to express the kind of moral intoxication produced by solitude (moral as well) in adolescence and youth. To you, and you alone, I will confide that this book is the *almost autobiographical novel* that one always writes, inevitably, sooner or later. I hope the critics won't be too harsh, but it's one of those books we write for ourselves, not really caring if others don't like it."[1] So wrote Némirovsky to her sometime mentor Gaston Chérau in February 1935, a few months before the publication of *The Wine of Solitude*. By then she was hardly in need of his help, having published several successful books after *David Golder* and being solidly established as a writer of note. If she had misgivings about the critics' response, warding them off, as it were, by proclaiming indifference, she had reason to rejoice when the book appeared in October, for it garnered plentiful praise from the establishment figures whose opinion mattered most to her. The Academician Henri de Régnier, who was following her career closely, reviewed the book in *Le Figaro* and praised her "harsh and powerful" talent. Ramon Fernandez, a well-known writer and public intellectual who had not yet abandoned his left-wing allegiances (a socialist since the 1920s, Fernandez converted to the extreme Right in 1937 and became an avowed collaborationist during the war but had the good fortune to die of a heart attack in August 1944 before he could be prosecuted), wrote in his review in the weekly *Marianne* that Némirovsky was "one of the most appealing novelists [un des romanciers les plus attachants— note the masculine noun]" in French letters.[2]

A Female Bildungsroman

The Wine of Solitude is indeed autobiographical, recounting the childhood and adolescence of a young woman, Hélène Karol, who resembles Némirovsky like a twin. Hélène, born in a city on the Dnieper River, "between the Ural Mountains and the Caspian Sea," is the only child of a mismatched, upwardly mobile Jewish couple. The family travels frequently to France and employs a French governess for Hélène, a sign of their social aspirations. Left largely on her own, between a vain, self-absorbed mother who cares more about her lovers than about her daughter and a father whose main preoccupation is to accumulate the wealth that seals his distance from his ghetto childhood, Hélène learns precociously to penetrate the secrets of the adults around her. She is especially watchful of her beautiful, emotionally cold mother, Bella, whom she observes with a mixture of longing and loathing. At the outbreak of the First World War the family moves to St. Petersburg, where financial speculation and war profiteering are at their peak. Boris Karol and his associates, both Jews and non-Jews, are caught up in the fever of moneymaking. This too Hélène observes with ironic precision: "'Ships . . .' 'Oil . . .' 'Pipelines . . .' 'Boots . . .' 'Sleeping bags . . .' 'Shares . . .' 'Millions . . . Millions . . . Millions. . . .' Money was the only thing that excited the men around Hélène. They were all getting rich. Gold flowed."[3] When Hélène sees her mother with her new lover, her young cousin Max, from the wealthy branch of the mother's family, which had always shunned the Karols until then, her first thought is, "Max, here? Oh, how rich they must be" (1233). Soon after the October Revolution, in 1917, the Karols, accompanied by Max, leave Russia for Finland and Sweden, arriving in Paris in 1919. During this time Hélène has grown into an attractive young woman. Fulfilling her childhood dreams of vengeance against her mother, she seduces Max, who falls in love with her and wants to marry her. But in the end she sends him away, her hatred of her mother now mingling with a kind of pity for the unhappy older woman. After her father has a stroke and dies, Hélène leaves the house for good, declaring herself finally "free, free from my childhood, my mother, free from everything I hated" (1362). Just before closing the door she looks at herself in the mirror and thinks she resembles "a child of immigrants who'd been forgotten in some port" (1361). But once out on the street, clutching her beloved cat to her bosom, she feels elated. Her life until now, she reflects, has been "simply the years of apprenticeship. They have been exceptionally hard, but they have forged my courage and my pride. That is mine, my inalienable treasure. I am alone, but my solitude is sharp and intoxicating."[4]

Critical commentaries on *The Wine of Solitude*, both nowadays and at the time, generally emphasize the mother–daughter conflict, a familiar and recurrent theme in Némirovsky's work. But Hélène's mention of her "years of apprenticeship" points us to a reading of this novel as a bildungsroman, a genre with a long history in European literature. Although the name was invented by a German philologist around 1820, the genre itself goes back at least to the Middle Ages, to tales of young knights setting out to find their way in the world. In its modern version, Johann Wolfgang von Goethe is usually credited as the inaugurator, with his novel of 1785 *Wilhelm*

Meister's Apprenticeship. Traditionally, the bildungsroman, literally, "novel of formation," featured a young male protagonist who, after a number of false starts, discovers his authentic self and his vocation in the world. In the best of circumstances the hero succeeds in melding individual autonomy with social integration and reaches manhood by assuming an active role in society. Negative versions, more numerous and varied than the positive ideal, emphasized the hero's failure or disillusionment. In Flaubert's *Sentimental Education*, the great example of a negative bildungsroman, the protagonist Frédéric Moreau is never able to move beyond the dreams of his youth and remains immature to the end. A specifically artistic version of the genre, the so-called *Künstlerroman*, recounts the "years of apprenticeship" of a young man who becomes an artist, more often than not a writer. In that case, exile and a refusal of social integration are the prelude to artistic achievement, as in James Joyce's *Portrait of the Artist as a Young Man*, probably the best-known example. Proust's *À la recherche du temps perdu* can also be considered as a Künstlerroman, in addition to being much else. According to one authoritative critic, the whole of that immense novel can be condensed into a single sentence: "Marcel becomes a writer."[5]

Traditionally, women protagonists did not easily fit into any version of the bildungsroman, no doubt because the genre presumes a degree of autonomy and choice as well as self-centeredness that were denied to most women. Women who sought to affirm their independence—usually defined in sexual terms, whether in adultery, prostitution, or merely a refusal to marry—generally incurred punishment, both in life and in fiction.[6] It was only toward the end of the nineteenth century, notably in England and the United States, where feminist movements were stronger than on the Continent, that novelists began to imagine destinies for women that included the possibility of self-realization through work, as opposed to marriage or motherhood. But even there, portraits of the artist as a young woman were virtually nonexistent, this despite the fact that quite a few women in both countries earned their living through writing fiction, without using male pseudonyms. In France too women participated increasingly in the literary marketplace, but their presence did not increase the number of fictional heroines who sought independence through work, let alone who affirmed themselves as art-

ists.[7] Colette's heroine in her novel *La Vagabonde* (1910) is a major
exception, and Némirovsky knew it well, as we shall see. Beauvoir,
growing up in the Paris of the 1910s and 1920s, dreamed of becoming a writer and became one, but in her novels all of the main characters who are writers are male.

Némirovsky, for her part, never presented herself as a feminist
or a radical in any way, but in *The Wine of Solitude* she tells a story
that ends on a note of female defiance. "I am not afraid to work,"
Hélène Karol assures herself at the end of the novel, as she affirms
her "courage and pride." Although we are not told what form her
work will take, everything that precedes this declaration of independence implies that Hélène will become an observer of other people's
secrets, one who describes the life around her without illusions—
in other words, a writer. "What always interests me," Némirovsky
stated in an interview in 1933, "is to try and discover the human soul
beneath the social exterior . . . , to *unmask*, in a word, the profound
truth that is almost always in opposition with appearance."[8] Hélène
thinks in exactly the same terms when she looks around at the crowd
at a fancy reception given by her parents in Paris: "There wasn't a
single face whose anxious, tense features Hélène could not perceive
beneath its mask of carefreeness and lust."[9] If Hélène becomes a
writer, she will be one who seeks to uncover the truth about people,
even if it is painful or unpleasant—in short, a writer like Némirovsky.
As we know, critics admired Némirovsky for the harsh quality of her
prose, her cruel but just insights into her characters. That's why they
called her a *romancier* and not a *romancière*. Yet it was as a woman
writer that she made her mark, sharing with Colette the enviable
status of a female literary star whose talent stood out all the more for
being "masculine." In Hélène Karol she created a portrait of the
artist as a young woman with similar qualities.

A Primal Scene of Writing

Even though Hélène's future career is not spelled out, Némirovsky
placed a highly elaborate scene toward the middle of the novel that
shows the heroine's "coming to writing" and the production of her
first literary text. A similar moment occurs in Proust's *Recherche* when
the narrator-hero writes his first text as a child, inspired by church

steeples appearing and disappearing as he observes them from a moving carriage. In Hélène's case the inspiration comes from her view of two scenes of family life, one fictional and the other real, that unfold before her eyes. Both scenes are built on lies, she decides, and it is the desire to unmask the lies that makes her take her pencil from her pocket and start to write.

The scene, set in St. Petersburg, occurs in a chapter that begins with an astonishingly concise summary of collective history: "The February Revolution came and went, then the October one. The city was haggard, hunkered down in snow" (1252). So much for the Russian Revolution! In her later novels, culminating in *Suite Française*, Némirovsky would pay more explicit, sustained attention to war, but her focus was always on how individual lives are affected by History. In her writing journal for *Suite Française* she notes that she has learned this from Tolstoy. In this scene the tension and anxiety felt by the characters are indicated by means of short, clipped sentences or else longer ones broken up by commas: "It was a Sunday in autumn. Lunch was over. Max was there. . . . Everyone was silent, listening absentmindedly to the muffled, distant gunfire that echoed in the suburbs, day and night, but that no one paid attention to any more."[10] Hélène is studying her German lesson while her parents and Max talk worriedly about how to leave the country and where they might go: Shanghai, Teheran, Constantinople?

Hélène's German textbook, by contrast, presents an idyllic scene, "the description of a close-knit family" accompanied by a color illustration. Hélène is supposed to memorize the sentences in the book, which she translates to herself (not always correctly) as she reads: "'*Eine glückliche Familie* (a happy family). *Der Vater* (the father) *ist ein frommer Mann* (the father is a humble man).'" The illustration shows the *Hausfrau* dusting the furniture while the father reads the paper; four children, playing quietly or doing their homework, plus a dog and a cat complete the picture. Hélène's reaction to this happy scene is immediate: "What a lie!" she thinks to herself. Looking at her own family, father, mother, mother's lover, she feels they are unreal, "half-hidden in a mist," and very far away: "She lived far from them, separated, in an imaginary world where she was mistress and queen." At that moment, she fishes out a pencil from her pocket and starts to write, on the page of the book itself: "*The father is thinking about a woman he met in the street, and the mother has only just said goodbye to her lover. They do not understand their children, and their children do not love them; the young girl is thinking about the boy she's in love with, and the boy about the bad words he learned at school. The little ones will grow up and be just like them. Books lie. There is no virtue, no love in the world. Every home is the same. In every family there is nothing but greed, lies and mutual misunderstanding.*"[11] Hélène literally overwrites the German text, as if she wanted to replace the lie she sees in it with her own view of the truth. Némirovsky emphasizes this by putting Hélène's text into italics. If "books lie," then Hélène seems to be saying that her own writing will not lie. Her jaundiced view of family life is subjective, presenting her individual experience as a universal one, but the main thing is that this act of writing produces an immense feeling of pleasure in her. Here again one thinks of Proust's episode about the church steeples, where after composing his text the boy is so pleased with himself that he begins to sing at the top of his lungs ("chanter à tue-tête").[12] In a similar way Hélène experiences a totally new pleasure as she writes "with a strange rapidity and dexterity she had never experienced before, an agility of all her thought"—and here the narrator introduces a striking simile: "as if she were watching tears flow down her face and hands on a winter evening, when the frost transforms them into icy flowers" (1254). Transforming tears into flowers could be a definition for the kind of writing Hélène—and, behind her, Némirovsky—considers valuable, for it makes something beautiful and pleasurable out of pain and alienation. She continues to write, and her own text (in italics) alternates with the narrative voice:

> It's the same everywhere. In our house as well, it's the same. The husband, the wife and . . .
> She hesitated, then wrote:
> *The lover . . .*
> She erased the last word, then wrote it in again, enthralled as it appeared before her eyes, then erased it again, crossed out each letter, spiking it with little arrows and curlicues until the word had lost its original appearance and

looked like a creature with a mass of antennae, or a plant with many thorns. It had a malevolent air about it, strange, secretive and crude, that pleased her.[13]

Suddenly her mother notices and demands to see what she has written. When Hélène, in a panic, tries to tear up the page, Bella grabs the book from her. Her enraged reaction is characteristic: "'She's gone mad!' she exclaimed. . . . When someone thinks, dares to think such things, so reckless, so stupid, they don't write them down at least, they keep them to themselves. How dare you judge your parents!" Hélène is an ungrateful, spoiled daughter, and the blame, according to Bella, must be placed on the governess, Mademoiselle Rose: "She's turning you against your parents. She's teaching you to look down on them! Well, she can just pack her bags, do you hear?"[14] In reality, the governess has been the only person to show real affection toward Hélène, who has always felt like an unwanted child. After being fired, Mademoiselle Rose has a breakdown and dies. Hélène, in despair, thinks about throwing herself into a canal but then steps back. From now on she will rely only on herself, she resolves, in terms that foreshadow her declaration of independence at the end of the novel: "'No, they won't get me,' she said out loud. 'I'm brave'" (1265).

Aside from offering a vivid dramatization of a young girl's artistic awakening, the scene of writing in *The Wine of Solitude* points to questions that preoccupied Némirovsky throughout her career, and nowhere more so than in this novel about a budding writer. The psychological knot that exists between mother and daughter is unmistakably a chief preoccupation in this scene. Hélène's text can be thought of as determined by and written against her mother, a fact Bella immediately understands, whence her rage upon reading it. But equally important is the focus on languages, in particular the role they play in delineating and complicating social, psychological, and generational differences. The scene puts into play French as the "language of truth" (Hélène's text is written in French) against the German textbook's lie and against the mother's lie as well. But since Bella's preferred language is French as a sign of distinction, this renders any simple opposition, whether between languages or between mother and daughter, impossible. To the extent that both mother and daughter speak French as their "chosen tongue," as opposed to a mother tongue, they are part of a dynamic in which contradiction and ambivalence predominate. If the mother is a source of rage and hatred, she is also a source of creation, as is emphasized by the language she shares with her daughter.

But the presence of Russian is also implied in the scene, for we know that the father, Boris Karol, does not speak French. When Bella speaks to him or to others in his presence it must be in Russian. The novel as a whole is, in a sense, written in translation, and Némirovsky occasionally calls the reader's attention to this fact. In an earlier scene, for instance, where the Jewish businessman Slivker is at the Karols' for dinner with the aristocratic Chestov, the latter says something to Bella "amiably, in French," the narrator states, thus pointing up the fact that until then the conversation was in Russian (1241)—and also marking Chestov's desire to differentiate himself from the more vulgar Slivker, with whom he nevertheless does business. When Hélène's grandmother calls her "my darling, my treasure made of sugar" (Ma chérie, mon trésor tout en sucre, 1204), we can be sure she is saying that in Russian. The published translation effaces this foreignness by rendering "trésor tout en sucre" as "sweet, sweet treasure." Above all, Russian emerges in moments of strong emotion, at least in the parents' generation. Thus toward the end, when Bella's love affair with Max is unraveling and she pleads with him on the telephone, the narrator specifies that she is speaking in Russian (1335). Like the mother of the ultracivilized Harry in *The Dogs and the Wolves*, who has lived in France for years and spoken French since the age of three but still reverts to Russian when she feels distressed, Bella lapses into her native tongue to express feelings of anxiety or rage. She must certainly not be speaking French when she berates Hélène for being an ungrateful daughter.

One language that does not appear in the writing scene but hovers in the background is Yiddish. As the language of the ghetto that upwardly mobile Jews have escaped or wish to have escaped, Yiddish is a primary marker of social differences. In her writing journal for *The Wine of Solitude*, which contains drafts she later discarded, Némirovsky develops the social difference that Bella and her family perceive between their own middle-class, albeit impoverished, status and Bella's husband, Boris, as a difference in their command of languages. The fact that Boris does not speak French is proof, in their eyes, that he is inferior to them socially. This lack marks him even in his own eyes, for although he is proud to be the family's financial mainstay, his pride, the narrator states, is mixed with humility: "He clearly did not belong to a 'good family'" (Il n'appartenait visiblement pas à une "bonne famille"). The fact that Némirovsky puts "bonne famille" in quotation marks suggests that she views such distinctions with a certain irony. In another discarded passage in her journal, she emphasizes that Bella's family, the Safronovs, including Bella herself, are not as far from their ghetto origins as they would like to think, for while they no longer speak Yiddish, they understand it. "Then, suddenly," Némirovsky writes, "Hélène no longer understood: her father was speaking in Yiddish. Her mother and grandparents replied in Russian, but they were laughing."[15] Since Némirovsky omitted these sentences as well as any explicit mention of Yiddish from the final version of the novel, the reader has to read between the lines to discern how intricately the theme of Jewish identity and its anxieties is linked to language. Bella, in the published version, refers to her family's view, which is also her own though she does not say so openly, that her husband, despite his millions, is "a little Jew who came out of nowhere." Her anxiety about her own social status is one reason she is so happy when Max becomes her lover, for he belongs to the wealthy branch of the Safronov family, more distant from Yiddish than she. In Max's family even French is not considered elevated enough—their preferred language is English. When Bella introduces Hélène to Max in St. Petersburg, his first words are to admonish the young girl to stand up straight, like his own sisters. And when Bella seconds him in criticizing Hélène, he remarks to her, in English, that his sisters have benefited from an *"English education, you know. . . . Cold baths and scraped knees and not encouraged to be sorry for themselves"* (1234). As if to tease the French reader, Némirovsky leaves these sentences untranslated.

She returns to the theme of social differentiation among Jews through language later in the novel, when the Karols and Max, along with others who have fled the Revolution, take refuge in Finland. The refugees, the narrator notes, get along well with each other, "like passengers caught in a storm," despite their belonging to diverse social groups: "Russians, Jews from 'good families' (those who spoke English together and followed the rites of their religion with proud humility), and the nouveaux riches, sceptics, free thinkers, with masses of money."[16] The remark about differences in religious practice is not necessarily accurate, given that many upper-class Jews in Russia and Europe were not at all strict in their observance of religious laws. But the contrast between those who felt sufficiently confident to maintain their ties to Judaism—like the Israélites who were members of the Consistoire in France—and those who, in their eagerness to distance themselves from their Jewish roots, abandoned all allegiance to Jewish groups or practice, is insightful. Significantly, Némirovsky does not delineate differences among Jews, either here or in her other works, in terms of ideology or politics. Many Jews who left Russia after the Revolution were not only anti-Bolshevik and "sceptics and free thinkers" but socialists, Zionists, working-class *Bundists*. In Némirovsky's mental and literary universe what separated Jews from each other was not so much their politics as their social standing, which in turn was defined by their relation to their Jewish roots; and the latter was expressed most often in familial, that is to say, psychological, terms. Némirovsky inflects the Jewish theme toward class and family rivalry, for instance, when she has Max recall the jealous attempts by his own mother to turn him away from Bella in the early days of their liaison: "'She doesn't love you. She wanted to take revenge on me, take you from me . . . You poor child . . . She who was nothing, *a mere nobody*,' she would say bitterly, finding some consolation in her misery by being able to express it in English, naturally, not like Bella, who had undoubtedly learned it from some lover or other."[17] One cannot be sure which of the two women, Max's snobbish mother—who may be right about Bella's English—or Bella herself, elicits the greater irony from the narrator in this observation.

Hélène too has her place in the linguistic and familial labyrinth. Speaking more than one language with ease, or "naturally," as Max's mother would say, Hélène is separated by one more generation from her Yiddish-speaking grandparents, her father's parents. In addition to French, the language in which she writes, she is learning German, a language that neither of her parents speaks. But given the relation of German to Yiddish, this could be a displaced form of bonding with her father or with her Jewish past. The narrator notes at one point that Hélène and her father have the same "dark humor," another link to Jewishness. Since she and her mother are united, willy-nilly, in their love of French, learning German also affords Hélène a way of separating herself from her mother or of finding a better substitute for her. When the family moves briefly to Helsingfors (Helsinki) before heading to Paris, Hélène is sent to board with a Finnish widow who teaches her German. But German is not a first language for Hélène, while French and Russian are. To have two first languages is, in one sense, a luxury, a sign of excess, as is suggested by Hélène Cixous in the epigraph to this chapter. In another sense it is an impoverishment, for it means that one has no true, that is, unique, home. The ambiguity of the in-between state, which is also a kind of nowhere state, suits Némirovsky's Hélène well, just as it had suited Némirovsky herself when she teased her "very French" friend Madeleine about the rowdiness of her Russian friends.

Hélène's in-betweenness is emphasized in a chapter devoted to the annual trips she takes as a child with her parents to Paris in the years before the war and Revolution. Here Némirovsky endows her heroine with a self-awareness well beyond her years. Hélène loves Paris, a "haven of light," but is no more than an observer of the life there, an outsider. At the same time, her native Russia, seen from Paris, appears like a "barbaric country where she didn't feel at home either" (1221). She dreams of being a French girl, with a name like "Jeanne Fournier or Loulou Massard or Henriette Durand, easy to understand, easy to remember"—but the next sentence brings a different thought: "No, she was not like the others . . . not completely . . . [. . .] It seemed to her at times that two souls inhabited her body without mingling, side by side, each one separate." This sense of doubleness, which could be experienced as an affliction, is turned by Hélène into a source of invention. Looking at the people on the street, she starts to imagine stories about them, endowing each with a name and a history. Not feeling at home either in France or in Russia, she is able to see her difference from others as a reason for pride: "In Russia, they [the Parisians she observes] would not understand the language of the country. They would not know the thoughts of a shopkeeper, a coachman, a farmer . . . But I know. . . .

I'm a little girl, but I've seen more things than they have in their whole long, boring life."[18]

Critics who think of Némirovsky as totally enamored of France and the French establishment, at least until the disillusionment of her last years, have overlooked this other side of her, which embraces and even celebrates foreignness. One can, it's true, see this in entirely negative terms, as a search for identity that ends in an impasse, with dissatisfaction in both East and West.[19] But that does not take account of the empowering possibilities of the in-between position. Hélène Karol, Némirovsky's alter ego, owes her creativity precisely to her doubleness, her bilingual, or even multilingual, if we count German and English, and bicultural status, which places her at once inside and outside any scene she observes. This is the position she occupies in the "scene of writing," making possible her critical view both of the German text and of the actual family tableau she is part of. Another bicultural Hélène, Hélène Cixous, writing a generation after Némirovsky, has called such a figure, with which she identifies, a *juifemme*, a "jewoman." Born in Algeria in 1937 of a German Jewish mother and a French Jewish father, Cixous grew up with two mother tongues and has written eloquently about the obstacles she faced in becoming a writer: "Everything about me conspired to forbid access to writing: History, my story, my origin, my gender. Everything that constituted my social and cultural self; starting with the most essential, the material out of which writing is tailored, which I lacked: language. . . . I learned to speak French in a garden from which I was about to be expelled, because I was a Jew. I belonged to the race of paradise-losers. Write in French? What right did I have to it?"[20] Although Némirovsky's career was by all indications unusually smooth and successful, she had in fact to overcome a triple exclusion from the "paradise" of French letters: as a woman, as a Jew, and as a foreigner.

"French Literature": Némirovsky and Colette

"There is not a book she hasn't read," gushed Némirovsky's admirer Janine Auscher in the interview she published with her a few months before *The Wine of Solitude* appeared.[21] But one finds relatively few literary allusions in Némirovsky's novels, including this one. Hélène, schooled by her French governess, has read classic authors like Jean Racine and Pierre Corneille, about whom she learns the usual clichés: "Racine paints men as they are, Corneille as they ought to be" (1267). More bizarrely, we are told that as an eight-year-old her favorite book was Napoleon's *Mémorial de Sainte-Hélène*, which she knew almost by heart. It's a curious book for a little girl to latch on to, but the *Mémorial* may be there to serve as an allusion to Stendhal's *The Red and the Black*, a bildungsroman of the negative type, ending in failure, whose hero, Julien Sorel, is also a fervent admirer of Napoleon's book and of its author. When we first meet him in Stendhal's novel, the adolescent Julien is reading the *Mémorial* and daydreaming about Napoleon's exploits. Hélène's version of this imaginative play is her construction of a fortress with the books in her library, where she reenacts Napoleon's victory at the battle of Wagram, playing the roles both of Napoleon and of the brave young lieutenant who dies while kissing the French flag!

Hélène's identification with male heroes tallies with the male model of the bildungsroman and generally of literature as a whole in those years. In numerous interviews in which Némirovsky was asked to name her favorite writers, she never cited a woman. This is hardly surprising, given the context—even Beauvoir, who was only five years younger than Némirovsky though she started publishing much later (her first novel appeared in 1943), imagined herself as Maurice Barrès or André Gide, two male literary giants at the time, when she dreamed of becoming a writer as an adolescent. Beauvoir adored George Eliot's Maggie Tulliver, the tragic heroine of *The Mill on the Floss*, but when it came to writers rather than their creations her thoughts focused on men.

Yet there was a woman on the French literary scene whom Némirovsky might well have mentioned among the writers she admired: Colette. Although Colette was thirty years Némirovsky's senior, the two shared space in the literary field. Both were considered to be noteworthy writers, rare among women. They shared a publisher, Albin Michel, and they contributed to some of the same journals, including *Gringoire*. They were both members of the Société des Gens de Lettres and had some friends in common, the playwright Tristan Bernard and the novelist Joseph Kessel among them. There is no indication they ever met in person, but they certainly knew of each other, as Colette was unavoidable and for a while Némirovsky was too. In 1931, when Duvivier's film adaptation of *David Golder* was released, Colette, along with fifteen other well-known writers, was asked to comment on it in *Le Figaro*. Duvivier had already made close to twenty highly successful silent films, and *David Golder* was his first talkie. Although in her comment Colette did not mention the novel on which the film was based and may well not have read it, she could not have been unaware of the young Russian immigrant woman whose début novel had made such a splash. Besides, Colette had been in charge of the literary page in the newspaper where Némirovsky published her first short story under her own name, and she may have remembered her.[22]

As for Némirovsky's awareness of Colette, it was real and it endured throughout her life. She started reading her as a teenager (a note in her journal dated 1919 includes one of the Claudine books in a list of works she wants to read or has read), and she mentioned Colette in her journal as late as 1941, saying she didn't think much of her last book![23] In a way Colette was for her both an older role model and a rival, which may explain, among other reasons, why Némirovsky didn't mention her in public. In *The Wine of Solitude*, however, she refers to Colette by allusion when she describes an expensive but vulgar resort in Normandy where "gigolos sprawled on the grass, cut-rate 'chéris' ['chéris' au rabais] with the hairy chests and damp red wrists of butcher boys" (1316). The published English version translates "chéris" as "darlings," thus eliminating the allusion to Colette. Némirovsky does not capitalize the noun whereas in Colette's novel it's the name of the young hero, but *Chéri*, published in 1920, was one of her best-known works, and readers would be sure to make the association. Némirovsky's allusion to it can be read as both an homage and a depreciation, for these "cut-rate 'chéris'" are a far cry from the seductive young man in Colette's novel, who is also a gigolo but a very refined one.

Colette is present, albeit unacknowledged, in another place in *The Wine of Solitude*, and, not by chance, it is in the scene where Hélène writes her first French text, the scene of writing I discussed earlier. Here again is the description of the word Hélène writes, erases, and finally transforms into a fantastic creature with her pen:

"She erased the last word, then wrote it in again, enthralled as it appeared before her eyes, then erased it again, crossed out each letter, *spiking it with little arrows and curlicues until the word had lost its original appearance and looked like a creature with a mass of antennae, or a plant with many thorns*" (italics added).[24] Now here is a passage from Colette's novel *La Vagabonde*, from 1910, in which the heroine, a writer turned music hall performer, reflects on what writing means to her: "To write! To be able to write! It meant a long reverie in front of the blank page, dreamy doodling, the pen circling around an inkblot, biting the word that doesn't belong, scratching it, *spiking it with little arrows, decorating it with antennae and legs until it lost its readable shape as a word, transformed into a fantastic insect.*"[25] I have italicized the words and phrases in the two passages that are nearly identical. The resemblance cannot be purely coincidental, for both passages contain rare combinations of words such as *hérisser de fléchettes*, spiking with little arrows, that build up to a strange metaphor: the written word becomes unreadable, a fantastic creature with antennae. Némirovsky was not plagiarizing Colette or imitating her in a systematic way. Instead, the passage suggests an unconscious echo, the way we sometimes find ourselves repeating almost word for word, without knowing it, a sentence we have heard or read and that has struck a chord in us. It confirms that Némirovsky knew Colette's work well enough to have assimilated it into her own creative process.

La Vagabonde was particularly suited to this kind of assimilation, as it too is an autobiographical novel and a female bildungsroman about a writer and artist. The heroine, Renée Néré, is no longer in the first bloom of youth, having been married and divorced, earning her living as a music hall performer when we first meet her. Colette herself, married at twenty, had divorced her first husband and spent several years as a music hall performer before she wrote *La Vagabonde*. She had allowed her husband, a journalist who wrote under the pen name Willy, to sign her first books, the enormously successful Claudine series. *La Vagabonde* was her coming out novel as an independent writer, and its theme is that of a woman's independence as well. When a rich, handsome man who becomes her lover asks Renée to marry him, she accepts, but in the end rejects him, preferring her vagabond life as an artist to the sedentary joys of bourgeois marriage. (Today's reader may be disappointed to learn that Colette's next novel, *L'Entrave [The Shackle]*, from 1912, has the same Renée Néré willingly accepting the shackle imposed on her by a man she is madly in love with! By then, Colette had married her next husband, Henry de Jouvenel.)

Némirovsky's Hélène too rejects a rich, handsome man who begs her to marry him. Are we totally surprised to learn that in both novels the rejected lover's name is Max? Yet another unconscious echo may be the title of Némirovsky's novel itself, for shortly before the above-quoted passage in *La Vagabonde* we find the following sentence: "There are days when solitude, for someone my age, is a heady wine that makes you drunk with freedom." Curiously, but understandably, since all this was below the level of consciousness, Némirovsky makes no mention of Colette's novel when she is trying out titles in her writing journal for *The Wine of Solitude*. Instead, she evokes two male poets, Charles Baudelaire and Alfred de Musset, who had both used "wine of" in some of their titles: "The beautiful Baudelairian phrases . . . The Wine of youth (A. de Musset), The Wine of memory, the Wine of Solitude."[26]

Colette, then, figures as an important but repressed predecessor and model in *The Wine of Solitude*. One can think of several interesting reasons for that repression, starting with Némirovsky's fraught relation to mothers and mother figures. If to her Colette was a literary mother of sorts, she would surely elicit some of the ambivalence, the combination of fascination and hatred or, in literary terms, of admiration and depreciation, that mothers always elicit in Némirovsky's works, especially in this one. Furthermore, Colette herself was known as a writer who idealized her mother, devoting several adoring books to her. While some recent critics have intimated that even Colette harbored ambivalent feelings toward her beloved Sido, her professed adoration for her mother would surely have struck Némirovsky as hard to tolerate.

Another reason for repressing Colette could be, as I mentioned earlier, that the literary models for a woman seeking to make a name for herself as a writer were, as if by definition, male. And not only in the years before the Second World War, but later as well. Beauvoir's acclaimed novel of 1954, *The Mandarins*, which won the Prix Goncourt that year, features two protagonists, a man who is a writer and a woman who is a psychoanalyst. In her memoirs Beauvoir explains why she made her writer figure male: "Depicting a writer, I wanted the reader to see in him a fellow human and not an odd beast [une bête curieuse]; but much more than a man, a woman whose vocation and profession are writing is an exception."[27] Némirovsky was already a sufficiently "odd beast" in France, being Jewish and Russian, with a foreign-sounding name, so we can understand why she chose to project herself into male rather than female literary role models. Unlike Beauvoir, however, she imagined her fictional writer-protagonist as a young woman, even if Hélène identifies herself at the end in the masculine terms of force, courage, autonomy. These "virile" traits in Némirovsky's heroine (and in Némirovsky herself, for, as we've seen, she was usually represented as a masculine writer) tend to confirm Virginia Woolf's observation that androgyny is a characteristic of creative minds—and, even more broadly, Freud's theory that bisexuality is a trait common to all humans. A male identification does not necessarily imply bisexuality in behavior, however: Némirovsky's sexual preference, like her heroine's, appears to have been exclusively heterosexual, while Woolf, Beauvoir, and Colette were all bisexual. Colette, when asked late in life about her happy marriage with Maurice Goudeket, who was decades younger than she, replied that what he loved about her was her virility.[28]

Finally, and perhaps most important, Némirovsky may have repressed Colette (but the repressed always manages to return, one way or another) because Colette was so unambiguously *French*. Just as she was known for her adoration of her mother, Colette was known for her celebration of her native province, Burgundy, where her mother lived, a place whose landscape and gardens and ways of speaking she dwelled on in many of her works. And when she wasn't writing about Burgundy or Provence, another of her preferred sites, she was lovingly depicting Paris and the ways of life of its inhabitants, from modest music hall performers and *demi-mondaines* to the artistic and social elite. One cannot imagine Colette ever saying to herself, as Némirovsky did in her journal, that she was writing a novel "about the French," since all of her works are unproblematically, that is, without any thought of alternate possibilities, set in France and feature French characters. Nary a foreigner nor a foreign word is to be found in their pages.

Némirovsky sought to be accepted by the same literary world as Colette, but on her own terms. Her preferred position, by now familiar to us, was the in-between, the position of emotional ambivalence and of an existential sense of otherness in relation to French or any other national or ethnic identity. This is one reason why her most interesting works feature Jews: Jews were the others par excellence in the world she lived in, as in the one she depicted. And surely it is also one reason Némirovsky, unlike some foreign-born writers in France, chose to keep her Russian-sounding name. The well-known novelist Romain Gary, who was born in Riga, Latvia, during the czarist regime and whose birth name was Roman Kacew, recounts with wonderful humor in his autobiography that as early as the age of thirteen, when he decided to become a writer in order to fulfill his mother's ambition for him, he started searching for an appropriate pseudonym, because, his mother told him, "a great French writer cannot have a Russian name."[29] Elsa Triolet and Nathalie Sarraute, both of them born in Russia and married to French husbands, used their married names to sign their books. Triolet did so even though she started publishing after she had divorced her first husband, André Triolet. But Némirovsky kept her name. She wrote under a French-sounding pseudonym only at two moments in her career. In the 1920s, as a totally unknown writer, she published two novellas, *L'Ennemie* (1928) and *Le Bal* (1929), that focused on a young girl's rage against her mother—evidently, she didn't want her own mother to see her name on them; in 1930, after the success of *David Golder*, she allowed Bernard Grasset to reissue *Le Bal* under her own name. The second moment, as we have seen, was just before her death, when she was forced into using a pseudonym by the Vichy laws that forbade Jews to publish in newspapers.

The Woman Artist as Foreigner and Keeper of Memory

While the heroine of *The Wine of Solitude* is on the threshold of becoming a writer, the heroine of *The Dogs and the Wolves*, published five years later, is shown evolving into a full-fledged artist. Ada Sinner is a painter, not a writer, but, like Hélène, she defines herself as an *étrangère* in France, both foreigner and stranger. Born in an unnamed city in Ukraine (again, the model is Kiev) in the early years

of the century, Ada arrives in Paris as a young girl before the First
World War. She continues to speak Russian with her immediate
family, including the cousin she marries, Ben, the go-getting wolf
of the title. As a result, she and Ben are perceived by their French
neighbors "with a profound distrust" (une profonde méfiance), notes
the narrator. This status as a kind of pariah is one that Ada accepts,
even chooses, as she considers the "French way of life" with irony.
On the same page where we are told that the neighbors are wary of
her, we get her view of them: "As for comfort, the home-cooked
dishes lovingly prepared, the hat you put together with a yard of
ribbon bought on sale, the evenings by lamplight, with a husband in
slippers who reads the newspaper while a child sleeps on his lap, that
lovely and harmonious French way of life, so enviable, it was . . . it
had to be, pleasant; but it was as difficult, and as foreign to Ben and
Ada, as the sedentary existence of rich plains dwellers is to nomads."[30]
In this tone of detached amusement (note the move from "it was" to
"it had to be," from the declarative to the doubtful), we recognize
the voice of the outsider who may yearn to belong to the majority
but only in part. Némirovsky's use of the word "foreign" here re-
verses the usual hierarchy, signaling that from Ada's perspective it is
France and the French that appear foreign. Later, she will refer to a
French woman as a foreigner. Like Hélène Karol, Ada loves France
but also derives satisfaction from not fully belonging to it. In fact,
her art is nourished by her sense of distance and difference. Némirovsky emphasizes this in a scene in which a group of French people
who admire her paintings makes an unexpected visit to Ada's studio.
They gush over her works, but the narrator compares their cries of
admiration to those of visitors "in a zoo, in front of a rare wild beast
[une bête sauvage et rare] in its cage" (621).

Ada resembles Hélène in yet another way: she too is a precocious child deprived of a mother's love. Her mother dies young and
is replaced as caretaker when Ada is five years old by a widowed
aunt, who cares more for her own children than for her niece. Ada's
first years are spent in her native city with her maternal grandfather
and her father, gentle souls who harbor great ambitions. The grandfather, a small-time jeweler, traveled and acquired some education
in his youth and now spends all his spare time writing his magnum
opus, "The Character and Rehabilitation of Shylock." Ada's father,

who ekes out a living by trading in "a little of this and a little of that," like the poor immigrant Rabinowitz in "Fraternité," dreams of a bright future for his daughter: perhaps she will become a great musician or actress? But Ada is not a performer. She is an observer, and she starts young: "She had just turned five, and she began to see what was around her" (517). When she turns ten, she receives her first box of paints and discovers her passion for reproducing what she sees, the snow-covered street beneath her windows, the gray and white sky of springtime, the faces of people she knows. As her father's fortunes improve, he agrees to send her, with her aunt and two cousins, to Paris to study—this is in May 1914, the narrator emphasizes. Soon the war and the Revolution will sweep away the Russia of Ada's childhood as well as the money for her studies. After her father's death, the family in France is forced to scramble for a living. A few years later, while still a teenager, Ada marries Ben. She does not love him, even expresses contempt for him, since in her view he cares only about making money, but by marrying him she gains the freedom to continue painting.

It will come as no surprise, to a reader of Némirovsky, that Ada's paintings do not feature "gracious young girls in beautiful gardens," as Ada puts it. Rather, her inspiration comes from people like her neighbor on the rue des Rosiers, the street of poor ethnic Jews that David Golder and his friend Soifer visit on occasion to reconnect with their impoverished childhoods. Examining her portrait-in-progress of the neighbor, Ada is satisfied with the way she has rendered her "full, voluptuous face, the hooked nose, the fake pearls and the satin dress, worn out at the elbows" as well as the woman's "lips painted a geranium red, with that humid glance sliding out from beneath her heavy lids." This portrait, which the artist herself finds both attractive and repelling at the same time, may remind us of Némirovsky's own fictional portraits of Jewish figures: the Jewish woman is observed without tenderness but with enormous precision and attention to detail. If one is so inclined, one can read the portrait as antisemitic: the hooked nose, the fake jewelry and tawdry dress, the voluptuous face and humid glance, hinting at the lubricity of Jewish women according to antisemitic myths. But it is more accurate, I believe, to see the portrait, as well as the artist's own feelings of attraction and repulsion when she examines it, as a self-reflexive commentary that refers both to Ada's work and to Némirovsky's. Ada asks herself why she doesn't paint instead "gracious young girls in beautiful gardens, light-colored hats, fountains, flowers in June" and immediately realizes she is incapable of that kind of work: "It wasn't her fault. She was driven to seek out, cruelly, tirelessly, the secrets hidden beneath sad faces and dark skies" (612).

This is as good a definition as any of Némirovsky's own vocation as a writer, and she seems to have been quite aware of it. In the spring and summer of 1938, as she was working on the novel she first titled "Le Charlatan" (now known as *Le maître des âmes*), she made numerous notations in her journal about the kind of writer she thought herself to be. In one of these she tries to define the character of her protagonist, Dario Asfar. He is a man "who sees people as they are and scorns them, hates them, desires with all his heart to be better than they, . . . and who in the end becomes just like the others and worse than the others." Then she adds, letting loose some expletives and even committing a spelling error in her indignation: "What will the assholes say? 'Madame Némirovsky stays true to the genre of the painful novel,' or other bulshit [coneries, misspelled]. . . . I should be hardened to it by now, but still . . . It's strange that in 1938 there should still be a desire to see life through rose-colored glasses."[31] She herself had no such desire and apparently had never had one. Whereas Tolstoy could claim that happy families are all alike, Némirovsky's novels show the resemblances among unhappy families, lacking in mutual love, displaced from home, if they ever had one, battered by historical upheavals, and, if they are east European Jews, like the families in *David Golder*, *The Wine of Solitude*, and *The Dogs and the Wolves*, battered as well by persecution and prejudice or merely by the daily anxieties of fitting in.

Némirovsky's Ada is cut from the same artistic cloth as her creator, and Ada's work has another aspect that is also present in Némirovsky's work. She depicts scenes remembered from her childhood in Russia, devoid of sentimentality but capable of arousing strong emotion in a viewer, at least if the viewer is a Jew or, better still, a displaced Russian Jew. Such a one is Harry, Ada's distant cousin, who plays the role of dog in the wolf–dog dichotomy that structures the novel. Although he resembles the wolfish Ben physically, shares the same last name as he, and hails from the same city in Russia,

Harry is socially and temperamentally Ben's opposite. The pampered only son of a wealthy Jewish banking family, Harry has grown up in a world of privilege, observed from afar by Ada, who became fixated on him even as a child. He is cultivated and a lover of fine books and art, and he apparently feels at home in the world of the Parisian bourgeoisie. Yet, after he marries a Catholic banker's daughter he is in love with, who had to overcome her father's prejudices against "foreigners from the East" in order to marry him, Harry falls in love with Ada through her art. One day while walking by the window of a bookshop he frequents, his attention is caught by two small paintings Ada has persuaded the bookseller to display, precisely in the hope that Harry would see them. The paintings, of a snowy street at dusk and a "half-wild garden in spring," represent Russian landscapes from her childhood. When Harry sees the works he is literally transported back to a "distant reality, long abolished," the snowstorms of his childhood, in March, when the first hyacinths were blooming inside. He remembers his birthday celebrations when, as a young boy, he would stare out melancholically at the falling snow while the chocolate cake, with its almost sickeningly rich odor, was brought in. Seeing the gray sky in Ada's painting, he suddenly rediscovers a whole world of objects and people he thought he had forgotten. One of these is his grandmother, who "spoke to him in a foreign language. She alone still spoke Yiddish, and everyone was scandalized by it" (615–16). Here, as in *The Wine of Solitude*, Yiddish serves as an indicator of social status, marking the relatively recent rise of the wealthy branch of the family, only a generation or two removed from their humble origins. And it marks as well their anxiety about it: that's why they are "scandalized" by the grandmother's speaking it.

Harry buys the paintings, thus setting in motion the somewhat implausible love story between him and Ada. This allows for dramatic scenes of jealousy and passion on both sides and several plot twists. But above all it allows for an extended questioning of Jewish identity and its relation to art, on the part of both the artist and the viewer. Ada's work and eventually Ada herself captivate Harry because he sees in them a key to who he is, to his "true self" rather than the social self he has constructed by marrying into the French bourgeois milieu. In a crucial scene he and his wife, Laurence, visit Ada's apartment studio along with other French friends, the episode in which the narrator remarks that Ada, compared to them, seems like a "rare beast in a zoo." In a brief exchange while they are alone Ada reminds Harry of the few times they had seen each other when they were children in Russia and asks him whether he remembers the climate and the air back there, the evenings by the river, the linden trees on the street where he lived. This precipitates a whole cluster of shared memories between them: of the "chouroum-bouroum" carpet merchant hawking his wares, of child acrobats who performed beneath people's windows, of the crazy old man who had been a singer at the Opera and now walked the streets in the snow, mouthing his songs silently. It was all so long ago, Harry remarks. Yes, she responds, but "what happened there may be more important than you think, more important than everything else, than your life here, your marriage. We were born there, our roots are there . . ." When Harry asks whether she means in Russia, she replies, "No. Further back . . . deeper . . ." [Non. Plus loin. . . . plus profond . . .] (621–23).

Ada is hinting here at their Jewish heritage, which binds them together beyond family and beyond nation. This idea is confirmed in the scene that immediately follows, when Harry is alone with his wife and they discuss their visit to the studio. Laurence is dismissive. Does he like those strange paintings? she asks, for instance, the one they saw on her easel, of men with curls on their face, trudging in the snow behind a sled bearing a coffin? Harry murmurs the work's title: *Burial of a Jew*. It's depressing and sordid, says Laurence—and besides, there is nothing original about Ada's use of color. But one mustn't look at her paintings with the eye of an art connoisseur, Harry responds: what matters is the effect they produce on him. "Her technique is weak, but her way of painting moves me so that I forget the painting and find myself instead. And that, probably, is the aim of her art. By all kinds of strange detours, I find myself" [Par des chemins détournés, étranges, je me retrouve] (625–27).

He then launches into a detailed commentary on the painting, which in his opinion captures an "imperishable essence." Of what, exactly? Of a way of life he sees suggested in every detail: the gray sky, the snow and the mud, the crude coffin thrown onto the sled, and the faces of the mourners, which show "no hope in an eternal

life" but are full of "avid attention" and passion. The wide-eyed child
in the corner, he says, resembles all the other Jewish children he saw
back there—in fact, he himself was such a Jewish child, just cleaner
and better dressed. As we might expect, Laurence pooh-poohs this
idea. She has seen photos of him as a child, she says, and he looked
nothing like the "personages of Madame Ada Sinner." When Harry
asks her to invite Ada to their home with other friends, Laurence
refuses. She invites only friends to her home, and Ada is too much
of an "odd beast" to be considered a friend. "I don't like her. I dislike
everything about her," Laurence continues. "You yourself have said
it many times: that specifically Jewish combination of insolence and
servility [ce mélange d'insolence et de servilité spécifiquement juif]
is . . ." (629–30). Then, seeing his face, she shifts abruptly. "I'm only
joking," she assures him. But the harm has been done. Harry, pale
with "fury and hurt pride," pushes the conversation to an out-and-
out fight and to a break in his marriage.

   This is all the more remarkable, given that earlier, when he had
first bought Ada's paintings, he had refused the bookseller's offer to
introduce him to the artist, who he said very much wanted Harry
to see her works. Harry's refusal on that occasion showed his own
suspicion of the "pushiness" of Jews. This young woman, doubtless
alone in Paris, was probably trying to take advantage of her distant
relation to the "rich Sinners." The narrator had commented that
"like all Jews, he was more sharply, more painfully shocked than a
Christian by specifically Jewish flaws. And that stubborn energy, that
quasi savage need to obtain what one desired, . . . all were summed
up in his mind by a single label: 'Jewish insolence'" (618). Harry
evidently worries that the "insolence" of some poor Jews may make
Jews like him look bad. But when his non-Jewish wife speaks of
"Jewish insolence," he becomes enraged, and we understand why:
it's for the same reason that Jews may enjoy telling deprecating jokes
about "Cohen and Schwartz" but feel uncomfortable when non-Jews
take that liberty.

   Ada's paintings, depicting a Jewish life that Harry himself never
experienced and that has become even for her no more than a distant memory, reveal to him an identity he finds both comforting and
inescapable. He becomes Ada's lover, bound to her not so much by
erotic passion as by "the obscure call of blood," as his wife puts it to

herself—against this call, she feels totally powerless. Harry's mother, as we might expect, is horrified at their liaison, seeing in Ada only the poor Jew, not the artist: "A simple girl from the slums! It's the worst thing that could have happened!," she wails to her daughter-in-law. Is Harry's infatuation with Ada a form of racial determinism? They are of the "same blood" not only as Jews but also as members of the same family. But his response to her paintings suggests that what unites them, rather, is a shared cultural heritage and a common history. As in Némirovsky's other works, not to mention debates still ongoing today about what it means to be a Jew, we see here a vacillation between two views of Jewishness: as biology, "race," or as ethnicity and culture. Clearly missing, however, is the third possibility, Jewishness as religious practice. The Jewish artist, although she feels neither group solidarity nor religious affiliation with Jews, nevertheless finds her inspiration in their world, both past, her childhood in Russia, and present, her neighbor on the rue des Rosiers. Her depictions are sufficiently true and sufficiently sympathetic to their subjects to reconnect her viewer emotionally to the Jewish past—if not exactly to his own past, then at least to a cultural memory (or is it a fantasy?) of Jewishness.

And there's the rub. In 1938–1939, when Némirovsky was working on this novel, was it possible seriously to envisage, if one was a realist writer (and Némirovsky was nothing if not a realist), a love story between two isolated Jews, with a happy ending based on their common, largely imagined cultural memories? Ada's and Harry's union is a mirage, a bubble, and Némirovsky bursts it with one of those sudden catastrophes she is so good at. One thinks of the way she dispatches the young, well-meaning priest Philippe Péricand in *Suite Française*, who is literally torn to pieces and drowned by the young delinquents he is shepherding; or of the way she kills off the despicable porcelain collector Charlie Langelet in that same novel, who is run over by a speeding automobile on his way to dinner. In *The Dogs and the Wolves* catastrophe arrives in the form of financial scandal, brought upon Harry's family's bank by the speculator Ben, who flees to South America. Ada, in a desperate move to save Harry, solicits the help of his wife, whose influential banker father can shield Harry from the scandal. In exchange Ada renounces Harry forever, letting him think that she has left the country with Ben.

In her first draft of the novel Némirovsky included a fairly long section on what happens after the scandal becomes public, including scenes in which Harry and Ada discuss what they should do.[32] When she proposes that they leave France together, he refuses: he is not a nomad, he tells her (Ada, we recall, was characterized as a nomad some chapters back). Némirovsky omitted these pages from the final version, in which Harry and Ada never see each other again after the scandal breaks. In fact, Harry never appears again, so we do not know how he responds to the news of Ben's misdeeds, to Ada's absence and his wife's help, or to anything else. In a sense Némirovsky loses interest in him, returning him to his former position as a haughty, assimilated Jew who looks down on "Jewish insolence." Instead, she follows the nomadic artist. Ada, technically still married to Ben, is expelled from France as an "undesirable alien" even though she is now living alone. She obtains a visa to an unnamed "small city in Eastern Europe," where she finds a place in a community of refugees who are not explicitly designated as Jews, but the context implies they are refugees from Nazi Germany. There she gives birth to a son. Her first thought, after he is born, carries an echo of Hélène's determination at the end of *The Wine of Solitude*: "She counted on her fingers, like a child surveying her possessions: 'Painting, the baby, courage: with that one can live. One can live very well'" [La peinture, le petit, le courage: avec cela on peut vivre. On peut très bien vivre] (699).

A few years earlier, in a note in her writing journal for the short story "Fraternité," Némirovsky had copied down a sentence she put in quotation marks, without indicating the source: "La forme de désespoir particulière au Judaisme comporte, en soi, une espérance formelle" (The form of despair that is particular to Judaism includes, inherently, a formal hope).[33] The implausibly upbeat ending she imagines for her artist heroine, stranded with a baby in a foreign city in eastern Europe on the eve of the Second World War, seems to bear out that claim.

Dogs, Wolves, and Jewish Fate

While I have emphasized the central role that Ada's activity as an artist plays in this novel, it would be wrong not to consider the larger setting, both the setting within the novel and the place of this work in Némirovsky's fiction. *The Dogs and the Wolves* was the last of her works to feature Jewish characters, and its writing coincided almost exactly with the process of her conversion to Catholicism. This work is in a sense her summing up of and farewell to Jewishness as she understood it, with all its shortcomings and impossibilities as well as its virtues. Intelligence, courage, resourcefulness, qualities bred by a long history of persecution, defined in her mind what it meant to be Jewish, along with anxiety, snobbishness, and an ambition to succeed that was so powerful it could on occasion turn into crime. This view was based on her perception of those she knew best, middle-class Ashkenazi Jews from Russia who were only a generation or two removed from the shtetl or its poor urban equivalent, the ghetto. In her interview of 1930 in *L'Univers Israélite*, when the journalist Nina Gourfinkel asked her why none of the Jewish characters in *David Golder* could produce a single "tender memory" of family or community, she answered, "They are Russian Jews," as if no further explanation was needed.[34]

In *The Dogs and the Wolves* she tries to provide an explanation, adopting a quasi-sociological analytic tone in some instances. Whereas in *The Wine of Solitude* the specifically Jewish story lies beneath the surface and must be read between the lines, here it is laid out explicitly. The novel begins with a description of the social and geographical strata among Jews in the "Ukrainian city that was home to the Sinner family." The very poorest Jews, the "riffraff" (la racaille) live in the teeming lower city near the river, while the members of the privileged elite reside in their villas in the hills, where Jews are not even allowed to live according to the law but where bribes pave their way. The rest live in the middle, among Russians and Poles, in an area that is itself divided into sectors: doctors and lawyers above tailors, shopkeepers, pharmacists. Traversing all three regions are the "intermediaries," who earn their living by making deals, finding buyers and sellers for whatever comes to hand. Ada's father is one of those middlemen, but there is also an elite branch of the family in the hills, doting on their only son and heir, Harry. One day, when she is seven years old, Ada goes with her older cousin, Ben's sister, for a walk in the upper city and catches a glimpse of a boy coming out of a sumptuous-looking house with his mother. He bears a striking physical resemblance to her other cousin, her playmate Ben, but everything else about him is different: dressed in a cream-colored suit with a fine lace collar, this boy is a vision of beauty such as she has never seen. From the start Harry is associated in Ada's mind with refinement and aesthetic pleasure as well as with a certain passivity. Later on, when they are lovers, she is the more active figure. She thinks of him as her "creation," and in her dreams he has "curls like a woman." This could also be an association to the sidelocks, or "curls," on the faces of religious Jews in Ada's paintings; the figure of the Jewish male is often feminized in popular antisemitic mythology.[35]

The narrator lingers over the class divisions among Jews in the city, emphasizing that they were not hereditary and fixed because the hope and ambition of all the poor Jews was to rise:

> So and so was born in the Ghetto. By the time he was twenty, he had saved a bit of money; he climbed a rung on the social ladder: he moved away and went to live far from the river [. . .]; by the time he married, he was already living on the even-numbered (forbidden) side of the street; later, he would rise even more: he would settle in the neighborhood where, according to the law, no Jew had the right to be born, to live, to die. People respected him; his own people thought of him as an object of envy and an image of hope: it was possible to climb to such heights.[36]

A few lines before this the narrator underlined the arrogance of Jews in the upper city, who take pleasure in "letting other Jews know that they [are] worth more than they."

Another Russian Jewish author with a love of France and conflicted feelings about Jewishness, Isaac Babel, just nine years Némirovsky's senior, wrote some wonderful stories about the distance between rich and poor Russian Jews around the time of the First World War. One of these is a comic tale titled "Guy de Maupassant," featuring an impoverished writer and a buxom lady, Raïsa, originally from Kiev, who lives in opulence on Nevsky Prospect in St. Petersburg and whose "only passion in life," she proclaims, is the nineteenth-century French author. The culture-loving Raïsa's husband, a "yellow-faced Jew" who made millions in war profiteering, interests her far less than the poor writer, whose knowledge of French and whose way with words she finds irresistible. Sholem Aleichem too emphasizes class differences among Jews in many of his stories, which are not only the stuff of comedy. One of Tevye's daughters drowns herself after the snobbish mother of her wealthy suitor, whom she loves dearly, forbids them to marry and spirits her son out of the reach of the dairyman's family. Not surprisingly, this daughter was left out of *Fiddler on the Roof*, the American musical version of *Tevye the Dairyman*, which had no place for such bitterness.[37]

The analysis of class differences spills over into questions of religious practice. The poor Jews of the ghetto, according to the narrator of *The Dogs and the Wolves*, are strictly observant by habit, unable to even imagine an alternative. Rich Jews are observant too but for a different reason: they consider strict adherence to tradition as a matter of "dignity, of moral distinction, as much as—perhaps even more than—genuine conviction." This recalls the narrator's remark in *The Wine of Solitude* that rich Jews "followed the rites of their religion with proud humility," which was not totally accurate historically. Yet evidently Némirovsky was convinced of it, having in mind perhaps families like the Rothschilds, who maintained formal ties to Judaism even if they no longer practiced it. As for the Jews in the middle, they are more lax in their observance, the narrator explains. Ada's father goes to synagogue occasionally, "the way one would visit a capitalist who could, if he wanted to, help you in your business, . . . but who is really too rich, too grand, too powerful to think about you, poor earthly creature." For this lesser branch of the Sinner family, the narrator concludes, "Judaism no longer brought any joys, but did still bring a lot of troubles" [le judaisme ne donnait plus de joies, mais procurait encore beaucoup d'ennuis] (541, 542).

Pogroms, for instance. Némirovsky devotes more than twenty pages to describing a pogrom that takes place in the city when Ada is eight years old. Historically, major pogroms occurred in or near Kiev in 1903 and 1905. In 1913, when Némirovsky herself was eight, Kiev was the site of the famous blood libel trial of Mendel Beilis, which caused some rioting in the city. In the novel she describes Cossacks riding through the poor neighborhoods, breaking and destroying—among other things, they burn Ada's grandfather's opus on Shylock, a loss he never recovers from. Ada and Ben find themselves in the street, separated from the servant who was taking them to stay with a Christian neighbor. The two children flee instinctively to the heights, beyond the reach of the Cossacks, and there Ada recognizes the grand house of the other Sinners. She and Ben are taken in, and she sees Harry again, but his mother and aunts try to relegate the two waifs to the kitchen until Harry's grandfather, the family patriarch, intervenes and treats them more kindly. This experience provides Ada with a major insight. Observing the arrogance of the women, she thinks to herself, "They are mean." But she immediately qualifies this simple thought:

> But, as sometimes happened to her, she found herself harboring two different thoughts at the same time: one naïve and childish, the other more mature, more understanding and insightful; she felt two Adas inside her, and one of them understood why they were casting her aside, why they spoke to her with anger: these famished children suddenly appeared before the rich Jews like an eternal reminder, a horrible and shameful memory of what they had been or what they could have been. Nobody dared to think: "what they could become again someday."[38]

This kind of understanding, which John Keats called "negative capability," allows one, in particular an artist, to take a step back from one's own concerns and identify with another person's feelings. The analysis given here is way beyond the capacity of an eight-year-old child, but it tallies perfectly with Némirovsky's own writerly interest in Jewish class differences and her engagement with the anxieties of assimilation. She was acutely aware of the discomfort that contact with poor, unassimilated Jews provoked among some upper-class Jews, whose fear of falling back into the ghetto was real. Of course, there were rich Jews who felt a moral responsibility to help their less fortunate brethren, but Némirovsky would probably have said they still felt uncomfortable around them, even if they were kinder than the women she imagines in this scene.

Her preoccupation with the social dichotomy is reflected in the metaphor that structures the novel: dogs versus wolves. Ben, ever hungry and restless, full of schemes to succeed in business, is the wolf to Harry's dog, the cultivated man of privilege. One is vulgar, unassimilated—when he is angry Ben curses in Russian and Yiddish—and fits the stereotype of the "pushy Jew." The other is sleek and refined and exclusively French-speaking, the quintessential assimilated Jew, even though he is perceived by his Gentile father-in-law as a "foreigner from the East." But this apparently stark dichotomy is complicated by the fact that Ben and Harry resemble each other physically and by the plot twist involving Ben's financial misdeeds. While Harry himself is unaware of Ben's shady dealings, Harry's uncles, who run the family bank, give Ben a free hand because they too have some of the wolf in them. Ada's character complicates the opposition even further: she loves Harry and despises Ben, but she shares Ben's energy and wildness. Harry himself, once he is in love with her, compares her admiringly to a "wild animal, not yet domesticated" because of her indifference to "feminine" niceties (660). And if she has some of the wolf in her, Ben has something of the artist in him. He "constructed gigantic schemes, imagined financial combinations the way an artist creates a world, out of nothing," notes the narrator (639). The Yiddish word for this kind of shrewd operator, *macher*—a figure who, as we know, fascinated Némirovsky—literally means "maker," which resonates quite nicely with "artist."

Possibly Némirovsky was evoking here the literary tradition's figure of the wolf, which is ambiguous. In fairy tales and fables this animal appears most often as a dangerous predator, but it can also embody a wild nobility, often in opposition to the domesticated dog. Jean de La Fontaine's fable "The Wolf and the Dog" presents the classic example of this opposition: the wolf in the fable appears as the starving but independent loner, while the dog is well fed but servile. Jack London's *The Call of the Wild* offers a variation on the same motif, transforming a domesticated dog into a quasi-wolf. The most romantic version of the noble wolf is probably Alfred de Vigny's narrative poem of 1843 "La Mort du Loup" (The death of the wolf), once known to all French schoolchildren. The wolf, killed by hunters, dies in stoical silence, but not before killing one of the hunters' dogs, and becomes an allegory of the suffering poet. Némirovsky too saw a kind of allegory in the wolf figure, not just of the striving Jewish macher/artist but of a certain human type. In the spring and summer of 1938, as she was starting on the novel she was calling *Le Charlatan* and thinking ahead to *The Dogs and the Wolves*, she speculated that her talent lay in the direction of Balzac, the great creator of types in social settings. "Faire mon petit Honoré" (doing my little Honoré [de Balzac]), as she put it in her journal, meant creating contemporary figures in contemporary situations but exaggerating their features to bring out the type. The protagonist of *Le Charlatan*, who desires to be better than other people but becomes worse, would have to be larger than life, she concluded, a quasi-tragic figure. At this point she imagined the character as a Frenchman, not a foreigner, but even in this early incarnation he appeared to her as a wolf. Immediately after her thought that he must be larger than life, she wrote, "Painting wolves, that's my business! I couldn't care less about animals in groups, nor about domestic animals. Wolves are my business, what I'm good at."[39] If we think back to the protagonist of *David Golder*, we see he was but the first of a series of such wolf characters, with all their ambiguous danger and charm.

But the dog–wolf metaphor in *The Dogs and the Wolves* raises more questions than it answers. Dogs and wolves are cousins in the animal realm, their difference being historical rather than biological. Is Némirovsky suggesting that beneath their varying exteriors Jews are a single, inalterable race? If so, then does history matter? Naomi Price, the British critic who found this novel horribly antisemitic, wrote, "The view of the novel is that Jews are all the same, whether poor and unpleasant or rich and unpleasant is simply an accident of birth. . . . Had a Nazi publishing house commissioned a novel stipulating the perpetuation of racial stereotypes, they would not have been disappointed with this as a result."[40] But if we accord history its due, then we might say Némirovsky was struggling to portray, as sympathetically as she could, the dilemmas of assimilation that European Jews faced in the first decades of the twentieth century and to anticipate as well the dead-ends that awaited them. When Ben, in a dramatic confrontation with Harry, whom he hates as a rival, hurls at him the taunt, "You who look at us from on high, who scorn us, who want nothing to do with the Jewish riffraff, just wait a bit! Wait! You'll be mixed up with them once more! And you'll be part of them, you who thought you had left them behind!,"[41] one cannot help thinking of cattle cars rolling to the East, with no dis-

tinctions among their occupants. Némirovsky could not foresee the
cattle cars—no one could. But during the time she was working on
this novel, roughly from the fall of 1938 to fall 1939 (it started appearing serially in *Candide* in October, after war had been declared),
one did not have to be clairvoyant to feel foreboding about the fate
of Jews in Europe. Hitler had annexed Austria in March 1938, creating a new wave of Jewish refugees, and a year later his troops occupied all of Czechoslovakia, breaking the agreement he had made
at Munich the previous September. In France, xenophobia and antisemitism ran rampant.

The last two chapters of *The Dogs and the Wolves*, after Ada receives her notice of expulsion from France, carry traces of this history. In fact, the chronology of the novel is perturbed by it, for
suddenly we are in the atmosphere of the late 1930s, whereas the
chapters devoted to Ada's years in Paris, the bulk of the novel, take
place in the decade after the Russian Revolution. The sudden leap
forward by a decade can be considered a flaw in terms of narrative
construction since it goes unacknowledged, but it corresponds to
Némirovsky's preoccupations at the time of writing. The Russian
refugee women Ada sees at her aunt's house worry about visas, asking themselves which countries still have places on their emigration
lists. Later, in her place of exile, Ada lives in a hotel full of "refugees
from Eastern Europe," including her neighbor, a Jewish woman
whose husband is in a concentration camp. This clearly points to
a time after 1933, when the Hitler regime set up the first camps for
political prisoners and other "undesirables" in Germany. Ada's neighbor, Rose Liebig, whose Germanic name evokes love, *Liebe*, helps
deliver Ada's baby and facilitates contact between her and the other
refugees. In a sense Ada in exile finds a community, but it is a community of outcasts.

That is as far as Némirovsky got in depicting the life of European Jews on the eve of the Second World War. Before she had finished the novel the war broke out, and soon afterward, in her story
"The Spectator," she imagined yet another outsider, Hugo Grayer,
who is comforted by a fellow sufferer as he awaits his death on the
high seas. I would like to think that in the wagon transporting her to
Auschwitz in July 1942 she as well found good neighbors, and that
she was one, too.

PART III

Denise and Elisabeth

CHAPTER SIX

Orphans of the Holocaust
Two Lives

When you have nothing to hang on to, neither a religion nor traditions nor an identity, it's not clear how to find a way out.

—DENISE EPSTEIN

To go on living after such a drama, one creates a kind of wall.

—ELISABETH GILLE

Two great dangers threaten the children of the Shoah. The first is to speak about it; the second is not to speak about it.

—BORIS CYRULNIK

PIECING TOGETHER THE LIVES of Némirovsky's daughters during the months and years that followed her arrest in July 1942 is a painstaking process. The scattered letters and bureaucratic documents that remain from that time provide only the barest outline, but they are precious for the historical exactitude they promise: on such and such a date something occurred or something was written down, and there is a historical record to prove it. The painstaking part is to discover how these records, necessarily incomplete, fit together to form a story. We can turn to the work of historians to find context, and to the memory of survivors to suggest how it felt, or, more exactly, how it was remembered years later. Decades after the events, hundreds of memoirs and testimonies by people who had survived the war as children became available through publications and video archives. Denise and Elisabeth too published books that evoked the traumas of their childhood and adolescence, and they were interviewed at various times on radio and television in relation to their mother. This was true especially for Denise after the enormous success of *Suite Française.* Elisabeth had died by then, but Denise became something of a celebrity herself. Like many other testimonial works by child survivors of the war, theirs are valuable not only for the stories they tell—or refuse to tell—but for the emotions they convey.

From One Arrest to Another

"We spent the three months of vacation trying not to see the ravaged face of our father," recalled Denise in the book of conversations she published in 2008. As she remembered it, Michel was unable to help her and her sister. In fact, he could barely stand the sight of them, for they sometimes laughed and played, as children do, while he himself was sunk in despair. She describes him spending his days trying to find out where his wife was and his nights drinking himself into oblivion. In *Le Mirador,* published almost twenty years before Denise's memoir, Elisabeth had already imagined an episode set in June 1942, when her mother realizes that Michel is an alcoholic and that he has been one ever since she has known him. But his drinking used to make him charming and playful, bubbly like the champagne he loved, whereas now he is a drunk on cheap red wine. It's a devastating moment in the book, since Elisabeth's vision is what we have here, not her mother's. Yet, according to a good friend of hers whom I interviewed, Arlette Stroumza, Elisabeth adored her father as a child.[1]

Reading Michel Epstein's letters from that summer, most of them addressed to Irène's editor André Sabatier, one has the impression that he is a desperate man. He fired off suggestions to Sabatier almost daily, asking him to contact people who might get new information on Irène's whereabouts and intervene on her behalf. He even sent him a letter addressed to the German ambassador in Paris, Otto Abetz, and asked him to forward it "URGENTLY" to someone who could make sure that Abetz received it. The pleading tone of the letter to Abetz, dated July 27, 1942 (by which time Irène was in Auschwitz), is evident in its opening sentences: "I know that writing to you directly is highly audacious on my part. Nevertheless, I am doing so because I believe that you alone can save my wife, you are my last hope." Michel went on to assure Abetz that his wife was a well-known novelist, that neither she nor anyone else in the family had ever been involved in politics, that although their grandparents were Jewish they themselves were Catholic, and that his wife had never shown any "tenderness" toward Jews in her novels. Nor did she have any sympathy for the Bolshevik régime, he told the ambassador.[2]

Sabatier was evidently not sure what to do with the letter, but he appears to have talked about it on the telephone with Paul Morand's wife, Hélène Morand, and he sent it to her with a note of his own on July 29. She was, in his opinion, in the best position to decide whether the letter should be sent to its addressee (he avoided spelling out Abetz's name). As for himself, Sabatier added, he thought that "certain sentences are not very felicitous."[3] He consulted Hélène Morand several times during those weeks and reported to Michel on August 12 that she had been "tireless" in her efforts on behalf of Irène. But in the same letter he mentioned that Madame Morand had read Irène's *Les Mouches d'automne* (*Snow in Autumn*), about a Russian aristocratic family that flees the Revolution and settles in Paris, and she did not find it sufficiently anti-Bolshevik to make a strong case. The work was "antirevolutionary, certainly, but not anti-Bolshevik," she had told him. One can only marvel at the fine distinctions Madame Morand was able to draw as she reflected on whether or not Némirovsky was ideologically worthy enough to be saved. In the end she appears to have taken the safe way out: Michel's best bet, she advised Sabatier, was to contact the "Union israélite" (that is, the Union Générale des Israélites de France, known by its initials UGIF, the official body set up by Vichy in November 1941 to represent

French Jews) to try and find out where his wife was and perhaps to send her news about the children.[4] Hélène Morand was well-known for her antisemitic views, reputed to be even more virulent than her husband's. The Morands had been on cordial, though superficial, terms with Irène and Michel before the war, and Irène had written Madame Morand earlier in 1942 to ask for help in obtaining permission to travel to Paris. Now, as then, the Epsteins' faith in her ability or willingness to go out of her way to help them appears to have been exaggerated.

Sabatier wrote to other highly placed people who were close to the Germans as well. Michel had suggested that Prime Minister Pierre Laval's son-in-law, the Comte de Chambrun, might act as go-between for his letter to Abetz—he thought perhaps Chambrun knew Irène's work. Sabatier had no personal connection to Laval's son-in-law, but he did as Michel asked. On July 28 he sent Chambrun a brief note about "the author of *David Golder*," with a copy of Michel's letter to the German ambassador. Chambrun did not respond, as Sabatier informed Michel two weeks later, on August 12. Sabatier was also in touch with his friend Jacques Bénoist-Méchin, a writer he had known and published since the 1920s and who was an active collaborationist working for Laval in Vichy. On July 15, two days after Irène's arrest, Sabatier sent a note to Bénoist-Méchin informing him that Némirovsky, "our author and friend," had been taken to Pithiviers. She was, he wrote, a "white Russian (*israélite*, as you know)," a novelist of great talent who had never engaged in politics, who had always brought great honor on her adopted country, and who was the mother of two young daughters.[5] Whether Bénoist-Méchin was sufficiently moved to intervene, or whether he could even have done so, is not clear. Given the efficiency of the post office at the time, with letters arriving the day after being mailed, it is possible he received Sabatier's letter on the sixteenth, which could have given him time to make a phone call before transport #6 left the station in Pithiviers the next morning. But Sabatier reported, in his letter of August 12 to Michel, "My friend has informed me categorically that his inquiries have led to the conclusion there was nothing he could do." Did Bénoist-Méchin know about transport #6 and where it was headed? Since he was working with Laval, who most certainly knew, it is very likely that he did, too. Did he tell his friend Sabatier everything he knew? We cannot know, but he told him there was nothing more to be done. Bénoist-Méchin was condemned to death for his collaborationist activities after the war, but the sentence was commuted, and, after spending a few years in prison, he was freed as part of a general amnesty in the early 1950s. He then enjoyed a long career as a journalist and writer until his death in 1983. The fact that Sabatier was his close friend, addressing him in the familiar "tu," does not necessarily reflect Sabatier's own political allegiances; as far as we know, he was not active in politics. Rather, it shows that personal relations and friendships could trump ideology, under Vichy as under other regimes.

As the summer wore on, the letters became rarer, but Michel still hoped to have news of Irène. On August 14 he wrote to Irène's friend Madeleine (Avot) Cabour, apparently in reply to a letter from her: "Unfortunately Irène has left—for where? I don't know. You can imagine how worried I am." Six days later, replying to another letter from Madeleine, he writes with more details about Irène's arrest and his attempts since then. He says he has tried everything, asking various people to help, but with no results so far: "If you can do anything at all, do it, I beg you, for this anxiety is unbearable. Just think, I can't even send her food, and she has neither clothes nor money."[6] By that time, if the official records are correct, Irène was dead. And so were Michel's two brothers, Paul and Samuel, and Samuel's wife, Alexandrine. They had been arrested in the big roundup of July 16 and 17 in Paris, the Rafle du Vél d'Hiv, and deported from the transit camp at Drancy, Paul on July 22, Samuel and Alexandrine on the twenty-fourth. Michel's sister Sophie (Mavlik) knew about their arrest and had written from Paris to tell him, although she did not know right away about their deportation. In her letter to Michel on July 29 she writes that Sam has left Drancy and is at Beaune-la-Rolande, the camp near Pithiviers, but actually his transport had already arrived in Auschwitz. She urged Michel to stay strong for Irène and for his daughters. "We don't have the right to lose heart, since we are believers [croyants]," she added. Her use of the word *croyant*, the term used to designate the Christian faithful, implies that she too had converted to Catholicism.[7]

Michel, for his part, kept writing more and more distraught letters to Sabatier. On August 9 he says he has found out from a "very serious source" that a train from Pithiviers had been sent "to the east" a few weeks earlier: "Until now, I thought my wife was in a camp somewhere in France, guarded by French soldiers. To know that she is in a savage country, under conditions that are probably atrocious, without money or food, among people whose language she doesn't even know, is unbearable." He feels as if he were himself in prison, unable to eat or sleep, and apologizes for the incoherence of his letter.[8] It is to this letter that Sabatier replies at length on August 12, trying to furnish as much precise information as he can. It appears, he says, that the measures against Irène were generalized, for in Paris too several thousand stateless people (apatrides) were arrested around the same time. Sabatier avoids the term *Jew*, as if the "apatrides" of those roundups had included other foreigners. According to Madame Morand, he reports, it's probable that Irène and the others were sent not to camps but to "cities in Poland where apatrides are assembled." Madame Morand was well informed, it appears, although she obviously did not know the exact nature of those "cities in Poland."[9]

A month later, on September 19, Michel comes up with an idea: could he not be allowed to take Irène's place, wherever she is, or, if that's impossible, could he not at least be allowed to join her? "Together we'd be better off," he writes. Sabatier replies on September 23, and this time he does use the word *camp*. It really won't be possible for Michel to take Irène's place, he explains, nor can he be with her in the same camp, for men and women are strictly separated. He too appears to be well informed.[10]

After that, there are only a few more letters. On September 29 Michel writes that he has promised not to overload Sabatier with more requests, and he is sticking to his promise. But he does have an urgent problem, as his foreigner's identity card will need to be renewed in November, and he is supposed to write to the prefect in Mâcon to request a renewal. He wouldn't want this to cause him any more troubles, for even though all his papers are "perfectly in order," people in his "category" have reason to fear bureaucratic problems. Would Sabatier please, therefore, intervene with the prefect on his behalf? This whole affair seems extremely odd because Mâcon was in the Unoccupied Zone, separated from Issy-l'Évêque by the heavily guarded demarcation line. As Michel well knew, all of his and

Irène's bureaucratic proceedings and requests until then had been addressed to the subprefect in Autun, who acted as prefect for the occupied part of Saône-et-Loire. Was this identity card something different? Whatever the case, Sabatier replied on October 5, briefly but firmly. He had consulted people, and their answer was unequivocal that Michel should do absolutely nothing, for any action on his part would be "extremely imprudent." Sabatier then adds a postscript: "Maybe you could consult my father in Dijon?"[11] Michel jumps at the suggestion, and on October 8 he sends a typewritten letter to Sabatier *père*, with a copy to André. It's a heartbreaking document, for it shows a man utterly overcome by events. After outlining the problem he had already explained to André Sabatier, Michel writes, "I find myself between two dilemmas: 1—Not to do anything, as André advises. My identity card will then be expired and I will be punishable by the full force of the law. 2—To request my card from Mâcon, but that would be, as André says, extremely imprudent. I beg you, Monsieur, please advise me, thinking only of my wife and children. I would have preferred to consult you in person, but unfortunately I don't have the right to leave here."[12] That same day Michel executed a legal document with the notaire at Issy-l'Évêque, Maître Vernet, in which he transferred to Julie Dumot the sweeping powers of attorney he himself had been given by Irène in 1933. Julie was henceforth authorized to act in his stead (and in Irène's) in all financial and legal transactions, which meant, among other things, that she became the legal guardian of the Epsteins' daughters.[13]

Michel did not have the right to leave Issy, as he wrote to André Sabatier's father, but he could be forced to do so. On the very day he wrote his letter, October 8, an official telegram went out from the regional prefect in Dijon to all the subprefects in his jurisdiction, which included the occupied part of Saône-et-Loire. The instructions were similar to the ones he had sent in July but with a few differences: this time foreign Jews were to be arrested regardless of age, children included, and they were to be transferred not to Pithiviers but to Drancy. On October 9, a Friday, Michel Epstein was arrested in Issy and taken to the prison in Le Creusot, an industrial town about thirty miles east of Issy. Denise and Elisabeth were also arrested, that day or later, but then allowed to go. From Le Creusot,

Michel was able to send two postcards to Julie, on October 16 and October 20, and he sounded serene for the first time since Irène had been taken away. He also sent a card to Sabatier, on October 19: "I am counting on your friendship toward my loved ones. They will need it. I am sure you will take care of them."[14] The prisoners in Le Creusot could evidently receive packages and visitors, for in his first card to Julie, Michel thanks her for her package, and in the second he mentions a visit from Norbert, possibly someone from Issy, which had made him happy. He asks her to send him tobacco. But in the end there was no time for that. On October 22 the camp registry in Drancy noted the arrival of 26 prisoners from Le Creusot. Two weeks later, on November 6, 25 of them, including Michel Epstein, were herded onto transport #42, along with 975 other Jews who had been shipped to Drancy from all over France. Michel's sister from Paris, Sophie Epstein, was on the same transport. They were among the 773 people, including 113 children under the age of twelve, who were gassed on arrival in Auschwitz.[15]

Denise and Elisabeth had become orphans.

Hidden Children

Most of the Jewish children who survived the war in France spent extended time in hiding under false identities, often separated from their parents temporarily or forever. Denise and Elisabeth were like these children in that regard. They both recalled, much later and with some variations, that they had been arrested at the same time as their father but let go by a German officer at the police station who was reminded of his own daughter when he saw Denise's blond hair. There is also a story, told by Denise and by one of the schoolteachers at Issy, that the teacher hid Denise (and, in one of the versions, Elisabeth as well) in her private apartment on the day the police came looking for them at school.[16] The variations in these narratives, all of them dating from the 1990s or later, demonstrate how hazy the memories of events that happened in the distant past can be. Usually, however, at least one or two kernels stand out as unvarying, in this case, the fact of having been hidden by the teacher and of having been let go by the German officer who saw a resemblance between Denise and his daughter. It is not clear exactly when all this happened. Michel's postcards to Julie indicate that she and the girls were still in Issy more than ten days after his arrest, while the story about the German officer ends with his telling them to "come back the next day," after which they left town in a hurry.

What is certain is that at some point in October, Julie and the girls left Issy-l'Évêque, carrying almost no luggage except for the precious suitcase Michel had confided to Denise, which contained her mother's notebooks and other papers and photos. They took the train to Bordeaux, and Denise later described the trip as terrifying because they were trying to avoid patrols that would ask for papers. Every time they heard one approaching, the girls would climb up into the baggage rack, which was "like a hammock" in those days, and Julie would cover them up, telling the other passengers they were sick. This is one of the memories that may have gotten revised over the years.[17] Bordeaux may not seem like the best choice of destination, for the city was a strategic site heavily occupied by the Germans. The Vichy police were very active there too, as witnesses recalled in detail during the trial in 1997 of Maurice Papon, the Vichy functionary who had been in charge of the roundups in the city. But Julie had relatives she could count on all over the region, some of whom were in the Resistance and proved very helpful. The previous spring she and Denise had spent time with her family in Audenge, a small seaside town about thirty miles southwest of Bordeaux. Over the next year and a half she moved around among several places where family members lived, including Cézac, a village about twenty-five miles north of Bordeaux, and Bruges, a suburb of Bordeaux where a cousin of hers lived. She was able to place the girls in a Catholic convent school in the city, the Cours Sainte-Thérèse, where only two of the Sisters knew their real identity. The family name they went by was Dumot. Denise recalled that in class she often failed to respond when the teacher called out her name of Dumot and was punished for it.[18]

Very few documents survive from that time, for obvious reasons: people in hiding try not to leave paper trails. The few letters from Julie Dumot that remain indicate that the girls were at the convent for about a year, possibly with a hiatus in the summer of 1943 and during other school vacations, when they stayed with Julie and her family. At Christmas 1942 both of them wrote to André Sabatier from Cézac to thank him for books he had sent them. Sabatier, who had no children, seems to have fulfilled Michel's hope that he would continue to look after the girls. Apart from the monthly checks that continued to be sent by Albin Michel, Sabatier took a personal interest in them. "There is nothing more we can wish for" (Pour nous rien ne laisse à désirer), Denise wrote to him in her letter of thanks at Christmas 1942. The literal meaning of that formulaic phrase strikes one as extraordinary under the circumstances. In fact, there was a lot more she and Elisabeth could have wished for, and very likely did, starting with the return of their parents. Children often cope with trauma by blocking it out, as if what was happening was normal. The shock is so great there is no way to process it at the time it occurs. Theorists of trauma have suggested that the inability to fully comprehend the traumatic event when it occurs applies to adults as well, but most adults can at least put a name on what is happening to them. Children, especially young children, have no such resource. Denise, who had turned thirteen in November 1942, seems to have been exceptionally mature for her age, judging by her letters. She had written a whole series of them to her parents while she was traveling with Julie in April and May 1942, and they are strikingly observant and well written for such a young girl; but still, it is doubtful that she understood what was happening during much of that time. She did, however, understand that she and her sister were in great danger, and that may be another reason she tried to sound normal in her Christmas letter to Sabatier. She reflected later that her one constant emotion at the time was fear and that she always had to be watchful. As for five-year-old Elisabeth, whose letter to Sabatier is on the back of Denise's and is full of misspelled words, she told him she was happy to play hide-and-seek with her sister and the other kids in the house and that she liked the books he had sent her.[19]

Many years later, when she was interviewed on radio and television as a well-known literary editor and then as a writer, Elisabeth Gille would sometimes mention that her "first book," the one that gave her a lifelong love of literature, was *Mon petit Trott*, a children's classic. Perhaps she remembered it was Sabatier who had sent it to her at Christmas 1942: "le petit trott mamuse beaucoup" (I realy lik little trott, to approximate her spelling), she wrote him. First published in 1898 and often reprinted in various versions after that, *Mon petit Trott* features a little boy who misses his Papa, a naval officer, while his "jolie maman" engages in a flirtation. Her would-be suitor is the wealthy Monsieur Aaron, who has an "ugly hooked nose" and whom Trott doesn't like, even though he gives him expensive presents. After Papa returns, there is trouble at home for a while, but little Trott prays that his parents will be happy again. Soon enough, Papa and Maman make up and order is restored. The author, André Lichtenberger (1870–1940), from an Alsatian Protestant family, was a historian and sociologist as well as a prolific novelist, although he is remembered today only for that one children's book. Lichtenberger was not an antisemite by those days' standards. Indeed, in a patriotic pamphlet published shortly before he died in 1940, *Why France Is at War*, he strongly condemned Hitler and the Nazis for their persecution of Jews. The fact that his children's book is nevertheless rife with antisemitic clichés about its only Jewish character—in the original version Monsieur Aaron is explicitly identified as a Jew, and Trott recalls that the Jews killed Jesus Christ—simply indicates how widespread and "normal" it was for Jews to appear as negative figures in the French (actually, European) cultural imagination. More likely than not the prejudicial stereotype was not even perceived as such by most readers—they took it for granted. The picture book version of 1935, probably the one Sabatier sent Elisabeth, considerably tones down the portrayal of Monsieur Aaron, who appears in only one paragraph, but he still has an "ugly hooked nose," and Trott still does not like him. A later edition, published in 1954, reproduces the original faithfully, including the part about Jews as Christ-killers.[20] To the very young reader who had seen both of her parents disappear in the space of a few months, the story may have provided comfort. Little Trott was almost exactly Elisabeth's age, and although his father was away for a long time he eventually returned.

In April 1943 Julie, who was still (or once again?) in Cézac, wrote to Sabatier that Elisabeth would have her first communion in a few weeks. Babet, as everyone called her, was barely six years old, and Julie thought she was too young for communion, but the Sisters wanted it, and they assured her that Babet was "very advanced and would be an angel." Julie also wrote to Madeleine Cabour, who had evidently kept in touch over the previous months, although no let-

ters from her are in the archives. But we know from Julie's letter to
her that Madeleine had recently sent clothing for the girls, for Julie
goes to great lengths to thank her and to describe the dress she would
make for Babet's communion. The girls were in need of everything,
she told Madeleine. Denise had been ill, and Julie had taken her to
her family to convalesce, but she would soon write to thank Madeleine as well. A sweet letter from Denise, who sounds very grown
up, went off to Madeleine on April 23: "Thanks to you, my little
Babet is dressed from head to toe." She hoped Madeleine and her
daughters were all well: "I feel a great deal of friendship [for your
daughters] without even knowing them."[21] Madeleine Cabour and
her brother René Avot, whose friendship with Irène Némirovsky
went back more than twenty years, would play an important role in
Elisabeth's life after the war.

Bordeaux was liberated a few days after Paris, on August 29,
1944, when the last German troops left the city. But during most of
the last year of the Occupation the pursuit of Jews all over France
and their transfer to Drancy, with final destination Auschwitz, continued and even intensified. The last transport from Bordeaux arrived in Drancy on May 14, 1944, and trains continued to leave
Drancy "for the East" until the end of July. Denise and Elisabeth
were therefore still in danger. One day in late 1943 or early 1944
(the exact date is uncertain), the Sisters at the convent received a
warning that the police were coming the next morning. Whether
they were looking specifically for Denise and Elisabeth, whose names
figured on lists of Jews in Saône-et-Loire but not in Bordeaux, or
were following up on a denunciation or merely searching for Jews is
not clear, although Denise thought she and Elisabeth had been specifically hunted by the police. Whatever the case, Julie took them
out of the school, and for the next several months they were almost
constantly on the run.[22] Denise generally refused to talk about their
time in Bordeaux when I questioned her later, even though she was
very generous with other remembrances, and when she evoked it in
her book of conversations with Clémence Boulouque, *Survivre et
vivre*, her account was extremely meager and disjointed. After they
left the convent "en catastrophe," she recalled, they moved from
place to place, and she could not remember any of them specifically.
She did remember "the system of frequent round-trips between

apartment and basement, depending on the circumstances and the time of day" and having to pretend they were "cousins or nieces from the provinces." She also recalled that Julie had told her to hide her nose because it could "betray her origins." For a very long time afterward, she told Boulouque, she had maintained the "reflex of bringing my hand to my nose whenever I passed a stranger," aware of the tragic as well as ridiculous aspect of that gesture.[23] But given that convoys of arrested Jews were leaving Drancy as late as July 1944, Julie's admonitions unfortunately made sense.

On October 1, 1944, Julie wrote to the director of Albin Michel, Robert Esménard, to thank him for the checks he was continuing to send and to give him news of Némirovsky's daughters: "You understand that I've been worried. For seven months I had to hide them again in various places. Now I hope that nightmare is over." She has put the girls back in school, she tells him, the one they had attended before. The following week, on October 10, she writes a similar letter to Sabatier to say the girls are very happy to be back with their schoolmates and the Sisters have been a great help. "I hope that now nothing more will come to torture us as we await the return of our exiles," she adds. On November 2 she sends a long letter to Madeleine Cabour: "We too had a lot of worries. For seven months I had to trundle these children from one side to the other." The girls had to interrupt their studies at the end of February, she tells Madeleine, but are finally back in school. Denise would like to go to Paris. She is a big girl now, will be turning fifteen on November 9, and her sister will be eight in a few months, but Julie would like her to finish out the year and take her exams. A lot "remains to be negotiated," and Julie is very grateful for Madeleine's interest in the children, as it makes her feel less alone. She sends her greetings to Madeleine's parents and to her brother and hopes that one day the girls will meet Madeleine's daughters. Meanwhile, she is hoping for the return of the "poor captives."[24]

But the captives did not return.

Postwar

At the end of the Second World War in France more than ten thousand Jewish children found themselves without one or both of their parents. Most had survived the war in hiding. Some adolescents from other countries who had survived concentration camps had been transported to France by Jewish rescue organizations after liberation and placed in children's homes. Elie Wiesel is doubtless the best known of these resettled orphans. While many of the non-French children eventually moved to Israel and elsewhere, the large majority of Jewish orphans who had lived in France before the war remained there, and an impressive number grew up to become distinguished, even world-renowned, writers, intellectuals, and public figures. A number of them eventually published memoirs and autobiographical novels that have entered the canon of Holocaust literature and of French literature tout court. Georges Perec's classic memoir *W, or the Memory of Childhood* is a prime example. Hundreds more have provided oral and written testimonies that have been archived or published over the past three decades, as the category of "child survivor of the Holocaust" has become part of our vocabulary. Until the 1980s many Jewish children who had survived the war in hiding did not think of themselves and were not perceived generally as Holocaust survivors since that label was reserved for people who had survived concentration camps. But as the children grew into maturity, associations of child survivors started to be formed in the United States and elsewhere. In France the Association des Enfants Cachés was formed in 1992, the same year Elisabeth Gille published *Le Mirador*, in which she included a few sketches of her memories of childhood and adolescence. Psychologists, historians, and literary scholars started to study the specific category of child survivors. This considerable body of work confirms that every individual survivor has a unique story. At the same time, it shows that Jewish children who survived the war in hiding share "family resemblances," both in their wartime and postwar lives and in their psychological profiles. Boris Cyrulnik, a French neuropsychiatrist and a specialist in theories of childhood resilience, who is himself a child survivor of the Holocaust orphaned at the age of five, has analyzed some of the psychological traits in such children. Surviving in hiding, pretending to be someone with a different name, always being on the lookout for possible disaster could lead to an excessive sense of power and invulnerability in later life ("Nothing can harm me"), Cyrulnik observes, or to its opposite ("I deserve to die"). Often, paradoxically, the two feelings may coexist in the same person.[25]

In the psychological literature on hidden children, one does not find a strong distinction made between children who lost one or both parents in the war and those who were reunited with their parents afterward. In one sense, all hidden children underwent similar experiences of dislocation and trauma, especially if they spent an extended period separated from their family. Many children whose parents returned from camps found their reunion difficult, for the parents had themselves been transformed by their experience. But no matter how troubled the relation to a parent is, the difference between having one and not having one or between losing a parent for a while and losing one or both forever is enormous for a child. Emile Copfermann (1931–1999), who became a journalist and novelist after doing odd jobs for a number of years, was eleven years old when his parents were arrested in September 1942 and deported to Auschwitz. An aunt had him and his two brothers baptized for extra protection and managed to send them to a family of farmers in the southwest, where they spent the rest of the war under false identities. Afterward, when it was clear that their parents were not coming back and the aunt could not take care of them, the boys were sent to a Jewish children's home, where they spent several years. In a memoir he published when he was in his late sixties, two years before he died, Copfermann wrote:

> A normal childhood and adolescence unfold under the influence of one's parents, so that later it becomes impossible to tell which of your memories you remember as something you lived through, and which were only told to you later, over and over. Our life as children was not only reduced to very little, but the memory of the years we spent with our parents was not revived by anyone. As an adult, no matter how hard I tried to assemble the pieces of the past, they didn't stick together: people were missing, places had become erased, even the years ran together. To reconstitute the puzzle, we would have had to question our elders, verify the facts with them. . . . Impossible, [for] most of our close relatives had also disappeared.[26]

Families like the Copfermanns, poor immigrants from Romania, did not keep archives. Perec, who came from a similar family, built *W, or the Memory of Childhood* around the absences he experienced, not only the physical absence of his parents but also that of the very traces of their existence. Perec had an aunt and older cousins who took care of him after the war and provided at least some answers to his questions. But the idea that pieces of his life were missing that could never be filled in, except by imagination and guesswork, still dominates his memoir, whose opening sentence has become famous for the way it contradicts the book's title: "I have no childhood memories." (Je n'ai pas de souvenirs d'enfance). The same is true of other orphans who have produced notable literary works about their experiences.[27]

Denise and Elisabeth Epstein were, in one way at least, luckier than most, for their mother's prewar fame constituted a unique heritage, and despite the destruction of many personal papers, a large archive relating to their mother's work was saved. Notwithstanding the terrible loss of their parents and other close relatives, the girls did not remain wholly without resources, either human or financial. Nonetheless, their postwar lives followed a pattern that has important points in common with other orphans' lives. Years of "putting the past behind," followed by attempts to recover it; feeling anxious about Jewishness or even wanting to escape it altogether, followed by a reclaiming of Jewish identity and memory: that, in brief, constituted the experience of many child survivors, and it was true (with variations, as always) of Denise and Elisabeth as well.

In the spring of 1945, the French public saw for the first time photographs and journalists' accounts of Buchenwald, Bergen Belsen, and other camps that American and British troops had liberated and were in the process of emptying. In April, trains carrying surviving deportees from the camps as well as prisoners of war and forced laborers started arriving at the Gare de l'Est in Paris. The newspapers were full of stories and images of these returnees. From the train station the former prisoners were transferred to the Hôtel Lutétia, a grand hotel on the Left Bank that had housed German headquarters during the Occupation, where a temporary receiving station with doctors and nurses in attendance had been set up. The large majority of the returnees from Nazi camps had been deported as members of the Resistance, not as Jews; only 3 percent of Jewish deportees from France returned, while roughly 50 percent of all deportees, Jews and *résistants*, did so. But many Jewish family members lined up with others on the sidewalk outside the Lutétia, hoping to see their loved ones and brandishing their photographs.[28]

Denise and Elisabeth Epstein were still enrolled in school in Bordeaux that spring, but both of them later recalled trips to the Lutétia to wait for their parents as well as a trip to the train station that had ended with Denise fainting at the sight of the emaciated people getting off the trains. Elisabeth, in *Le Mirador*, dates the fainting episode to September 1945, but that could not have been the right date because by then all camp survivors had returned, save perhaps for a few individuals arriving separately. According to the historian Annette Wieviorka, a specialist on the subject, by August 1945 all prisoners liberated from camps, whether by American, British, or Soviet troops, had been repatriated. Most of them had returned in April, May, and June.[29]

The September date may have been a case of erroneous memory due to retrospective "smoothing out," for Denise and Elisabeth did return to Paris permanently in September 1945. But if their kernel of memory about waiting at the train station and at the Lutétia is correct—and there is no reason to doubt it—they must have gone to Paris at least briefly with Julie Dumot earlier that year, when trainloads of deportees were still arriving. In her autobiographical novel of 1996 about her childhood, *Un paysage de cendres* (*Shadows of a Childhood*), Elisabeth imagines her young heroine, Léa Lévy, being taken to Paris by a Sister from the convent to look for her parents in April 1945. Their visit to the Lutétia is described with details that suggest Gille based it on historical accounts (Wieviorka's book on the return of deportees had been published just a few years earlier, in 1992), but there was probably a trace of personal memory in her description as well. We know that Julie Dumot was actively seeking information about Michel and Irène that spring. According to a note on the back of Irène's Pithiviers camp registration card, a certificate about her deportation was delivered to "Mlle Dumot" on March 28, 1945. The girls could have been with her in Paris for a few weeks, at that time or later. In an undated letter with a Paris return address, written most likely in late spring or early summer 1945, Julie wrote to Madeleine Cabour that she would "bring the children back" to her in early September. In a letter dated September 8 she wrote that she and the girls sent Madeleine their "meilleur souvenir," which implies they had already met earlier that year, given that a "best remembrance" can be sent only to somebody one has met in person.[30]

Another episode from that time, one which has attained almost legendary status among Némirovsky fans, is the story of the girls' failed visit, early in 1945, to their grandmother Fanny, Irène's mother. Fanny Némirovsky had survived the war on the Côte d'Azur with a fake Lithuanian passport and had returned to her Paris apartment in the elegant 16th arrondissement. The story told by Denise and Elisabeth is that they and Julie went knocking on her door, perhaps in January 1945, the date Elisabeth gives in *Le Mirador*, or perhaps later. The old lady wouldn't let them in: she had no granddaughters, she said from behind the closed door. When Julie told her that Denise was sick with pleurisy, she supposedly replied, "There are sanatoria for the poor." Elisabeth recounted in a radio interview after the publication of *Le Mirador* that when she was sixteen she telephoned her grandmother, pretending she was a journalist seeking information about Irène Némirovsky. Her grandmother replied that she knew no one by that name.[31] Anecdotes like this have earned Fanny Némirovsky the title of "monster mother," and it certainly seems well deserved. She was by all accounts an exceptionally vain, narcissistic, ungenerous woman. As we know, Irène's relationship with her had been terrible from her early childhood on, and the two hadn't seen each other in many years by the time Irène was deported. It comes as something of a shock to read, therefore, in Julie's undated letter of 1945 to Madeleine Cabour, a sentence which states that "the 1,000 Francs that Mme Némirowsky sends me are not enough to pay for amusements for the children [les sorties des enfants]." This is the sole reference in any of this correspondence to a "Mme Némirowsky," and it can refer only to Irène's mother. The name of a male relative named Némirovsky appears in some of the postwar documents, but no "Madame Némirovsky" other than Fanny is mentioned anywhere. Did the dragon lady, if it was indeed she, send regular checks or just one? The sentence structure suggests the former since Julie uses the present tense of the verb. A thousand francs was not very much, it's true: she complains in the same letter that the three-thousand-franc monthly check from the publisher (five hundred dollars in today's terms) is insufficient to live on.[32] But still, this

is one of those pieces of historical documentation that cannot logically be fitted into the story. According to the story, Fanny Némirovsky died at close to the age of one hundred, in 1972, without ever
having seen or otherwise acknowledged her granddaughters, and
the only thing found in her safe deposit box after her death were two
books by her daughter Irène: *David Golder* and *Jézabel,* both of which
feature monstrously self-centered mothers.

If their grandmother wanted nothing to do with the girls, other
adults were eager to help. Madeleine Cabour had been involved since
1942, and René Avot and his wife, Hortense, would soon be as well.
Sabatier and Esménard continued their support. The authors' guild,
the Société des Gens de Lettres, showed interest in contributing
to the girls' education, and Michel Epstein's former employer, the
Banque des Pays du Nord, which had fired him unceremoniously
in June 1940, sent a letter to Dumot five years later stating that "in
memory of Mr. Epstein" they would like "to do something for these
children."[33] Irène Némirovsky's name and fame had spread even to
New York, for in April 1945 a certain Marc Aldanov, representing
the Fund for the Relief of Men of Letters and Scientists of Russia,
wrote to Esménard. Unfortunately the fund had no money and not
too many members, he explained, but they were admirers of Némirovsky's work and hoped that as her publisher he would perhaps find
some back royalties to pay to her children. Esménard replied that
since Irène's arrest his firm had sent 151,000 francs to Mademoiselle
Dumot, who had saved the children, and that it was continuing to
send monthly checks.[34] Indeed, Albin Michel continued its monthly
payments until each of the girls reached the age of twenty-one, and
other institutions did likewise. A committee was formed in 1945 to
oversee the girls' education. We don't have the names of all the
members of the committee, but at least one of them is mentioned
in a note Esménard dictated to his secretary in December 1945. Esménard himself was involved, on behalf of Albin Michel. In the note,
he reports that he had gone to see Madame Simone Saint-Clair, a
member of the committee, to discuss Albin Michel's contribution.
Saint-Clair (1896–1975) was a journalist and novelist and a member
of the Société des Gens de Lettres who may have known Irène
Némirovsky before the war. She had been active in the Resistance
and had been deported to the women's camp in Ravensbrück. After

her return, in 1945, she published one of the first testimonies about the camp, *Ravensbrück: L'enfer des femmes* (Ravensbrück: Women's hell). According to Esménard's note, she had told him that a number of individuals and organizations would contribute monthly sums until both of the girls had obtained their *baccalauréat*, or secondary school diploma, roughly equivalent at the time to a year of college, and that further moneys would be collected to constitute a fund for the girls. A designated *notaire* in Paris would receive and distribute the payments, starting with sums due to Julie Dumot to defray her expenses during the war.[35] (A number of letters and accounts from the *notaire*, André Oudard, are in the Némirovsky archives.) In addition to the funds provided by the committee, Denise and Elisabeth were entitled to some support from the French government, as *pupilles de la Nation* (wards of the nation). This legal category was created during the First World War to help children whose parents had died in the war, and it is still in existence, although the definition has been updated several times after different wars.

Denise and Elisabeth spent several weeks in the summer of 1945 in Brittany at the vacation home of Madeleine Cabour, but René and Hortense soon took over as guardians of Elisabeth. The Avots had three children of their own, two girls and a boy. Their older daughter, Edwige, was exactly Elisabeth's age, a fact which no doubt played a role in their willingness to take her as their charge. They did not feel they could do the same for Denise, which led to some resentment later.[36]

In the fall of 1945 Denise and Elisabeth entered as boarders the elite Catholic school for girls Notre Dame de Sion, located in Évry, a sleepy suburb south of Paris. The tuition fees were paid out of the funds deposited with Maître Oudard. Admission to the school took some pulling of strings by Sabatier and others, for Sion was a fashionable school attended by the daughters of wealthy professionals and industrialists. It had been founded in the nineteenth century by Father Théodore Ratisbonne and his younger brother Alphonse, both of whom were Jewish converts to Catholicism. Dumot, a devout Catholic herself, was thrilled that Denise and Elisabeth had been admitted to the school. It was exactly what their mother had wished for, she wrote to Sabatier after he told her the news.[37] Denise Epstein, by the time I met her in 2008, strongly denied that her mother had wished for anything of the sort. In her book as well as in personal conversations she had harsh things to say about the way she and Elisabeth had been treated at Sion, as "poor little Jewish orphans."[38] The reality is hard to judge, but we can imagine that both of the girls felt bereft and out of place there (and elsewhere too, no doubt), at least at the start, even if they were surrounded by kind, well-meaning adults.

Today, Notre Dame de Sion is a flourishing coeducational establishment with more than fifteen hundred students from diverse backgrounds, very few of them boarders. When I visited the school in June 2011, it looked like an open and welcoming place. It organizes educational trips to Auschwitz for the older students, with the aim of teaching them about the "reality of the Shoah" and the "importance of memory," according to the account on the school's website. In 1945 things were rather different. For one thing, no one wanted to talk about what had happened during the war, least of all the Jewish orphans themselves. Most children whose parents had been deported were silent about it for decades. In addition, social differences were much more pronounced than today, and the old tradition of French Catholic antisemitism was still alive and well in many places. The Sisters at Sion were not antisemitic, Denise told me, but nevertheless they thought it was "better to be Christian than Jewish."[39] None of this made for a comfortable situation for Denise and Elisabeth, even if they were technically Catholics and the daughters of a once-famous mother who had occupied a place among the privileged members of society. Denise recalled with some anger that the Sisters had urged her to become a nun, for she had no resources and that way at least she would be taken care of.

Happy or not, the girls stayed at Sion for several years. According to the school's records, Denise obtained her baccalauréat degree in June 1949, when she was nineteen, being slightly behind because of the delay caused by the war. Elisabeth remained at the school for six years, but at the end of the 1950–1951 school year she was apparently asked to leave.[40] The school records make no mention of that fact, merely listing her years of attendance, but a number of people I interviewed recalled her dismissal with some amusement. She was too outspoken and a "troublemaker," according to family legend. The Avots, who by then considered her almost a member of their

family, Edwige Avot Becquart told me, found a new boarding school
for her about twenty miles from Versailles, where they lived. She
became a boarder at the Institution du Sacré Coeur in Saint-Maur-
les-Fossés (today the Lycée Teilhard de Chardin) until 1953, when
she obtained her baccalauréat.

Like his father, René Avot was in the paper manufacturing business. The family firm in northern France had been bombed during
the war, and Avot and his family moved to Paris at that time because his wife was convinced "Paris would never be destroyed," their
daughter recalled. After the war he built a new factory in Nanterre,
just outside Paris, and moved his family to a large house on a leafy
street in Versailles, not far from the celebrated Château. Edwige
Avot Becquart still lives in that house with her husband, although
they now occupy only part of it. Elisabeth had been going to stay
with the Avots on school vacations ever since Christmas 1945, and
she and Edwige were close friends. In fact, the Avots had enrolled
Edwige at Notre Dame de Sion in 1945 because of Elisabeth, and
both girls left the school at the same time. The family spent one
month every summer at Madeleine Cabour's summer house in Car-
nac and another month in Le Havre with Madeleine's and René's
parents, who had met Irène Némirovsky as a young woman and who
were very fond of Elisabeth.

By this time the two Epstein sisters' lives had diverged dramatically. Denise, a few months short of her twentieth birthday when she
left Notre Dame de Sion in June 1949, found herself on her own,
harboring haunting memories of her parents and her prewar life and
a feeling of utter abandonment. After the summer of 1945 she no
longer spent vacations with Elisabeth, who was with the Avots. She
remembered spending one or two summers with her mother's friend
Jean-Jacques Bernard and his wife, who had opened their house in
Normandy to her and to other orphans. But they were mourning the
death of their son in the war, and she stopped seeing them—it was
too depressing, she told me. She was poor and would soon cease receiving stipends as an orphan. They stopped when she reached the
age of twenty-one, though the notaire received some other income
for her for a year or two after that. Her father's old bank gave her a
job, but she was untrained for it, and they didn't particularly care—
they were employing her out of charity, she felt, and it made her

angry rather than grateful. She was living in a seventh-floor walk-up maid's room with running water on the landing, like many other poor young people at the time. One day her old nurse, Cécile Michaud, the one whose mother lived in Issy, came to visit her after not hearing from her and found her shivering and ill. It turned out she had typhus, requiring a hospital stay and several months in a rehabilitation facility in the country. It must have been around this time or shortly before that an unnamed person wrote a letter on what looks like a page torn out of a notebook: "I went to see Denise in the attic [the writer had first put "room," then crossed it out] where she is staying. . . . I think it my duty to tell you that I was shocked and upset to see the material conditions in which she lives. Her furniture consists of a small couch on which she sleeps. Furthermore, she is alone, with no one who could give her the care her state of health requires." The writer of the letter appears to be a member of the committee overseeing the girls' education since he or she refers to Denise as "our ward" (notre pupille) and requests a meeting with the addressee (also unknown, unfortunately) to discuss the matter. The date of this letter, which bears no other identifying mark, is given at the bottom in what appears to be a different hand, in different ink: "23 June 1950." This seems to have been the absolute low point in Denise Epstein's postwar life.[41]

Elisabeth's life at this time was a lot more cheerful. More than seven years younger than her sister, she had no real memories of her parents or of her mother's arrest, although she said she did recall her father's, and she felt less burdened by the past, at least on the surface. Her personality seems to have been different as well. Many people I interviewed remembered Denise as "the woman who cried," but they recalled Elisabeth as a woman who loved to laugh. Laughter, like tears, can be a coping mechanism in response to trauma, and Denise too laughed a lot, at least by the time I met her. Nevertheless, it seems Elisabeth wanted to avoid the sadness she associated with her sister. In 1994, in her radio interview about her childhood, she said that for a long time she refused to think about the past, in part because she had seen her older sister, who had been incapable of "creating a wall," "go under" several times as a result. But coping mechanisms may also depend on personality. By all indications Elisabeth was an irrepressible child from an early age, sparkling with

intelligence and talking a blue streak. Denise recounted how on a
few occasions when they were hiding in Bordeaux she had had to tie
a scarf over her little sister's mouth to keep her quiet. Edwige Becquart also remembers Elisabeth as being very lively and far more
"intellectual" than she. Everyone in the Avot family was "in admiration of Babet," she said. Edwige's mother, Hortense, was especially
close to Elisabeth because they both loved to read; the two of them
would go on book-buying sprees together.

Although Elisabeth later claimed in several interviews, including
the radio interview of 1994, that she had felt like a "nettle in a field
of tulips" among the Avot family (une ortie dans un champ de tu-
lipes), she actually remained close to the Avots well into her adult-
hood. Edwige Becquart showed me several letters Elisabeth had
written to her parents in 1974 and 1976 that manifest a great deal of
affection and familiarity. She uses the familiar "tu" in addressing
both of them and calls them Tonton (uncle) and Mamie, terms of
endearment usually reserved for family members. She gives them
detailed news about her children and husband and thanks Hortense
for photos of recent get-togethers as well as for checks she had sent
as Christmas presents to Elisabeth's son and daughter. "There was
no question of celebrating Christmas without Babet," Becquart explained. Elisabeth's son, Fabrice, who was born in 1963 and whom
I interviewed in 2010, remembers frequent visits to the Avots with
his mother when he was a child. He was especially fond of Edwige
and thought of her children as his cousins, going horseback riding
and taking tennis lessons with them in Versailles. The relationship
cooled after the 1970s, however, in part because Elisabeth didn't
want to tell Hortense about her divorce and ran out of excuses why
her husband was not with her on her visits. Fabrice Gille, who has
lived in the United States for the past two decades, has not seen the
Avot family in a long time, he told me.[42]

Despite her cordial relations with the Avots, Elisabeth kept her
distance from them after graduating from the Sacré Coeur lycée.
"She took flight" (Elle a fait son envol) is how Edwige Becquart put
it. After obtaining her baccalauréat in 1953, she enrolled in two years
of "classes préparatoires" (*hypokhâgne* and *khâgne*), which prepare
students for the highly competitive entrance examinations to the
École Normale Supérieure, France's premier institution of higher

learning. Most students at Normale aim for an academic career, but many famous writers and philosophers, including Sartre and Simone Weil, have also been alumni of the school (women and men went to separate branches until 1985). In the end Elisabeth did not sit for the entrance examinations to Normale, but she did obtain several Certificats from the Sorbonne, based on year-end examinations in English language and literature. The examination records, which are conserved at the French National Archives, show that her grades were respectable although not brilliant: "Assez bien," about a *B+*, was her usual grade (the next grades up would have been "Bien" and "Très bien," the latter very rarely given). To the chagrin of Hortense, who admired her so, she did not obtain the *licence* degree, roughly equivalent to a bachelor of arts or a one-year master of arts today, apparently because she did not take the one remaining examination, in American literature and civilization, that would have granted it automatically with a passing grade.[43]

But even if somewhat short on academic achievement, her years of study at university endowed her with a good enough knowledge of English to become, not long afterward, a successful literary translator. And they opened doors to a whole new world for her. While she lived in the Avots' home in Versailles during her first year, attending hypokhâgne at the lycée in Versailles, she soon found places to stay in Paris. Her student card shows the Versailles address of 1953–1954 crossed out for subsequent years and replaced by addresses in the capital. Among the people she met there was her much older cousin Natacha, whose parents, Samuel Epstein and his wife, Alexandrine, had been deported to Auschwitz. Natacha, already a young woman during the war, had escaped to North Africa and survived that way. A full generation older than her cousins, Natacha Epstein Duché was a colorful figure, enjoying many friends and lovers of both sexes, according to Denise, who spoke about her with great verve and humor. To the twenty-year-old Elisabeth, she represented above all the allure of the intellectual life. Married to a prolific journalist and writer, Jean Duché, Natacha lived in an apartment full of books, which Elisabeth thought of as a kind of paradise, she told her friend Anka Muhlstein years later.[44] Natacha was one of the people, along with Denise and Elisabeth's children, to whom Elisabeth dedicated *Le Mirador* in 1992.

At the Sorbonne, Elisabeth made friends closer to her own age. One of these was Odile Roux, from a provincial Protestant family, who was also studying English literature. The two women remained best friends until Odile's untimely death from lung cancer in 1986. In 1960 Odile married Jean-Luc Pidoux-Payot, who ran his family's publishing firm, the venerable Éditions Payot, and who became a lifelong friend to Elisabeth as well as, eventually, to Denise. During her university years Elisabeth also met her future husband, Claude Gille, who worked for a children's publisher, the Éditions des Deux Coqs d'Or. They were married in 1957, when she was twenty and he twenty-three. Most of her friends were unimpressed by Claude and viewed Elisabeth as far superior in intelligence and personality (the couple eventually divorced).[45] Claude was not at all an intellectual, one of Elisabeth's friends told me, but still, he was part of a Parisian cultural milieu very far from the suburb of devout Catholics and wealthy businessmen in which she had grown up after the war. Marrying him may have facilitated her "taking flight" from the Avots and setting her sights on Paris and on literature. In September 1953, just before embarking on her university studies, she had gone to see her mother's old friend Jean-Jacques Bernard, who was one of Albin Michel's authors. Elisabeth had probably not read his book about his imprisonment during the war, *Le camp de la mort lente,* but she had no doubt read the moving preface he had written to Némirovsky's biography of Chekhov, published in 1946. After his meeting with her, Bernard wrote to the secretary at Albin Michel, asking her to send Elisabeth four volumes of his plays. This "younger daughter of Irène Némirovsky," he explained, was sixteen years old and "hungry for things to read."[46]

Over the next four decades Elisabeth Epstein Gille had plenty of opportunity to satisfy that hunger. She became a well-known, highly respected fiction editor in Paris, occupying increasingly powerful positions at some of France's top publishing houses. She also translated more than sixty books by English-language authors, from Mordecai Richler to J. G. Ballard, Patricia Highsmith, Alison Lurie, Kate Millett, and many others. During the last few years of her life, she became an author herself, publishing three widely praised books.

Denise, meanwhile, had found a different milieu in Paris. After two years at the bank, where she felt inept and out of place, even though everyone treated her with pity as her father's daughter (that was one reason she felt out of place, she later said), she quit her job. By then she had met her future husband, André Dauplé, a young veteran of the war in Indochina three years her senior who, like her, was living from hand to mouth doing odd jobs. As Denise told me, all their friends were in the same situation, "down and out and drifting," as per the very expressive French word *paumés*. But, she added, they were not unhappy. In the early 1950s Paris was still a place where you could spend a whole day in your favorite café without ordering more than a glass of water and then at night go to a Left Bank club to dance and listen to Juliette Greco sing. Existentialism was at its apogee, which meant, among other things, that "everyone wore black. So we always looked properly dressed!" Besides, "no one cared whether you were well dressed or not. We were all wounded, very wounded, but we shared what we had."[47] The accounting sent to Denise by the notaire Oudard in early 1952 shows that she still had 176,000 francs, equivalent to about $4,600 today, not exactly a fortune but something. Five years later, in January 1957, Maître Oudard reported, regretfully, that she had no more funds at all.[48]

Certain social niceties persisted despite the bohemian existence. On April 30, 1953, Denise Epstein-Némirovsky and André Dauplé were married in the Saint-Séverin church in the Latin Quarter and sent out printed announcements to that effect.[49] André's family, lower-middle-class provincial Catholics, "as boring as the town they lived in," according to Denise, were not happy when he told them he was marrying a Jewish woman—even though she had been Catholic since the age of nine. They insisted on a church wedding, and she did not object since she was still obsessed by a need for security. Getting the priest's "stamp" on her papers was very important to her at the time, she told me in 2011. The wedding announcement lists the couple's address as 35, rue de la Harpe, not far from the church; it is a building dating from the eighteenth century and looks quite beautiful today. Denise and André may have lived there briefly, but in October Denise wrote to André Sabatier to say that she was expecting a child in February and that she and her husband were living in a hotel room, badly in need of money.[50] The following year, at the end of December 1954, she writes a New Year's greeting to Robert Esménard: her husband has lost his job, and their family of three is living in a hotel room. The return address is in Montmartre, where Denise recalled living for two and a half years from the time of her first pregnancy.[51]

Her son Emmanuel was born in February 1954, followed two years later by another son, Nicolas, and three years after that by a daughter, whom she named Irène. By that time the family was living in a working-class suburb south of Paris called Villejuif (literally, "Jewtown," but the name is a corruption of the Latin Villa Juvius and has nothing to do with Jews). A few years later they moved to neighboring Massy, another working-class town, where they were able to buy a house and where Denise's husband and eventually Denise herself settled into modest jobs. André worked for a now-defunct company, SVP (S'il Vous Plaît, "please"), which provided "facts on demand" to subscribers, a useful tool in pre-Google days. Denise eventually found a job as a *documentaliste*, or archivist/researcher, in a government agency, the bureau for "repression of agricultural fraud." They both became active in union activities, and Denise also got involved in various left-wing movements, as did her older son, Emmanuel, when he came of age. Her husband was a union man, very respectful of legality, she told me, whereas she was willing to break the law from time to time, as she did in sheltering deserters during the Algerian war around 1960 and revolutionaries on the run from Chile and elsewhere a few years later. In the basement of their house she had a mimeograph machine, for printing leaflets she typed on an old typewriter. Denise attributed her rebellious streak and her always siding with those she considered unjustly persecuted to her own wartime drama. "With a past like mine," she told me, "we know what intolerance is, so why would we accept it when it concerns others? We can't."[52]

And where was the faithful Julie Dumot during those years? In light of how central a role she had played during the war and right after, when her name appeared on several official documents concerning the two girls, it is hard to believe she simply dropped out of their lives. But that is pretty close to what happened. After the war she obtained another position as companion to an aristocratic family in Paris. In March 1948, according to an identity card issued by the U.S. Immigration and Naturalization Service, she arrived in New York (whether alone or accompanied is not indicated) and was

admitted as an immigrant for permanent residence. She kept her
French citizenship, and in March 1952 she renewed her French
identity card at the consulate in New York, giving as her place of
residence an address in Allamuchy, New Jersey. By October 1954,
however, she was back in France. In a letter to a government office
she states she has returned definitively. This letter was somewhat
bizarre, requesting payments due to her for her "wards," but Denise
was already married and a mother, definitely not a ward. Elisabeth,
at seventeen, could still be considered technically Julie's ward but
had not been under her care for years.[53] On May 31, 1956, at the age
of seventy-one, Julie Dumot died of cancer in Bordeaux and was
buried in Cézac. During her last years she evidently had some contact with Denise, as some of her personal documents ended up in
Denise's possession after her death. But, curiously, Denise had few
kind words to say about her. Whereas Denise spoke with great affection about her "nounou" Cécile Michaud and continued to see
her and her family (Cécile's daughter is still in touch with Denise's
children), she largely avoided speaking about Julie, and, in fact, she
mostly refused to do so. She was grateful to Julie for having saved
her and her sister, she said, but Julie had "behaved badly" after the
war. Even Denise's children don't know exactly what she held against
Julie. They think there were some issues about money and property,
but, given Denise's refusal to speak about her, no one knows anything for sure. Denise did note in her book, however, that Elisabeth's
memories of Julie were more positive than her own.[54] Elisabeth's
friend Anka Muhlstein, who had worked with her in publishing in
the 1970s and maintained contact with her until her death, recalls
that Elisabeth sometimes spoke of Julie, always quite fondly. Indeed,
by a strange lapse of memory she told Anka she was hoping to hear
from Julie after she published *Le Mirador*, in 1992! At the time, Julie
Dumot would have been over 110 years old.[55]

Jewishness and Memory

Among the shared experiences of children hidden during the war
was that of having to deny their identity. The change of name carried with it the requirement to pretend to be someone else, and the
most important thing about that someone was that he or she was not

Jewish. Very often this involved actual baptism, but even a child who
was not baptized had to learn some basic rituals that were part of the
everyday life of many people in France, especially in the provinces:
attending Mass, if not regularly at least from time to time, making
the sign of the cross, kneeling, reciting prayers. The psychologist
Marion Feldman has posited, in her study of hidden children in
France, that all such children experienced psychological disturbances
in their relation to their personal past and to their family after the
war. She calls these disturbances "troubles de filiation," in distinction
to broader problems relating to group identity, "troubles d'affiliation."[56] In fact, Jewishness is both a family issue and a group issue, as
is Catholicism or any other religious identity, one can say. But given
the particular history of Jews in Europe, with its ongoing conflicts
both internal, including class differences (modernists versus tradi-
tionalists, Zionists versus assimilationists), and external, such as antisemitism and persecution, Jewish identity has always been more
problematic than the religious identity of the majority. This was
especially true for children who had lost their family in the war,
when their personalities were not yet formed and they lacked any
sense of stability or historical continuity.

It is extraordinary how often and how consistently one comes
across the theme of self-division or ambivalence linked to religion
in the memoirs of orphaned Jewish children. Emile Copfermann,
whose book I quoted earlier, writes that his aunt had him and his
brothers baptized "as an extra measure" before sending them to the
farm, which resulted in their going to church every Sunday. Ironi-
cally, the farmers they were living with had stopped going to church
years earlier but started going again because of the boys. Copfermann adds that he can still recite "Our Father" and "Hail Mary" but
has no knowledge whatever of the Torah or the Mishna. And while
he knows perfectly well how to make the sign of the cross, it was only
when he was over sixty years old that he learned how and why to
light Hanukkah candles.[57] Georges Perec, who was not only a Jewish
orphan but one of France's great twentieth-century writers, made
inner division the structural principle as well as a major theme in *W,
or the Memory of Childhood*, which alternates autobiographical chapters about the fragments of memory he retains from his childhood
with chapters of a science fiction novel that is itself broken in two.

And the philosopher Sarah Kofman, who lost her father when she was seven years old, recounts with shattering precision, in the memoir she wrote shortly before committing suicide, the struggle for her soul that went on between her Polish Jewish mother and the French Catholic woman who saved her during the war.[58]

One way to avoid inner conflict is not to think about it. And one way not to think about is to "forget" what one went through—or, at the very least, not to talk about it. The writer Berthe Burko-Falcman's father, Aron Falcman, a poor Polish tailor, served in the French army in 1940 but was arrested in 1941 as a foreign Jew and sent to the camp at Pithiviers, from where he was deported to Auschwitz on June 25, 1942, a few weeks before Irène Némirovsky. In the spring of 1942, when Berthe was seven years old, her mother arranged for her to live with farmers in Normandy, where she learned all the Catholic prayers and was due to be baptized on her eighth birthday. A week before her birthday, in February 1943, a messenger came to pick her up and take her to join her mother in a village in the southwest, where they survived the war together. But, she writes, "despite the missed baptism, for several years I felt Catholic in my own way." Berthe eventually married, became a teacher, and published three novels in the 1980s and 1990s based on her wartime and postwar experiences. But her memoir of childhood, *Un prénom républicain* (A republican first name), perhaps her most compelling work, did not appear until 2007, when she was seventy-two years old. She recalls that in the Yiddish-speaking summer camps where she and other Jewish children who had lost parents were sent after the war, none of the children talked about what they had gone through: "Maybe we didn't know that what had happened to us was unusual. With a few variations, we all had the same story. There was therefore nothing to say, and we didn't speak about it."[59] The psychoanalyst Denise Weill, who as a teenager was active in a group of Jewish scouts that took care of orphaned children in 1942, told me that after the war she and her surviving friends would get together to dance all night and have a good time: "We had worn the yellow star, we had lost parents, but we never talked about the past. We wanted to study, get married, have children," she said. Later, as an analyst, she realized that many child survivors, including herself, didn't talk about their past even in analysis. "Repression is a useful

defense mechanism," she observed. "It allows you to go on living."[60]
The neuropsychiatrist Boris Cyrulnik, in his slender book of reflections about how he survived the war after the deportation of his parents, explains that the compulsion to "always keep going forward"
(aller toujours de l'avant) became his strategy of survival for many
years, a defense against depression and helplessness.[61] This ability to
bracket off the most painful aspects of the past is an important com-
ponent of what Cyrulnik and other theorists of childhood trauma
call resilience, but it generally comes at a cost.

With a few notable exceptions most of the memoirs and testimonies by French child survivors of the Holocaust date from the
1990s or later. During the decade after the war, many children were
not only too young to give coherent accounts of their experience but
also, as Burko-Falcman and others make clear, unable to talk about
it, even with those who had lived through similar events. This temporal delay in recalling the painful past, while particularly poignant
in the case of children who had suffered the traumatic loss of a parent, is well known to theorists of trauma and occurs in adults as well.
Historians have pointed out that as far as the Holocaust is concerned,
the phenomenon of "forgetting" and delayed remembrance also occurred on a collective level. In the postwar years, in France and elsewhere, after a first brief flurry of fascination as the full horror of the
Nazi concentration camps became known, the public lost interest in
hearing survivors' stories. Annette Wieviorka, in her important book
Déportation et génocide, documents the large number of testimonies
by camp survivors that appeared right after the war but notes that
the public tired of them very quickly. Like the survivors themselves,
those who might have listened to them felt it necessary to move
on.[62] In her subsequent book, *L'ère du témoin* (*The Era of the Witness*),
Wieviorka concurs with other historians that the change in public
attitudes occurred after the trial of Adolf Eichmann in 1961. The
sudden recovery of public memory that followed the trial, gathering
speed and force over the following decades, occurred on both an individual and a collective level.

Like so many others, Denise and Elisabeth remained silent about
their childhood suffering for many years, even with each other—or
maybe especially with each other. "My aunt and her sister, my mother,
found it very hard to speak about all that, for decades," recalled Fab-

rice Gille. According to him, it was Elisabeth who most resisted speaking about the war, perhaps because she had so few personal memories of that time. "They had some fairly stormy conversations, when my mother said, 'Listen, I can't talk about it. I don't have your memories, I can't talk about it. It's not possible.'" The spell was broken one night when Denise was visiting them, sometime in the late 1970s—he couldn't remember the exact year, but it was after his parents had divorced, he thought. Elisabeth and her husband separated in 1975 and divorced two years later. "I had had enough of those conversations that didn't go anywhere. So I sat down with my aunt and said to her, 'Tell me my story.' My aunt started to talk and my mother was listening from the kitchen, and she started to hear things they had never been able to discuss between them . . . but it was a story told to me, not face-to-face between the two sisters."[63]

The importance of this moment was confirmed by Denise Epstein in 2011, when I interviewed her for the last time. This was our longest, most productive recorded conversation, maybe because by then I had known Denise for three years and we both felt relaxed. Toward the end she remarked that a life never moves in a straight line but in zigzags, especially for people who "lived through that." Her sister, for example, was focused on her career as an editor for many years, which was understandable. Elisabeth had eventually turned to writing only as a means of getting to know her past, and that was due above all to Fabrice. Denise then told me about that evening when Fabrice sat her down and asked her to "tell the story."

This anecdote illustrates beautifully what theorists of testimony have devoted many pages to explaining. In order for a story of trauma to be told, a sympathetic listener must ask to hear it, and it may take many years for that to happen. A close family member is not always the one who asks the crucial question. Denise Epstein's daughter, Irène, told me that her mother almost never spoke about her childhood with her own children but spoke about it freely with some of their friends. The friends asked, whereas her children, aware of how painful the subject was to her, made a point of not asking. "With someone who has suffered a lot," Irène said, "it's hard to say to them, 'Tell me. What exactly made you suffer?' So I have the impression that my own history is something I learned in fragments. And then, little by little, I glued the pieces together."[64] The feeling of a past cut off, one which can be reassembled only in pieces, is experienced not only by child survivors but also by their children and grandchildren.

If remembering and telling the story came late to Denise and Elisabeth, so did a proclaimed identification with Jewishness. Although Denise often said, in interviews and publications after the success of *Suite Française,* that her baptism meant nothing to her and that soon after she arrived at Notre Dame de Sion she insisted on no longer going to Mass because she was Jewish, her public behavior for many years points toward a fear of being identified as Jewish. She herself emphasized that for a long time she felt anxious and afraid, eager to get the Catholic "stamp" on her papers. She had a church wedding, made sure that all of her children were baptized, sent them to catechism to prepare them for their first communions, which they all had, and used the name Epstein only on occasion. Even in her last years, when she was very outspoken about her Jewishness, her mailbox in Toulouse bore the name Dauplé, not Epstein. Emmanuel recalls that up to the age of fourteen he was quite religious, going to church with his mother. He thought of the family as left-wing Catholics, and even after he had started asking questions and become an atheist, it never occurred to him they might be Jewish. Denise was afraid that the "whole thing could start over," and she wanted to protect her kids, make sure they were "just like everyone else." Her reaction was not at all unusual for that generation of Jews, Emmanuel remarked. Indeed, more Jews changed their names to sound "less Jewish" during the decade after the Second World War than in the preceding century and a half combined.[65] When I asked Emmanuel how he found out about his Jewish background, he said it was on the day he came home from a pro-Palestinian demonstration (he was very involved in left-wing politics as a young man) and found her crying. Why? Because she thought the demonstration was antisemitic—but it wasn't, he assured her, it was anti-Zionist. This was in the early 1970s, when he was eighteen or nineteen years old, he recalled. The discovery of his Jewish origins did not make much difference to him, as by then he was an atheist and opposed to all organized religions.[66]

As for Elisabeth, she rebelled against the conventional Catholicism of the Avots as soon as she had left the convent lycée. She did not marry in church, did not have her children baptized, and declared herself an atheist, as did her husband. She knew the story of her mother and father, of course, and had already read all of her mother's books as a teenager. But the question of Jewishness and Jewish identity did not concern her much, according to her own account as well as those of her friends whom I interviewed. For a long time she held the view that Sartre had made famous in his *Réflexions sur la question juive* (*Antisemite and Jew*): a Jew is someone whom others call Jew, there is no positive content to the term. She later said that she began to change after the birth of her children, at which point she "felt a genuine continuity" and "accepted the heritage of [her] parents."[67] Elisabeth's son was born in 1963 and her daughter in 1973, but it seems likely that her interest in Jewish history and culture as well as in her own past started in the late seventies, precisely at the time when Jewish memory of the Holocaust became a widespread collective phenomenon in France. It was not by pure chance that young Fabrice Gille asked his aunt to "tell the story" just around then: a desire to know and to tell was in the air.

These were the years when the first testimonies by orphans of the Holocaust were published in France (or anywhere, for that matter). Perec's *W, or the Memory of Childhood*, a book Elisabeth Gille admired greatly, appeared in 1975. In 1978 the historian Saul Friedländer, whose family had arrived in France from Prague in 1938 and whose parents had died in Auschwitz, published a moving memoir in which he captured the belated and fragmentary nature of his own and other child survivors' memories. The following year the psychologist Claudine Vegh, whose father had died in deportation, published her pioneering account of the life stories of eighteen men and women she had interviewed who had lost one or both of their parents, and in some cases their whole immediate family. Her interviewees had never told their stories until then, more than thirty years after the end of the war.[68]

Meanwhile, in 1978 Serge Klarsfeld, whose father had been deported to Auschwitz in 1943 and never returned, completed his monumental *Mémorial de la déportation des Juifs de France*, with its chronology of all the transports that had left France during the Occupation and the names of all the persons on each transport, based on the lists prepared by German and French authorities. Klarsfeld also indicated how many people each transport carried, where it left from and where it was heading (almost all to Auschwitz), and how many people were murdered immediately on arrival—they were the ones who were not even registered in the camp. Klarsfeld's book, the fruit of years of painstaking research, was self-published and available at first only to those in the know. Over the years it has undergone several new editions and is today known as a major landmark in Holocaust studies as well as in the furthering of Jewish memory. Many Jews in France have stated that "until Klarsfeld" they had never known exactly how and when and with whom their loved ones had been sent "to the East."

But in the 1950s, the outpouring of Jewish memory was barely on the horizon. In one of the autobiographical fragments in *Le Mirador*, Elisabeth Gille recounts that in 1957 she went to see *Night and Fog*, Alain Resnais's newly released documentary film about Nazi camps, and found the experience so wrenching that she stayed away from Holocaust-related works for many years. Resnais's short film, with its haunting music and poetic voiceover text written by a camp survivor, Jean Cayrol, who had been deported as a member of the Resistance, is rightly considered a masterpiece among Holocaust documentaries, but it never mentions that the huge majority of the Nazis' victims were Jews, and the word *Jew* hardly appears in it. In the 1950s and early 1960s no public distinction was made in France between men and women who had been deported because they had been members of the Resistance and those, including children and the elderly, who had been taken away and murdered for no reason other than who they were. The first French memorial to the deportation, the Mémorial des Martyrs de la Déportation near Notre Dame Cathedral, which was inaugurated in 1962 during Charles de Gaulle's first term as president, lumped all deportees together as having "died for France." This seems difficult to imagine today, when concentration camps are so overwhelmingly associated, in public memory, with the persecution of Jews. But it was of a piece with de Gaulle's long-standing policy of smoothing over internal divisions and remembering the war as a time of heroic resistance by "all of France." Odd as it may seem now, it was possible even for Jews, in the France of the immediate postwar years, to be outraged at Nazi crimes without necessarily confronting the specific issue of Jewish persecution or of Vichy's role in it.[69]

Elisabeth Gille was no exception. But as we know, the repressed has a way of returning in indirect ways. Starting in 1959 Elisabeth worked for more than nine years as a freelance translator before taking on her first full-time job as an editor at the Denoël publishing firm in October 1968.[70] The many books she translated during those years included literary fiction, thrillers, and children's books as well as essay collections and narrative nonfiction. Among her very first translations, published in 1960 when she was twenty-three, was Mordecai Richler's breakthrough novel, *The Apprenticeship of Duddy Kravitz*, which had appeared in English the previous year. Richler, the son and grandson of orthodox Polish Jewish immigrants who had settled in Montreal around the time of the First World War, was twenty-eight years old when he published *Duddy Kravitz*. It was his third novel, the one for which he is most widely remembered and the one that made him famous. It also made him controversial. Like his contemporary Philip Roth, whose *Goodbye, Columbus* was published the same year, Richler was blamed by some readers for making his Jewish characters look bad. The novel's protagonist is a fast-talking, wheeling-dealing young man who rises from his impoverished childhood in a Montreal slum to become a formidable real estate speculator, committing more than a few sins along the way. Duddy Kravitz is a fully realized character, sympathetically drawn with a largely comic brush, but he is also despicable in many ways. Fiercely loyal to his family, he is willing to betray friends and lovers who are devoted to him in order to get what he wants. Richler surrounds Duddy with a whole gallery of Jewish types, ranging from his pious grandfather and his studious older brother who becomes a doctor to the local Jewish gangster known as the Boy Wonder, much admired for his chutzpah by Duddy's father, a taxi driver.

The underlying question for many of the Jews who populate Richler's novel is how to define themselves in relation to other Jews and to Jewish traditions, in a society that is itself divided linguistically and religiously. Richler, an Anglo-Canadian who wrote the book partly in France while living in London, was the inhabitant of several worlds, not fully at home in any of them. When he returned to Montreal in 1960 he was often challenged by Jewish readers who faulted him for not being more positive in his portrayals of Jews. One of his published replies will sound familiar to readers who recall Némirovsky's attempts to explain herself to Jewish journalists after the publication of *David Golder*—or, for that matter, Roth's attempts to do the same regarding *Goodbye, Columbus*. Richler wrote, "Anyone who writes seriously is a moralist. But moralists are critical, and, to a large degree, no-saying. What I know best is my own background and so to some I appear to be only critical of the Jews."[71]

Considering the debates that still swirl around *David Golder*, there is an uncanny rightness about the fact that it was Némirovsky's daughter who rendered *Duddy Kravitz* into French. At the age of twenty-three, Elisabeth Gille, an alumna of many years of Catholic schooling who felt personally separated from anything resembling Jewish identity, suddenly found herself explaining Yiddish words and Jewish customs to French readers. Her translation of Richler's novel contains a noticeable number of translator's notes at the bottom of the page, which are of course not present in the original. Where a Richler character orders a "lean on rye," she has him ordering *pickle-fleich*, with a note that gives the recipe for corned beef; where Richler writes "dreck" or "shul," she reproduces the words (*choule* is a whole new experience in French), with a dictionary definition at the bottom of the page; and when it comes to words like B'nai Brith or Oneg Shabbat, she explains them, occasionally incorrectly, as when she defines *Oneg Shabbat*, a communal Sabbath celebration, as a "traditional meeting in Jewish youth movements." It is strange and wonderful to imagine the young translator poring over dictionaries and encyclopedias in order to learn something about the language and customs of the world her parents had sought so determinedly to leave behind.[72]

She signed her translation as Elisabeth Gille-Némirovsky, a hyphenated name she used only one other time in her prolific career as a translator and writer—and by another uncanny coincidence, that other time was in her translation of Isaac Deutscher's *"The Non-Jewish Jew" and Other Essays* (1969), which appeared in French under the title *Essais sur le problème juif* (Essays on the Jewish problem). Deutscher's most pithy statement, in the famous title essay from 1958, was that "the Jewish heretic who transcends Jewry belongs to a Jewish tradition." In other words, even those Jews who reject Judaism belong, paradoxically, to a Jewish lineage. Deutscher, a distinguished historian of Marxism who had been a child prodigy of the Talmud in his native Poland before abandoning Judaism and joining the Communist Party, clearly placed himself in the "heretic" category, along with an impressive list of those he called the "great revolutionaries of modern thought: Spinoza, Heine, Marx, Rosa Luxemburg, Trotsky, and Freud." Aside from their "heretical" Jewishness, which in the case of Heine and Marx included conversion, these thinkers all shared, according to Deutscher, the experience of living "on the borderlines of various civilizations, religions, and national cultures. . . . It was this that enabled them to rise in thought above their societies, above their nations, above their times and generations, and to strike out mentally into wide new horizons and far into the future."[73] In other essays in the book Deutscher writes with great acuity about Jewish history, literature, and art, focusing especially on eastern Europe and Russia, the areas he knew best from his own life and scholarship. He especially admired the works of Marc Chagall, who in his opinion combined a deeply Jewish sensibility with the avant-garde's rejection of conventions, including religious ones.

One can only speculate on what it meant to Elisabeth Gille, just starting out on her own career, to translate these works by Jewish writers, both of whom had obvious points in common with her mother. Like Némirovsky, Richler and Deutscher came from eastern European Jewish families, spoke several languages, and "lived on the borderlines of various civilizations" even while achieving literary and intellectual success in one. Like her, they were deeply aware of the dilemmas and contradictions of Jewish identity in modern times and explored them in their writings. Also like her, they were viewed with suspicion and anger by many Jews while being admired by others. One major difference among them was that Richler and Deutscher grew up in orthodox Jewish homes where Yiddish was spoken, while Némirovsky's parents were alienated from Jewish practice and from Yiddish. But she herself did know a few Yiddish words, which she used to great effect in *David Golder*. And it was from personal experience that she wrote about the disdain many Jews on their way to assimilation felt toward their more traditional, generally much poorer, coreligionists, who were sometimes members of their own family. Elisabeth Gille translated dozens of books in the decade between *Duddy Kravitz* and *The Non-Jewish Jew*, but these were the only two works on which she put her mother's name as well as her own.

It was not until a decade later, however, when she was a well-known Parisian editor, that Gille went public in identifying herself as a Jew and as a child survivor of the Holocaust who had lost both her parents to deportation. On April 18, 1979, she published an op-ed article in the daily *Le Monde*, which appeared directly beneath a report about four separate incidents involving Nazi graffiti and other vandalism of synagogues and of a Jewish community center over the previous week, during Passover. Her article, labeled a "Témoignage," or personal testimony, was titled "We Are Afraid" (Nous avons peur). "The events of the last few weeks have put me in such a state of anger and indignation that I feel obliged to be a witness," she began. She was referring not to the antisemitic incidents detailed in the article above hers but to a whole series of controversies involving the Holocaust that had occupied the public over the previous year. The latest of these was the indictment of a former Vichy official, Jean Leguay, for crimes against humanity because of his role in the mass roundup of Jews in Paris in July 1942. Gille mentions the Leguay indictment in her article as well as two other recent events: the screening of the television series *Holocaust* in February and March, which had occasioned heated debates, first about whether it should be shown at all and then about whether it was any good; and the sensational interview with another former Vichy official, the notoriously antisemitic Louis Darquier de Pellepoix, that had appeared in the liberal weekly *L'Express* a few months earlier. Darquier had headed the General Commissariat on Jewish Questions from 1942 to 1944 and had been tried after the war—but it was in absentia, for he had escaped to Spain after the Liberation and lived there undisturbed ever since. The interview, with a journalist who had traveled to Spain to see him, had been featured on the magazine's cover under a sensational headline quoting Darquier: "In Auschwitz, the only things that were gassed were lice." *L'Express* was not endorsing the opinions of this unrepentant Nazi sympathizer, but the magazine was still blamed by many people for the provocative way it had presented them.[74]

Elisabeth Gille expresses outrage at these and other recent exploitations of the Holocaust, but the real interest of her article lies elsewhere. This was the first piece she published as an author rather than a translator, and the first piece in which she told her family's story, even if only in summary form. In the opening paragraphs she evokes the deportation of her parents and other relatives and emphasizes her mother's life and career: "My mother's name was Irène Némirovsky." Assuming, quite correctly, that most readers have not heard of Némirovsky, she provides details: her Russian immigrant background, her prominence as a writer after the success of *David Golder*, her conversion to Catholicism. Gille emphasizes that her parents were arrested by French *gendarmes* and that she and her sister escaped arrest only at the last minute. She then declares that "the time for discretion being over" (l'heure n'étant plus à la pudeur), she wants to say what it means to be an orphan in such circumstances. Aside from the pain experienced by any child who loses her parents and is therefore unable to express "normal feelings of love or hate" toward them, it means the loss of "roots and identity, since there is no one there to tell you where you came from, and you possess neither tombs nor memories." And it means that "you yourself are negated," part of an "immense attempt to abolish the Jewish people." This is quite a surprising statement on the part of a woman who not that many years earlier had subscribed to the idea that Jews existed as a people only in the minds of antisemites. The moment appears to have been a turning point in Elisabeth Gille's life, as in the lives of many other Jews in France—and like most turning points it was part of a much longer process that unfolded over many years and became visible when the time was right.

This was that time, Elisabeth affirmed. The only real reason for dwelling on the past is to make it illuminate the present, she wrote in conclusion. The current obsession with the Holocaust was justified only if it led to reflections on *contemporary* antisemitism. The French must "ask themselves why they are, still now, antisemites, racists, and xenophobes." She then reports that in her son's high school the walls are covered with Nazi slogans and graffiti, and a teacher who refused to allow a student to attend Carnival in a Nazi costume was jeered at as a "whore for Jews." She adds that she has been asked to join the suit against Leguay as one of the plaintiffs and has not yet decided whether to do so, but if she does, it will not be in order to honor the memory of her parents, "who don't need that and who died horribly, for nothing." Rather, it will be in order to defend herself and her children and the other children at the lycée who had gone to their teacher and told her, "*Madame*, defend us, we are afraid." The title of the article thus is a quote, referring to a general fear among Jewish children (and adults?) in France. This information too may come as a surprise to a reader today. We are used to hearing about the fear and unease of French and European Jews in the wake of recent terrorist attacks but may not be aware of similar fears that existed more than thirty years ago. Elisabeth Gille was writing at a time when "Islamic judeophobia," a frequently used term today that exempts non-Muslim French people, was not yet in circulation.[75] She was protesting against good old-fashioned French antisemitism and xenophobia, as represented by Leguay and his ilk.

Was she right in claiming that these noxious prejudices were still alive in France, unchanged? Fortunately, we don't need to decide that question, for to do so adequately would require a whole other book. (The short answer is yes and no.) One thing we can say with assurance is that over a period of many years, under the pressure of both internal and external events, Elisabeth Gille evolved from a position of indifference to questions of Jewish identity and Jewish existence to a position of personal engagement. And her evolution mirrored that of a number of other Jewish intellectuals in France, including some who, like herself, had lost their parents in the Holocaust.

Pierre Vidal-Naquet, a world-renowned classicist and one of France's most respected public intellectuals—he had been among the first to protest against the use of torture by the French army in Algeria in the 1950s—was among them. He came from a family of Israélites long established in France, but that fact did not prevent both of his parents from being deported to Auschwitz. Like most Israélites, Vidal-Naquet grew up in a highly secular household, revering the French Republic and knowing very little about Jewish traditions and Jewish history. But starting in the 1960s, when he first studied the history of the Dreyfus Affair, he wrote increasingly about issues concerning Jews, and in the late 1970s he led the charge against Holocaust denial, a rabid version of which had hit France

during those years in the work of Robert Faurisson. In the preface
to his first collection of essays on Jewish themes, published in 1981,
Vidal-Naquet wrote touchingly, "It is not so much because I'm Jewish that I wrote these pages, but rather the opposite: it was in writing
this book, and a few other works, that I became a Jew, a voluntary
Jew one might say, or a Jew through reflection."[76]

This was the time when Elisabeth Gille published her article in
Le Monde. Over the next decade and a half, discussions and debates
about the Holocaust and its consequences would become the regular stuff of front-page news in France, as the trials of Klaus Barbie,
the notorious Nazi official captured in Bolivia in 1984 and extradited
to France, and of prominent Vichy functionaries, most notably
Maurice Papon, who had organized the roundups of Jews in Bordeaux, ground their way through the courts. Jewish memory, at first
a trickle, would become a torrent as literally thousands of survivor
testimonies were collected and many were published.

During these years Elisabeth Gille and Denise Epstein mounted
serious efforts to revive their mother's writings and to study the life
that had made them possible. In the process, they saw their own lives
transformed.

CHAPTER SEVEN

Gifts of Life

A Mother and Her Daughters

Every book of my mother's that is published brings her back into the world of the living.

—DENISE EPSTEIN

Suddenly, we had a family heritage.

—LÉA DAUPLÉ, Némirovsky's great-granddaughter

ACCORDING TO LEGEND, THE manuscript of Némirovsky's *Suite Française*, written in a notebook in tiny lettering to save paper, lay for decades in a suitcase, unread. The suitcase, containing papers and photographs as well as the precious notebook, had been handed to Denise by her father on the day he was arrested, with the admonition to never let go of it. After the war she and her sister had continued to treasure it, but they thought the notebook contained their mother's personal journal and were not able to bring themselves to read it. Then one day decades later, Denise opened the notebook, saw that it was a novel, transcribed it—and the rest is history.

The story is "beautiful and tragic," wrote a journalist who repeated the oft-told tale in October 2014.[1] Like all legends, however,
this one has only an approximate link to reality. The reality, in this
case, is just as compelling and has the advantage of being true. But
as usual, the truth is complicated and messy and requires patience in
the telling. Here are a few facts to start with: Denise and Elisabeth
knew about their mother's novel from early on and did not try to
hide that fact. Denise showed the manuscript to at least one journalist in the 1950s, who thought it unpublishable because it was "unfinished." Denise's son Emmanuel Dauplé recalls that his mother transcribed the manuscript more than once, while her daughter Irène
remembers knowing about it since she was a child. Denise herself
mentioned it, "a fat manuscript in my possession," on a radio program in 1992, when Némirovsky's name started to crop up again
after the publication of Elisabeth's *Le Mirador*, which also mentions
it several times. When I first met her, in 2008, Denise told me she
and her sister had been aware of the work for many years but were
uncertain about publishing it. Elisabeth especially, ever the professional editor, worried about the fact that it was unfinished and that
their mother had not had the chance to polish it. As we know, Némirovsky herself had offered to send part 1 of the novel to the editor of
Gringoire, Horace de Carbuccia, as soon as she had finished it, in
June 1941. The Némirovsky archives contain a very old typescript
of the whole work on onionskin, probably done by Michel Epstein,
who typed Irène's manuscripts during the war. The typescript dif-
fers from the handwritten version, sometimes considerably. It is not
clear who did the editing and revisions or exactly when, but after a
quick perusal my impression was that they did not improve on the
original. The revisions show signs of overwriting and striving for
effects—for example, where the manuscript speaks simply of "birds
singing," the typescript chooses the more precious "sparrows chirp-
ing." Denise was right to use only the original manuscript for the
publication of 2004.[2]

This chapter will tell a complicated story with a happy ending,
at least as far as the fortunes of Irène Némirovsky and her descendants are concerned. But even the happiest tale may have a bitter
undertone, especially if it involves Jewish identity in modern times.

In Limbo: Némirovsky in the Postwar

At the time she was deported, in July 1942, Némirovsky had been urging Albin Michel to publish two books of hers that were ready and waiting, the novel *Les Biens de ce monde* (*All Our Worldly Goods*), which had been serialized in *Gringoire* under a pseudonym in 1941, and *La Vie de Tchekhov*, which she had completed around the same time. She had also finished another novel, *Les Feux de l'automne* (*The Fires of Autumn*), written hastily in 1941–1942, which had never been published. In addition, there were some unpublished stories, a novel serialized in 1939 but never published as a book, and a novella, *Chaleur du sang* (*Fire in the Blood*), that was found by her biographers in the Albin Michel archives only after *Suite Française* had appeared. And there was *Suite Française* itself. Some of these works took decades to be published, but three were issued relatively soon after the war.

Albin Michel had contracted, while Némirovsky was still alive, to publish the Chekhov biography and *All Our Worldly Goods*, and they fulfilled their obligation by issuing them as soon as it became possible to do so after the war. *La Vie de Tchekhov* appeared in October 1946 with a substantial preface by Jean-Jacques Bernard, who succeeded in expressing his admiration and affection for Némirovsky and his outrage at the murder of "six million victims" of the Nazis without ever pronouncing the word *Jew*. "Born in the East, Irène went on to perish in the East," he wrote. But she was deeply integrated into her adopted country, he added. Her writing shows no trace of her "foreign origin," and she must be mourned as a "French writer."[3] Less than a year later, in March 1947, Albin Michel brought out *All Our Worldly Goods*, with no preface. These posthumous works received very few reviews, generally positive but quite short. Ineluctably, Némirovsky's name was slipping into oblivion. The war had brought into prominence a whole new set of writers, including a few women, who were identified, rightly or wrongly, with the Resistance and with the Left. Sartre, Camus, Gary, Beauvoir, Elsa Triolet were among the newly famous. At the same time, the "chers Maîtres" of the Académie Française who had constituted the prewar establishment and on whose support Némirovsky had always counted were discredited by their less-than-stellar record of resistance to the occupant, to put it understatedly, for some were outright collaborators during the war. Besides, most of these Académiciens were now elders displaced by the new generation, whether Left or Right politically. Némirovsky had never been part of the aesthetic avant-garde, which also gained new prominence in the years after the war. The worldwide recognition of Samuel Beckett and Nathalie Sarraute, both of whom had published before the war but became known only with their postwar works, was accompanied in the 1950s and early 1960s by the rise of the *nouveau roman,* the so-called new novel, whose practitioners rejected the kind of social and psychological realism in fiction that Némirovsky had excelled at.

In the immediate postwar years Denise and Elisabeth were too young to have any role in promoting their mother's work. Whatever negotiations occurred would have to be between the publisher and the girls' guardian, Julie Dumot, who was not qualified for the task. By the time *The Fires of Autumn* appeared, in the spring of 1957, Némirovsky's daughters, especially Denise, who was not employed at the time, could be more actively involved. In April 1957, soon after its publication, the French-language Swiss newspaper *Tribune de Lausanne* ran a long article on Némirovsky in its Sunday edition, featuring it as the main piece on its literary page. Signed by one J. Daven, it was actually written by the journalist and artist Catherine Descargues, who had interviewed Denise and corresponded with her in preparing it. Illustrated with two photos of Némirovsky furnished by Denise, the article was headlined, "At the moment when her last book appears: Remember Irène Némirovsky." It began as follows: "There was no news of her since 1939, but with this publication we see the reappearance of Irène Némirovsky, one of the most famous women novelists before the war." The journalist goes on to evoke Némirovsky's death in Auschwitz, then gives a detailed, very positive review of the new book. Most important, from our point of view, she refers to the writer's older daughter, who had told her about the family's refuge in a village during the war. "*The Fires of Autumn* was written then, under those conditions, along with another book, unfortunately unfinished, which would no doubt have counted among the writer's major works: '*Suite Française.*'" For a very long time, the existence of these works was unknown, the article states, but when the guardian of Irène Némirovsky's two daughters died, among her belongings was found a suitcase containing "the novelist's last writings."[4]

When I discovered this obscure article in the online archives of a Swiss newspaper that no longer exists under that name (the *Tribune de Lausanne* became the tabloid *Le Matin*, which is still in existence), I experienced one of those moments that researchers long for: an important piece in a puzzle had fallen into place. Julie Dumot, who died in 1956, must have stowed the suitcase away for safekeeping during the war, which made perfectly good sense, for how could she or, more improbably still, the twelve-year-old Denise have carried the thing around with them during their years in hiding? But it was troubling to think that Julie had hung on to the suitcase after the war, when by all rights she should have turned it over to Némirovsky's publisher or to the notaire who was handling the girls' assets. If the article is right about dates, she did not part with the suitcase even when she returned from the United States in 1954, by which time Denise, one of its rightful owners, was a grown woman. Denise often hinted that Julie had done something dishonest, without further explanation. If this article is correct, it explains both Denise's anger at Julie and the ten-year gap between the publication of the two earlier posthumous books and *The Fires of Autumn*. We know that Albin Michel paid an advance on royalties for *The Fires of Autumn* to Denise and Elisabeth in November 1956, just a few months after Julie Dumot's death.[5]

So the story about the suitcase revealing its contents after many years is not completely wrong—it merely simplifies things for greater dramatic effect. One can only wonder what would have happened if *Suite Française* had been published when it first came to light, circa 1957. Denise had apparently sent the manuscript to Descargues with the idea of publishing it, and the journalist wrote to her a few days before the *Tribune de Lausanne* article appeared, returning the photos Denise had sent and promising to return the manuscript very soon. She had found it "altogether remarkable," she wrote, then added, "It's really a pity that, being unfinished, it can't be published."[6] In fact, *Suite Française* as it currently exists has a perfectly acceptable ending with the departure of German troops from the occupied village in June 1941, almost exactly one year after the story begins.

Némirovsky made copious notes for a sequel, but the novel as it is, spanning the first year of German occupation, stands on its own. She had been willing even to publish just the first part, "Storm in June," separately. Her failure to find a publisher for it in 1941, which made her feel so bitter, turned out to be providential, and quite possibly the categorical response Denise received from the journalist in 1957, that "being unfinished, it can't be published," was fortunate as well. It is not at all certain, given the literary context at the time, that *Suite Française* would have been met with the same admiration it received in 2004. The nouveau roman was just gaining momentum, and *Suite Française* was definitely not that. Nor was there much interest in fiction about the Second World War or the Holocaust. The first French novel to evoke the Holocaust, André Schwarz-Bart's *The Last of the Just*, did not appear until 1959. Even nonfiction works now considered classics, like Elie Wiesel's *Night*, Charlotte Delbo's *None of Us Will Return*, and Primo Levi's *If This Is a Man* (known in America as *Survival in Auschwitz*), were either unknown or not yet published. *Night* appeared in French in 1958 and was translated into English two years later; Delbo's book, written quite early, was not published until 1970; and Levi's book, published in Italy in 1946, had sold only a few hundred copies and was not translated into French until 1961. Besides, *Suite Française* was not a book about the Holocaust but a historical novel about French civilian life during the first year of German occupation. Realist historical fiction about the Second World War that did not deal with heroic feats, preferably by men, was not much of a sell in the France of the 1950s. In fact, after the flurry of novels and memoirs published right after the war had died down, there was little interest even in heroic stories. Beauvoir's *The Mandarins*, which won the Prix Goncourt in 1954, could be considered an exception, but its subject was the postwar, with only glancing references to the period of the Occupation. The historian Henry Rousso has called the 1950s the period of repression about the Vichy years in France. By the time *Suite Française* finally appeared, fifty years later, France had acquired a huge appetite for works about the Second World War and the Holocaust, so huge that Rousso has qualified it as an obsession.[7]

In fact, the obsession had started quite a bit earlier, in the 1980s, and one may wonder why *Suite Française* was not published then. It could probably have found a publisher, especially given Elisabeth Gille's connections. The people I spoke with offered various explanations for the delay, none of them documented. According to some, Gille was against publication because she too considered the novel unfinished, and not as good as it would have been had her mother lived to complete and revise it. Others claim that Elisabeth wanted to write her own book about Némirovsky before publishing the novel and that her sister went along with that. No doubt a host of factors created the delay, some based on conscious choice, some on the demands of everyday life, and some on pure chance.

Meanwhile, after the publication of *The Fires of Autumn*, which received almost no reviews even though it was advertised by Albin Michel as the posthumous work of a "great woman novelist who died in deportation," Némirovsky's fortunes in public memory continued to decline. *David Golder* remained in print at Grasset throughout all those years. But in 1965 Albin Michel still had several thousand unsold copies of the Chekhov biography and *The Fires of Autumn*; only a hundred or so of *All Our Worldly Goods* remained, but that was because they had pulped five thousand copies two years earlier. The books they had published during Némirovsky's lifetime were all out of print, except for two titles of which a few hundred copies remained. These were the numbers Albin Michel provided to Elisabeth's husband, Claude Gille, in response to a letter in which he requested an accounting (he signed the letter C. Gille-Némirovsky).[8]

After that, it was close to total silence for many years. But in July 1983 Albin Michel received a letter from someone who said he was doing research on Némirovsky and who wondered which of her books were still available. He had recently acquired her letters to André Sabatier, he said (Sabatier had died ten years earlier). Could they send him the addresses of her daughters? The publisher supplied the addresses but then cautioned, "Please be aware that our last correspondence with the heirs dates back to June 1972."[9] During the intervening years Denise's children had grown up and left home, and she and her husband had gotten divorced. A few years later she moved to Toulouse, where her older son and daughter lived. Elisabeth too was divorced by then and had already published her article in *Le Monde* about being a child survivor of the Holocaust. And she had met, through her friend Odile Pidoux-Payot, the Yiddishist and specialist in American Jewish literature Rachel Ertel, who introduced her to the Cercle Gaston Crémieux, a group of secular Jewish intellectuals she would be involved with until her death.[10] The Cercle, named after a nineteenth-century liberal Jewish writer, had been founded in 1967 by Richard Marienstras, a professor of Elizabethan literature at the Sorbonne whose family had emigrated to France from Poland before the war. Ertel, herself an immigrant from Poland who had survived the war as a child with her mother in the Soviet Union, was among the Cercle's earliest members, along with Pierre Vidal-Naquet and Berthe Burko-Falcman, both of whom had lost parents to deportation. Jacques Burko, the latter's husband, edited the group's journal, *Diasporiques,* for many years (it ceased publication in 2007). The Cercle defined itself, and still does, on its website, as "a Jewish, secular, diasporist discussion group committed to the Left."[11] A few years before Elisabeth Gille joined them, Marienstras had published a book whose title sounds like a manifesto: *Être un peuple en diaspora* (Being a people in diaspora). According to Marienstras, Jews were a people, perhaps even a nation, but not a *nation-state.* He supported the existence of Israel but opposed the idea that all Jews should emigrate to Israel. His view of Jewish existence was, as he put it, that of a dreamer, for he thought it possible to affirm one's Jewishness and to belong to a Jewish community even while rejecting all three of the major solutions, Zionism, assimilationism, religious orthodoxy.[12] "Diasporism" as he defined it was a fine line to walk. Basically, he called for the embrace of multiple identities and allegiances, for "dispersion" as a way of life, but one in which Jewishness as a cultural and historical belonging would play a vital role. How this balancing act was to be achieved remained unclear and has not become clearer since then.

One of Elisabeth's close friends at the time told me that Elisabeth had several circles of friends, which she kept quite separate.[13] The Cercle Gaston Crémieux was only one of them, but it doubtless played a role in her growing affirmation of a certain Jewishness. It would lead her to request, when she was dying of cancer in 1996, that she be buried according to Jewish funeral rites, presided over by a rabbi. It would also lead her, in the last decade of her life, to delve more and more deeply into her own and her mother's past—and to write about them.

Out of the Shadows: *Le Mirador*

In the late 1980s Némirovsky's publishers started, somewhat cautiously, to reissue her works. Grasset, in addition to *David Golder*, which it had always kept in print, brought out *Le Bal* in their quality paperback series Les Cahiers Rouges in 1985 and followed it a few years later with the two other works they owned by her, *Les Mouches d'automne* (*Snow in Autumn*) and *L'Affaire Courilof* (*The Courilof Affair*). Albin Michel, not to be left behind, reissued *The Wine of Solitude* and *The Dogs and the Wolves* in 1988, and *The Life of Tchekhov* a year later. No one noticed these books, but at least they were available. And in the meantime Elisabeth and Denise were talking seriously about writing a biography of their mother. As Elisabeth Gille explained in interviews, someone had contacted Némirovsky's publisher, presumably Albin Michel, with a proposal for a biography. But she did not like that idea, and she and Denise decided to write one together. It was to be a "classic biography, coauthored, based on documents."[14] Denise, putting to use her experience as a researcher and her excellent typing skills, went to work gathering her mother's papers and transcribing some of her journals and other manuscripts. Albin Michel had all the professional correspondence in its archives, and Madeleine Cabour had handed over the letters Irène and Michel had sent her during the Sorbonne years and during the war. Denise also combed through the periodicals at the National Library, digging up dozens of stories and articles Némirovsky had published in newspapers and magazines. Perhaps most precious of all, she could refer to personal memories of her mother, from a time when Elisabeth was not even born. She later recalled that working on the book brought her and her sister together in a new and very positive way. It also brought them closer to their shared childhood: they visited Issy-l'Évêque together in the summer of 1990, for what appears to have been the first time since the war.[15]

Many children of famous parents have written books about them. But even if they avoid the "Mommy Dearest" genre of recrimination, their emotional involvement makes the usual stance of a biographer, sympathetic but distant, engaged but dispassionate, impossible to maintain. The most successful such books take the form of "My Father [or, more rarely, My Mother] the Writer, Artist, etc.," with the child clearly implicating him- or herself as a privileged, if sometimes pained, observer. Alexandra Styron's and Susan Cheever's books about their self-centered, brilliant fathers come to mind, as does, closer to home, Dominique Fernandez's book about his father, who became a collaborator during the war.[16] The solution Elisabeth and Denise finally settled on was different and highly original. Elisabeth decided to write the book herself, with Denise contributing documents and memories—but it would not be a "classic biography." Instead, she would write it in the voice of her mother, producing something between a biography and a first-person novel. *Le Mirador* is subtitled "mémoires rêvées," dreamed memories. Irène was the presumed memoirist, but Elisabeth was the dreamer/author and historian as well, for she did a tremendous amount of background reading, as she explains in her acknowledgments, and incorporated many documents from Némirovsky's archives into the book. This is where Denise's help was precious. Adding yet another layer, Elisabeth inserted occasional brief fragments about "the child," herself, bearing dates from March 1937, just after her birth, to October 1991. The book opens and closes with these fragments, which are written in the third person, as if to emphasize the difficulty of drawing clear boundaries between history, objective or at least verifiable, and dream, or invention. It is the autobiographical fragments that appear as history, told by an objective voice, while the subjective account of Irène Némirovsky's life and thoughts is a literary invention, even if one based on historical research. Elisabeth Gille was a great admirer of Perec's *W, or the Memory of Childhood* (she even quotes from it on the first page of *Le Mirador*), which consists of two parallel narratives, one totally fictional and one autobiographical. Perec is famous for this formal innovation, which allowed him to compensate for his lack of childhood memories—his father died in the war, and his mother was deported when he was six years old—by inventing a fictional story that mirrored both his and his mother's stories indirectly. Elisabeth created her own version of a split narrative by interspersing Irène's reconstructed story with her own and Denise's scattered but actual memories.

She had to confront another problem, however: How to tell her mother's story, most of which took place "before Auschwitz," without imposing on it her own post-Holocaust perspective? In concrete terms, without judging it? As we have seen throughout this book, some of Irène Némirovsky's choices during the 1930s and even in the first years of the war appear unfortunate, if not downright reprehensible, in retrospect. Elisabeth allowed herself to criticize her mother in interviews, including the one that appeared as a postface to the new edition of *Le Mirador* in 2000, and she had no trouble speaking about her mother with a certain distance, which was why she never referred to Némirovsky in public as Maman, always by her name. But in the book itself she did not want to adopt the position of a judge, which is the usual consequence of "backshadowing," that is, expecting a person in the past to have known what we know later. As Elisabeth told Myriam Anissimov in 1992, "I had to confront the problem of their [her parents'] blindness. That is one reason I wrote [Irène's story] in the first person. I didn't want to set myself up in an attitude of reproach toward them."[17]

Still, the problem obviously bothered her: How to tell the story without papering over those choices made by her parents that she, and no doubt others of her generation, found questionable or even deplorable but without condemning them or standing in judgment over them? This is a problem that confronts anyone writing about Némirovsky, as about many other assimilated Jews in Europe during the interwar period, but it is especially vexed if the writer is the subject's own daughter. Elisabeth Gille solved the problem, as she herself explained, by dividing the book into two parts. In part 1 she imagines Irène writing about her life in November 1929, shortly after the birth of her daughter Denise. She recounts her childhood in Kiev, including the pogrom of 1905, the trips to France before the First World War, the upheavals of the Revolution and exile, before ending on a highly optimistic note: Her family had made the right choice by settling in France, "the country of moderation and freedom, and generosity too," which had "definitively adopted" her as she had adopted it.

After this bit of tragic irony, we skip to July 1942: Irène is sitting in her favorite spot for writing, the woods outside Issy-l'Évêque, wearing the yellow star—and she is no longer optimistic. By constructing the book this way, Elisabeth told Anissimov, "I could have my mother say things in 1929 that she no longer recognized in 1942."[18] More to the point, she could have her mother say things in

1942 that showed remorse over her earlier choices. In the opening chapter of part 2 (chapter 9), Elisabeth imagines Némirovsky just days before she was deported, "crying with rage" when she rereads the pages written by her younger self. How could she have been so blind to what was happening around her? Even if a certain obliviousness was excusable in a "frivolous young girl" who had already seen too much death and destruction, was it not downright "criminal on the part of the happy and fulfilled woman I was in 1929, and that I remained until I arrived here?"[19] The "crime" she reproaches herself for was her indifference to the rise of right-wing, antisemitic movements in France as early as the 1920s and her later hostility to "foreigners" fleeing Hitler's Germany.

Elisabeth Gille's solution as author, then, consisted in having Némirovsky herself express a judgment that her daughter refused to pronounce. She even imagines her mother foreseeing her daughters' dilemma, for on the same page where Némirovsky calls her earlier self practically a criminal, she also asks, "If things go badly, very badly, what will my daughters think of me? What will they reproach me for, with good reason, in ten or twenty years, when they will be grown women?" One has the impression at moments like this that Elisabeth Gille wanted to "tell all" about her mother, holding nothing back, but also wanted to protect her and in a sense to excuse her or at least to explain her choices to a later generation. The temporal distance between subject and author, or reader, is hinted at in the book's title. A mirador, from the Spanish *mirar*, "to look," is an observation tower, most often associated these days with prisons and concentration camps. The word emphasizes the importance of seeing and being seen but also of perspective and point of view, which shift with time. In the book's original edition the title appeared on the cover above a photo of Némirovsky in her youth, looking radiant. Elisabeth Gille explained to a journalist that she had sought that contrast: "I wanted the tragedy to be present, next to my mother's smiling face."[20]

A persecuted woman who bitterly regrets her earlier errors and even imagines her daughters reproaching her for them after her death necessarily elicits sympathy. In real life none of Némirovsky's wartime writings suggest that she underwent that kind of transformation. She expressed rage and despair at what was happening to her, and she judged the French elites harshly, both in her journals and in the narrator's ironic observations in *Suite Française*. But she showed no remorse over her own earlier views and never sought to justify or explain them. Elisabeth Gille, by contrast, provides fairly detailed explanations and comparisons, based on her historical research, that serve as a kind of apology for her mother. For example, she imagines a dinner party at Némirovsky's home in 1933, shortly after Hitler had come to power, when the first influx of Jewish refugees was arriving from Germany. Among the guests are two visitors from New York, the psychoanalyst Alfred Adler and his wife, Raïssa, who was a relative of Michel Epstein. The others are Emmanuel Berl and Daniel Halévy, two French intellectuals with Israélite pedigrees (though Halévy's family had converted to Protestantism before he was born), who both express hostility toward the newly arriving foreigners. The presence of these immigrants will harm the "integrated Jews who have been in France for centuries," says Berl. The historical Berl railed against "undesirable" immigrants in his political articles of the late 1930s, calling them a threat to French culture, but he didn't explicitly frame his arguments in terms of Jews.[21] Alfred and Raïssa, who have left-wing sympathies, are appalled at Berl's statement. But Gille's Némirovsky writes, "I confess I shared Berl's ideas: I took the measure of his blindness, and of my own, only in 1940, when I learned that he had followed Pétain to Vichy and even wrote two of his speeches."

Berl did indeed write Pétain's first speeches, including the famous one of June 25, 1940, in which Pétain condemned the "left-wing" ideas he associated with the 1930s—and with Jews and Freemasons. A sentence from that speech, "I hate the lies that did you [France] so much harm," is among Pétain's most-often-quoted statements, partly because of its poetic cadence. Elisabeth too quotes it in her book (on page 354). But it is not certain that Némirovsky herself would have blamed Berl for writing that speech (his authorship was not public knowledge at the time), and even less so that she realized his and her own "blindness." As we know, she herself wrote to Pétain in September 1940 to request that he consider her an honorable foreigner, not an undesirable one. Elisabeth Gille reproduces her letter in full, but she has Irène say it was her husband who had insisted she write it (387). This is a perfect example of the "tell all but protect" impulse that dominates the book. The same impulse accounts for the historical explanations and analyses she puts into Némirovsky's mouth, such as this one: "My arrival in France after the Great War had persuaded me that antisemitism no longer existed here. We foreigners had a very elevated idea of this country: the land of the Revolution, of freedom, of the rights of man. . . . We would never have imagined that it could betray us" (355). Or, a few pages later, "In Israélite milieux like mine, discretion was the rule. . . . In our crowd, everyone insisted on the distinction that Maurras himself [Charles Maurras, the founder of the right-wing Action Française] drew, between 'well-born Jews,' those who had been in France for generations and had given their blood for the fatherland, and those people that we ourselves considered to be 'immigrants of the dregs' [immigration de déchet]" (358–59).

There was one issue on which Elisabeth Gille was not in a position to tell all. It concerns Louis-Ferdinand Céline, the brilliant writer whose pathological antisemitism has presented a problem for several generations of critics. In 1932 Céline had become justly famous with his first novel, Journey to the End of Night (Voyage au bout de la nuit), which revolutionized French fiction by introducing the rhythms and vocabulary of slang into a highly stylized, poetic language. Journey is an angry book, lashing out at the whole world, but there can be no doubt that it is a masterpiece, and one would have to look very carefully to detect any sign of antisemitism in its pages. Five years later, however, after another novel, Mort à crédit (Death on the Installment Plan), in which he pushed his ranting style even further, Céline published Bagatelles pour un massacre, the first of his so-called antisemitic "pamphlets." Bagatelles is not a slim pamphlet but another long rant of a novel, featuring as narrator Céline's alter ego Ferdinand, whose favorite mode of expression is the incomplete sentence ending in three dots or an exclamation point. But this time the target of Ferdinand's anger and hatred is specified: it's the Jews, who are to blame for both his own and the whole world's miseries. Bagatelles became a runaway best seller and was followed by two other similarly hateful works, L'École des cadavres in 1938 and Les Beaux draps in 1941. All three "pamphlets" were banned from Céline's complete works by his and his heirs' decision, but they are available as PDFs online and have also recently been published together in a scholarly edition in Canada.²² Despite the general acknowledgment of his extraordinary linguistic gifts, which were again manifested in several novels published after the war, Céline remains to many readers even today a writer to be shunned, or if not shunned then read with an extremely critical eye. He fled France in 1944, fearing reprisals for his collaborationist writings, and did not return until 1951. He had been tried and condemned in absentia after the war but was eventually amnestied and enjoyed a decade of literary acclaim for the novels he published in the 1950s. He died in 1961.

Elisabeth Gille has Némirovsky refer to Céline as a madman with abhorrent views (351). But she had not read her mother's writing journals from the 1930s, which were still lying in the storage rooms of Albin Michel, undiscovered until 2005. (They were no doubt among the manuscripts Némirovsky had given to André Sabatier for safekeeping in March 1942.) Céline is not a steady reference in Némirovsky's journals, but the one or two times she mentions him are significant. At the end of May 1938, after arriving at the summer house in Hendaye, she expresses relief that her mood has changed: "Blue sky. Sun. Ecstasy." She had left Paris feeling terrible, lower than low: "36 degrees below zero. As Céline says, 'You've got an ugly character, Ferdinand' [T'es une sale nature, Ferdinand]."²³ The quote, referring self-ironically to Céline's hero, is from *Death on the Installment Plan*, which Némirovsky had evidently relished. By identifying herself with Céline's angry alter ego, she gives her own depression a literary sheen. She notes, however, that it was the memoirs of Rudyard Kipling, "blessed be he," that had brought her out of her "crisis of blackness."

Among Némirovsky's ideas that summer was the novel she planned to call "Le Charlatan," which would feature an illegitimate child, Gabriel Dario, who grows up to be a crook. Eventually, she transformed him into Dario Asfar, a poor, ambitious immigrant doctor from the Levant, one of those shady but compelling "foreigners" that had always fascinated her. Dario Asfar is another version of David Golder and would soon be followed by Ben Sinner of *The Dogs and the Wolves*, both of whom are presented and indeed analyzed as Jewish characters. But even though he fits the model perfectly, Némirovsky decided not to specify Dario Asfar's ethnicity, possibly because of the difficulties she had had in publishing her short story "Fraternité" two years earlier. (The editor of the *Revue des Deux Mondes*, we recall, had rejected the story as antisemitic.) In the midst of her notes for "Le Charlatan," in June 1938, on a page where she also talks about her desire to find peace of mind, perhaps by converting to Catholicism, there is suddenly the following: "Ah, God, if I were to describe the Jew . . . Yes, obviously, there was Golder, but . . . But I don't dare, I'm afraid, Céline is right. I quite like *Bagatelles* [J'aime bien *Bagatelles*]."[24]

It came as a shock when I read those lines a few years ago, sitting in the high-ceilinged reading room, once the church of an abbey, of the Institut Mémoires de l'Édition Contemporaine in Normandy, where Némirovsky's papers are deposited. True, it was a brief outburst written in a private journal, evidently at a time of great psychological stress and depression. But still, how could she say she liked *Bagatelles?* Was this her equivalent of Kafka's outburst, in a letter to his lover Milena, that sometimes he would like to "stuff all Jews in a drawer," including himself, and suffocate them?[25] André Gide, in his review article in the *Nouvelle Revue Française*, treated *Bagatelles* as a kind of joke on Céline's part since it displayed his usual stylistic verve and listed Cézanne, Picasso, and other modern artists among the Jews—and also because Gide could not believe this talented writer would say such hateful things in earnest.[26] But Némirovsky does not appear to have been in a joking mood, nor was she referring only to Céline's style, when she said she liked the book. This seems to have been one of those truly low moments when all her anxieties were let loose, at least momentarily. If Céline was "right," then Jewishness was the cause of all her problems.

Elisabeth Gille's version of Némirovsky voices nothing but indignation at *Bagatelles pour un massacre*. She hasn't read the book, writes the "dreamed" Irène in 1942, but she has heard it is "a horrible pamphlet" and a "veritable call to murder" (351). Elisabeth's ignorance of the facts can be called fortunate since it allowed her to reinforce her two-part schema for the narrative, with the older Irène wiser than her younger self. Curiously, however, Elisabeth invents another literary reference on the same page, this time somewhat to her mother's detriment: her Irène mentions Robert Brasillach and Drieu La Rochelle, two notorious antisemites, in a list of "genuine writers," among them Jacques Chardonne and Paul Morand, whom she had once loved and who had loved her, or at least pretended to, but who have now abandoned her. In reality, Némirovsky's biographer Olivier Philipponnat has confirmed to me that Némirovsky had no personal relations whatsoever with Drieu and never mentions him in her journals; she may have met Brasillach, but there was hardly any "love" between them. She mentions him in her journal once, in 1934, after reading his negative review of *Le Pion sur l'échiquier*, which distressed her.[27] Generally respected as a literary critic, Brasillach had written positive reviews of her works until then. His political views took a virulently antisemitic turn after 1934, when he first visited Nazi Germany. Chardonne and Morand, whom the real Némirovsky did know and correspond with, were bad enough, we could say. Chardonne was tried after the war for collaboration but was eventually acquitted, while Morand's name figured for a while on a black list of collaborationist writers, although he was never tried.[28]

   Le Mirador was published in February 1992 by a small press, the Presses de la Renaissance, where Elisabeth's good friend Arlette Stroumza was her editor. Stroumza recalled, in 2010, that she and Elisabeth had talked about the book for many years, "whether to do it or not." Elisabeth, she said, "was afraid it would bring back too many memories."[29] The book received admiring reviews in major newspapers and magazines, from *Le Monde* and *Libération* to *L'Express*, *Elle*, and the Jewish weekly *Actualité Juive Hebdo*. Their focus was on Elisabeth Gille as author and daughter, but above all on Irène Némirovsky, whose name suddenly reappeared in the press after a decades-long absence. The reviewers all emphasized her tragic death at the age of thirty-nine, but many also praised her work. Lionel Rocheman, himself a writer, declared in *Actualité Juive Hebdo* that he considered Némirovsky "one of the great French authors of the 20th century" and singled out *David Golder*, *Le Bal*, and *The Dogs and the Wolves* as among her best works.[30] Elisabeth Gille was widely interviewed, both in the press—the *International Herald Tribune* headlined its article "A Daughter's Painful Quest"—and on radio and television. She and Denise were featured in a ninety-minute-long program on the radio devoted to Némirovsky. The other participants on the program, all of them great admirers of Némirovsky's work, were Françoise Ducout, a journalist from *Elle*; Maurice Schumann, an elder statesman and former minister and a member of the Académie

Française who had been the "voice of Free France" on the radio in London during the war; and Lionel Rocheman, who recalled seeing a copy of *David Golder* on his parents' bookshelf when he was a young boy—in his family's milieu of Polish Jewish immigrants, he said, the novel was considered a masterpiece.[31]

Despite this flurry of interest, Irène Némirovsky's work remained largely unknown for another decade. But her daughter's book had breathed new life into her, and she returned the favor: with *Le Mirador* Elisabeth Gille became a writer. In the too few years that remained to her, she published two more books, including a novel that has entered the canon of autobiographical fiction by child survivors of the Holocaust.

Elisabeth Gille, Writer

Elisabeth had always had a particular respect for writers, "a kind of veneration," her friend René de Ceccatty recalls. A novelist and essayist as well as a translator, Ceccatty was one of the authors she took under her editor's wing. "She was like that with everyone," he said, "extraordinarily kind and considerate. One could feel that writers fascinated her." She always protested, even after the positive reception of *Le Mirador*, that she was "not a writer but an editor" and that the writer was her mother, he said.[32] But when she was diagnosed with lung cancer in 1992, after treatment for a less malignant cancer a few years earlier, her primary way of dealing with it was to write a book. *Le Crabe sur la banquette arrière* (The crab on the backseat), published in 1994, is that rarest of entities, a hilariously funny memoir/novel about a cancer patient who is fired from her prestigious job at a Parisian publishing firm because her boss thinks it would harm the morale of the editorial team to see her "looking thin, wearing a wig." Elisabeth Gille was in fact asked to leave the new position she had accepted around that time, as director of literary fiction at the Rivages publishing firm. Characteristically, she treated this blow with withering humor. Her book is written in the form of brief dialogues between the unnamed patient ("la malade") and her well-meaning friends, colleagues, doctors, nurses, and family members, all of whom fail to recognize what is happening to her and how she feels about it. They assure her she will "do just fine," that she will "come out of this because [she is] strong." Besides, cancer is becoming very curable, and then they proceed to tell her about friends of friends who have died of the disease or committed suicide! The nurses are incompetent and underpaid, as they keep reminding her, the doctors are in competition with each other, and her twenty-year-old daughter borrows her good jacket and her cosmetics since she is "not going out these days." Meanwhile, she is trying to write.

Le Crabe is the kind of book that has the reader laughing out loud, all the while aware of its devastating underside. At one point the patient calls the cemetery where her grandparents are buried in the Jewish section and explains that she wants to be buried rather than cremated, even though she knows cremation is cleaner and takes up less space. "But I think my family has already contributed," she declares, no doubt to the bewilderment of the employee at the other end. The reader knows what she is referring to, however, just as we can guess why she tells some friends who are talking about ways to lose weight that "there were no overweight people at Auschwitz." If ever there was gallows humor, this is it. Freud, in his essay "Humor," defined this kind of humor as a way of asserting control over a desperate situation, like the man being taken to be hanged who observes the sunshine and declares, "It's a nice day."

At the end of the book the patient feels better after months of treatment, and her friends surprise her one evening bearing food and presents to celebrate her cure. But she knows that it is not a cure, at best a temporary reprieve. And she also realizes, raging at the thought, that her friends cannot understand this, for they live in a different "spatio-temporal universe" from hers. One thinks here of Susan Sontag's famous observation about the two kingdoms, the kingdom of the well and the kingdom of the sick. All humans are potentially citizens of both, but the distance between them is unbridgeable. The patient throws her friends out and is left alone, as "the curtain falls."[33] A television film adaptation broadcast shortly after Elisabeth Gilles's death considerably sweetened this ending. The patient and her daughter, with whom she has had a quite stormy relation until now, come together, finally reconciled, and the last image we see is of them hugging.[34]

Le Crabe sur la banquette arrière was published in September 1994, timed for the fall literary season. It received respectful attention in the press and on radio and television. Elisabeth Gille was featured on an hour-long radio program devoted to writers' childhoods, during which she spoke a great deal about her mother, the war years, and *Le Mirador*. When the conversation turned to *Le Crabe*, the interviewer remarked that it was rare to see a comical book on illness. Elisabeth responded that what is terrible about death is the death of others, not one's own—she thought her mother herself may have faced death with a certain "gaiety." Many of Elisabeth's friends told me they saw in her a toughness belied by her petite frame. She did not suffer fools gladly and let them know it, but she was hard on herself as well: self-pity was not in her repertory. "Not to feel sorry for yourself, I learned that during the war," she told her interviewer on this radio program. "But writing is a therapy. Books have always given me strength."[35] The previous evening she had participated in one of the most popular programs on television, a weekly talk show featuring writers and artists, moderated by the iconic journalist Bernard Pivot. To be invited "chez Pivot" was a coveted prize. On the program with Elisabeth that September evening were the Polish director Krzysztof Kieslowski, who had just completed his celebrated trilogy of films in French, and two famous actors, Jean-Louis Trintignant, the star of Kieslowski's *Three Colors: Red*, and Michel Bouquet, who was starring in a production of Eugène Ionesco's *Exit the King*. Ionesco himself had died recently, and Pivot showed an excerpt from an interview Elisabeth Gille had conducted with him a few years earlier.

This was not the first time she found herself the only woman in a gathering of high-powered men, nor, for that matter, her first time chez Pivot. He had invited her in 1978, when she was a young editor at Denoël, to talk about new science fiction with seven other editors and authors, all of them men. Seeing the archived version of this program gives one a lot of insight into Elisabeth Gille's success in the Paris publishing world. Petite, with short, dark curly hair and deep-set eyes, she sits at first silently smoking while the men talk animatedly among themselves without ever addressing her. But when Pivot finally turns to her and asks her to tell about the series she is in charge of, she becomes unstoppable. Science fiction is a kind of ghetto in the literary world, she explains, with its own rigid rules and conventions. It is written almost exclusively by men, and the characters are mere stereotypes, not really human. Girls don't read it, generally, and she herself never read it as a child in her "personal ghetto," the Catholic boarding school where she was educated, she says with a smile. But now that women writers are entering the field, she hopes they will bring more psychological depth to the genre. She speaks in a low voice, with great composure and authority, without a trace of shrillness: an intelligent, attractive professional woman.

Sixteen years later, once again surrounded by high-powered men, she gives the same impression. One would hardly know, were it not for her pallor, that she had undergone a year of intensive treatments for cancer. She had lost her job, but her good friend and neighbor Claude Cherki, who had recently become head of a major publishing firm, the Éditions du Seuil, offered her an editorial position evaluating manuscripts. It was not a full-time job, more like piecework, but it allowed her to keep her hand in.[36] Above all, it allowed her to work on her next book, a novel, which Seuil would publish. She herself chose an editor to work with, Patrick Salvain, who was trained in philosophy and psychoanalysis and had been a practicing analyst when he started working at Seuil. When I interviewed him in 2010 he recalled that they had discussed her book very often while she was working on it. Her public persona was that of a highly self-assured woman, he said, but in private, at least with him, she revealed her more "tormented and vulnerable" side. Also, she was now racing against time, for her cancer had returned with a vengeance.[37]

Un paysage de cendres (A landscape of ashes, translated as *Shadows of a Childhood*) tells the story of a young child, Léa Lévy, whose parents are deported from Bordeaux in 1942 and who survives the war in a convent school under a false name. In *Le Mirador* Elisabeth had written the autobiographical fragments about the child in the third person, and in *Le Crabe sur la banquette arrière* she had sought the objective tone of theatrical dialogue, as if the closer she came to autobiography, the more she found it necessary to create distance. The novel too is written in the objective mode, from a classically omniscient perspective, and it too appears in large measure to be autobiographical. Léa comes from a wealthy, cultivated family of Russian immigrants in Paris and is five years old when her parents disappear. She is lively and highly intelligent, with a strong mind of her own even as a little girl. Baptized and attending only Catholic schools, Léa for a long time does not consider herself Jewish, citing Sartre's *Antisemite and Jew* as her guide. But when she is at university, in Paris, she discovers the writings of a Jewish philosophy professor at the Sorbonne, Vladimir Jankélévitch, and she begins to think about a possible new way to be Jewish: neither as a religious practice nor as Zionism but as an "identity freely consented to." Jankélévitch, born in the same year as Irène Némirovsky (1903), had been fired from his university position in 1940 as a Jew; he had been a supporter of the Popular Front in the 1930s and a member of the Resistance during the war. Aside from his many books on music and on moral philosophy, he wrote widely after the war on issues of Jewish identity and on the Holocaust, and participated in the "Colloquia of French-Speaking Jewish Intellectuals" that met annually in Paris starting in 1957. Elisabeth Gille mentioned her admiration of Jankélévitch in an interview in 1992 and paid him homage in this novel.[38] Having her young heroine come under his influence may also have been a way of affirming her own intellectual and political distance from her mother.

Elisabeth put much of herself into Léa Lévy, but the differences between them are important too. Léa is a nightmare version of herself, as if she wanted to explore through this character the most extreme consequences of childhood trauma in orphans of the Holocaust. Brutally separated from her parents at an early age, Léa has no older sibling who remembers them, no nanny who knew them, no personal memories, no documents or other traces of their lives, absolutely nothing to hold onto. Even her beloved doll is thrown into the fire, along with her Parisian clothes, when she arrives at the convent. Her one connection to life is her best friend, Bénédicte, two years older, whose kindly parents bring up Léa with their own daughter after the war. But despite their well-meaning attempt to shield the child from knowledge about Nazi atrocities, Léa becomes obsessed with them. Secretly, before she even turns ten, she collects magazine articles with photographs of mass graves and other horrifying images of Nazi camps and listens to radio broadcasts of the postwar trials, dreaming of vengeance. Later, as an adolescent, she succeeds, by a stratagem that strains the reader's suspension of disbelief, in gaining entry, over a period of several years, into the court-

room of the military tribunals in Bordeaux where collaborationists
are being tried. One day she goes berserk when she realizes that
those tribunals are starting to grant very light sentences to defen-
dants whom she thinks of as the murderers of her parents. In fact, by
the early 1950s almost all those who had been tried for collaboration
were amnestied. Her outburst in the courtroom is like the lancing of
an abscess, promising recovery. But at the end of the novel, just as
Léa seems to be emerging from the deep, studying in Paris and living with her friend Bénédicte, Gille suddenly kills off Bénédicte in
an automobile accident. Deprived of the one person who mattered
to her, Léa is literally cut off from the outside world. She shuts herself in her room, scratches her face with her nails and "tears her hair
out by the handful," then curls up into a ball on the floor. She wakes
to the sound of knocking on the door but doesn't answer, covered
by a "rain of ashes, which enveloped her in a thick grey shroud that
shut out all sound." Earlier, Bénédicte's mother had used a similar
metaphor: Léa, she feared, was "nothing but scorched earth, a landscape of ashes."[39]

Burning and drowning, along with ashes, are recurrent images
in literary works by survivors of the Holocaust. "To sink is the easi-
est of matters," writes Levi in *Survival in Auschwitz;* "Burned child
seeks the fire" is the title of Cordelia Edvardson's poetic memoir
about persecution and survival; Saul Friedländer, in his memoir
about his orphaned childhood, writes, "Those who have descended
never completely rise again."[40] Elisabeth Gille obviously knew many
of these works and drew on her own experiences as well in creating
the portrait of Léa. She herself had succeeded, brilliantly, where her
heroine failed (if we take the ending of the novel as an indication of
Léa's future). But in the end she too fell victim, albeit to a different
enemy: she was "vanquished by the crab," as one obituary put it in
October 1996.[41] She lived long enough to hold a copy of her novel
in her hand as she lay in her hospital bed. By the time the first glowing reviews appeared, however, she was not able to read them. Nor
was she present to see her book nominated for all the major literary
prizes that fall. All three of her books are available now in paperback
editions, and *Shadows of a Childhood* is becoming a classic of autobiographical Holocaust fiction.

Elisabeth Gille died on September 30, 1996. Her death was re-

ported on the eight o'clock news that evening on national television.[42] She was buried according to her wishes, in the Jewish section
of the Belleville cemetery, next to her grandparents Léon and Fanny
Némirovsky.

Toward the Renaudot Prize and Beyond

Next it was Denise's turn. After moving to Toulouse in the late
1970s she had started to frequent Reform Jewish groups, which in
France are called "les libéraux," and visit schools to talk about the
persecution of Jews in France during the war, including her parents
and herself. Before Elisabeth died, the two sisters donated what
they possessed of their mother's papers to the Institut Mémoires de
l'Édition Contemporaine, thus making them available to researchers. Although the general public was still unaware of Némirovsky's
name, her work had started to be discussed by scholars of modern
French literature at home and abroad. Jonathan Weiss, a professor
of French literature at Bowdoin College who would publish the first
biography of Némirovsky in 2004, contacted Elisabeth shortly before her death and met with her. After she died he met frequently
with Denise, who gave him access to her personal archives.[43]

It was a good time to think about publishing some of the stories
Denise had unearthed during her earlier research trips to the library. She had often traveled to Paris during Elisabeth's final illness
and had met many of her sister's colleagues in the publishing world.
In 2000 Jean-Marc Roberts, the head of the Stock publishing firm,
who had been one of Elisabeth's closest friends and had published
a heartfelt eulogy in a Sunday paper after her death, brought out
twin volumes bound in Stock's signature dark blue covers: Elisabeth
Gille's *Le Mirador*, with a new preface by René de Ceccatty and an
interview with the author that Ceccatty had published in an Italian
newspaper after the book first appeared; and *Dimanche*, a selection
of short stories by Némirovsky, originally published between 1934
and 1941 and never previously collected. The two books were often
reviewed together. In fact, it was upon reading Edgar Reichmann's
review of them in *Le Monde*, in June 2000, that I started to be in-
trigued by the figure of Irène Némirovsky.

Not long after that, Denise found a small publisher near Toulouse to bring out another selection of her mother's stories, in a limited edition for which she wrote the preface. Pasted onto the first page was a photograph of Irène and Michel with their daughters, smiling, in the garden of the summer house in Hendaye in August 1939. Denise's preface is a commentary on this image, in which she sees "the last happy days" of her childhood. Her tone is mournful, her style eloquent: "Memory, which often causes so much pain, is warmed by the remembrance of a childhood filled with the love of a mother and a father who, for me, remain eternally young." Denise Epstein had a very strong sense of her role as a witness to her parents' tragic history. Twice in this brief text she expresses her desire to bring her mother back to life, with "her talent and her personality at once tender but often cruel [à la fois tendre, mais souvent cruelle], with her clear-eyed gaze on the world around her." The importance of memory and testimony, which has dominated public discourse about the Holocaust worldwide in the past half century, had acquired a particular resonance in France during the 1980s and 1990s, when a number of highly publicized trials brought the Vichy period and, most notably, Vichy's responsibility in the deportation of Jews, back into the limelight. The "duty to remember" (devoir de mémoire) became a slogan that Denise, like many others, adopted with fervor. In her case, the duty to remember was reinforced by the status of her mother, a writer once celebrated but now forgotten. She ended her preface with the hopeful declaration I have excerpted as an epigraph to this chapter: "I am the only one left now who still speaks of them [her parents], but every book of my mother's that is published brings her back into the world of the living."[44]

This book of stories, aptly titled *Destinées* (Destinies—it's the title of one of the stories), appeared in April 2004. A few months later Irène Némirovsky returned to the "world of the living" with a bang. Denise had made a new transcription of the manuscript of *Suite Française* and had spoken about it with Myriam Anissimov, who was visiting Toulouse on a book tour. Anissimov, who had published an interview with Denise and Elisabeth a decade earlier, after *Le Mirador* appeared, read the typescript and showed it to her publisher at Denoël, Olivier Rubinstein, who took it immediately. Denise had also typed up excerpts from Némirovsky's wartime writing journal and correspondence, which were added as an appendix. A preface by

Anissimov outlining Némirovsky's brilliant career and tragic end completed the volume, which appeared in bookstores at the end of September 2004. Right from the start the novel garnered excellent reviews in France and a great deal of interest from foreign publishers at the Frankfurt Book Fair. But major success came when it was awarded the Renaudot Prize on November 8 that year. A few writers and journalists, pointing out that the literary prizes were awarded in order to "encourage living writers," criticized the posthumous award, for which there was no precedent. But the general opinion, about the prize as well as the book, was enthusiastic. By the beginning of December *Suite Française* had sold more than two hundred thousand copies in France, earning a place among the top twenty best sellers of 2004.[45] And it had made Denise Epstein, at the age of seventy-five, into a minor literary celebrity. In fact, the main television station, TF 1, had filmed, some time earlier, a long segment devoted to the book for its prime-time Sunday evening news program, which they ran on the night before the prize was announced. The segment focused on Némirovsky and *Suite Française*, but the starring role was played by her daughter. Denise, dressed in slacks and a turtleneck sweater, is shown in the back seat of a car heading to Issy-l'Évêque. Later, the camera records her joyful reunions in the village with a few people she had known as a child and her tearful visit to the house her family had lived in, now inhabited by a Dutch lady. Later still, we see Denise in her book-lined living room in Toulouse, with pictures of her mother on the wall. Finally, she reads from *Suite Française* to a packed audience at the local bookstore and fields questions with great poise.[46]

Thus began a whole new life for Denise Epstein. For the first time she found herself free of financial constraints. After years of living in cramped quarters, she bought a large, airy apartment on the top floor of a modern building. And she "worried over the high taxes she had to pay, after years of not paying any!" her son Nicolas Dauplé told me with a laugh. But characteristically, he added, she did not move into the fancy downtown section of Toulouse, preferring to stay in her old neighborhood near the outskirts, where all the shopkeepers knew her. Over the next eight years she traveled the world as her mother's representative and occasionally, after the publication of her book of conversations about her life, *Survivre et vivre*, as an author herself. Already a local celebrity in Toulouse, she was invited as the guest of honor to the ceremony that took place in Issy-l'Évêque in September 2005, when a memorial tablet was placed on the wall of the house where the Epstein family had lived in 1941–1942 and the square in front was renamed Place Irène Némirovsky.[47] As Némirovsky's heir and copyright holder, Denise had the final say over adaptations and other uses of her mother's work. She attended museum exhibits, literary festivals, and theatrical performances in New York, London, Paris, Tel Aviv, Hamburg, Milan, Reykjavik, and other world cities. In 2010 she even made a trip to her mother's birthplace, Kiev, at the invitation of the Alliance Française and then traveled to another Ukrainian city, Lviv, where *The Wine of Solitude* had just appeared in a Ukrainian translation. On these trips she was accompanied by various younger friends and representatives of her publisher and occasionally by her daughter Irène. She relied particularly on Olivier Philipponnat, who had become a good friend during the time he was working on his and Patrick Lienhardt's massive biography of Némirovsky (2007), to which Denise had contributed documents and reminiscences. A few years later he acted as the editor of the two-volume edition of Némirovsky's complete works.

Philipponnat, like many others I have spoken with, including Denise's children and grandchildren, remembers her as a woman of extraordinary energy and vitality, with a real talent for friendship. Her granddaughter Léa, who was eleven years old when *Suite Française* was published, thinks of her as different from the "cookies and hugs kind of grandmother." Denise was more like a *copine*, Léa told me, a girlfriend with whom she could talk about books and the world, who told cool stories about her travels and knew "so many things." If some people who had known Denise years earlier remembered her as a sad woman, that certainly could not be said of her in the last decade of her life. In June 2008, after I first met her, I wrote in my notes, "Denise is a small woman with a youthful air, despite her wrinkled face and her almost 79 years. She dresses casually, smokes a lot, laughs easily, and affirms often that she 'lives as she likes, not according to conventions or rules,' and has brought up her children that way too." Elisabeth's old friend René de Ceccatty, when I spoke with him in 2010, used the word *radiant* to describe the impression Denise made on him when they met again after many years.

Her son Nicolas described her as transfigured after the success of *Suite Française.* "It was as if she had been on radio and television all her life," he said.[48]

The last time I interviewed Denise, in June 2011, we spent a while talking about Elisabeth's funeral, but despite the rather solemn subject our conversation was full of laughter. Denise took delight in recounting her efforts to organize a Jewish ceremony, her ignorance of traditional rituals notwithstanding. The requirement of a *minyan*, a quorum of ten Jews to say the prayers, was news to her, she said. Luckily, the "liberal" rabbi who had been recommended to her was very understanding, even when she told him that Elisabeth had been a convinced atheist. As for herself, Denise said, she hadn't decided yet how she would be buried, in a casket or an urn, but she had reserved a place for herself next to her sister. She knew that Jewish law forbade cremation, but the liberals had assured her that a Kaddish could be said for her even in an urn.

The following year she was diagnosed with lung cancer, the same illness that had killed her sister. Despite the debilitating chemotherapies, she continued her e-mail correspondence as long as she could, always interested in work about her mother; her last e-mail to me dates from October 2012. Up to the very end, according to Nicolas, she maintained her courage and good humor and her love of life. A favorite photo that Nicolas's sister Irène sent to friends after Denise's death shows her sitting on a fall day on a beach in Hendaye, her childhood vacation spot, where her children had taken her as a surprise gift for her eightieth birthday. She is bundled up in a sweater and scarf, with a bottle of champagne at her feet. Her arms are raised in a gesture of victory, and she is smiling.

Denise Epstein died on April 1, 2013, at her home in Toulouse, surrounded by her family. Her ashes are buried in the Belleville cemetery beside Elisabeth and next to an inscription that records the deaths of their parents at Auschwitz.

Legacy

The publication of *Suite Française* and everything that followed it affected the lives of all of Némirovsky's descendants. Aside from the monetary rewards and the occasional notoriety when a new book or film or television or radio program featuring Némirovsky appears, they have suddenly experienced what Némirovsky's great-granddaughter Léa calls a family heritage. Léa considers *Suite Française* to have been a "unifying factor" for the family. But she also found it daunting, for "we would have to rise to the occasion [il faudrait être à la hauteur]." This is no small task in a country that values its literary tradition as highly as France does. The heirs of great writers, and even of less-than-great ones, are often kept very busy managing their ancestor's legacy—not so much in terms of finances as in terms of the specifically French juridical notion of "droit moral," the moral right of authors to protect their name and their works. Copyrights and the royalties that go with them are limited in time—seventy years after the author's death is the international standard—but moral right is timeless, according to French law, as long as there is someone to represent the author in that regard. Such a person or persons, most often a direct descendant of the writer, is called an *ayant-droit*, literally, the "possessor of rights." The literary executor in U.S. copyright law plays a similar role but not as sweeping. The rights of an ayant-droit are of two kinds: first, as long as copyright is in effect, he or she, or they if more than one direct descendant exists, is entitled to receive royalties on behalf of the author. Royalties for Némirovsky's works would normally have expired in 2012, but as she is considered to have "died for France" (the irony of that label, in her case, is quite sharp), her works were accorded a thirty-year extension, maintaining royalties until 2042. Second, an ayant-droit possesses the moral right to authorize or refuse to authorize adaptations and other uses of the author's work, according to her or his judgment of their appropriateness. Not long ago the descendants of the eighteenth-century playwright Pierre-Augustin Beaumarchais, the author of *The Marriage of Figaro* among other works, succeeded in preventing the publication of an adaptation they considered harmful to his name.

To complicate things further, the two kinds of rights can be separated: the moral right can be bestowed, by the author or her representative, on someone other than the author's heirs. While they were alive, Denise Epstein and her sister were Némirovsky's ayant-droit in both senses, but after Elisabeth's death her share of royalties went to her children, while Denise continued in her double role. At

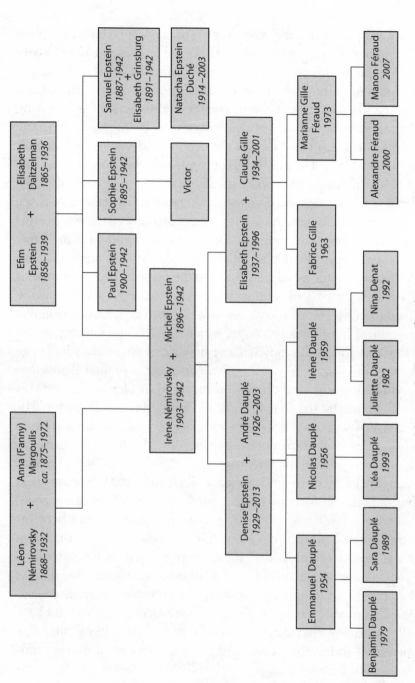

Némirovsky/Epstein family tree.

her death, however, the roles were separated, for Denise assigned the moral right to Némirovsky's works to her trusted friend Olivier Philipponnat. It is an unpaid responsibility and a heavy one, but one he could not refuse when Denise asked him, Philipponnat told me. Technically speaking, if there were ever a disagreement involving the moral right to one of Némirovsky's works, he would have the final say. It helps that he is on very good terms with Denise's children, he added.[49] He and Nicolas Dauplé, who has taken on the role of family representative since his mother's death, discuss all of the decisions and have agreed on everything so far. On his side, Nicolas, who consults on everything with his brother and sister and his two cousins, expresses nothing but admiration for Philipponnat: "They don't make guys like that anymore," he said. In 2015 alone they authorized a graphic novel adaptation of the first part of *Suite Française*, "Storm in June," which appeared in January, and a television film adaptation of Némirovsky's novel *Deux* (1939), a rather resigned portrait of bourgeois marriage, which aired at the end of March. They also followed from afar the making of an English-language feature film based on part 2 of *Suite Française*, a Franco-British co-production whose script had been approved by Denise Epstein.[50]

Directed by the British director Saul Dibb and featuring Michelle Williams as the young Frenchwoman Lucile, Kristin Scott Thomas as her stern mother-in-law, and Mathias Schoenarts as the soulful German officer who is Lucile's impossible love, the film opened in Paris and other European cities in April 2015. Némirovsky's descendants were among those invited to the preopening screening and party a few weeks earlier. (As of April 2016 it had not been released in the United States.) The film is a well-done reconstruction of the period, costumes and all, with gorgeous photography of the French countryside and plenty of dramatic incidents. But it lacks the presence of the novel's narrator, whose "pitiless gaze" and occasionally sardonic tone contribute to the reader's sense, which I have called uncanny, that this work is both of its time and of ours. The one place we get that sense, and it is the film's most moving moment, is in the final credits, which roll over an image of the manuscript in Némirovsky's tiny handwriting, followed by the dedication of the film to Denise Epstein.[51]

The critical reception was mixed, in France and elsewhere, but the film did quite well at the box office. More to the point, Nicolas Dauplé was asked to attend several public screenings and to answer questions afterward. He talked about Némirovsky and about the importance of remembering what happened during the war. He admits freely that he became interested in all this relatively recently, especially since his mother's death. Now that Denise is no longer here, he feels it is up to him to represent the family and help preserve the memory of his grandmother.

Nicolas, who is a gym teacher at a lycée near Grenoble and has become a local celebrity of late, is a friendly, athletic-looking man nearing retirement age. He was an ace volleyball player in his youth, he told me, and still plays on a team every week. He takes pride in his good relations with his young students and has written some short stories for adolescents, having started by inventing fairy-tales for his daughter Léa when she was a baby. Léa herself wants to be a journalist and has already published many articles in the regional newspaper, *Le Dauphiné Libéré*, he said, showing me the clippings, carefully preserved in a special folder. Léa is the only child of Nicolas and his wife, Julie, and they obviously dote on her. A few days later I met her in Paris, where she was completing an internship for the weekly news magazine *L'Express*. She had just finished her next to last year at "Sciences Po," the prestigious School of Social Sciences in Grenoble, where she studied modern European history with an emphasis on the Second World War, among other subjects. She was getting ready to spend the summer in New York, having obtained an internship with a French-language online newspaper that would allow her to come up with ideas for stories and write them. I had a chance later to read some of her articles: this young woman knows how to turn a phrase.[52] Léa had applied for her internships without referring to her illustrious great-grandmother, for despite her pride in the family heritage she wants to succeed on her own merits. In June 2015 she was admitted to the highly competitive school of journalism the Ecole Supérieure du Journalisme, in Lille.

Denise Epstein had told me that she had raised her children to be independent spirits. By all indications she succeeded, helped no doubt by the social upheavals of the 1960s and 1970s. During the years when her children were coming of age, experimentation and freedom from social conventions became a way of life for many young people. Nicolas Dauplé jokes that he is Denise's most conventional child, having been interested mainly in volleyball and girls as a teenager, then attending university and becoming a teacher. Denise's older son, Emmanuel, devoted himself to far-left politics throughout his teenage years. He remembers with great pride the time he and his group broke up a meeting of the extreme-right-wing Ordre Nouveau, a precursor to the Front National, in 1973. He worked for years as a computer programmer and a consultant to industrial firms, until he became "too old for the tech industry" (he was around forty). He never learned any of his skills in school but taught himself, he told me. After the tech jobs, he moved to Toulouse and started a construction business, once again learning on the job. When I met him, in June 2013, he had just come from work and was dressed in dust-covered jeans and a T-shirt, sporting a gray ponytail. Soon he would be retiring, he said. He has read Némirovsky's novels, but she is not his kind of writer. His favorite author is Emile Zola, whose series of novels about late nineteenth-century French society and politics, the Rougon-Macquart, he has read several times. During our conversation he laughed often, although not in a particularly lighthearted way, and we talked for a while about the meaning of such laughter. His mother laughed a lot too, he said: "It's a way of hiding your despair."[53] Emmanuel is the father of two grown children, Benjamin and Sara, who live in Paris.

Denise Epstein's youngest child, Irène, has led a similarly varied life. She left home right after obtaining her *baccalauréat* at the age of eighteen and lived for several years in an agricultural region in the southwest, near Perpignan, where she could do seasonal work and relax or travel during the off months. Her daughter Juliette, who is a member of a modern dance troupe in Montreal, was born around that time (in 1982). Juliette visits her family in Toulouse regularly, and I interviewed her with her mother in June 2011. Juliette knows her mother's story well—she referred to those years near Perpignan as her "hippy period, *Baba cool,* and all that." Eventually, Irène moved to Toulouse and enrolled in university, earning a degree in Russian, which she had studied in high school. But after several years of study she still couldn't speak the language with sufficient ease, so she packed up Juliette and the two of them went off to Orenburg, in the

Urals, to spend a few weeks with a Russian couple she had become friends with in Toulouse. It was the time of perestroika, and everything was opening up in the former Soviet Union, Irène recalled. Her immersion in the language having proved successful, she returned to Toulouse and worked for several years in the aerospace industry as a translator and interpreter from Russian—the MIR space station project had an outpost in Toulouse. But when the United States joined the project and interpreters had to be proficient in English as well, she gave it up and started to work seasonally again, as a stage manager for a summer theater troupe. Recently, she and some friends opened a summer dance hall and music venue (she calls it a *guinguette*, evoking the nineteenth-century *vie de bohème*) on the outskirts of Toulouse, where she is in charge of programming. Money has never been very important to her, she told me. She has simple tastes, loves to move around, and has always preferred to work at something she enjoyed.

Irène Dauplé and her daughters—her younger daughter Nina was born in Toulouse in 1992—are all avid readers and have read many of Némirovsky's works, sometimes more than once. Irène recalls reading them for the first time as a teenager, in the original editions her mother had at their house. When I interviewed them, she and Juliette both spoke admiringly about Némirovsky's keen understanding of human nature. "I find it astonishing how, despite her very protected and strict upbringing, she still had such a profound sense of life, of what human beings are, with all their good and bad qualities," Irène said. "A sense of human misery," Juliette added.[54] As for Nina, she was still in elementary school when *Suite Française* was published, but she read it and became very interested in her great-grandmother's story, so Irène gave her a copy of *Le Mirador* (this was before any biography had appeared). Nina, whom I interviewed in 2016, told me that her good friends know the story as well, and she is proud to be a part of it.[55]

All of Denise's children and grandchildren with whom I have spoken express affection for the family, although they don't see each other very often. "We don't have that strong 'family feeling,'" said Juliette, and her sister Nina said it more recently as well. Their cousin Benjamin, Emmanuel's son, whom I interviewed in June 2015, agreed.

"We lead our individual lives," he said. Their younger cousin Léa, who considers *Suite Française* a unifying factor in the family, noted that it was mostly Denise who brought them together. But she and Nina are quite close, born only a year apart, and by a happy coincidence they were both at university in Lille for a few months in 2015 and 2016, Léa studying journalism and Nina earning a degree in teaching French as a second language. Like her mother and her sister, Nina likes to travel, and when I met her she was about to leave for Berlin as part of her degree work. It's wondrous to see how a heritage of "foreignness," which was a weight to bear for Némirovsky and her generation, can be transformed into a light-footed wanderlust. Being a native-born young French woman with a valid passport helps.

Denise's children grew up quite separately from Elisabeth's, and they don't see each other often. Elisabeth's daughter Marianne, born in 1973, is considerably younger than her first cousins. Marianne's brother Fabrice, closer to the cousins in age, is in regular contact with them, but he has lived in the United States for many years. Still, all of Némirovsky's descendants have read *Suite Française* and at least one or two of her earlier works, *David Golder* and *Le Bal* being the most popular. Even those who don't consider themselves avid readers feel an obligation to have at least some familiarity with their great-grandmother's writings and with her story. Elisabeth Gille's children have the added heritage of their own mother's books, which some of their cousins have also read. And whether consciously or not, at least a few of Némirovsky's descendants seem to be following in the footsteps of their ancestor. Nicolas Dauplé writes fiction, and his daughter Léa is on her way to becoming a successful journalist; on Elisabeth's side, Marianne has translated, under her married name, Marianne Féraud, more than a dozen books by British and American writers. She considers her mother to have been the more serious translator, while she does pop genres like romance and fantasy, but there is clearly a lineage there. Marianne's son Alexandre, who was around ten years old when I met him with his mother in 2010, is interested in history, he told me. He knew that his grandmother and his great-aunt had lost their parents during the war and were left alone, but he didn't know the name of Irène Némirovsky or anything about her, at least not yet. Marianne said she would tell him and his little sister Manon about "all that" when they were older.[56]

The Weight of History

Is Jewish identification part of the heritage? After speaking with so many members of the family, my sense is that the answer, as is so often true with regard to Jews in France, is yes and no. Largely no, if by identification one means a sense of personal belonging to a group or community, and definitely no, if one has in mind some form of religious practice or knowledge about Jewish rites and traditions. Every one of Némirovsky's descendants, as far as I can tell, including those who went to church as children, is today resolutely secular (*laïque*, in the lingo), if not downright hostile to organized religion. In this they resemble many other French people, indeed, people all over Western Europe. As survey after survey shows, church attendance and religious practice are way down and decreasing every year. A survey published by *Le Monde des religions* in January 2007 concerning France showed that only 51 percent of respondents identified themselves as Catholic, down from 80 percent in the early 1990s—this in a country that was historically known as the "oldest daughter of the Church." Only half of that half said they believed in God, and the number of practicing Catholics is much smaller, estimated at 3 percent of the population in 2014.[57] Among minority religions in France, which include Protestants, Jews number around five hundred thousand, representing less than 1 percent of the population, and practicing Jews are a small minority among them. Muslims, whether practicing or not, hover around 10 percent.

Némirovsky's grandchildren did not baptize their children, but neither did they marry Jews, if they married at all. If some of their children—Léa, Benjamin, Sara—have Jewish-sounding names, it is by coincidence, they say. But there is at least one way that many of them reply yes when asked whether they feel Jewish: it concerns antisemitism. Part of the heritage they discovered after the publication of *Suite Française*, if they were not fully aware of it before, was what it means to be "of Jewish origin," as the euphemism goes. It may not seem like much, but it makes a difference. "If I hear an antisemitic remark around the table, I say I'm Jewish," Irène Dauplé says. Her daughter Juliette feels the same way: "I never introduce myself to people by saying 'I'm Jewish,' because I practice no religion, I'm completely agnostic. But if I hear people talking about Jews or making antisemitic remarks, my hair stands on end. And I go on the attack!" It's a matter of history, they both say—if nothing else, Jewishness is a heritage. It is not necessarily a happy one. When I asked Nicolas Dauplé what it meant to him, he replied, "I feel sufficiently Jewish to know that one day somebody could beat me up or call me a 'dirty Jew.'" And what would he do in that case, I asked him. "I would say to myself, 'So, it has finally happened,'" he replied. His nephew Benjamin, who is an elementary school teacher in a northern suburb of Paris where 80 percent of his pupils are Muslims from poor immigrant families, has a somewhat different view. He is against all racism and discrimination, he says, and tries to communicate that to his students, without necessarily singling out racism against Jews. His school is not far from the former camp of Drancy, where Jews were imprisoned during the war before being deported. There is a memorial and museum there now, and he takes his ten- and eleven-year-old students on class visits. The Shoah, in his view, was a horror not because it murdered Jews but because it tried to destroy a whole people.

Benjamin Dauplé is a highly articulate, thoughtful man who studied sociology at university and decided to become a teacher because he wanted to contribute to society. He is firmly against all forms of religion and would no more consider himself Jewish than any other denomination. Above all, he says, he is an advocate of individual freedom. At the same time, he recognizes that this position is possible because he lives in France, in a generally peaceful time. What would happen, he wonders, if one day he had to "choose sides," if there were an armed conflict between Muslims and Jews in his suburb, for example? That would be a real problem, but, luckily, it is not one he has to confront now or in the near future, he said.[58] This was in June 2015, six months after the terrorist attacks of January 2015 in Paris that had targeted journalists at the satirical newspaper *Charlie Hebdo* and, a day later, Jewish shoppers at a kosher supermarket.

That Jewishness in modern times may be nothing more—but nothing less—than a heritage, for better or worse, is not a new idea or a new feeling. It has been the starting point of countless works of existential questioning by Jewish writers and philosophers, both before and after the Holocaust. In 1930 the novelist Albert Cohen, the son of Jewish immigrants to France from Corfu, created his larger-than-life hero Solal, a Cephalonian Jew who achieves brilliant success in French society. Dashing, handsome, and fablelike in his intelligence and talent, Solal becomes a newspaper editor in Paris and a government minister by the time he is twenty-five years old (this is not a realist novel!), marries a beautiful young Catholic noblewoman who adores him, and seemingly leaves all Jewishness behind. In a paroxysmal moment he repudiates his own father, a rabbi, at a public reception. But in the end we discover he has made amends, harboring a whole village of Jews from all over the world, most of them his relatives, also named Solal, in the basement of his chateau, where he visits them in secret every night. He is so tormented by the incongruities in his life that he ends up committing suicide; but true to the fable mode, he is resuscitated in the final chapter. Solal was a character, or at least a name, that haunted Cohen, returning in different incarnations in two more of his novels, including the international best seller *Belle du seigneur*, which appeared in 1964, when the author was in his seventies.

One cannot get rid of Jewishness, even if one tries. A similar conclusion, as we have seen, was reached by Némirovsky in her novels featuring Jewish protagonists. Némirovsky and Cohen were very different writers, and different too in their identification with Jewishness; Cohen even edited a short-lived Jewish literary journal in Paris, *La Revue Juive*, during the 1920s.[59] But in their novels about Jews both of them emphasized the contradictions and dilemmas, the sorrows as well as the satisfactions of Jewish existence in the modern world.

For many individuals, in life as in fiction, Jewishness is a bitter heritage and even a mere "Jewish origin" is a burden, especially in hard times. "In times of persecution, there is probably not a single Jew . . . who has not blamed the heavens for his Jewishness," wrote the philosopher Alain Finkielkraut in 1980, in his reflections on what it meant to him to be a Jew in France after the Holocaust.[60] But that is only one side of the existential puzzle. On the other side, simultaneously, is a possibility that Finkielkraut also recognized: Jewishness as a positive link to something larger than one's individual self, a mode of transcendence. This may not be much, which is why Finkielkraut called himself and others of his generation "imaginary Jews," who have neither a personal experience of suffering, as their parents do, nor any genuine knowledge of Jewish history or Jewish practice. The son of Polish Holocaust survivors, Finkielkraut emphasizes that he himself was born "after." But being an "imaginary Jew" is not nothing, and it may be enough to awaken a feeling of solidarity in times of crisis. Finkielkraut is proud of his name, which marks him as an East European Jew. Even without being thus marked, Irène Dauplé and her daughter Juliette affirm their Jewishness when they hear antisemitic remarks made in their presence, and Nicolas Dauplé wrote to me, after the latest incident of anti-Jewish terror in France in January 2015, "I believe that my family's past and my Jewish origins have forever prepared me for the folly of humans."[61]

Over the past decade and a half, the "folly of humans" in its specifically anti-Jewish form has manifested itself in Europe, especially in France, with increasing frequency and violence, prompting anguished, often heated discussions among Jews and non-Jews alike. This is not the place to rehearse the full list of attacks against Jews that have created shock waves, from the kidnapping and murder of Ilan Halimi in Paris in 2006 to the murder of Jewish schoolchildren and a teacher in a religious school in Toulouse in 2012 to the murder of Jews in a kosher supermarket in Paris following the bombing of the offices of the satirical newspaper *Charlie Hebdo* in January 2015. Religious Jews, who constitute a visible target, have been the most affected. Guards and heavily protected entrances have been the rule in most synagogues and other Jewish institutions for years now, including the Mémorial de la Shoah in the center of Paris, and after January 2015 they were reinforced by armed troopers in military garb. Threats and attacks against businesses owned by Jews as well as antisemitic incidents in some public schools, which have occurred at intervals for several decades, have also multiplied in recent years. And for the first time since the 1930s, cries of "Death to the Jews" and "Jews, France is not for you" have been heard on the streets of Paris. In a mass antigovernment demonstration in January 2014 dubbed Day of Wrath by its organizers, far-right Catholic groups—the so-called *identitaires*, who rail against gay marriage, "gender theory," and other social phenomena they blame for France's supposed decline, attributing them largely to Jewish influence—

marched side by side, shouting antisemitic slogans, with militant Islamists from the ghettoized suburbs, who identify all Jews with the state of Israel and its current policies. Joining them were various left-wing groups that define themselves as "anti-Zionist but not antisemitic," some of whose members have long associations with Holocaust denial. Six months later, in July 2014, mass demonstrations against the Israeli incursion in Gaza featured many of the same participants and produced similar slogans.

The historian and political scientist Pierre Birnbaum, whose many books on Jews in France make him an authority on the subject, is in agreement with the noted specialist on contemporary Islam Gilles Kepel in calling this a totally new alliance between partners who otherwise have nothing in common. Birnbaum sees in this alliance "a new antisemitic moment" that both recalls and reconfigures earlier such moments during the Dreyfus Affair and the Vichy years. Pierre-André Taguieff, the author of many books on racism and antisemitism, does not fully share this assessment. According to him, the "new Judeophobia" of the twenty-first century, founded mainly on religious and ideological grounds, cannot be compared to the old, racial antisemitism that predominated during the Dreyfus Affair and Vichy. This seems like too fine a point, however, for it's not always possible to distinguish "racial" from "ideological" antisemitism: the old and the new can coexist quite comfortably in that domain. Thus the far-right politician Jean-Marie Le Pen (though not his daughter Marine, who currently heads the Front National and is seeking political legitimacy for the party), whose brand of antisemitism is of the old, racial variety, has no trouble marching with the "anticapitalist" and "anti-Zionist" ideologue Alain Soral, who blames all of France's current problems on what he calls the empire of worldwide Jewish dominance. They are united in their espousal of Holocaust denial, among other convictions they share with some radical Islamists, and they are all united in their support of the militantly antisemitic comedian Dieudonné, who was among the first to defend the terrorists of January 2015.[62] He was arrested, and his performances were forbidden by the French government as a result.

All this is cause for worry, though perhaps it was eclipsed by the terrorist attacks of November 2015 that targeted not just Jews and journalists the murderers considered offensive, but all Parisians at random. Jewish emigration from France, mostly to Israel, increased dramatically between 2012 and 2014 and continued to do so in 2015. In September 2014 the liberal daily *Libération* published a special section on the theme "Are the Jews Leaving France?" in which they quoted some well-known, fully integrated secular Jewish intellectuals who said that for the first time they had felt scared when they heard the marchers earlier that year shouting slogans from the 1930s. In the United States, alarm bells have been rung: the journalist Jeffrey Goldberg published a long article in the *Atlantic* in March 2015 with a title whose question is merely rhetorical: "Is It Time for the Jews to Leave Europe?"

In fact, most Jews in France are staying put. The writer Diana Pinto, who identifies herself as a "daughter of Italian Jews who lives in Paris," responded specifically to Goldberg's article in her own long piece in the *New Republic:* "I'm a European Jew—and No, I'm Not Leaving." Robert Zaretsky, an American intellectual historian who is a frequent commentator on developments in France, concluded, after interviewing a number of French Jewish leaders and scholars as well as journalists in May 2015, that their concern is "not about leaving France. [Their] question is how to stay."[63] Birnbaum and others stress that, despite the identical slogans one may hear on the street, there is an enormous difference between the current situation and the one in the thirties, let alone the war years. Today, the French government is not party to antisemitic agitation. On the contrary, Prime Minister Manuel Valls declared very soon after the murders of January 2015, when Prime Minister Benjamin Netanyahu of Israel had invited French Jews to emigrate to Israel, that "France without the Jews of France is not France." He repeated the message in January 2016 at a ceremony commemorating the anniversary of the event.[64]

I end this book in the fervent hope that history will not repeat itself, for Jews or any other vulnerable minority. And that Némirovsky's descendants, along with all the many other kinds of Jews in France—from those who consider themselves merely of distant "Jewish origin" to orthodox observers of all 613 Jewish laws, or *mitsvot*—will be able to continue asking themselves, and each other, the endless questions that have characterized Jewish existence for centuries.

Notes

Introduction

1. Interview with Denise Epstein (Dauplé was her married name, which she continued to use on official documents), Toulouse, June 6–7, 2008.
2. In fact, Denise Epstein was aware of the manuscript's existence as early as 1957. For the full story, see chapter 7 below.
3. Némirovsky, *Suite Française*, trans. Sandra Smith, 221.
4. The radio and television programs in which Gille participated are preserved in the archives of the Institut National de l'Audiovisuel (INA), at the Bibliothèque Nationale in Paris. For full references, see chapters 6 and 7.
5. I conducted interviews with a number of people who worked with Gille at various publishing firms and reference them in chapters 6 and 7.
6. Suleiman, *Crises of Memory and the Second World War*, chaps. 2, 4.
7. René de Ceccatty, interview with Elisabeth Gille in *Il Messagero*, January 1992; reprinted as "Postface" to Gille, *Le Mirador*, 418.
8. Némirovsky, "L'enfant génial," 211.
9. Among the notable American reviews were Paul Gray's front-page review in the *New York Times Book Review*, Alice Kaplan's in *The Nation*, and Ruth Kluger's in the *Washington Post*. I reviewed it in the *Boston Globe*.
10. Franklin, "Scandale Française"; Weiss, *Irène Némirovsky*. Franklin wrote a very positive review of Elisabeth Gille's *Le Mirador* a few years later—in which she reiterated her views about Némirovsky, however. Franklin, "Elisabeth Gille's Devastating Account of Her Mother, Irène Némirovsky."
11. Price, "Out of the Ghetto."
12. Dan Kagan-Kans, "Portrait of the Artist as a Self-Hating Jew," was posted on October 25, 2011, and received numerous responses from readers over the next few weeks: http://www.jewishideasdaily.com/990/features/portrait-of-the-artist-as-a-self-hating-jew/. The *JID* ceased publication

in June 2013, but its archive is still available; it was replaced by the online daily *Mosaic*.

13. Coetzee, "Irène Némirovsky: The Dogs and the Wolves," 35.

Chapter 1. The "Jewish Question"

1. Arendt, *Rahel Varnhagen*. Varnhagen was among those featured in the exhibition on *Jewish Women and Their Salons: The Power of Conversation* (2005), at the Jewish Museum in New York City—see the exhibition catalog by that title. An excellent history of the Jews in Germany, among hundreds of books on the subject, is Amos Elon's *The Pity of It All*.

2. Lessing's book has not been translated into English but has been into French: Lessing, *La Haine de soi*.

3. Reitter, *On the Origins of Jewish Self-Hatred*, 36. Reitter's book is an extremely thorough and balanced discussion of this term.

4. Gilman, *Jewish Self-Hatred*, 11.

5. Marx's essay, in two parts, with substantive excerpts from Bauer's, is in Marx, *Selected Writings*.

6. Toury, "The Jewish Question," 99; for a massive historical study, see Bein, *The Jewish Question*.

7. Toury, "The Jewish Question," 92, 100 (italics added).

8. Caron, "The 'Jewish Question' from Dreyfus to Vichy," 176. Caron sees the "Jewish question" as synonymous with antisemitism; her essay is about the historiography of antisemitism in France.

9. Brasillach's article "La Question Juive" appeared on the front page of *Je suis partout* on April 15, 1938; Rebatet's "Esquisse de quelques conclusions" appeared on page 9. A note on page 1 states that the articles in this special issue, which also contains a large number of antisemitic cartoons, were written and assembled by Rebatet.

10. See Robertson, *The "Jewish Question" in German Literature, 1749–1939*, especially on the period after emancipation, 1871 in Germany and 1867 in Austria.

11. This material is taken in large part from what I wrote in the long introduction to Suleiman and Forgács, *Contemporary Jewish Writing in Hungary*, xxiii–xxiv.

12. See Hanák, ed., *Zsidókérdés*, 21; this volume reprints some of the responses to the survey. My translation.

13. Bein, *The Jewish Question*, 20.

14. Hanák, *Zsidókérdés*, 58, 59.

15. For the classic work on this division in the German context, see Aschheim, *Brothers and Strangers*. In his reflections on the critical reception of the book, which figured as the introduction to the updated edition, Aschheim noted that his emphasis on "intra-Jewish tensions" had caused "acute dis-

comfort" among some readers, so much so that a major German publishing house had refused to publish the book in translation (xxii).

16. Quoted in Fejtő, *Hongrois et juifs*, 209–10. Fejtő gives an excellent summary of the 1917 survey and of its significance.
17. Jankélévitch, "Le Judaisme, problème intérieur," 55, 56.
18. Arendt, *The Origins of Totalitarianism*, 66.
19. "Stefan Zweig: Jews in the World of Yesterday," in Arendt, *The Jewish Writings*, 328.
20. "We Refugees," in ibid., 272.
21. "Letter to Gershom Scholem," in ibid., 466.
22. Kafka, *Diaries, 1910–1923*, quoted in Begley, *The Tremendous World I Have Inside My Head*, 63.
23. Birnbaum, *Les Fous de la République*. For an excellent general history of Jews in France, see Becker and Wieviorka, eds., *Les Juifs en France de la Révolution à nos Jours*.
24. Hyman, *From Dreyfus to Vichy*, chap. 2, "The Golden Age of Symbiosis."
25. Samuels, *Inventing the Israelite*, 46.
26. For Arendt's discussion of Lazare in "The Jew as Pariah: A Hidden Tradition," see Arendt, *The Jewish Writings*, 183–86. Most of Lazare's articles on Jewish issues, written between 1890 and 1901, are collected in Lazare, *Juifs et antisémites*. For an excellent, detailed account of the Dreyfus Affair, including Lazare's role in it, see Bredin, *The Affair*.
27. "We Refugees," in Arendt, *The Jewish Writings*, 270.
28. See *Les Temps Modernes*, December 1945, 535–47; the article "Vie d'un Juif" appeared in November 1945, 338–43; no author is credited for either article, but "Vie d'un Juif" was reprinted in Robert Misrahi's book *Un Juif laïque en France* (2004). I thank Pierre-Emmanuel Dauzat for alerting me to this fact. A note in the inaugural issue of *Les Temps Modernes* in October explained that these "Lives" of typical individuals would be published regularly as quasi-ethnographic documents, but the series does not seem to have been continued beyond the first few issues.
29. Berl explained himself to Patrick Modiano shortly before his death in their joint book, *Interrogatoire;* see also the biography by Revah, *Berl, un Juif de France;* and Raczymow, *Mélancolie d'Emmanuel Berl*.
30. Guedj, "Les Juifs français face aux Juifs étrangers," p. 21 of online version: http://cdlm.revues.org/index4637.html.
31. Meyer, "Les Juifs et la littérature," *L'Univers israélite*, October 30, 1925.
32. Weinberg, *A Community on Trial*, 26.
33. For a set of photographs and useful timeline of Némirovsky's life, see the lavishly illustrated catalog of the exhibit at the Museum of Jewish Heritage, *Woman of Letters: Irène Némirovsky and Suite Française* (2008).
34. Journal and draft of "Fraternité," IMEC, ALM 2999.13.
35. "Ses lèvres, toujours sèches, semblaient fanées par une soif millénaire,

une fièvre transmise de génération en génération. 'Mon nez, ma bouche, les seuls traits spécifiquement juifs que j'aie gardés.' " Némirovsky, "Fraternité," *OC* 1:1623.

36. "C'était donc avant votre père. Tous les Rabinovitch viennent de là-bas" (*OC* 1: 1629); "Qu'y avait-il de commun entre ce pauvre Juif et lui?" (1630).

37. "Où Dieu ne jette-t-il pas le Juif? Seigneur, si seulement on pouvait être tranquille! Mais jamais, jamais, on n'est tranquille! A peine a-t-on gagné, à la sueur de son front, du pain dur, quatre murs, un toit pour sa tête, qu'arrive une guerre, une révolution, un pogrom, ou autre chose, et adieu! 'Ramassez vos paquets, filez. Allez vivre dans une autre ville, dans un autre pays. Apprenez une nouvelle langue—à votre âge, on n'est pas découragé, hein?' Non, mais on est fatigué." *OC* 1:1631.

38. "Heureux ceux qui sont nés ici. Voyez, à vous regarder, à quelle richesse on peut arriver! Et, sans doute, votre grand-père venait d'Odessa, ou de Berditchev, comme moi. C'était un pauvre homme ... Les riches, les heureux, ne partaient pas, vous pensez! Oui, c'était un pauvre homme. Et vous ... Un jour peut-être, celui-là ..." Ibid., 1631–32, ellipses in the text.

39. "Misérable créature! Était-il possible qu'il fût, lui, du même sang que cet homme? De nouveau il pensa: 'Qu'y a-t-il de commun entre lui et moi? Il n'y a pas plus de ressemblance entre ce Juif et moi qu'entre Sestres et les laquais qui le servent! Le contraire est impossible, grotesque! Un abîme, un gouffre! Il me touche parce qu'il est pittoresque, un témoin des âges disparus. Oui, voilà comment, pourquoi il me touche, parce qu'il est loin, si loin de moi ...' " Ibid., 1632–33, ellipses in the text.

40. "C'est de cela que je souffre. ... C'est cela que je paie dans mon corps, dans mon esprit. Des siècles de misère, de maladie, d'oppression. ... Des milliers de pauvres os, faibles, fatigués, ont fait les miens." Ibid., 1633.

41. Journal and draft of "Fraternité," IMEC, ALM 2999.13. The French quotes in this paragraph are "le riche est (se croit) délivré de sa religion, mais le pauvre aussi. La fraternité ne réside pas dans la religion, mais dans la race, oh Hitler, tu n'as pas tort." "Et pourtant, il y a, avant tout, au-dessus de tout, le droit imprescriptible de la vérité." "Recommencer, et encore recommencer, plier le dos, et recommencer. Mais celui qui n'a pas eu besoin de ça, le riche, il lui reste *sickening fear,* cet héritage." "En somme, je démontre l'inassimilabilité, quel mot, Seigneur ... Je sais que c'est vrai."

42. Philipponnat and Lienhardt, *La Vie d'Irène Némirovsky,* 284–85; cf. Gille, *Le Mirador,* 366.

43. "Une expérience communiste. KON, DIT BELA KUN," Récit historique inédit par Georges Oudard, *Gringoire,* February 5, 1937.

44. Suleiman and Forgács, introduction to *Contemporary Jewish Writing in Hungary,* xxvii–xxviii.

45. P. Loewel, *Tableau du Palais.*

46. Journal and draft of "Fraternité," IMEC, ALM 2999.13.
47. "Toi qui nous regardes de haut, qui nous méprises, qui ne veux rien avoir de commun avec la racaille juive! Attends un peu! Attends! et on te confondra de nouveau avec elle. Et tu te mêleras à elle, toi qui en est sorti, toi qui as cru en échapper!" *Les chiens et les loups* (1940), in *OC* 2:645.
48. Endelman, *Leaving the Jewish Fold*, 4.
49. "C'était son tour maintenant. Ce n'était plus d'un enfant chinois, d'une femme espagnole, d'un Juif d'Europe centrale, de ces pauvres charmants Français qu'il s'agissait, mais de lui, Hugo Grayer!" "Le Spectateur," in *OC* 2:448–49.
50. I discussed "Le Spectateur" and Némirovsky's other wartime stories at the conference "Between Collaboration and Resistance," organized by the New York Public Library in conjunction with their exhibition by that title: April 3, 2009. Nathan Bracher has argued persuasively that Némirovsky's "ethical turn" largely preceded the writing of *Suite Française*. In particular, he contests Angela Kershaw's claim that this ethical turn was a sign of her espousal of "Pétainist and Vichy themes," since these stories date from earlier in the war. See Bracher, "Mere Humanity."
51. "Ces foules ressemblaient aux volailles qui laissent égorger leurs mères, leurs soeurs en continuant à glousser et à picorer leurs grains, sans comprendre que c'est cette passivité, ce consentement intérieur qui les livrerait, elles aussi, le jour venu, à une main forte et dure." *OC* 2:449.
52. Bracher, *After the Fall*, esp. chap. 4. Bracher discusses several other contemporary accounts of the 1940 defeat and of the *exode* (including works by Jews), none of which singled out the situation of Jews at that time. In fact, the Vichy anti-Jewish laws came several months later.

Chapter 2. Némirovsky's Choices, 1920–1939

Epigraph: "Croire de tout son cœur que la vie est peuplée de monstres. Et plus tard, la vie n'arrivera pas à vous détromper. Elle fera de son mieux souvent. Elle vous comblera des biens de ce monde, richesses, honneurs, et même affections vraies. Vous la verrez jusqu'au dernier jour avec vos yeux d'enfant: une mêlée horrible." IMEC, ALM 2999.1.

1. Interview with René de Ceccatty, published in the Italian newspaper *Il Messagero* in January 1992; reprinted as "Postface" to the 2000 edition of Gille, *Le Mirador*, 417–18.
2. Bérard-Zarzycka, "Les écrivains russes," 352. The historian Catherine Gousseff, who has studied this in detail, writes that the great majority of Russian exiles left the country in 1920, with only a small minority (around 7 percent) leaving in 1917 and 1918, the year the Némirovskys left. See Gousseff, *L'exil russe*, 23.
3. Claude Perrey, article in *Chantecler*, March 8, 1930; reprinted in Philipponnat and Lienhardt, *La Vie d'Irène Némirovsky*, 429. The photos men-

tioned here, along with many others, are reproduced in the exhibition catalogue *Woman of Letters: Irène Némirovsky and* Suite Française. I saw the original photos in the album shown to me by Denise Epstein when I first visited her in Toulouse, June, 6–7, 2008; all the photos have since been deposited at IMEC.

4. Beauvoir, *Mémoires d'une jeune fille rangée*, 106. While a realist about her situation, Beauvoir's father, as she explains later in the book, was not happy that his older daughter harbored serious intellectual ambitions.

5. Kershaw, *Before Auschwitz*, 43–44. Philipponnat and Lienhardt mention only 1921–24, but Kershaw also found a dossier recording Némirovsky's *certificat* in Russian philology in March 1925.

6. One notebook (IMEC, NMR 7.1) contains a number of poems in Russian, written around 1919. Némirovsky used empty pages in this notebook to make much later notations, dated 1937 and later.

7. See Berberova's autobiography, *The Italics Are Mine.*

8. "Nonoche chez l'extra-lucide" appeared on August 1, 1921, in the biweekly *Fantasio* and is the inaugural text in Némirovsky's two-volume Complete Works. (*OC* 1:49–55.) The three other pieces about Nonoche, which remained unpublished, are also included in this volume.

9. Letter dated "Paris le lundi," with no date, but one can piece together that it is from July 1922. Most of the letters to Madeleine are undated. They are all at IMEC, NMR 5.2.

10. Undated letter, "Paris-Plage, le vendredi," possibly summer 1921 since it refers to a costume ball at the beach resort, where Irène was dressed as a "bohémienne," a gypsy. There are several photos of her in this costume, one of them reproduced in the exhibition catalogue *Woman of Letters*, 31.

11. Weiss, *Irène Némirovsky*, 26.

12. Letter dated March 15, 1922.

13. Letter dated "Paris, le lundi," probably from 1922.

14. Courrière, *Pierre Lazareff*, 223–25. Lazareff was Hélène Gordon's second husband.

15. *Le Vin de solitude,* in *OC* 1:1275–76.

16. Undated letter, "Paris, le lundi," most likely from 1922 or 1923.

17. Undated letter, "Paris le jeudi" [January 1925].

18. See Philipponnat and Lienhardt, *La Vie d'Irène Némirovsky*, 134.

19. E. Epstein, *Les Banques de commerce russes*, 110.

20. Philipponnat and Lienhardt, *La Vie d'Irène Némirovsky*, 134–37. Samuel Epstein's connection to the film production company Albatros doubtless came through Alexandre Kamenka, the major stockholder of the company, whose father was president of the Bank of Azov-Don, where Samuel's father had held an important post. The strong presence of Russian emigrés in the film business in Paris during the 1920s is studied in detail by François Albera in *Albatros: des Russes à Paris.* Samuel Epstein's name is mentioned, as S. Epstein, on p. 93; Kamenka's bank connection, on p. 92.

21. Interview with Denise Epstein, Toulouse, June 7, 2008.
22. Courrière, *Pierre Lazareff*, 223–27.
23. See the detailed chronology in Sarraute, *Œuvres complètes.*
24. For a recent biography, see Bona, *Clara Malraux.* Clara Malraux's most important works are her six volumes of autobiography, published between 1963 and 1979.
25. For a brief biography of Simone Kahn, see Rosemont, ed., *Surrealist Women*, 16–17. On the ups and downs of Kahn's marriage with Breton (they divorced in 1929), see also the chatty book by Georges Sebbag, *André Breton, L'amour-folie*, 82 and passim. The biography of reference for Breton is Mark Polizzotti's *Revolution of the Mind.*
26. Sylvia Bataille is mentioned briefly in biographies of Georges Bataille and Jacques Lacan; her best-known film role was in Jean Renoir's *A Day in the Country (Partie de campagne*, 1936). A mini-biography by David Stevens is on the movie database IMDb: http://www.imdb.com/name/nm0060663/bio?ref_=nm_ov_bio_sm.
27. Aragon and Triolet, *Œuvres romanesques croisées d'Elsa Triolet et Aragon.*
28. Arban, *Je me retournerai souvent.* A literary critic and essayist after the war, Arban wrote several books on Dostoevsky as well as other works before publishing her autobiography in 1990. Massis was the author of dozens of books, including *Défense de l'Occident (1927).* He was elected to the Académie Française in 1960.
29. Quoted by Arendt in her introduction to Walter Benjamin, *Illuminations*, 53 n. 12. The full letter appears in a slightly different translation in Kafka, *Letters to Friends, Family and Editors*, 289.
30. On women writers in the interwar years, see Milligan, *The Forgotten Generation*, esp. chaps. 1–2. The Swedish writer Selma Lagerlöf was the first woman to be awarded the Nobel Prize in Literature, in 1909; three other women, including the American Pearl Buck (1938), received the prize in the years before the Second World War.
31. "Êtes-vous partisan de l'entrée d'une femme à l'Académie Française ?," *Toute l'édition*, April 15, 1939.
32. On Bernard Grasset, see Bothorel, *Bernard Grasset.*
33. Némirovsky tells this story in her interview with Frédéric Lefèvre in *Les Nouvelles Littéraires*, January 11, 1930, which I discuss below.
34. Courrière, *Joseph Kessel*, 242.
35. Bourget-Pailleron, "La nouvelle équipe."
36. The website of the current *Revue des Deux Mondes* contains the tables of contents of every issue since 1829, with the notable exception of the months between June and December 1940, the first months of the Vichy regime inaugurated by Maréchal Pétain, who contributed two articles to the *Revue* during those months: http://www.revuedesdeuxmondes.fr/archive/tocs. I discuss the effect of Vichy on Némirovsky's life and career in chapter 3.

37. I am grateful to Olivier Philipponnat, who discovered this cache of manuscript letters in 2010, for directing my attention to it. All of the quotes that follow are from letters at the Bibliothèque de l'Arsenal, Paris, cat. MS 15621.

38. Chérau, "Irène Némirovsky," *L'Intransigeant*, October 25, 1933, 6.

39. Letters to Henri de Régnier dated January 29, 1930 and June 21, 1934, at the Bibliothèque de l'Institut, cat. 5708.

40. Telegram to Marie de Régnier, date stamp unreadable but probably May 1936, at the Bibliothèque de l'Institut, cat. 5696. Under the pen name Gérard d'Houville, Marie de Régnier published music criticism throughout the 1930s in the *Revue des Deux Mondes* and was the author of more than a dozen novels, none of which is remembered today. She had a somewhat scandalous reputation for her many amorous liaisons with well-known writers.

41. The author of a long article published in July 1925, for example, argued that although the Jews fleeing pogroms deserved "all our sympathy," they must be encouraged to get rid of their old habits, stop speaking Yiddish, and learn "the beautiful French language" if they were to be welcomed in France. Meyer, "L'assimilation des Israélites étrangers." An excellent recent overview of French Jews' attitudes toward Jewish immigrants in the interwar period is provided by Jérémy Guedj, "Les Juifs français face aux Juifs étrangers," A classic study of the subject is David Weinberg, *A Community on Trial.*

42. Weinberg, *A Community on Trial*, 81–82. For a good recent biography of Blum that emphasizes his Jewish ties, see Birnbaum, *Léon Blum.*

43. "Nativité" appeared on December 8, 1933. Despite its title and its allusion to Christmas, the story was more about death than about birth. It features an exhausted woman who gives birth to a premature baby and lies dying while her younger sister, recently engaged, wonders whether she will suffer the same fate one day.

44. These figures are given by Courrière, *Joseph Kessel*, 330.

45. Gary, *La promesse de l'aube*, 212–13; see also Anissimov, *Romain Gary le caméléon*, 145. Anissimov notes that his first stories in *Gringoire* appeared under his real name, Romain Kacew.

46. Courrière, *Joseph Kessel*, 330.

47. Carbuccia, *Le Massacre de la Victoire, 1919–1934*, 410–11.

48. Béraud, "Assez!," in Béraud, *Gringoire: Écrits, 1928–1937*, 143–46.

49. "Minuit, Chrétiens," in ibid., 361–65.

50. "Je vais te répondre," in ibid., 371–74. It is doubtful that Alexander Kerensky was Jewish, but Béraud evidently thought he was. The others he lists came from assimilated Jewish families.

51. IMEC, NMR 4.13.

52. Béraud, "Encore Blum, toujours Blum," *Gringoire*, May 1, 1941, 1. On

January 9 an unsigned front-page text appearing beneath a stereotyped caricature of Blum called him a "Jew without nationality."

53. Henriot, "Place aux Français de France!," *Gringoire*, April 10, 1941, 2.

54. Béraud, *Les derniers beaux jours*.

55. Biographical information on the database of the French National Assembly, where Carbuccia held a seat as deputy from Corsica from 1932 to 1936, is online at http://www.assembleenationale.fr/sycomore/fiche.asp?num_dept=1435.

56. See my discussion of "Fraternité" in chapter 1.

57. Journal entry for June 25, 1938, in journal and notes for *Le Charlatan*, IMEC, ALM 2999.1. The earlier entry is dated June 13 and begins as follows: "I have just learned that we owe 50,000 to a dirty Jewess [Je viens d'apprendre que l'on doit à une sale Juive 50.000]. Absolutely nothing in the cash drawer. M. even took a month's advance. The only salvation lies in selling the novel, and even if that succeeds it will only go to pay what we owe." She then uses their own situation as a way of understanding the main character of the novel she is working on, a dishonest doctor who is always in need of money.

58. Kershaw, *Before Auschwitz*, 33–34.

59. Foreword by Olivier Philipponnat to "Rois d'une heure," deposited along with copies of the article in Némirovsky's papers at IMEC, not yet catalogued. I thank Olivier Philipponnat for sharing his discovery with me. The only known copies of *Le Magazine d'aujourd'hui* are at the Bibliothèque Carnegie in Reims.

60. Némirovsky, "Rois d'une heure," *1934, Le magazine d'aujourd'hui*, May 16, 1932, 3. The full article ran on May 16, 23, and 30, 1934 (issues 32–34).

61. Review of "*Les Races*, 8 tableaux de Ferdinand Brückner, adaptation de René Cave," *Aujourd'hui*, no. 323, March 10, 1934, 14. *Aujourd'hui* was a daily newspaper unrelated to the weekly *Magazine d'Aujourd'hui*, where "Rois d'une heure" appeared. It was owned by Paul Lévy, an Israélite of quite conservative but anti-Nazi political views. I thank Olivier Philipponnat for sharing this article with me.

62. Philipponnat, introduction to Némirovsky, *Oeuvres complètes*, 1:10.

63. On the complicated zigzagging of naturalization laws in the 1920s and 1930s, see Weil, *Qu'est-ce qu'un Français?*, chap. 3. The law of 1927 is discussed on 76–78, and the statistics cited are on 79, 80. See also Caron, *Uneasy Asylum*.

64. Quoted by Schor, "Le Paris des libertés," 30.

65. Weil, *Qu'est-ce qu'un Français?*, chap. 4.

66. These figures are given by Guedj in "Les Juifs français face aux Juifs étrangers," pp. 3–4 in the online version: http://cdlm.revues.org/index4637.html.

67. Spire, "Devenir français en 1931," 106.

68. Letter from Jean Vignaud, September 1, 1939, IMEC 5.38. Other letters and documents concerning the application for naturalization are also in this dossier.

69. Letter to Gaston Chérau, October 22, 1930, Bibliothèque de l'Arsenal, cat. MS 15621.

70. "Deux questions," unsigned item under the weekly rubric "À Paris et ailleurs," *Les Nouvelles Littéraires*, November 22, 1930, 2.

71. The differences between France and Germany as far as opportunities for Jews were concerned have been a subject of constant interest to historians. Among the more recent works on this is the volume edited by Brenner, Caron, and Kaufman, *Jewish Emancipation Reconsidered: The French and German Models.*

72. See, for example, Dreyfus's retrospective look reaffirming his faith in France, in the book of "memories and correspondence" published by his son Pierre after Dreyfus's death: Dreyfus, *Souvenirs et correspondance.*

73. Gugelot, *La conversion des intellectuels*, 203. Gugelot's detailed study is my chief source for the information on conversions given here.

74. On the figure of 769, see ibid., 173, and also Gugelot's article "De Ratisbonne à Lustiger," 9. On the Jewish population in Paris between the wars, see Benbassa, *Histoire des Juifs de France*, 226. On the estimate, by Raymond-Raoul Lambert, of the total conversions in France between 1910 and 1930, see Gugelot, "De Ratisbonne à Lustiger," 9.

75. Gugelot, *La conversion des intellectuels*, chap. 9.

76. Chalier, *Le désir de conversion*, 108.

77. Valéry's speech is available on the Académie's website: http://www.acade mie-francaise.fr/allocution-prononcee-loccasion-de-la-mort-de-m-henri -bergson.

78. Chalier, *Le désir de conversion*, 142–43; also Gugelot, *La conversion des intellectuels*, 177 n. 15.

79. Gille, *Le Mirador*, 385.

80. This wording appears on the baptism certificates of Michel Epstein, "husband of Irène-Irma Némirovsky," Denyse-France-Catherine Epstein-Némirovsky, and Irène-Irma Némirovsky, "wife of Michel Epstein," all duly signed and dated February 2, 1939. There is no certificate for Elisabeth Epstein, possibly because she was not yet two years old and could therefore not sign it and make a profession of faith.

81. Gugelot, "De Ratisbonne à Lustiger," 21. In the pages of *L'Univers Israélite* one finds frequent condemnations of conversion by Jews.

82. IMEC, ALM 2999.1, dossier on *Le Charlatan*. The French text, dated June 15, 1938, reads, "Je mêle à tout ceci, je ne sais pourquoi, une idée de Grâce. Un roman devrait toujours être par la plupart des côtés sordide, sombre, plein des intérêts et des passions humaines, et par d'autres, que l'on entrevoit les âmes. Jésus n'est qu'un homme comme nous; c'est à dire qu'il est un Dieu. Cette parole: 'Vous ne pensez pas aux choses du Ciel;

vous n'aimez que les choses de la terre.' Humainement, humblement, raisonnablement, on ne peut, on ne doit s'attacher qu'à décrire ceux-là." And on the reverse side: "La parole de Jésus: 'Vous, soyez des enfants de lumière.'" The biblical verse (John 12:36) reads, in French: "Croyez en la lumière, afin que vous soyez des enfants de lumière" (Believe in the light, so that you may be children of light).

83. Ibid. "Vu C. hier. Mieux marché que je ne l'espérais, Dieu merci. Et, parallèlement à ceci, une sorte de paix. Si on pouvait ne pas désirer, ne pas craindre surtout. Non, ne pas désirer, c'est impossible. Mais ne pas craindre et, en même temps, sourire, se résigner, s'effacer, que la vie se-rait facile! Il y a une parole que je ne peux me lasser de répéter: Ne crains pas, Zaïre, crois seulement . . ."

84. Voltaire, *Zaïre*, act III, scene 5.

85. Morand met Hélène Christoveloni Soutzo in 1916, when she was still married. She divorced Dimitri Soutzo in 1924 and married Morand three years later. See the detailed chronology in Morand, *Nouvelles complètes*, 1:xlii, xlvi, xlviii.

86. Letter to Vladimir Ghika, December 21, 1938, in the Archives of the Institut Vladimir Ghika (Châtillon-sur-Seine). I am grateful to Olivier Philipponnat for having given me copies of the fifteen manuscript letters Némirovsky addressed to Monsigner Ghika between December 21, 1938, and July 3, 1939.

87. Philipponnat and Lienhardt, *La Vie d'Irène Némirovsky*, 317–18.

88. In a letter to Hélène Soutzo Morand dated February 12, 1942, Némirovsky mentions that she has tried to contact Monsignor Ghika recently but has received no reply. However, the Némirovsky papers contain a postcard from him from Bucharest, dated March 2, 1942, whose battered state (it's partly torn and full of official stamps from government censors) suggests that it took a long time getting to its destination (IMEC, NMR 5.25). Némirovsky's letter to Hélène Soutzo Morand is in the Archives of the Bibliothèque de l'Institut. It was shown in the exhibit on Némirovsky at the Mémorial de la Shoah, Paris, Fall–Winter 2009–10.

89. Because of the beatification a great deal of information on Monsignor Ghika is available online. I consulted the biography written by Pierre Hayet, secretary-general of the Institut Vladimir Ghika: http://blog .lanef.net/index.php?post/2013/08/01/Mgr-Vladimir-Ghika-b%C3 %A9atifi%C3%A9-%C3%A0-Bucarest-le-31-ao%C3%BBt-2013.

90. His certificate of baptism is dated October 7, 1943. He wrote later that his wife and grown children also converted (Bernard, *Mon père Tristan Bernard*, 263). However, the Archives of the Catholic Archdiocese in Paris, which sent me a copy of his baptism certificate, have no documents for the rest of his family.

91. Bernard, "Judaïsme et Christianisme," *Le Figaro*, November 1, 1946, 2.

92. Bernard, *Mon père Tristan Bernard*, 259.

93. Bernard, *Le camp de la mort lente*, 69.
94. Ibid., 68.
95. Weiss, *Irène Némirovsky*, 90.

Chapter 3. Choices and Choicelessness, 1939–1942

Epigraph: "Sa vie devrait se poursuivre, longue et féconde, mais tout se passe comme si quelqu'un avait prononcé la phrase si souvent entendue par Tchekhov: 'L'ouvrage doit être prêt à telle date . . .' Sur la page on trace déjà le mot: fin." *OC* 2:800.

 1. Interview with René de Ceccatty, published in the Italian newspaper *Il Messagero* in January 1992; reprinted as "Postface" to the 2000 edition of Gille, *Le Mirador*, 417–18.
 2. Eiland and Jennings, *Walter Benjamin*, 671–76. Recent historical studies focusing in detail on the wartime lives of Jews in France include Semelin, *Persécutions et entraides dans la France occupée*, and Mariot and Zalc, *Face à la persécution*. One of the earlier works to pay close attention to individual stories is Poznanski, *Les Juifs en France pendant la Seconde Guerre mondiale*.
 3. The figures for France cited here and below are those arrived at by Serge Klarsfeld, who has done the most thorough research on this subject. His four-volume work *La Shoah en France*, published in 2001, consists of updated individual studies he originally published between 1983 and 1995. I cite his figures here as reported by Semelin, *Persécutions et entraides*, 25–26. The figures for Holland and Belgium are given by Dawidowicz, *The War Against the Jews*, 402.
 4. As it turned out, many children were separated from their parents and deported separately. On Laval's behavior in this matter, see the detailed discussion by Marrus and Paxton, *Vichy France and the Jews*, 163–69. As for French versus foreign Jews, it's true that Laval and Pétain were generally more hostile to the latter, but that didn't prevent their persecution of the former.
 5. "C'était la première nuit de la guerre. Dans les guerres et les révolutions, rien de plus extravagant que ces premiers instants où l'on est précipité d'une vie dans une autre, le souffle coupé, comme on tomberait tout habillé du haut d'un pont dans une rivière profonde, sans comprendre ce qui vous arrive, en conservant au coeur un absurde espoir." "La nuit en wagon," in *OC* 2:389; originally published in *Gringoire*, October 5, 1939, and later collected in a volume prepared by Denise Epstein, *Destinées et autres nouvelles*.
 6. Quoted in Eiland and Jennings, *Walter Benjamin*, 669.
 7. "Brusquement, les gens ne paraissaient plus se connaître. . . . Les voyageurs s'étaient séparés sans un mot." Ibid., 404.
 8. Sartre, *Carnets de la drôle de guerre*. This four-hundred-page volume, pub-

lished after Sartre's death, contains one of several notebooks he filled
between September and May; the others were lost.

9. Beauvoir, *Journal de guerre*.

10. Gille, *Le Mirador*, 385.

11. Denise Epstein, *Survivre et Vivre*, 59–60. This slim book of recorded conversations with the writer Clémence Boulouque appeared in 2008. Denise Epstein sometimes spoke of writing a full-fledged memoir but did
not consider herself an author. She died before undertaking the project.

12. See Drake, *Paris at War*, 13–15. Henri Borland, in his memoir *Merci
d'avoir survécu*, remembers being sent away from Paris at that time.

13. Several letters were exchanged between Michel Epstein and his former
employers after June 1940, letters in which he asks to be reinstated, to no
avail; IMEC, NMR 5.15 and 5.45.

14. "Je sens bien qu'il faudrait faire une ou deux nouvelles, tant qu'on peut
encore—peut-être—les placer. Mais . . . incertitude, inquiétude, angoisse
partout: la guerre, Michel, la petite, les petites, l'argent, l'avenir. Le
roman, l'élan du roman coupé net." Journal entry dated June 6, 1940,
Issy-l'Évêque; IMEC, ALM 3000.2.

15. I base my historical summary of France under Vichy, here and in what
follows, mainly on Robert Paxton's classic study, *Vichy France: Old Guard
and New Order*, and on Julian Jackson's more recent *France: The Dark Years,
1940–1944*.

16. See Revah, *Berl, un Juif de France*, 253–61; also Raczymow, *Mélancolie
d'Emmanuel Berl*.

17. The annotated document is reproduced in the exhibition catalogue:
Peschanski and Fontaine, *La Collaboration*, 36. The curators note that
it was discovered only in 2010, when an anonymous donor gave it to the
Mémorial de la Shoah in Paris.

18. Paxton, *Vichy France*, 170–71.

19. Marrus and Paxton, *Vichy France and the Jews*, 4.

20. "Loi du 3 octobre 1940," published in the *Journal Officiel* on October 18,
1940. Full text on http://pages.livresdeguerre.net/pages/sujet.php?id=doc
ddp&su=103&np=876. This site contains full texts of all the Vichy anti-
Jewish legislation between July 1940 and December 1942.

21. Marrus and Paxton, *Vichy France and the Jews*, 3.

22. Archives départementales de Saône-et-Loire, dossier 1714W127. A copy
of this report is also at the Centre de Documentation Juive Contemporaine in Paris (Document DCCCXCII-12).

23. Marrus and Paxton, *Vichy France and the Jews*, 13–15; Jackson, *France: The
Dark Years*, 355 and passim. Jackson writes that Vichy issued its first anti-
Jewish statute in October 1940 "almost apologetically" (354), but I detect
no note of apology in the text of the statute, and none of the administrative correspondence I have read, by and to Vichy prefects (admittedly,

only a sampling) suggests unease. On the contrary, everything sounds extremely cold and bureaucratic, with no hint of apology.

24. Serge Klarsfeld, in his four-volume "calendar" of Jewish persecution in France, reproduces some of these cards as well as registration forms: see Klarsfeld, *Le Calendrier de la persécution des Juifs de France*, 1:40–45, 166–69.

25. Mariot and Zalc, *Face à la persécution*.

26. Semelin, *Persécutions et entraides*, 212.

27. According to his biographer, Kessel was courted by Vichy officials in the summer of 1940 and was even offered a job at Vichy that he refused. He remained somewhat optimistic even after the Statut des Juifs of October 1940, writing to his brother in Hollywood that France was not "nazified and not antisemitic." But he lost all illusions by June 1941, participated in Resistance activities, and left the country illegally via Spain after the Germans occupied all of France in November 1942. He spent the rest of the war mostly in London as a journalist, writing in support of de Gaulle and the Resistance, and also published a novel that Jean-Pierre Melville later adapted into the now-classic film *L'Armée des ombres* (Army of shadows). In 1943 Kessel wrote the lyrics for what became the most famous song of the Resistance in France, "Le Chant des Partisans." See Courrière, *Joseph Kessel*, 541–94.

28. Ibid., 197.

29. Badinter, "Mort d'un Israélite français," 103–4.

30. Semelin, *Persécutions et entraides*, 196.

31. Ibid., 123–24. Semelin relies here on reports given by survivors, and some historians have reproached him for not distinguishing between such sources, which may not always be totally reliable as to precise facts, and more objective documentary ones.

32. "Aujourd'hui, pluie, froid, hier neige. Ma chambre pleine de fumée. 6 ou 7 hommes silencieux, doux d'aspect, courtois qui boivent de la bière et sourient à 'Elissabeth.' Ce matin, 2 prisonniers emmenés entre 2 hommes au fusil. On leur a donné un quart d'heure pour se préparer. Radio française—chansonnettes idiotes. Je suppose que la radio française est pour faire plaisir aux enfants." IMEC, ALM 3000.2.

33. "Je ne puis croire, Monsieur le Maréchal, que l'on ne fasse aucune distinction entre les indésirables et les étrangers honorables qui, s'ils ont reçu de la France une hospitalité royale, ont conscience d'avoir fait tous leurs efforts pour la mériter. Je sollicite donc de votre haute bienveillance que ma famille et moi-même soyons compris dans cette deuxième catégorie de personnes, qu'il nous soit permis de résider librement en France et que je puisse continuer à y exercer ma profession de romancière." Letter to Maréchal Pétain, carbon copy at IMEC, NMR 5.39. The letter is reproduced in full in Gille, *Le Mirador*, 388–89.

34. Pétain, "L'Éducation nationale." The rewriting of "Liberté, égalité, fra-

ternité" is the last sentence, p. 253. This article was later reprinted as a separate pamphlet by the Comité France-Amérique, *Cahiers de Politique Nationale* no. 2, n.d. [1941?].

35. Pétain, "La politique sociale de l'avenir." The phrases quoted are on p. 116.

36. Robert Esménard to IN, August 28, 1939; IMEC, NMR 6.6.

37. IN to Mademoiselle Le Fur, September 8, 1940; IMEC, NMR 6.11.

38. The correspondence with Esménard is at IMEC, in the folders of general correspondence with Albin Michel. His and her letters are separated, making them difficult to read in sequence; his are in dossier NMR 6.1– 6.8, hers in 6.9–6.12. A few of these letters are reproduced in the appendix to *Suite Française*.

39. "Par moments, angoisse insupportable. Sensation de cauchemar. Ne crois pas à la réalité. Espoir (ténu?) et absurde. Si je savais trouver un chemin seulement pour me tirer d'affaire, et les miens avec moi. Impossible de croire que Paris est perdu pour moi. Impossible. La seule issue me paraît 'l'homme de paille', mais je ne me fais aucune illusion sur les difficultés folles que ce plan présente. Pourtant, il faut." IMEC, ALM 3000.2.

40. "Réalisme absolu et mystère." Ibid. The story whose kernel she describes here, featuring a painter and his two grotesque, hidden offsprings, was "L'incendie" (The fire), published in *Gringoire* on February 27, 1942. It was the last work of hers to appear in *Gringoire*.

41. See Némirovsky, *OC* 2:859–60. However, this letter (which I discuss below) was written in February 1942, not December 1940. As far as I know, there is no trace of an earlier letter from her to Carbuccia, but the fact that he published her work for over a year under pseudonyms suggests that she had an understanding with him.

42. Taguieff, ed., *L'Antisémitisme de plume*. This book includes a selection of articles by Coston and other antisemitic ideologues, most of them unknown today, that appeared in the collaborationist press in Paris, endlessly repeating the same argument: the Jews, an international conspiracy, were depraved and bloodthirsty and solely responsible for the war as well as for Bolshevism. Béraud was arrested in September 1944 and condemned to death for his writings in February 1945, around the time Brasillach was executed for his. These condemnations fell under the heading of "intelligence with the enemy" (article 75 of the penal code), that is, treason, and were not linked to antisemitism. Béraud's sentence was commuted to life in prison by de Gaulle, and no other writer was executed after Brasillach. Brasillach was an outspoken advocate of collaboration with Germany, while Béraud hammered home his enmity toward England and the United States. Carbuccia, for his part, began to soften the tone of *Gringoire* after the Allied victories of November 1942 in North Africa and the occupation of all of France by the Germans—to the point that Béraud, who was no longer welcome at the paper, even published a pamphlet against him

in June 1944. Carbuccia fled the country in 1945, was condemned to prison in absentia in 1950, then retried in person and acquitted of all charges in 1955. See Pascal Fouché, *L'Édition française sous l'Occupation*, 2:250–51. All of Béraud's articles published during the Occupation have been collected in Béraud, *Gringoire: Ecrits 1940–1943;* his pamphlet against Carbuccia, *Les Raisons d'un silence*, and Carbuccia's unpublished response, written after 1945 (made available by his son Jean-Luc de Carbuccia), are in Fouché, 437–67.

43. See Taguieff's introduction in *L'Antisémitisme de plume*, esp. 30–41, and his essay in the same book, "L'antisémitisme à l'époque de Vichy: la haine, la lettre et la loi."

44. IN to Robert Esménard, May 10, 1941; IMEC, NMR 6.12; reprinted in the appendix to *Suite Française*, 545. She writes to thank him on May 17. The average salary of a worker in the Paris region in 1940 was around twelve hundred francs per month (counting a six-day workweek), so Némirovsky's monthly stipend of three thousand to support the family in the countryside was quite comfortable, though by no means luxurious. For a table of salaries in 1940, see http://noisy93160.histoire.free.fr/documents/2013-01-17_priL'x_et_salaires_19_&_20eme_siecles_RP.pdf.

45. Letter from Robert Esménard to Julie Dumot, May 27, 1942. He addresses the letter to her instead of to Némirovsky because Dumot was the one receiving the stipends. IMEC, NMR 6.14.

46. IN to André Sabatier, October 14, 1941, IMEC, NMR 6.13; IN to Robert Esménard, October 30, 1941, IMEC, NMR 6.12. The originals of all of Némirovsky's letters to Sabatier are at the Bibliothèque Marguerite Durand in Paris. Copies are at IMEC, where I consulted them: NMR 6.13. Hereafter I will mention only their dates in the text, with no note.

47. Robert Esménard to IN, October 27, 1941, IMEC, NMR 6.8; IN to Esménard, October 30, 1941, IMEC, NMR 6.12.

48. Letters exchanged between "Julie" and Sabatier or Esménard in 1941 and early 1942 (before Irène's arrest) are at IMEC, NMR 6.14–15. Olivier Philipponnat, in his foreword to *Les Biens de ce monde* in Némirovsky's Complete Works (*OC* 2:906), mentions a contract with Julie's name on it, signed in December 1941, but I was not able to find it among Némirovsky's papers at IMEC. The letters, however, clearly indicate that Esménard was willing to go along with the fiction of Julie as the author of Némirovsky's wartime writings.

49. IMEC, NMR 6.8. According to this report, *The Dogs and the Wolves* had sold quite well (though Esménard had complained about few sales in 1940), with two printings and more than 17,000 copies sold. The biggest seller was *Deux*, recounting a bourgeois marriage from its passionate beginnings to the "resigned" middle age of husband and wife; it had had four printings, with 21,600 copies sold.

50. An updated bilingual edition of the 1942 list, titled "Undesirable Litera-

ture in France" (Unerwünschte Literatur in Frankreich/Ouvrages Lit-téraires Non-Désirables en France), appeared in May 1943. It contained an appendix of hundreds of names of Jewish authors writing in French, along with their publishers. Némirovsky's name was on it, spelled Némi-rowsky, but curiously her publisher was listed as Flammarion, the owner of the journal where she had published her very first works. The 1940 and 1943 publications are available online through the Bibliothèque Natio-nale de France: http://gallica.bnf.fr/ark:/12148/btv1b8626072f and http://gallica.bnf.fr/ark:/12148/btv1b86260674/f11.item.r=Ouvrages%20litter aires%20francais%20non-desirables, respectively.

51. IN to Madeleine (Avot) Cabour, December 5, 1940; IMEC, NMR 5.1.
52. IN to Madeleine Cabour, April 14, 1941, IMEC, NMR 5.1.
53. IN to Madeleine Cabour, September 9, 1941, at IMEC, NMR 5.1.
54. IN to André Sabatier, November 20, 1941.
55. I read these reports in Mâcon in October 2013 and would like to thank the archivist Cécile Mariotte and her colleagues for their help.
56. IN to Julie Dumot, June 22, 1941; IMEC, NMR 5.40.
57. There is a fascinating exchange of letters between Némirovsky and an agent of her mother's, one W. I. Pahlen Heyberg, who wrote to her in August 1941 demanding that she return the furs she had taken from her mother's trunk. Némirovsky replied that she had indeed taken the furs and a few other items and sold them immediately. She assumed her mother would be happy to know that this had allowed her granddaughters to subsist for a while, "[for] she must have guessed that I had neither money nor work at the time she fled from Paris" (IMEC, NMR 5.1). The poi-sonous relationship between Irène and her mother obviously persisted into the war.
58. Postcard from Raïssa Adler, October 13, 1944; IMEC, NMR 6.16.
59. Louis Bazy's secretary replied to Michel Epstein on August 3, 1942, men-tioning that he was traveling on business but had received the letter and would do everything he could to help. Michel mentions him to Sabatier in his letter of August 9. Both of these are reprinted in the appendix to *Suite Française*, 558–59.
60. I consulted the minutes from February 1941, when Louis Bazy was elected president, to October 1942, when he was forced out by Pierre Laval and replaced by Albert de Mun, at the Germans' insistence. Available at the headquarters of Croix Rouge Française, Paris.
61. On the history of Pithiviers and Beaune-la Rolande, see the essays by Katy Hazan ("Comment en est-on arrivé là?") and Benoît Verny ("Les camps d'internement du Loiret") in Hazan et al., eds., *Pithiviers–Auschwitz 17 juillet 1942, 6h15*, 8–20. The Centre d'Étude et de Recherche sur les Camps d'Internement dans le Loiret (Cercil), which is both a research center and a museum (its full name now is Cercil-Musée-Mémorial des Enfants du Vél d'Hiv), was founded in 1991 and is supported by the mu-

nicipalities of Orléans, Pithiviers, and Beaune-la-Rolande as well as the Fondation de la Mémoire de la Shoah and various government agencies. Its current president and one of its founders, Hélène Mouchard-Zay, is the daughter of Jean Zay, who was minister of education and held other government posts in the 1930s; his father was Jewish, and he was murdered by the French Milice in 1944. I thank Hélène Mouchard-Zay for kindly guiding me through Pithiviers and introducing me to the staff of the Centre in Orléans, who were very helpful in providing documents about the camp.

62. Klarsfeld, *Le Calendrier de la persécution*, 1:345–48. The full listing of all the transports from France, in chronological order, with deportees listed alphabetically, was assembled and first published by Serge Klarsfeld in 1978. His *Mémorial de la déportation des Juifs de France* was the work that first provided family members of deportees who had perished access to this information. Today, a number of online summaries list the numbers and dates of all the transports and the number of survivors (the latter not always accurate).

63. One such letter of instructions, addressed by the Préfet of the Department of Haute-Saône to police commissioners of the areas under his jurisdiction, is reprinted by Klarsfeld in *Le Calendrier de la persécution*, 1:385–86. The Préfet underlines that Jews are to bring their "carte de textile" ration card with them when they pick up their stars at the police stations.

64. The report, dated Orléans, June 29, 1942, and signed by S.S. Hauptsturmführer Westphal, is included, in French translation, in Klarsfeld, *Le Calendrier de la persécution*, 1:431.

65. See Olivier Philipponnat's note on the text of *Les Feux de l'automne* in *OC* 2:1182.

66. Letter from IN to the Kreiskommandantur, February 11, 1942; IMEC, NMR 5.13.

67. Letter to Hélène Soutzo Morand, Archives de l'Institut, 2 AP7 MS 442.

68. Ibid.

69. These letters were deposited at IMEC by Denise Epstein in 2011: NMR 25.2. She and Julie were away during most of April and May, starting and ending their trip in Paris, with several weeks in between in the Bordeaux region, where Julie Dumot's family lived.

70. Alan Riding has chronicled this in his highly readable account *And the Show Went On: Cultural Life in Nazi-Occupied Paris*.

71. Thurman, *Secrets of the Flesh: A Life of Colette*, 454–67.

72. Manuscript draft of letter to Horace de Carbuccia, no date, but his reply in March mentions the date of her letter: February 20, 1942. IMEC, NMR 5.30, 5.33.

73. Horace de Carbuccia, typed letter to IN, Paris, March 17, 1942. IMEC, NMR 5.33.

74. The report of the sous-préfet at Autun, R. P. Coldefy, sent to the Police des Questions Juives in Dijon, dated June 16, 1942, is at the Archives Départementales de Saône et Loire, Mâcon, AD71 1081W1. Elisabeth Gille, in her mother's voice, refers to the star in *Le Mirador*, 283. I thank Madeleine and Denise Jobert for sharing their memories with me and also for showing me the church registry in which Denise Epstein's first communion is recorded. Copies of school registries showing Denise's and Elisabeth's names were kindly given to me by the secretary of the *mairie*, M. Granger, whom I wish to thank.

75. "Mon cher aimé, mes petites adorées, je crois que nous partons aujourd'hui. Courage et espoir. Vous êtes dans mon coeur, mes biens-aimés. Que Dieu nous aide tous." Copies of all three letters are at IMEC, NMR 5.7 (the originals are at the Centre de Documentation Juive Contemporaine, CDJC); the first and third, erroneously designated as the "last two" she wrote, are reprinted in the appendix to *Suite Française*, 549–50. These three letters were her last ones.

76. These lists are reproduced in Hazan et al., *Pithiviers–Auschwitz*, 348–49.

77. I wish to thank Catherine Thion, an archivist at the Cercil-Musée-Mémorial des Enfants du Vél d'Hiv in Orléans, for explaining this notation to me. Copies of all the detainees' *fiches* from Pithiviers can be seen at the CDJC in Paris as well as at the Center for Advanced Holocaust Studies of the U.S. Holocaust Memorial Museum in Washington, D.C.

78. For these and other details on transport #6, see Klarsfeld, *Le Calendrier de la persécution*, 1:530–31. The seven departments under the jurisdiction of Dijon, including the Saône et Loire, are listed in Hazan et al., *Pithiviers–Auschwitz*, 359.

79. The text of the telegram is cited in the work of two local historians, Roger Marchandeau and Georges Legras, *La Tragédie des Juifs montcelliens (1940–1945)*, which is deposited at the Archives Départementales de Saône et Loire in Mâcon (cat. 2950).

80. These numbers are furnished in ibid., 21.

81. All of this correspondence, right up to Michel's arrest in October, is at IMEC, NMR 6.26. Much of it is reprinted in the appendix to *Suite Française*, 549–65. I discuss it in detail in chapter 6.

82. The complete list, often difficult to read, is reproduced in Hazan et al., *Pithiviers–Auschwitz*, 337–49. Némirovsky's name appears on the list of women, where her name is again misspelled, as Nimierovsky (349). On the same page there is a separate list of fifteen names, of women who arrived in the camp on July 16, which does not include her. This book contains brief biographies of some victims from the transport, written by members of their family. Némirovsky's, written by Denise Epstein, is on pages 273–75. This particular transport is especially well documented, for there exists another volume with testimonies and brief biographies of other victims: Antoine Mercier, *Convoi No. 6. Destination: Auschwitz*.

juillet 1942 (Le Cherche Midi, 2005), reissued in 2008 in an updated version under the title *Un Train parmi tant d'autres, 17 juillet 1942*. According to the list published in the latter, ninety-four people survived, almost all of them men.

Chapter 4. Foreigners and Strangers

Epigraphs: Roth, "Writing about Jews," in *Reading Myself and Others*, 200; "Ce qui me tient le plus à coeur: le Juif," undated entry, journal and drafts of "Le Charlatan," IMEC, ALM 2999.1.

1. Shteyngart, *Little Failure*, 29–30.
2. Reed, "Fade to White," *New York Times*, February 5, 2010.
3. The most recent report, published in October 2013, is the 314-page "A Portrait of Jewish Americans." It is available in full and in summaries on the Pew Center's website: http://www.pewforum.org/files/2013/10/jewish -american-full-report-for-web.pdf.
4. "Defender of the Faith" appeared in the *New Yorker* in April 1959. Roth tells the story about letters to the editor from Jewish readers in *Reading Myself and Others*, 203–4.
5. Ibid., 201. "Writing about Jews" was first published in *Commentary*, December 1963.
6. Quoted by Jules Chametzky, in his introduction to Cahan, *The Rise of David Levinsky*, xvi.
7. Ibid.
8. Ibid., xviii.
9. Ertel, *Le roman juif américain*, 39 and passim; Homberger, "Some Uses for Jewish Ambivalence: Abraham Cahan and Michael Gold," in Cheyette, ed., *Between "Race" and Culture*, 168.
10. Robert le Diable [Robert Brasillach], review of *David Golder*, in *L'Action Française*, January 9, 1930. Other, similarly positive reviews appeared in *Le Figaro*, January 28, 1930, *Le Temps*, January 10, 1930, the weekly *Gringoire*, January 31, 1930—all establishment papers, it must be said—and many others. An unsigned American review appeared in the *New York Times*, November 23, 1930. For an extended discussion of the press reception, see Philipponnat and Lienhardt, *La Vie d'Irène Némirovsky*, chap. 6.
11. Unsigned review of *David Golder*, *La Tribune Juive*, no. 19 (May 1930): 285–86. Ida R. See, "Un chef-d'oeuvre?," *Réveil Juif*, January 31, 1930.
12. Interview with Madame Denise Weill, Paris, July 12, 2010.
13. The letter was reproduced in Auscher, "Nos Interviews: Irène Némirovsky," 669.
14. "Rue des Rosiers," unsigned article under the rubric "Nos Échos," *L'Univers Israélite*, January 31, 1930.
15. Gourfinkel, "L'expérience juive d'Irène Némirovsky," 677.
16. Lacretelle, *Le Retour de Silbermann*, 104.

17. I have analyzed some of the unintended "antisemitic effects" in Sartre's portrayal of "the Jew" in *Antisemite and Jew* in three articles: "The Jew in Sartre's *Réflexions*" (1995); "Rereading: Further Reflections" (1999); and "Réflexions sur la question américaine" (2005). The first of these occasioned some heated discussions, which is why I wrote the other two, but they failed to persuade those who disagreed with me—yet another demonstration of the subject I am treating in these pages.

18. Gourfinkel, "L'expérience juive d'Irène Némirovsky," 678.

19. Auscher, "Sous la lampe: Irène Némirowsky [*sic*]," *Marianne*, February 13, 1935. Auscher's earlier interview with Némirovsky was "L'actualité littéraire: Les romancières et leur métier," *Marianne*, May 16, 1934.

20. Auscher, "Nos interviews: Irène Némirovsky," 669.

21. Deutscher, "The Non-Jewish Jew," in *The Non-Jewish Jew and Other Essays*. This essay was first delivered as a lecture to the World Jewish Congress in London in 1958.

22. Derrida, "Avouer—l'impossible," in *Le dernier des Juifs*, 15–65; this paper first appeared in the proceedings of the 1998 colloquium *Comment vivre ensemble?*, ed. Halpérin and Hansson, 179–216.

23. Auscher, "Nos interviews," 670.

24. A few titles that come to mind, among many others: Angenot, *Ce que l'on dit des juifs en 1889*; Bartov, *The "Jew" in Cinema*; Cheyette, ed., *Between "Race" and Culture*; Cheyette and Valman, eds., *The Image of the Jew in European Liberal Culture*; Nochlin and Garb, eds., *The Jew in the Text*.

25. Julius, *T. S. Eliot, Anti-Semitism, and Literary Form*, new edition and a response to the critics, 1–2; hereafter, page references to this work will be given in parentheses in the text.

26. Amossy and Herschberg Pierrot, *Stéréotypes et clichés*, 35. This short book offers a thorough, useful survey of the large body of work done by social scientists on stereotypes, from Walter Lippmann to Erving Goffman and others.

27. I owe this information to my Harvard colleague Karen Thornber, who is a specialist in the culture of contemporary China.

28. A recent discussion of this gender dichotomy is in Maurice Samuels's essay, "Jews and the Construction of French Identity from Balzac to Proust," 407.

29. This example is given by Amossy and Herschberg Pierrot, *Stéréotypes et clichés*, 99.

30. Julius, *T. S. Eliot*, 61, 73.

31. The "pamphlets" are *Bagatelles pour un massacre* (1937), *L'École des cadavres* (1938), and *Les Beaux Draps* (1939). There is very little difference in style or in the persona of the narrator between the pamphlets and Céline's late novels.

32. Aleichem, *Tevye the Dairyman and The Railroad Stories*, 123.

33. Bragin, "British Film Gives 'An Education' in Anti-Semitism," film re-

view, *Jewish Journal*, Los Angeles, December 1, 2009. Consulted online: http://www.jewishjournal.com/film/article/british_film_gives_an_education _in_anti-semitism_20091201/.

34. Suleiman, "Ideological Dissent from Works of Fiction."

35. Jonathan Weiss, in his discussion of this work, writes that Mr. and Mrs. Kampf are "converted Jews" who had become Catholics out of social ambition (*Irène Némirovsky*, 59). But the novella mentions only Mr. Kampf's conversion (he is the only converted Jew in Némirovsky's fiction), and he is still described as a "dry little Jew." His wife, Rosine, is his former mistress, whom he married when their daughter was about to be born. Rosine is not Jewish: she reminds her husband that her relatives had stopped seeing her when she married a Jew. See *Le Bal*, *OC*, 1:360, 368.

36. "Je continue à peindre la société que je connais le mieux et qui se compose de désaxés, sortis du milieu où ils eussent normalement vécu, et qui ne s'adaptent pas sans choc ni sans souffrances à une vie nouvelle." Radio interview, 1934, quoted as wall text at the exhibit, "Irène Némirovsky: 'Il me semble parfois que je suis étrangère,'" Mémorial de la Shoah, Paris, October 2010–March 2011.

37. Durkheim's *Le Suicide: Étude de sociologie* appeared in 1897 and has been continuously reprinted since then. See his chapter titled "Anomic suicide," book 2, chap. 5.

38. Du Bois, *The Souls of Black Folk*, 8.

39. Quoted in Begley, *The Tremendous World I Have Inside My Head*, 74. For an excellent discussion of Proust's ambivalence toward Jews and Jewishness in *À la recherche du temps perdu*, see Samuels, *Inventing the Israelite*, 239–61. Piperno, by contrast, accuses Proust bluntly of antisemitism: *Proust antijuif.*

40. Beauvoir, *La Force des choses*, 188.

41. "A mesure qu'il devenait plus vieux et malade, il se fatiguait davantage des gens, de leur tumulte, de sa famille et de la vie." *OC* 1:436–37.

42. "Quel besoin avait eu Gloria de l'inviter, celui-là? Il le regarda avec une sorte de haine comme une caricature cruelle. Il se tenait debout sur le pas de la porte, un petit Juif gras, roux et rose, l'air comique, ignoble, un peu sinistre, avec ses yeux brillants d'intelligence derrière les fines lunettes à branches dorées, son ventre, ses petites jambes faibles, courtes et tordues, ses mains d'assassin qui tenaient tranquillement une boîte de porcelaine, pleine de caviar frais, collée contre son coeur." *OC* 1:436–37.

43. Franklin, "Scandale Française," 40.

44. "Plus tard, Soifer devait mourir seul, comme un chien, sans un ami, sans une couronne de fleurs sur sa tombe, enterré dans le cimetière le meilleur marché de Paris, par sa famille qui le haïssait, et qu'il avait haïe, à qui il laissait pourtant une fortune de plus de 30 millions, accomplissant ainsi jusqu'au bout l'incompréhensible destin de tout bon Juif sur cette terre." *OC* 1:511.

45. "Il possédait une espèce de sombre humour qui était assez semblable à celui de Golder lui-même et les faisait se plaire ensemble." Ibid.

46. "'Quelle sale juiverie, hein? dit-il tendrement: qu'est-ce que ça vous rappelle?' 'Rien de bon,' dit sombrement Golder." Ibid., 514.

47. "'C'est un long chemin,' dit-il tout haut. 'Oui,' dit le vieux Soifer, 'long, dur et inutile.'" Ibid., 516.

48. This interpretation of the novel's ending was offered by Ruth Franklin in a public discussion we had, with Maurice Samuels, at the Museum of Jewish Heritage in New York City, December 8, 2008.

49. Price, "Out of the Ghetto," 21.

50. Ezrahi, "After Such Knowledge, What Laughter?," 290.

51. Weiss, *Irène Némirovsky*, 10.

52. See, for example, the thoughtful article by Michel Leymarie, "Les frères Tharaud," which starts by asking how the Tharauds' "indubitably anti-semitic" works could have had such success at the time, even among many Jewish readers. Leymarie suggests that the ambivalence of the Tharauds' "exotic portraits of foreign Jews" led readers astray (89).

53. "Les enfants naissaient dans le quartier comme pullule la vermine." *OC* 1:212; "[Ils] prospéraient comme les rats qui couraient sur la plage autour des vieux bateaux." Ibid., 1:213.

54. "Jamais le petit ne réfléchissait d'avance à ce qu'il allait dire: les paroles s'éveillaient en lui comme des oiseaux mystérieux auxquels il n'y avait qu'à donner l'essor, et la musique qui convenait les accompagnait aussi naturellement." Ibid., 216.

55. "Autrefois, il avait été un enfant génial; à présent, il n'était plus qu'un garçon gauche et stupide, comme les autres . . . La Princesse le regardait de ses yeux froids." Ibid., 241 (ellipsis in the text). The definition of *peiss* is on page 211.

56. "Awakening" (1930), in Babel, *The Collected Stories*, 305, 309. I thank Steve Zipperstein for directing me to this story.

57. Weiss, *Irène Némirovsky*, 11.

58. "Pourquoi s'étaient-elles tues, les chansons qui naissaient autrefois spontanément sur ses lèvres? . . . Son génie avait-il été une espèce de morbide fleur, éclose seulement parce que sa vie avait été violente, excessive, malsaine? . . . Hélas! C'était tout simplement qu'il entrait dans la difficile période de l'adolescence. . . . Mais personne ne le lui disait; personne ne lui faisait espérer retrouver plus tard le don délicieux et fatal, plus tard, quand il serait un homme. . . . Personne n'était là pour lui chuchoter: 'Attends, espère. . . .' Ils étaient tous penchés sur lui, autour de lui, accrochés à lui, comme des humains qui veulent ouvrir de force de leurs doigts sacrilèges une fleur." *OC* 1:243.

59. "Écoute, je vais te dire. Ne le répète à personne. Peut-être . . . je n'ose pas le dire tout haut . . . peut-être qu'ils sont morts, mes oiseaux merveilleux." *OC* 1:246.

60. I owe the insight about Ismael's name to Elena Quaglia, who is completing a doctoral dissertation in Italy on Jewish identity in Némirovsky and other French writers. See Quaglia, *"L'Enfant génial* di Irène Némirovsky."

Chapter 5. Portraits of the Artist as a Young Jewish Woman

Epigraphs: Cixous, "Coming to Writing," in *Coming to Writing and Other Essays*, 21 (in French, *La Venue à l'écriture*, 28); *Le Vin de solitude, OC* 1:1201.

1. "Le sujet n'est pas la confession d'un ivrogne solitaire, quoique ce serait, ma foi, assez amusant à traiter, ne le pensez-vous pas? Non, ce titre dans ma pensée veut exprimer l'espèce d'enivrement moral que donne la solitude (morale également) dans l'adolescence et la jeunesse. À vous, mais à vous seul, je confierai que ce livre-ci est *le roman presque autobiographique* que l'on écrit toujours, fatalement, tôt ou tard. J'espère qu'on ne l'éreintera pas trop, mais c'est un de ces livres surtout pour soi que l'on se résigne facilement à ne pas voir aimés ..." Letter to Gaston Chérau, February 11, 1935. Bibliothèque de l'Arsenal, cat. MS 15621. Emphasis added.

2. Ramon Fernandez, review of *Le Vin de solitude, Marianne*, October 9, 1935. Henri de Régnier's review appeared in *Le Figaro*, November 2, 1935.

3. "'Les bateaux ... Le pétrole ... Les pipe-lines ... Les bottes ... Les sacs de couchage ... Le paquet d'actions ... Millions ... Millions ... Millions ...' [...] Seul l'argent passionnait les hommes autour d'Hélène. Tous s'enrichissaient. L'or coulait." *OC* 1:1245–46. Hereafter I give the French text in notes only for longer quotes; for others, page numbers will be cited in parentheses after the quote.

4. "'Ce ne sont que les années d'apprentissage. Elles ont été exceptionnellement dures, mais elles ont trempé mon courage et mon orgueil. Cela, c'est à moi, ma richesse inaliénable. Je suis seule, mais ma solitude est âpre et envirante.'" *OC* 1:1363.

5. "Marcel devient écrivain" is how Gérard Genette sums up, with a bit of irony, the plot of the novel in his classic study of narrative, "Discours du récit."

6. Abel et al., eds., *The Voyage In: Fictions of Female Development*. See also Miller, *The Heroine's Text*, for a study of the punishment/reward pattern in eighteenth-century fiction about women.

7. Showalter, *A Literature of their Own;* Gilbert and Gubar, *The Madwoman in the Attic;* Milligan, *The Forgotten Generation*.

8. "Ce qui m'intéresse toujours c'est d'essayer de surprendre l'âme humaine sous les dehors sociaux ..., de *démasquer,* en un mot, la vérité profonde qui est presque toujours en opposition avec l'apparence." Frédéric Lefèvre, "En marge de *L'Affaire Courilof,* Radio-dialogue entre F. Lefèvre et Mme I. Némirovsky," *Sud de Montpellier,* June 7, 1933; reprinted in Philipponnat and Lienhardt, *La Vie d'Irène Némirovsky*, 432 (emphasis added).

9. "Il n'y avait pas une figure sur laquelle Hélène en esprit ne pût lever le

masque d'insouciance et de luxure qui recouvrait des traits tirés et anxieux." *OC* 1:1352.

10. "C'était un dimanche d'automne. Le déjeuner finissait. Max était là. . . . Tous se taisaient et écoutaient distraitement les coups de feu, légers et lointains, qui, jour et nuit, résonnaient dans les faubourgs, mais auxquels personne ne prenait plus garde." *OC* 1:1252.

11. "Le père pense à une femme qu'il a rencontrée dans la rue, et la mère vient seulement de quitter un amant. Ils ne comprennent pas leurs enfants, et leurs enfants ne les aiment pas; la jeune fille pense à son amoureux, et le garçon aux vilains mots qu'il a appris au lycée. Les petits enfants grandiront et seront pareils à eux. Les livres mentent. Il n'y a pas de vertu, ni d'amour dans le monde. Toutes les maisons sont pareilles. Dans chaque famille il y a le lucre seulement, le mensonge et l'incompréhension mutuelle." *OC* 1:1253.

12. Proust, *Du côté de chez Swann*, 180.

13. "C'est partout pareil. Et chez nous aussi, c'est pareil. Le mari, la femme et . . .

Elle hésita et écrivit:
L'amant . . .

Elle effaça le dernier mot, puis l'écrivit encore, jouissant de le voir sous ses yeux, puis, de nouveau, l'effaça, ratura chaque lettre, la hérissa de fléchettes, de boucles, jusqu'à ce que le mot eût perdu son apparence première et fût devenu semblable à une bête bardée d'antennes, à une plante ornée de piquants. Ainsi, il avait un aspect maléfique bizarre, secret et rude qui lui plaisait." *OC* 1:1254.

14. "Mais elle est folle! . . . [. . .] Quand on pense, quand on ose penser des choses pareilles, aussi imprudentes, aussi idiotes, on ne les écrit pas, du moins, on les garde pour soi! Oser juger ses parents!" "Elle te détache de tes parents! Elle t'apprend à les mépriser! Eh bien, elle peut faire ses paquets, tu entends!" *OC* 1:1255.

15. Journal and drafts for *Le Vin de solitude*, IMEC, ALM 2998.9. The excerpt about Yiddish was published in *Le Magazine Littéraire*, no. 454 (June 2006): 97.

16. "Des Russes, des Juifs de 'bonne famille' (ceux qui parlaient anglais entre eux et suivaient avec une orgueilleuse humilité les rites de leur religion), et les nouveaux riches, sceptiques, libres penseurs, et bourrés d'argent." *OC* 1:1275–76.

17. "'Elle ne t'aime pas. Elle a voulu se venger de moi, te prendre à moi . . . Malheureux enfant . . . Elle qui n'était rien, *a mere nobody*,' disait-elle amèrement, trouvant dans son malheur une consolation de pouvoir l'exprimer en anglais, naturellement, et non comme Bella, qui l'avait appris, sans doute, d'un amant de passage." *OC* 1:1325.

18. "Non, elle n'était pas comme les autres . . . pas tout à fait [. . .]. Il lui semblait parfois que dans son corps deux âmes habitaient sans se mêler, se juxtaposaient sans se confondre"; "En Russie, ils ne comprendraient pas la langue du pays. Ils ne sauraient pas ce que pense un marchand, un cocher, un paysan . . . Moi, je le sais. [. . .] Je suis une petite fille, mais j'ai vu plus de choses qu'eux dans toute leur longue, ennuyeuse vie." *OC* 1:1222.

19. This is the conclusion arrived at by Norman David Thau, in his study of five French and German novelists of the interwar period, including Némirovsky: *Romans de l'impossible identité*, 217–18.

20. *Coming to Writing and Other Essays*, 12–13; *La Venue à l'écriture*, 20.

21. Auscher, "Sous la lampe, Irène Némirowsky [*sic*]," *Marianne*, February 13, 1935.

22. The story, "La Niania," appeared in the daily *Le Matin* on May 9, 1924, under a rubric run by Colette, "Les Mille et un Matins." Colette's comment on Duvivier's *David Golder* was published in *Le Figaro*, along with comments by fifteen other writers and artists, on March 6, 1931; only four mentioned the novel on which the film was based.

23. "Lu le livre de Colette. Si c'est tout ce qu'elle a pu tirer de juin je suis tranquille." (Read Colette's book. If that's all she was able to do with June, I'm not worried). Entry dated April 24, 1941, IMEC, ALM 3000.2. The book by Colette she refers to is *Journal à rebours*, a collection of short pieces that contains a section on "June 1940." Némirovsky had just finished the first part of *Suite Française*, "Storm in June," which describes the exode of June 1940. She was obviously relieved that Colette had not "done more" with the theme.

24. "Elle effaça le dernier mot, puis l'écrivit encore, jouissant de le voir sous ses yeux, puis, de nouveau, l'effaça, ratura chaque lettre, *la hérissa de fléchettes, de boucles, jusqu'à ce que le mot eût perdu son apparence première et fût devenu semblable à une bête bardée d'antennes, à une plante ornée de piquants*" (italics added).

25. "Écrire! Pouvoir écrire! cela signifie la longue rêverie devant la feuille blanche, le griffonnage inconscient, les jeux de la plume qui tourne en rond autour d'une tache d'encre, qui mordille le mot imparfait, le griffe, *le hérisse de fléchettes, l'orne d'antennes, de pattes, jusqu'à ce qu'il perde sa figure lisible de mot, mué en insecte fantastique*." *La Vagabonde*, in Colette, *Oeuvres*, ed. Claude Pichois (Gallimard, 1984), 1:1074.

26. Journal and drafts for *Le Vin de solitude*, IMEC, ALM 2998.9. Colette's sentence about solitude and wine is in *La Vagabonde*, 1073. For details about Colette's life, see the chronology in *Oeuvres*, vol. 1, and Thurman, *Secrets of the Flesh*.

27. Beauvoir, *La Force des choses*, 284.

28. Thurman, *Secrets of the Flesh*, 470.

29. Gary, *La Promesse de l'aube*, 24.

30. "Quant au confort, aux petits plats tendrement préparés, au chapeau que l'on chiffonne avec un mètre de ruban acheté en solde, quant aux douces veillées sous la lampe, en face d'un mari qui, les pieds dans ses pantoufles, lit son journal, un enfant endormi sur ses genoux, quant à cette vie française si belle, si harmonieuse, si enviable, c'était... ce devait être agréable, mais aussi difficile, aussi étranger à Ben et Ada que pour les nomades l'existence des sédentaires dans de riches plaines . . ." *Les chiens et les loups,* in *OC* 2:611. Hereafter, for shorter quotes I will give page numbers in parentheses after the quote.

31. "Que diront les couillons? 'Mme Némirovsky reste fidèle au roman pénible . . .' ou d'autres coneries [*sic*]. Je devrais être blindée, mais enfin . . . C'est drôle qu'en 1938 il y ait encore ce désir de voir la vie en rose." Dossier on "Le Charlatan," IMEC, ALM 2999.1: journal entry dated June 9, 1938.

32. An early draft of the novel is at IMEC, ALM 2999.3. The first page is dated January 24, 1939.

33. Journal and draft for "Fraternité," IMEC, ALM 2999.13.

34. Gourfinkel, "L'expérience juive d'Irène Némirovsky," 678.

35. The quasi-pathological association of Jewishness with a devalued femininity found one expression in Otto Weininger's *Sex and Character* (1903), a remarkably influential book which is often cited as the ultimate example of Jewish self-hatred. Weininger, a Viennese Jew slated for philosophical stardom, committed suicide in 1903 at the age of twenty-three, shortly after publishing his book.

36. "Un tel était né dans le Ghetto. A vingt ans, il avait quelques sous; il montait d'un échelon dans la vie sociale: il déménageait et allait s'installer loin du fleuve . . . ; à son mariage il habiterait déjà le côté pair (interdit) de la rue; plus tard, il monterait encore: il s'établirait dans le quartier où, selon la loi, aucun Juif n'avait le droit de naître, d'exister, de mourir. On le respectait; il était en même temps pour les siens un objet d'envie et une image d'espoir: on pouvait monter jusqu'à de telles hauteurs." *OC* 2:516.

37. "Guy de Maupassant," in Babel, *The Collected Stories;* Aleichem, "Shprintze," in *Tevye the Dairyman.*

38. "Mais, ainsi que cela lui arrivait parfois, elle était habitée en même temps par deux pensées différentes: l'une naïve, enfantine, et l'autre plus mûre, indulgente et sage; elle sentait en elle deux Ada, et l'une des deux comprenait pourquoi on la chassait, pourquoi on lui parlait avec colère: ces enfants affamés surgissaient devant les riches Juifs comme un rappel éternel, un souvenir atroce et honteux de ce qu'ils avaient été ou de ce qu'ils auraient pu être. Personne n'osait penser: 'ce qu'ils pourraient redevenir un jour.'" *OC* 2:562.

39. "Mon affaire, peindre les loups! Je n'ai que faire des animaux en tribu, ni les animaux domestiques. Les loups, c'est mon affaire, mon talent." Entry

dated May 26, 1938, dossier on "Le Charlatan," IMEC, ALM 2999.1. The first mention of a novel about Russian Jews, involving two opposing types of men and a woman, is in ALM 2999.2 and is dated July 21, 1938.

40. Price, "Out of the Ghetto."

41. "Toi qui nous regardes de haut, qui nous méprises, qui ne veux rien avoir de commun avec la racaille juive! Attends un peu! Attends! Et on te confondra de nouveau avec elle! Et tu te mêleras à elle, toi qui en es sorti, toi qui as cru en échapper!" *OC* 2:645.

Chapter 6. Orphans of the Holocaust

Epigraphs: Cyrulnik, preface to Jablonka, ed., *L'Enfant-Shoah*, 7; Gille, on radio program "Pentimento," France Inter, September 4, 1994; Epstein, *Survivre et vivre*, 87.

1. Interview with Arlette Stroumza, December 13, 2010. For the other information in this paragraph, see Gille, *Le Mirador*, 315–23, and Epstein, *Survivre et vivre*, 69.

2. Michel Epstein (henceforth ME) to Ambassador Otto Abetz, July 27, 1942. IMEC, NMR 5.10. Much of this correspondence was reproduced in the appendix to *Suite Française*. I consulted the original documents at IMEC.

3. André Sabatier to Hélène Morand, July 29, 1942. IMEC, NMR 6.25.

4. André Sabatier to ME, August 12, 1942. IMEC, NMR 5.19.

5. André Sabatier to Jacques Bénoist-Méchin, July 15, 1942. IMEC, NMR 6.25.

6. ME to Madeleine Cabour, August 14 and 20, 1942. IMEC, NMR 5.10.

7. Mavlik to Michel Epstein, July 29, 1942, IMEC NMR 5.17. The Drancy camp registration cards as well as the Préfecture de Police cards (from October 1940) for Paul, Samuel, and Alexandrine Epstein are at the Centre de Documentation Juive Contemporaine (CDJC) in Paris and are on microfilm at the U.S. Holocaust Memorial Museum in Washington, D.C. All the cards bear stamped or handwritten notes indicating the dates they were deported.

8. IMEC, NMR 5.14.

9. IMEC, NMR 5.19.

10. ME to Sabatier, September 19, 1942. IMEC, NMR 6.26; Sabatier to ME, September 23, 1942. IMEC, NMR 5.19.

11. IMEC, NMR 6.26.

12. Copy of letter to M. Sabatier senior, enclosed with letter to André Sabatier, October 8, 1942; IMEC, NMR 6.26.

13. A copy of this document, bearing the stamp of Maître Charles Vernet, is at IMEC, NMR 8.12.

14. The postcards to Julie Dumot are at IMEC, NMR 5.12; the card to Sabatier is in NMR 5.14.

15. The telegram of October 8 from Dijon is referred to in a police report from Montceau-les-Mines, sent to the souspréfet in Autun, René Coldefy—cited in Marchandeau and Legras, *La Tragédie des Juifs montcéliens (1940/1945)*, 25. Michel Epstein's two postcards to Julie were dated by him and also stamped by the post office in Le Creusot with the dates clearly indicated; his postcard to Sabatier is dated by him, "19–10–42." The record of the arrival of Jews from Le Creusot to Drancy is cited by Klarsfeld, *Le Calendrier de la Persécution des Juifs de France, 1940–1944*, 3:1228. The statistics given for the transport of November 6, 1942, are in ibid., 1255–56. Michel's and Sophie Epstein's names appear on the alphabetical list of the transport in Klarsfeld, *Le Mémorial de la déportation des Juifs de France*.

16. The teacher, Madame Ravaud, wrote Denise Epstein two letters, dated August 8 [1990] and April 16 [1992], containing slightly different accounts of the incident in which she hid her (or, in one version, Elisabeth as well) in her apartment; copies of both are at IMEC, NMR 5.27. The originals were given by Denise Epstein to Madame Ravaud's daughter, Elisabeth Kulik, a retired English teacher who now lives in Issy-l'Évêque. Mme Kulik kindly showed me around Issy in June 2014 and told me about her mother. The story of the German officer who let the girls go after their arrest was told by Denise and Elisabeth on numerous occasions—see, for example, Epstein, *Survivre et vivre*, 69–70; Dupont, "A Daughter's Painful Quest" [interview with Elisabeth Gille], *International Herald Tribune*, March 31, 1992; Anissimov, "Les filles d'Irène Némirovski," 74.

17. Epstein, *Survivre et vivre*, 74–75.

18. Ibid., 72; also in Anissimov, "Les filles d'Irène Némirovski," 74.

19. Denise's and Elisabeth's letter of December 25, 1942, to Sabatier is at IMEC, NMR 6.14. Denise's letters to her parents went from April 8 to May 21, 1942. IMEC, NMR 25.2. A few letters from Irène to Denise during that time are in NMR 5.42.

20. The full version of Lichtenberger's book that I summarized is titled *Mon Petit Trott* (Plon, 1931); the picture book of 1935 is *Le Petit Trott*. *Le Noel de Trott*, with illustrations by Paule Gaillard de Champris (Plon, 1935); the illustrated version from 1954 is *Mon petit Trott* (Bibliothèque Rouge et Or, Plon, 1954). Lichtenberger's pamphlet *Pourquoi la France est en guerre* (1940) was published by the Comité Protestant des Amitiés Françaises à l'Étranger, a Protestant organization of which he was a member; it was translated into English.

21. Denise Epstein to Madeleine Cabour, April 23, 1943, in Denise Epstein's personal archive; Julie Dumot's letter of April 25, 1943, to André Sabatier, from "Cézac par Cavignac," is at IMEC, NMR 6.14. Julie's letter to Madeleine Cabour, also from Cézac, is undated, but internal evidence, including the reference to Babet's upcoming communion, allows us to date it from around the third week of April 1943. IMEC, NMR 5.46.

Copies of the documents I cite from Denise Epstein's personal archive were kindly provided to me by Olivier Philipponnat.

22. The information about transports of Jews from Bordeaux is in Klarsfeld, *Le Calendrier de le persécution des Juifs de France*, vol. 3, by date: the last convoy from Bordeaux to Drancy arrived on May 14, 1944; the last transport from Drancy to Auschwitz was on July 31. The exact date when Denise and Elisabeth were taken out of the convent school is not certain, although Denise Epstein recalled it as being in October 1943. This date was repeated by Elisabeth Gille in *Le Mirador*, but she based all of the wartime dates on Denise's memory. Julie Dumot, in a letter to Madeleine Cabour dated November 2, 1944, wrote that the "girls had not been in school since the end of February," which suggests that they left the school at that time, not the previous October (IMEC, NMR 5.46). The only certain fact is that they left the school no later than the end of February and spent several months in hiding.

23. Epstein, *Survivre et vivre*, 74–75.

24. Julie Dumot to Madeleine Cabour, November 2, 1944. IMEC, NMR 5.46.

25. Cyrulnik, *Un merveilleux malheur*, 47–51. Psychological studies of hidden children have multiplied in France in recent years. Among the most important ones, in addition to Cyrulnik, are Frydman, *Le Traumatisme de l'enfant caché* (2002); Feldman, *Entre trauma et protection* (2009); Zajde, *Les enfant cachés en France* (2012). I have proposed the term "1.5 generation" to designate the specific age group of child survivors: Suleiman, "The 1.5 Generation."

26. Copfermann, *Dès les premiers jours de l'automne*, 95.

27. See Suleiman, *Crises of Memory and the Second World War*, chap. 8, "The Edge of Memory."

28. For a detailed study of the return of the deportees, see Wieviorka, *Déportation et Génocide*.

29. Ibid., 101, 118.

30. Julie Dumot to Madeleine Cabour, undated (summer 1945?) and September 8, 1945. Both are at IMEC, NMR 5.46.

31. "Pentimento," radio program on writers' childhoods, France Inter, September 4, 1994. Inathèque de France, DL R 19940904 FIT 12.

32. Julie mentions three thousand francs as the monthly amount in this letter, although Esménard had written shortly before Irène was deported that he was raising it to five thousand. I don't know whether the increase ever took place.

33. Typed letter from M. Ginoux, who identifies herself as former secretary of Michel Epstein, to Julie Dumot, June 22, 1945. In Denise Epstein's personal archive.

34. Letter from Marc Aldanov, April 5, 1945, and reply from R. Esménard, April 11, 1945; IMEC, NMR 6.16.

35. Robert Esménard to Mlle Le Fur, December 7, 1945, IMEC, NMR 6.16.
36. The information that follows about the Avot family is based in large part on my interview with Madame Edwige (Avot) Becquart, Versailles, October 9, 2014. I thank Madame Becquart for showing me family photographs and letters as well as sharing her personal memories of Elisabeth.
37. Julie Dumot to André Sabatier, August 29, 1945. IMEC, NMR 6.15.
38. Epstein, *Survivre et vivre*, 91.
39. Interview with Denise Epstein, Toulouse, June 23, 2011.
40. The school records for Denise and Elisabeth Epstein were communicated to me over the telephone by the school secretary on June 25, 2010. Student transcripts are destroyed after seven years, I was told, but the school keeps records of students' years of attendance.
41. Letter in Denise Epstein's personal archive. The biographical information is based on my interviews and conversations with Denise Epstein in Toulouse, in June 2008 and June 2011. She also recounts much of it in her book *Survivre et vivre*, 95–99.
42. Interview with Fabrice Gille, San Diego, April 29, 2010; interview with Edwige Becquart, Versailles, October 9, 2014. The four letters I saw from Elisabeth Gille to René and Hortense Avot are dated January 25, 1974 (to Hortense), July 5, 1974 (to René), December 23, 1974 (Hortense), and December 27, 1976 (Hortense).
43. Elisabeth Epstein's exam results and diplomas are in the following cartons at the Archives Nationales: June 1954, carton 19910563/1, "Certificats d'études littéraires générales," did not count toward the *licence*; November 1955, carton 19910563/79, "Certificat d'Études Supérieures, Littérature étrangère (anglais)" and "Études pratiques (anglais)"; June 1956, "Certificat d'Études Supérieures, Philologie anglaise." Her individual student registration card, in carton 19800246/58, shows that she was registered at the Sorbonne from 1953 to 1958 and lists the American literature and civilization course in 1957–58. But there are no exam results in either 1958 or 1959, which bears out Edwige Becquart's remark that her mother was chagrined at Elisabeth's not obtaining a *licence*.
44. Interview with Anka Muhlstein, New York City, February 26, 2015. Anka Muhlstein was a close friend of Elisabeth Gille in the 1970s, when they both worked at the Denoël publishing firm. They remained in touch and saw each other regularly after Anka moved to New York, where she lives with her husband, the novelist Louis Begley.
45. Interview with Jean-Luc Pidoux-Payot, Paris, June 21, 2012.
46. Jean-Jacques Bernard to Mme Pasquier at Albin Michel, October 1, 1953; IMEC, NMR 6.20. I discuss Bernard's *Le camp de la mort lente* in chapter 3.
47. Interview with Denise Epstein, Toulouse, June 23, 2011.
48. André Oudard to Madame [Denise] Dauplé, January 14, 1957. Personal archive of Denise Epstein.

49. IMEC, NMR 6.20.

50. The letter is signed "D. Dauplé, daughter of Irène Némirovsky." IMEC, NMR 6.20.

51. Denise Epstein (signature) to Robert Esménard, December 31, 1954; IMEC, NMR 6.21.

52. Interview with Denise Epstein, Toulouse, June 23, 2011; the information about André Dauplé's job at SVP was provided by Denise's daughter, Irène Dauplé, whom I interviewed separately on the same day. See also Epstein, *Survivre et vivre*, chap. 5, "Militantisme." Denise's son Nicolas, whom I interviewed in June 2014, provided the information about her job at the government agency. I have not been able to find any official documents relating to it.

53. Julie Dumot to the Payeur Général, October 26, 1954. A copy of this letter was in Denise Epstein's personal archives, along with Julie Dumot's American identity cards. They must have been among Dumot's papers found after her death, many of which were given to Denise.

54. *Survivre et vivre*, 64–65. I met Cécile Michaud's daughter Renée in Issy-l'Évêque in June 2014. She graciously showed me the house, now renovated, where her mother had grown up and where Denise and Elisabeth had been sent to live during the first months of the war.

55. Interview with Anka Muhlstein, New York City, February 26, 2015.

56. Feldman, *Entre trauma et protection*, 233–70.

57. Copfermann, *Dès les premiers jours de l'automne*, 99.

58. Kofman, *Rue Ordener rue Labat*.

59. Burko-Falcman, *Un prénom républicain*, 92; the earlier quote, about feeling Catholic in her own way, is on page 203. Burko-Falcman's earlier works are novels loosely based on her wartime experiences: *La Dernière vie de madame K.* (1982), *Chronique de la source rouge* (1984), *L'enfant caché* (1997).

60. Interview with Denise Weill, Paris, July 10, 2010. Denise Weill, the mother of the journalist and essayist Nicolas Weill, was born in 1926 and died in 2015.

61. Cyrulnik, *Je me souviens*, 49. In 2012 Cyrulnik published a full-length memoir about his childhood and youth in which he juxtaposes his personal story with general observations about the psychology of trauma and survival: Cyrulnik, *Sauve-toi, la vie t'appelle*.

62. Wieviorka, *Déportation et génocide*, 167–76.

63. Interview with Fabrice Gille, San Diego, April 29, 2010.

64. Interview with Irène Dauplé, Toulouse, June 23, 2011.

65. Of all the name changes in France between 1803 and 1957, 85 percent were done after 1945. See Grynberg, "Après la tourmente," 262–68.

66. Interview with Emmanuel Dauplé, Toulouse, June 25, 2013.

67. "Pentimento," radio program, France Inter, April 4, 1994.

68. Friedlander, *Quand vient le souvenir* (When memory comes); Vegh, *Je ne lui ai pas dit au revoir* (I didn't say goodbye).

69. Rousso, *Le syndrome de Vichy;* Samuel Moyn has argued that the specificity of Jewish deportation first came to the fore in 1966, when Jean-François Steiner published his "nonficton novel" *Treblinka*. The novel caused a brief but fiery controversy, some critics accusing Steiner of Jewish racism because of his emphasis on Jewish deportation (vs. that of *résistants*). See Moyn, *A Holocaust Controversy.*

70. Interview with Jean-Luc Pidoux-Payot, June 23, 2012. He kindly gave me a copy of Elisabeth Gille's official record of employment, established by French Social Security, which lists October 1968 as the date of her employment by Denoël. Pidoux-Payot was a good friend of Gille's and helped the family with bureaucratic details after her death.

71. Quoted in Foran, *Mordecai, the Life and Times,* 263.

72. Richler, *L'Apprentissage de Duddy Kravitz,* trans. Elisabeth Gille.

73. Deutscher, "The Non-Jewish Jew," in *The Non-Jewish Jew and Other Essays,* 26–27, for the quotes in this paragraph. Elisabeth's translation was published by Editions Payot, Paris, 1969.

74. *L'Express,* October 28, 1978. The interview, by the journalist Philippe Ganier Raymond, created a huge stir. Henry Rousso, in his book *Le syndrome de Vichy* (*The Vichy Syndrome*), analyzes this incident as a major step in the revival of "Jewish memory" in France in the 1970s.

75. The term "nouvelle judéophobie," referring specifically to Islamic anti-Judaism, was put into circulation by Pierre-André Taguieff in his book by that title (*La nouvelle judéophobie*), published in 2002. The exemption of traditional French antisemitism seems to have been premature, however.

76. Vidal-Naquet, *Les Juifs, la mémoire et le présent,* 12.

Chapter 7. Gifts of Life

Epigraphs: Denise Epstein, "Une photographie," preface to Irène Némirovsky, *Destinées et autres nouvelles,* 10; interview with Léa Dauplé, Paris, June 9, 2014.

1. Macha Séry, "Le pays où l'archive est reine," *Le Monde,* October 10, 2014, p. 6 of book section.

2. The typescript on onionskin is at IMEC, NMR 2.5–2.10. Denise showed the manuscript to the journalist Catherine Descargues in 1957, as I discuss below. Her mention of the "fat manuscript" came during the radio program devoted to Némirovsky, "Une vie, une oeuvre," France Culture, March 12, 1992, INA 00740130; Elisabeth mentions it in *Le Mirador,* 286, 308, 370. That Denise's children knew about the manuscript of *Suite Française* from an early age was told to me by her daughter Irène Dauplé (interview June 11, 2011) as well as by her son Emmanuel Dauplé (interview June 25, 2013), who repeated it in an interview published online in

the newspaper *La Dépêche.fr* on April 5, 2015: http://www.ladepeche.fr/article/2015/04/05/2081288-irene-nemirovsky-suite-francaise-eu-fin-tragique.html.

3. Bernard, preface *to La Vie de Tchekhov, OC* 2:709.

4. "Au moment où paraît son dernier livre: Souvenez-vous d'Irène Némirovsky," *Tribune de Lausanne*, April 14, 1957, 7. Accessed online on April 8, 2015: http://scriptorium.bcu-lausanne.ch/#.

5. IMEC, NMR 6.21 mentions the sum of 125,000 francs (about 2,600 euros or $3,000 in today's terms), with 75,000 to Denise and 50,000 to Elisabeth.

6. Catherine Descargues to Denise Epstein Dauplé, April 12, 1957. Personal archives of Denise Epstein.

7. Rousso, *Le syndrome de Vichy*; Conan and Rousso, *Vichy: Un passé qui ne passe pas.*

8. Letter from C. Gille-Némirovsky to Albin Michel, February 1, 1965; Albin Michel sent the accounting on February 4. Both are at IMEC, NMR 6.23.

9. Letter from Jean-Louis Meunier to Albin Michel, requesting information, July 12, 1983. IMEC, NMR 6.26.

10. Interview with Rachel Ertel, Paris, July 7, 2010.

11. www.cercle-gaston-cremieux.org. Vidal-Naquet discusses his own early participation in the group in his *Mémoires* 2:261–62.

12. Marienstras, *Être un peuple en diaspora*, 101.

13. Interview with Arlette Stroumza, December 13, 2010.

14. Anissimov, "Les filles d'Irène Némirovski," 70. This interview provides the most details about the original project and its evolution. Denise spoke about it with me in personal interviews, June 2008 and June 2009.

15. The date of the return visit to Issy-l'Évêque is referred to in the schoolteacher Madame Ravaud's letter of August 8 [1990]: she expresses regret at having been out of town and not seeing them, "after so many years" (IMEC, 5.27).

16. Styron, *Reading My Father*; Cheever, *Home Before Dark*; Fernandez, *Ramon.*

17. Anissimov, "Les filles d'Irène Némirovski," 72.

18. Ibid., 72–73.

19. Gille, *Le Mirador*, 287.

20. P.R., "Grand Prix des Lectrices 1992," *Elle*, March 23, 1992, 67. *Le Mirador* was a finalist for this annual prize awarded by the magazine, though it did not win.

21. Revah, in his biography of Berl, quotes his articles in *Pavés de Paris*, a weekly publication he wrote and edited almost singlehandedly. Berl's attitude toward immigrants, not only Jews but including them, was extremely hostile and was praised by antisemites like Charles Maurras. See Revah, *Berl, un Juif de France*, 232–34.

22. Céline, *Écrits polémiques.*

23. Journal entry dated May 26, 1938, IMEC, ALM 2999.1.

24. "Ah, Dieu, si je le décrivais, moi, le Juif . . . Oui, évidemment, il y a eu Golder, mais . . . Mais je n'ose pas, j'ai peur, il a raison Céline. J'aime bien *Bagatelles.*" Journal entry dated June 17, 1938. Ibid.

25. Quoted in Begley, *The Tremendous World I Have Inside My Head*, 74.

26. Gide, "Les Juifs, Céline et Maritain," *Nouvelle Revue Française*, April 1938.

27. Email communication from Olivier Philipponnat, June 15, 2015.

28. Sapiro, *La Guerre des écrivains*, chap. 8.

29. Interview with Arlette Stroumza, Paris, December 13, 2010.

30. Rocheman, "Spectatrice malgré elle," *Actualité Juive Hebdo*, no. 282, February 13, 1992. The other reviews referred to in this paragraph are Edgar Reichmann, "La Comète Némirovsky," *Le Monde*, February 7, 1992; Gérard Maudel, "Ma mère, mon héroïne," *Libération*, February 13, 1992; Jacques Bonnet, "Ma mère, souviens-toi," *L'Express*, May 12–18, 1992; P.R., "Irène," *Elle*, March 2, 1992.

31. "Une vie, une oeuvre," France Culture, March 12, 1992; INA, 00740130. The interview in the *International Herald Tribune*, by Joan Dupont, appeared on March 31, 1992.

32. Interview with René de Ceccatty, Paris, July 7, 2010.

33. Gille, *Le Crabe sur la banquette arrière*, 140; Sontag, *Illness as Metaphor*, 3.

34. "Le Crabe sur la banquette arrière," telefilm directed by Jean-Pierre Viergne, aired on France 2 on December 4, 1996; at INA, CPB96008153.

35. "Pentimento," France Inter, September 4, 1994, INA DLR 19940904 FIT 12.

36. Interview with René de Ceccatty, Paris, July 7, 2010.

37. Interview with Patrick Salvain, Paris, December 13, 2010.

38. Anissimov, "Les filles d'Irène Némirovsky," 72. The "Colloques d'intellectuels juifs de langue française" published its conferences, and Jankélévitch's name appears regularly until the early 1970s; he died in 1985.

39. Gille, *Un Paysage de cendres*, 201, 185.

40. Levi, *Survival in Auschwitz*, 81; Friedländer, *Quand vient le souvenir*, 162.

41. Anne Diatkine, "L'éditrice Elisabeth Gille rattrapée par le 'crabe,'" *Libération*, October 1, 1996. Elisabeth's friends René de Ceccatty and Jean-Marc Roberts published moving obituaries as well, in *Le Monde* (October 2, 1996) and *Journal du Dimanche* (October 6, 1996).

42. TF 1, "20 heures," INA 0410837001025.

43. Email correspondence from Jonathan Weiss, May 4, 2015.

44. Epstein, "Une photographie," preface to Irène Némirovsky, *Destinées et autres nouvelles*, 10; the other quotes in this paragraph are on pp. 7–8.

45. Christine Rousseau, "La fiction au 'top,'" *Le Monde*, February 10, 2005, consulted online, April 29, 2015: http://abonnes.lemonde.fr/archives/article/2005/02/10/la-fiction-au-top_397. Criticisms of the posthumous award were reported in an unsigned article in *Le Monde*: "Le Renaudot attribué, à titre posthume, à Irène Némirovsky," November 9, 2004; con-

sulted online, April 29, 2015: http://abonnes.lemonde.fr/archives/article/
2004/11/09/le-renaudot-attribue-a . . . . See also Josyane Savigneau, "Renaudot, Goncourt et marketing littéraire," *Le Monde*, November 11, 2004.
Savigneau mentions the book's success at the Frankfurt Book Fair. Consulted online, April 29, 2015: http://abonnes.lemonde.fr/archives/article/
2004/11/11/renaudot-goncourt-et . . .

46. "Sept à huit," segment on *Suite Française:* TF 1, November 7, 2004; INA
CLT 20041107 TF1 16h.

47. Letter from Denise Epstein to Gilbert Vachet, then mayor of Issy-
l'Évêque, September 6, 2005, in which she thanks him for the "unforget-
table day" of the ceremony. A copy was given to me in June 2014 by
the current mayor's office, along with other materials relating to the
ceremony.

48. Interview with René de Ceccatty, Paris, July 7, 2010. Interview with
Nicolas Dauplé, Volnaveys-le-Bas, near Grenoble, June 6, 2014; interview with Léa Dauplé, Paris, June 9, 2014.

49. Email communications from Olivier Philipponnat, May 13 and 14, 2015.

50. The graphic novel is by Emmanuel Moynot: *Suite Française: Tempête en
juin;* the telefilm "Deux" aired on the Franco-German station Arte on
March 27, 2015; the feature film is *Suite Française,* dir. Saul Dibb.

51. I saw the film at the preopening screening in Paris, on March 10, 2015.

52. http://frenchmorning.com/villes-americaines-aux-accents-francais/; and
http://frenchmorning.com/travailler-moins-mieux-france-francais
-revue-de-presse/.

53. Interview with Emmanuel Dauplé, Toulouse, June 25, 2013.

54. Interview with Irène Dauplé and her daughter Juliette, Toulouse, June
23, 2011.

55. Interview with Nina Denat, Lille, January 20, 2016.

56. Interview with Marianne Féraud, Aix-en-Provence, July 20, 2010.

57. The results of the survey of 2007 (conducted in December 2006) were
reported by the British newspaper the *Telegraph* on January 10, 2007, in a
story headlined "France No Longer a Catholic Country." http://www
.telegraph.co.uk/news/worldnews/1539093/France-no-longer-a-Catholic
-country.html, accessed May 22, 2015. The figure of 3 percent for devout
Catholics in 2014 is given by Birnbaum, *Sur un nouveau moment antisémite,* 45.

58. Interview with Benjamin Dauplé, Paris, June 15, 2015.

59. Schaffner, "L'échec de *La Revue Juive* d'Albert Cohen," consulted online:
http://id.erudit.org/iderudit/1013324ar.

60. Finkielkraut, *Le Juif imaginaire,* 126.

61. Email from Nicolas Dauplé, January 9, 2015.

62. See Birnbaum, *Sur un nouveau moment antisémite,* 57–122. Taguieff explicitly contests the analogy with earlier forms of antisemitism in *La nouvelle
judéophobie,* 28–29, and *Une France antijuive?,* 22. Birnbaum cites Gilles

Kepel's remarks about the joining of two different strains of antisemitism in *Sur un nouveau moment*, 118, 143–44.

63. Zaretsky, "Next Year in Paris," *The Forward*, May 11, 2015; Pinto, *New Republic*, March 16, 2015; the special section of *Libération* mentioned in the preceding paragraph, "Juifs français, la tentation du départ," by Bernadette Sauvaget, appeared on September 26, 2014.

64. Reported in *Le Figaro*, among other newspapers, on January 10, 2016: http://www.lefigaro.fr/flash-actu/2016/01/10/97001-20160110FILWWW 00025-valls-sans-les-juifs-de-france-la-france-ne-serait-pas-la-france .php, consulted on April 16, 2016.

Bibliography and Sources

Works Cited

Unless otherwise stated, the place of publication for all works in French is Paris.

Works by Irène Némirovsky

The references below cite both the original publication information and the page numbers in Némirovsky's complete works: *Oeuvres complètes*, 2 vols., ed. Olivier Philipponnat. Librairie Générale Française (Pochothèque), 2009. Abbreviated as *OC*. Where English translations are available, their titles are indicated after the French.

"Nonoche chez l'extra-lucide," *Fantasio*, August 1, 1921; *OC* 1:49–56.

"La Niania," *Le Matin*, 9 May 1924; *OC* 1:80–88.

Le Malentendu. In *Les Oeuvres Libres*, February 1926; *OC* 1:89–206. *The Misunderstanding*. Translated by Sandra Smith. London: Chatto and Windus, 2012.

L'Enfant génial. In *Les Oeuvres Libres*, April 1927; reissued as *Un enfant prodige*, with a preface by Elisabeth Gille. Gallimard Jeunesse, 1992; *OC* 1:207–48. "The Child Prodigy." Translated by Julia Elsky. *Yale French Studies* 121 (2012): 229–61.

L'Ennemie (pseud. Pierre Nérey). In *Les Oeuvres Libres*, February 1928; *OC* 1:249–353.

Le Bal. In *Les Oeuvres Libres* [pseud. Pierre Nérey], February 1929; Grasset, 1930; *OC* 1:353–400. *The Ball*, in *David Golder, The Ball, Snow in Autumn, The Courilof Affair*. Translated by Sandra Smith, with an introduction by Claire Messud. New York: Knopf, 2008.

David Golder. Grasset, 1929; *OC* 1:401–550. *David Golder*—see above.

Les Mouches d'automne. Kra, 1931; *OC* 1:551–98. *Snow in Autumn*, see above.

L'Affaire Courilof. Grasset, 1933; *OC* 1:661–798. *The Courilof Affair*, see above.

Le Pion sur l'échiquier. Albin Michel, 1934. *OC* 1:833–967.

"Rois d'une heure." *1934. Le Magazine d'Aujourd'hui,* May 16, 23, 30, 1934.

Le Vin de solitude. Albin Michel, 1935; *OC* 1:1169–1368. *The Wine of Solitude.* Translated by Sandra Smith. New York: Knopf.

"Fraternité." *Gringoire,* February 5, 1937; in *Dimanche et autres nouvelles* (2000); *OC* 1:1623–34. In *Dimanche and Other Stories.* Translated by Bridget Patterson. New York: Random House, 2010.

Deux. Albin Michel, 1939.

Les Échelles du Levant. Gringoire, May–August 1939; retitled *Le Maître des âmes,* with a preface by Olivier Philipponnat and Patrick Lienhardt. Denoël, 2005; *OC* 2:201–388.

"La nuit en wagon." *Gringoire,* October 5, 1939; in *Dimanche et autres nouvelles; OC* 2:389–404.

"Le Spectateur." *Gringoire,* December 7, 1939; in *Dimanche et autres nouvelles; OC* 2:435–54. In *Dimanche and other stories.*

Les Chiens et les loups. Albin Michel, 1940; *OC* 2:509–700. *The Dogs and the Wolves.* Translated by Sandra Smith. London: Chatto and Windus, 2009.

"M. Rose." *Gringoire,* August 28, 1940; in *Dimanche et autres nouvelles; OC* 2:861–76. In *Dimanche and Other Stories.*

"L'incendie." *Gringoire,* February 27, 1942; in *Dimanche et autres nouvelles; OC* 2:1405–20.

La Vie de Tchekhov. Preface by Jean-Jacques Bernard. Albin Michel, 1946; *OC* 2:701–855.

Les Biens de ce monde. Albin Michel, 1947; *OC* 2:901–1088. *All Our Worldly Goods.* Translated by Sandra Smith. London: Chatto and Windus, 2008.

Les Feux de l'automne. Albin Michel, 1957; *OC* 2:1177–1374.

Dimanche et autres nouvelles. Preface by Laure Adler. Stock, 2000.

Destinées et autres nouvelles. Preface by Denise Epstein. Pin-Balma: Sables, 2004.

Suite Française. Preface by Myriam Anissimov. Denoël, 2004. *OC* 2:1455–1840. *Suite Française.* Translated by Sandra Smith. New York: Knopf, 2006.

Chaleur du sang. Edited with a preface by Olivier Philipponnat and Patrick Lienhardt. Denoël, 2007; *OC* 2:1841–1934. *Fire in the Blood.* Translated by Sandra Smith. New York: Knopf, 2007.

Other Books and Articles

Only some of the articles from newspapers and websites are listed below. Full references for others are given in the notes.

"A Portrait of Jewish Americans." Pew Center. October 2013, http://www.pewforum.org/files/2013/10/jewish-american-full-report-for-web.pdf.

Abel, Elizabeth, Marianne Hirsch, and Elizabeth Langland, eds. *The Voyage In: Fictions of Female Development.* Hanover, N.H.: University Press of New England, 1983.

Albera, François. *Albatros: des Russes à Paris, 1919–1929.* Cinémathèque française, 1995.

Aleichem, Sholem. *Tevye the Dairyman and the Railroad Stories.* Translated by Hillel Halkin. New York: Schocken Books, 1987.

Amossy, Ruth, and Anne Herschberg Pierrot. *Stéréotypes et clichés: Langue, discours, société.* Nathan Éditions, 1997.

Angenot, Marc. *Ce que l'on dit juifs en 1989: Antisémitisme et discours social.* Vincennes: Presses Universitaires de Vincennes, 1989.

Anissimov, Myriam. "Les filles d'Irène Némirovski." *Les Nouveaux Cahiers,* no. 108 (Spring 1992): 70–74.

———. *Romain Gary le caméléon.* Éditions Denoël, 2006.

Aragon, Louis, and Elsa Triolet. *Œuvres romanesques croisées d'Elsa Triolet et Aragon.* 26 vols. Robert Laffont, 1964–73.

Arban, Dominique. *Je me retournerai souvent . . . Souvenirs.* Flammarion, 1990.

Arendt, Hannah. *The Jewish Writings.* Edited by Jerome Kohn and Ron H. Feldman. New York: Schocken Books, 2007.

———. *The Origins of Totalitarianism,* 2d ed. New York: World Publishing, Meridian, 1958.

———. *Rahel Varnhagen: The Life of a Jewess.* Edited by Lilian Weissberg. Translated by Richard Winston. Baltimore: Johns Hopkins University Press, 1997. First published by the Leo Baeck Institute in 1957.

Aschheim, Steven. *Brothers and Strangers: The East European Jew in German and German Jewish Consciousness, 1800–1923.* Updated edition, with new introduction. Madison: University of Wisconsin Press, 1999.

"Au moment où paraît son dernier livre: Souvenez-vous d'Irène Némirovsky." *Tribune de Lausanne,* April 14, 1957. http://scriptorium.bcu-lausanne.ch/#.

Auscher, Janine. "L'actualité littéraire: Les romancières et leur métier." *Marianne,* May 16, 1934.

———. "Nos Interviews: Irène Némirovsky." *L'Univers Israélite,* July 5, 1935, 669–70.

———. "Sous la lampe: Irène Némirowsky." *Marianne,* February 13, 1935.

Babel, Isaac. *The Collected Stories of Isaac Babel.* Translated by Lionel Trilling. New York: Meridian Fiction, 1960.

Badinter, Robert. "Mort d'un Israélite français: Hommage à Maître Pierre Masse." *Le Débat,* no. 158 (2010): 101–7.

Bartov, Omer. *The "Jew" in Cinema: From the Golem to Don't Touch My Holocaust.* Bloomington: Indiana University Press, 2004.

Beauvoir, Simone de. *La Force des choses.* Gallimard, 1963.

———. *Journal de guerre, Septembre 1939–Janvier 1941.* Gallimard, 1990.

———. *Les Mandarins.* Gallimard, 1954.

———. *Mémoires d'une jeune fille rangée.* Gallimard, 1958.

Becker, Jean-Jacques, and Annette Wieviorka, eds. *Les Juifs de France de la Révolution à nos jours.* Éditions Liana Levi, 1998.

Bein, Alex. *The Jewish Question: Biography of a World Problem*. Translated by Harry Zohn. London: Associated University Presses, 1990.

Begley, Louis. *The Tremendous World I Have Inside My Head. Franz Kafka: A Biographical Essay*. New Haven: Yale University Press, 2008.

Benbassa, Esther. *Histoire des Juifs de France*. Éditions du Seuil, Collection Points Histoire, 1997.

Benjamin, Walter. *Illuminations*. Edited with an introduction by Hannah Arendt. Translated by Harry Zohn. New York: Schocken Books, 1968.

Bérard-Zarzycka, Ewa. "Les écrivains russes—Blancs et Rouges—à Paris dans les années 20." In *Le "Paris des étrangers" depuis un siècle*, ed. André Kaspi and Antoine Marès. Imprimerie nationale, 1989.

Béraud, Henri. *Gringoire: Écrits 1928–1937*. Edited by Georges Dupont. Consep, 2004.

———. *Gringoire: Écrits 1940–1943*. Edited by Georges Dupont. Consep, 2005.

———. *Les derniers beaux jours*. Plon, 1953.

Berberova, Nina Nikolaevna. *The Italics Are Mine*. New York: Harcourt, Brace and World, 1969.

Berl, Emmanuel, and Patrick Modiano. *Interrogatoire suivi de Il fait beau, allons au cimetière*. Gallimard, 1976.

Bernard, Jean-Jacques. "Judaïsme et Christianisme." *Le Figaro*, November 1, 1946.

———. *Le camp de la mort lente*. Éditions Albin Michel, 1944.

———. *Mon père Tristan Bernard*. Éditions Albin Michel, 1955.

Bernstein, Michel-André. *Foregone Conclusions: Against Apocalyptic History*. Berkeley: University of California Press, 1994.

Birnbaum, Pierre. *Les Fous de la République: Histoire politique des Juifs d'Etat, de Gambetta à Vichy*. Fayard, 1992.

———. *Léon Blum. Prime Minister, Socialist, Zionist*. New Haven: Yale University Press, 2015.

———. *Sur un nouveau moment antisémite*. Éditions Fayard, 2014.

Bona, Dominique. *Clara Malraux*. Éditions Grasset, 2010.

Bonnet, Jacques. "Ma mère, souviens-toi." *L'Express*, May 12–18, 1992.

Borland, Henri. *Merci d'avoir survécu*. Éditions du Seuil, 2011.

Bothorel, Jean. *Bernard Grasset: Vie et passions d'un éditeur*. Éditions Grasset, 1989.

Bourget-Pailleron, Robert. "La nouvelle équipe." *Revue des Deux Mondes*, November 1, 1936.

Bragin, Irina. 2009. "British Film Gives 'An Education' in Anti-Semitism." *Jewish Journal*, Los Angeles, December 2, 2009. http://www.jewishjournal.com/film/article/british_film_gives_an_education_in_anti-semitism_20091201/.

Bracher, Nathan. *After the Fall: War and Occupation in Irène Némirovsky's* Suite Française. Washington: Catholic University of America Press, 2010.

————. "Mere Humanity: The Ethical Turn in the Shorter Wartime Narratives of Irène Némirovsky." *Yale French Studies* 121 (2012): 34–53.

Brasillach, Robert. "La question juive." *Je suis partout*, April 15, 1938.

————. Review of *David Golder*, *L'Action Française*, January 9, 1930.

Bredin, Denis. *The Affair: The Case of Alfred Dreyfus*. Translated by Jeffrey Mehlman. New York: George Braziller, 1986.

Brenner, Michael, Vicki Caron, and Uri R. Kaufman eds. *Jewish Emancipation Reconsidered: The French and German Models*. London: Leo Baeck Institute, 2003.

Burko-Falcman, Berthe. *Un prénom républicain*. Seuil, 2007.

Cahen, Edmond. *Juif, non! . . . Israélite*. Librairie de France, 1930.

Carbuccia, Horace de. *Le Massacre de la Victoire, 1919–1934*. Plon, 1973.

Caron, Vicki. "The 'Jewish Question' from Dreyfus to Vichy." In *French History Since Napoleon*, ed. Martin S. Alexander. London: Arnold, 1999.

————. *Uneasy Asylum: France and the Jewish Refugee Crisis, 1933–1942*. Stanford: Stanford University Press, 1999.

Céline, Louis-Ferdinand. *Écrits polémiques*. Critical edition, ed. Régis Tettamanzi. Québec: Éditions 8, 2012.

————. *Mort à crédit*. Denoël, 1936.

————. *Voyage au bout de la nuit*. Denoël, 1932.

Chalier, Catherine. *Le désir de conversion*. Éditions du Seuil, 2011.

Chametzky, Jules. Introduction to *The Rise of David Levinsky*, by Abraham Cahan. New York: Penguin Books, 1993.

Cheever, Susan. *Home Before Dark*. Boston: Houghton Mifflin, 1984.

Chérau, Gaston. "Irène Némirovsky." *L'Intransigeant*, October 25, 1933.

Cheyette, Bryan, ed. *Between "Race" and Culture: Representations of "the Jew" in English and American Literature*. Stanford: Stanford University Press, 1996.

Cheyette, Bryan, and Nadia Valman, eds. *The Image of the Jew in European Liberal Culture 1789–1914*. Portland: Vallentine Mitchell, 2004.

Cixous, Hélène. "Coming to Writing." In *Coming to Writing and Other Essays*. Edited by Deborah Jenson. Cambridge: Harvard University Press, 1992.

Coetzee, J. M. "Irène Némirovsky: The Dogs and the Wolves." *New York Review of Books*, November 30, 2008, 34–38.

Cohen, Albert. *Solal*. Gallimard, 1930.

Colette. *Œuvres*. Edited by Claude Pichois. 4 vols. Gallimard, 1984–2001.

Conan, Éric, and Henry Rousso. *Vichy: Un passé qui ne passe pas*. Gallimard, 1996.

Copfermann, Emile. *Dès les premiers jours de l'automne*. Gallimard, 1997.

Courrière, Yves. *Pierre Lazareff, le vagabond de l'actualité*. Gallimard 1995.

————. *Joseph Kessel, ou Sur la piste du lion*. Plon, 1986.

Cyrulnik, Boris. *Je me souviens*. Éditions Odile Jacob, 2010.

————. *Sauve-toi, la vie t'appelle*. Éditions Odile Jacob, 2012.

————. *Un merveilleux malheur*. Éditions Odile Jacob, 2002.

Dawidowicz, Lucy S. *The War Against the Jews.* New York: Holt, Rinehart and Winston, 1975.

Deutscher, Isaac. *The Non-Jewish Jew and Other Essays,* ed. Tamara Deutscher. London: Oxford University Press, 1968.

Derrida, Jacques. "Avouer—l'impossible." *Le Dernier des Juifs.* Éditions Galilée, 2014.

Drake, David. *Paris at War, 1939–1944.* Cambridge: Harvard University Press, 2015.

Dreyfus, Alfred. *Capitaine Alfred Dreyfus, Souvenirs et correspondance publiés par son fils.* Éditions Grasset, 1936.

Du Bois, W. E. B. *The Souls of Black Folk.* Edited with an introduction and notes by Brent Hayes Edwards. New York: Oxford University Press, 2007.

Dupont, Joan. "A Daughter's Painful Quest." *International Herald Tribune,* March 31, 1992.

Durkheim, Émile. *Le Suicide: Etude de sociologie.* 1897; repr. Presses Universitaires de France, 1960.

Eiland, Howard, and Michael W. Jennings. *Walter Benjamin: A Critical Life.* Cambridge: Harvard University Press, 2014.

Elon, Amos. *The Pity of It All: A History of Jews in Germany, 1743–1933.* New York: Henry Holt, 2002.

Endelman, Todd. *Leaving the Jewish Fold: Conversion and Radical Assimilation in Modern Jewish History.* Princeton: Princeton University Press, 2015.

Epstein, Denise. *Survivre et Vivre: Entretiens avec Clémence Boulouque.* Gallimard, 2015.

Epstein, Efim. *Les Banques de commerce russes: Leur rôle dans l'évolution économique de la Russie, leur nationalisation.* Marcel Giard, 1925.

Ertel, Rachel. *Le roman juif américain: Une écriture minoritaire.* Éditions Payot, 1980.

"Êtes-vous partisan de l'entrée d'une femme à l'Académie Française?" *Toute l'édition,* April 15, 1939.

Ezrahi, Sidra DeKoven. "After Such Knowledge, What Laughter?" *Yale Journal of Criticism* 14, no. 1 (Spring 2001): 287–313.

Fejtő, François. *Hongrois et juifs.* Fayard, 1997.

Feldman, Marion. *Entre trauma et protection: quel devenir pour les enfants juifs cachés en France (1940–1944).* Toulouse: Éditions Érès, 2009.

Fernandez, Dominique. *Ramon.* Éditions Grasset, 2008.

Fernandez, Ramon. Review of *Le Vin de solitude. Marianne,* October 9, 1935.

Finkielkraut, Alain. *Le Juif imaginaire.* 1980; repr. Éditions du Seuil.

Foran, Charles. *Mordecai, the Life and Times.* Toronto: Alfred A. Knopf Canada, 2010.

Fouché, Pascal. *L'Édition française sous l'Occupation, 1940–1944.* Bibliothèque de Littérature contemporaine de l'Université de Paris 7, 1987.

Franklin, Ruth. "Scandale Française: The Nasty Truth About a New Literary Heroine." *New Republic,* January 30, 2008: 28–43.

———. "Elisabeth Gille's Devastating Account of Her Mother, Irène Némirovsky." *New Republic*, September 11, 2011.

Freud, Sigmund. *Three Essays on the Theory of Sexuality*. Translated by James Strachey. New York: Basic Books, 1905.

Friedländer, Saul. *Quand vient le souvenir.* 1978; repr. Éditions du Seuil.

Frydman, Marcel. *Le Traumatisme de l'enfant caché*. L'Harmattan, 2002.

Gary, Romain. *La promesse de l'aube*. 1960; repr. Gallimard, 1960.

Genette, Gérard. "Discours du récit." In *Figures III*. Éditions du Seuil, 1972.

Gilbert, Sandra, and Susan Gubar. *The Madwoman in the Attic: The Woman Writer and the Nineteenth-Century Literary Imagination*. New Haven: Yale University Press, 1979.

Gille, Elisabeth. *Le Mirador.* 1992; repr. with preface by René de Ceccatty, Éditions Stock, 2000.

———. *Le Crabe sur la banquette arrière*. Mercure de France, 1994.

———. "Nous avons peur." *Le Monde*, April 18, 1979.

———. *Un Paysage de cendres*. Éditions du Seuil, 1996.

Gilman, Sander L. *Jewish Self-Hatred: Anti-Semitism and the Hidden Language of the Jews*. Baltimore: Johns Hopkins University Press, 1986.

Gourfinkel, Nina. "L'expérience juive d'Irène Némirovsky: Une interview de l'auteur de *David Golder*." *L'Univers Israélite*, February 28, 1930, 677–78.

Gousseff, Catherine. *L'exil russe: La fabrique du réfugié apatride (1920–1939)*. CNRS Éditions, 2008.

Gray, Paul. "As France Burned." Review of *Suite Française*. *New York Times Sunday Book Review*, April 9, 2006.

Grynberg, Anne. "Après la tourmente." In *Les Juifs de France de la Révolution à nos jours*, ed. Jean-Jacques Becker and Annette Wieviorka, 249–86. Éditions Liana Levi, 1998.

Guedj, Jérémy. "Les Juifs français face aux Juifs étrangers dans la France de l'entre-deux-guerres." *Cahiers de la Méditerranée* 78 (2009): 43–73.

Gugelot, Frédéric. *La conversion des intellectuels au catholicisme en France (1885–1935)*. CNRS Éditions, 2010.

———. "De Ratisbonne à Lustiger: Les convertis à l'époque contemporaine," *Archives Juives*, no. 35 (2002/1): 8–26.

Halpérin, Jean, and Nelly Hansson, eds. *Comment vivre ensemble?* Albin Michel, 2001.

Hanák, Péter, ed. *Zsidókérdés, asszimiláció, antiszemitizmus*. Budapest: Gondolat, 1984.

Hazan, Katy, Benoît Verny, and Nadine Fresco, eds. *Pithiviers–Auschwitz 17 juillet 1942, 6h15*. Orléans: Éditions Cercil, 2006.

Hayet, Pierre. "Mgr Vladimir Ghika béatifié à Bucarest le 31 août 2013." http://blog.lanef.net/index.php?post/2013/08/01/Mgr-Vladimir-Ghika-b%C3%A9atifi%C3%A9-%C3%A0o-Bucarest-le-31-ao%C3%BBt-2013.

Hyman, Paula. *From Dreyfus to Vichy: The Remaking of French Jewry, 1906–1939*. New York: Columbia University Press, 1979.

Jackson, Julian. *France: The Dark Years, 1940–1944.* Oxford: Oxford University Press, 2001.

Jankélévitch, Vladimir. "Le Judaïsme, problème intérieur." In *La Conscience juive, données et débats,* ed. Eliane Amado Lévy-Valensi and Jean Halperin. Presses Universitaires de France, 1963.

Jewish Women and Their Salons: The Power of Conversation. Edited by Emily D. Bilski and Emily Braun. New York: The Jewish Museum and New Haven: Yale University Press, 2005. Exhibition catalog.

Julius, Anthony. *T. S. Eliot, Anti-Semitism, and Literary Form.* London: Thames and Hudson, 2003.

Kafka, Franz. *Diaries, 1910–1923.* Edited by Max Brod. Translated by Joseph Kresh and Martin Greenberg. New York: Schocken Books, 1975.

———. *Letters to Friends, Family and Editors.* Translated by Richard and Clara Winston. New York: Schocken Books, 1977.

Kaplan, Alice. *The Collaborator: The Trial and Execution of Robert Brasillach.* Chicago: University of Chicago Press, 2000.

———. "Love in the Ruins." Review of *Suite Française. The Nation,* May 29, 2006.

Kershaw, Angela. *Before Auschwitz: Irène Némirovsky and the Cultural Landscape of Interwar France.* New York: Routledge, 2010.

Klarsfeld, Serge. *Le Calendrier de la persécution des Juifs de France, 1940–1944.* Vol. 2: 1er juillet 1940–31 août 1942; and Vol. 3: septembre 1942–août 1944. Éditions Fayard, 2001.

———. *Mémorial de la déportation des Juifs de France.* Klarsfeld, 1978.

Kofman, Sara. *Rue Ordener rue Labat.* Éditions Galilée, 1994.

Kruger, Ruth. "Bearing Witness." Review of *Suite Française. Washington Post,* May 14, 2006.

Lacretelle, Jacques de. *Le Retour de Silbermann.* Gallimard, 1929.

———. *Silbermann.* Gallimard, 1922.

Lazare, Bernard. *Juifs et antisémites.* Edited by Philippe Oriol. Allia, 1992.

"Le Renaudot attribué, à titre posthume, à Irène Némirovsky," November 9, 2004. http://abonnes.lemonde.fr/archives/article/2004/11/09/le-renaudot -attribue-a.

Lefèvre, Frédéric. "Une révélation: une heure avec Irène Némirovsky." *Les Nouvelles Littéraires,* January 11, 1930.

Lessing, Thedor. *La Haine de soi: le refus d'être juif.* Translated by Maurice-Ruben Hayoun. Berg International, 1990.

Levi, Primo. *Survival in Auschwitz [Se questo è un uomo].* Translated by Stuart Wolf. New York: Collier Books, 1961.

Leymarie, Michel. "Les frères Tharaud: De l'ambiguïté du 'filon juif' dans la littérature des années vingt." *Archives juives* 2006/1, no. 39: 89–109.

Lichtenberger, André. *Mon Petit Trott.* Librairie Plon, 1931.

———. *Pourquoi la France est en guerre.* Comité Protestant des amitiés françaises à l'étranger, 1940.

Loewel, Pierre. *Tableau du Palais*. Gallimard, 1929.

"Loi du 3 octobre 1940." *Journal Officiel*, October 18, 1940. http://pages.livres deguerre.net/pages/sujet.php?id=docddp&su=103&np=876.

Marchandeau, Roger, and Georges Legras. *La Tragédie des Juifs montcelliens (1940–1945)*. Montceaux-les-Mines: la Physiophile, 2010.

Marienstras, Richard. *Être un peuple en diaspora*. François Maspero, 1975.

Marrus, Michael R., and Robert O. Paxton. *Vichy France and the Jews*. With a new foreword by Stanley Hoffmann. Stanford: Stanford University Press, 1995. Originally published in France in 1981 as *Vichy et les juifs* by Éditions Calmann-Lévy, and in English in 1982 by Basic Books.

Mariot, Nicolas, and Claire Zalc. *Face à la persécution: 991 Juifs dans la guerre*. Éditions Odile Jacob, 2010.

Marx, Karl. *Selected Writings*. Edited by Lawrence H. Simon. Indianapolis: Hackett, 1994.

Maudel, Gérard. "Ma mère, mon héroïne." Review of Gille, *Le Mirador*. *Libération*, February 13, 1992.

Meyer, Jules. "Les Juifs et la littérature." *L'Univers israélite*, October 30, 1925.

———. "L'assimilation des Israélites étrangers," *L'Univers Israélite*, July 3, 1925.

Mercier, Antoine. *Convoi No. 6: Destination Auschwitz 17 juillet 1942*. Le Cherche Midi, 2005.

———. *Un train parmi tant d'autre, 17 juillet 1942*. Le Cherche Midi, 2009.

Milligan, Jennifer. *The Forgotten Generation: French Women Writers of the Interwar Period*. Oxford: Berg, 1996.

Morand, Paul. *France la doulce*. Gallimard, 1934.

———. *Nouvelles complètes*. Vol. I. Edited by Michel Collomb. Gallimard, Bibliothèque de la Pléiade, 1992.

Moyn, Samuel. *A Holocaust Controversy: The Treblinka Affair in Postwar France*. Waltham: Brandeis University Press, 2005.

Moynot, Emmanuel. *Suite Française: Tempête en juin*. Éditions Denoël, 2015.

Nochlin, Linda, and Tamar Garb, eds. *The Jew in the Text: Modernity and the Construction of Identity*. London: Thames and Hudson, 1996.

Oudard, Georges. "Une expérience communiste. KON, DIT BELA KUN." *Gringoire*, February 5, 1937.

Paxton, Robert O. *Vichy France: Old Guard and New Order 1940–1944*. 1972; repr. New York: Columbia University Press, 2001.

Perec, Georges. *W, ou le souvenir d'enfance*. Gallimard, 1975.

Peschanski, Denis, and Thomas Fontaine. *La Collaboration, Vichy-Paris-Berlin, 1940–1945*. Éditions Tallandier, 2014.

Pétain, Philippe. "L'Éducation nationale." *La Revue des Deux Mondes*, August 15, 1940.

———. "La politique sociale de l'avenir." *La Revue des Deux Mondes*, September 15, 1940.

Philipponnat, Olivier, and Patrick Lienhardt. *La vie d'Irène Némirovsky*. Éditions Denoël, 2007.

Pinto, Diana. "I'm a European Jew—and No, I'm Not Leaving." *New Republic,* March 26, 2015.

Piperno, Alessandro. *Proust antijuif.* Translated by Franchita Gonzalez Batlle. Éditions Liana Levi, 2007.

Polizzotti, Mark. *Revolution of the Mind: The Life of André Breton.* London: Bloomsbury, 1995.

Poznanski, Renée. *Les Juifs en France pendant la Seconde Guerre mondiale.* Éditions Hachette, 1997.

Price, Naomi. "Out of the Ghetto." Review of *The Dogs and the Wolves. Times Literary Supplement,* October 30, 2009.

Proust, Marcel. *Du côté de chez Swann.* In *À la recherche du temps perdu.* Vol. 1, edited by Jean-Yves Tadié. Gallimard, Bibliothèque de la Pléiade, 1987.

Quaglia, Elena. "*L'Enfant génial* di Irène Némirovsky: il problema delle origini, tra appartenenza, allontanamento e impossibile ritorno." *Enfances francophones,* ed. Sara Arena et al. *Publif@rum,* n.22, 2014: http://www.publifarum .farum.it/ ezine_articles.php?art_id=302.

Raczymow, Henri. *Mélancolie d'Emmanuel Berl.* Gallimard, 2015.

Rebatet, Lucien. "Esquisse de quelques conclusions." *Je suis partout,* April 15, 1938.

Reed, Ishmael. "Fade to White." *New York Times,* February 5, 2010.

Reichmann, Edgar. "La Comète Némirovsky." *Le Monde,* February 7, 1992.

———. "Némirovsky, ou l'insouciance coupable de l'étre." *Le Monde,* June 9, 2000.

Reitter, Paul. *On the Origins of Jewish Self-Hatred.* Princeton: Princeton University Press, 2012.

Revah, Louis-Albert. *Berl, un Juif de France.* Éditions Grasset, 2003.

Richler, Mordecai. *The Apprenticeship of Duddy Kravitz.* London: André Deutsch, 1959.

———. *L'Apprentissage de Duddy Kravitz.* Translated by Elisabeth Gille-Némirovsky. Éditions Julliard, 1960.

Riding, Alan. *And the Show Went On: Cultural Life in Nazi-Occupied Paris.* New York: Alfred A. Knopf, 2010.

Robertson, Ritchie. *The "Jewish Question" in German Literature, 1749–1939: Emancipation and Its Discontents.* New York, Oxford University Press, 1999.

Rocheman, Lionel. "Spectatrice malgré elle." *Actualité Juive Hebdo,* no. 282, February 13, 1992.

Rosemont, Penelope, ed. *Surrealist Women: An International Anthology.* Austin: University of Texas Press, 1998.

Roth, Philip. "Defender of the Faith." *New Yorker,* March 14, 1959: 44–50.

———. *Goodbye Columbus and Five Short Stories.* New York: Houghton-Mifflin, 1959.

———. "Writing about Jews." In *Reading Myself and Others.* New York: Vintage, 2001.

Rousseau, Christine. "La fiction au 'top.'" *Le Monde*, February 10, 2005. http://abonnes.lemonde.fr/archives/article/2005/02/10/la-fiction-au-top_397.

Rousso, Henry. *Le syndrome de Vichy 1944–1987*. 2d rev. ed. Éditions du Seuil, 1990.

"Rue des Rosiers." Nos Échos. *L'Univers Israélite*, January 31, 1930.

Saint-Clair, Simone. *Ravensbrück: L'enfer des femmes*. Éditions Tallandier, 1945.

Samuel, Henry. "France 'no longer a Catholic country.'" *Telegraph*, January 10, 2007, http://www.telegraph.co.uk/news/worldnews/1539093/France-no-longer-a-Catholic-country.html.

Samuels, Maurice. *Inventing the Israelite: Jewish Fiction in Nineteenth-Century France*. Stanford: Stanford University Press, 2009.

———. "Jews and the Construction of French Identity from Balzac to Proust." In *French Global: A New Approach to Literary History*, ed. Christie McDonald and Susan Rubin Suleiman. New York: Columbia University Press, 2011.

Sapiro, Gisèle. *La Guerre des écrivains, 1940–1953*. Éditions Fayard, 1999.

Sarraute, Nathalie. *Œuvres complètes*. Edited by Jean-Yves Tadié. Gallimard, Bibliothèque de la Pléiade, 1996.

Sartre, Jean-Paul. *Carnets de la drôle de guerre, Novembre 1939–Mars 1940*. Gallimard, 1983.

Savigneau, Josyane. "Renaudot, Goncourt et marketing littéraire." *Le Monde*, November 11, 2004. http://abonnes.lemonde.fr/archives/article/2004/11/11/renaudot-goncourt-et.

Schaffner, Alain. "L'échec de *La Revue Juive* d'Albert Cohen." *Mémoires du livre / Studies in Book Culture* 4, no. 1 (Autumn 2012), http://id.erudit.org/iderudit/1013324ar.

Schor, Ralph. "Le Paris des libertés." In *Le Paris des étrangers depuis un siècle*, ed. André Kaspi and Antoine Marès. Imprimerie Nationale, 1989.

Sebbag, Georges. *André Breton, L'amour-folie: Suzanna Nadja Lise Simone*. Jean-Michel Place, 2004.

Semelin, Jacques. *Persécutions et entraides dans la France occupée*. Éditions du Seuil/Les Arènes, 2013.

Séry, Macha. "Le pays où l'archive est reine." *Le Monde*, October 10, 2014.

Showalter, Elaine. *A Literature of Their Own: British Women Novelists from Brontë to Lessing*. Princeton: Princeton University Press, 1977.

Shteyngart, Gary. *Little Failure: A Memoir*. New York: Random House, 2014.

Spire, Alexis. "Devenir français en 1931." In *Les étrangers au temps de l'Exposition coloniale*, ed. Laure Blévis, Hélène Lafont-Couturier, Nanette Jacomijn Snoep, and Claire Zalc. Gallimard/CNHI, 2008.

Sontag, Susan. *Illness as Metaphor and Aids and Its Metaphors*. New York: Doubleday Anchor, 1990.

Stevens, David. "Sylvia Bataille: Biography." Internet Movie Database (IMDb), http://www.imdb.com/name/nm0060663/bio?ref_=nm_ov_bio_sm.

Styron, Alexandra. *Reading My Father: A Memoir*. New York: Scribner, 2011.

342 Bibliography and Sources

Suleiman, Susan Rubin. *Authoritarian Fictions: The Ideological Novel as a Literary Genre.* New York: Columbia University Press, 1983.

———. *Crises of Memory and the Second World War.* Cambridge: Harvard University Press, 2006.

———. "The 1.5 Generation: Thinking about Child Survivors and the Holocaust." *American Imago* 59, no. 3 (Fall 2002): 277–95.

———. "Ideological Dissent from Works of Fiction: Toward a Rhetoric of the *roman à thèse.*" *Neophilologus* 60, no. 2 (April 1976): 162–77.

———. "The Jew in Jean-Paul Sartre's *Réflexions sur la question juive*: An Exercise in Historical Reading." In *The Jew in the Text*, ed. Linda Nochlin and Tamar Garb. London: Thames and Hudson, 1995.

———. "Réflexions sur la question américaine." In *Sartre et les Juifs*, ed. Ingrid Galster. La Découverte, 2005.

———. "Rereading Rereading, Further Reflections on Sartre's *Réflexions*," *October 87* (Winter 1999): 129–38.

Suleiman, Susan Rubin, and Éva Forgács, eds. *Contemporary Jewish Writing in Hungary: An Anthology.* Lincoln: University of Nebraska Press, 2003.

Taguieff, Pierre-André. *La nouvelle judéophobie.* Mille et une nuits / Fayard, 2002.

———. *Une France antijuive? Regards sur la nouvelle configuration judéophobe.* CNRS Éditions, 2015.

———, ed. *L'Antisémitisme de plume 1940–1944: Études et Documents.* Editions Berg International, 1999.

Thau, Norman David. *Romans de l'impossible identité: Être Juif en Europe occidentale (1918–1940).* Oxford: Peter Lang, 2001.

Thurman, Judith. *Secrets of the Flesh: A Life of Colette.* New York: Knopf, 1999.

Toury, Jacob. "'The Jewish Question': A Semantic Approach." *Yearbook of the Leo Baeck Institute.* Volume 2. London: Horovitz, 1996.

Valéry, Paul. "Allocution prononcée à l'occasion de la mort de M. Henri Bergson." Le 9 janvier 1941. http://www.academie-francaise.fr/allocution -prononcee-loccasion-de-la-mort-de-m-henri-bergson.

Vegh, Claudine. *Je ne lui ai pas dit au revoir.* Gallimard, 1979.

Vidal-Naquet, Pierre. *Les Juifs, la mémoire et le présent.* François Maspero, 1981.

———. *Mémoires.* 2 vols. Seuil / La Découverte, 1995.

Weil, Patrick. *Qu'est-ce qu'un Français? Histoire de la nationalité française depuis la Révolution.* Éditions Grasset, 2002.

Weinberg, David. *A Community on Trial: The Jews of Paris in the 1930s.* Chicago: University of Chicago Press, 1977.

Weininger, Otto. *Sex and Character: An Investigation of Fundamental Principles.* Edited by Daniel Steuer and Laura Marcus. Translated by Ladislas Löb. Bloomington: Indiana University Press, 2005.

Weiss, Jonathan. *Irène Némirovsky: Her Life and Works.* Stanford: Stanford University Press, 2006.

Wieviorka, Annette. *Déportation et génocide: Entre la mémoire et l'oubli.* Éditions Plon, 1992.

———. *L'ère du témoin*. Éditions Plon, 1998.

Woman of Letters: Irène Némirovsky and Suite Française. Edited by Olivier Corpet and Garrett White. New York: Five Ties, 2008. Exhibition catalog.

Zajde, Nathalie. *Les Enfants cachés en France*. Éditions Odile Jacob, 2012.

Zaretsky, Robert. "Next Year in Paris." *The Forward*, May 11, 2015.

Archives

Institut Mémoires de l'Édition Contemporaine (IMEC), Abbaye d'Ardenne, Caen. Fonds Némirovsky (NMR and ALM).

Institut National de l'Audiovisuel (INA), Bibliothèque Nationale, Paris.

Archives Départementales de Saône-et-Loire, Mâcon.

United States Holocaust Memorial Museum, Washington, D.C.

Centre de Documentation Juive Contemporaine, Paris.

Cercil-Musée des Enfants du Vél d'Hiv, Orléans.

Bibliothèque de l'Arsenal, Paris.

Bibliothèque de l'Institut, Paris.

Archives Nationales, Pierrefitte, France.

Interviews

Edwige Becquart (née Avot), Versailles, October 9, 2014.

René de Ceccatty, Montrouge, July 7, 2010.

Benjamin Dauplé, Paris, June 14, 2015.

Emmanuel Dauplé, Toulouse, June 25, 2013.

Irène Dauplé, Toulouse, June 23, 2011.

Juliette Dauplé, Toulouse, June 23, 2011.

Léa Dauplé, Paris, June 9, 2014.

Nicolas Dauplé, Volnaveys-le-Bas, June 5, 2014.

Nina Denat, Lille, January 20, 2016.

Denise Epstein, Toulouse, June 6, 2008, and June 23, 2011.

Rachel Ertel, Paris, July 5, 2010.

Marianne Féraud (née Gille), Aix-en-Provence, July 20, 2010.

Fabrice Gille, San Diego, Calif., April 29, 2010.

Anka Muhlstein, New York City, February 26, 2015.

Jean-Luc Pidoux-Payot, Paris, June 21, 2012.

Jean-Marc Roberts, Paris, July 23, 2010.

Patrick Salvain, Paris, December 13, 2010.

André Schiffrin, Paris, June 21, 2011.

Arlette Stroumza, Paris, December 13, 2010.

Denise Weill, Paris, July 12, 2010.

Acknowledgments

Many people and institutions have contributed to the making of this book. The Bacon Fund of the Department of Romance Languages and Literature at Harvard made possible my frequent research trips to France over a seven-year period. The Center for Advanced Holocaust Studies at the U.S. Holocaust Memorial Museum in Washington provided, through its invitation to occupy the Shapiro Senior Scholar position, an indispensable year of reading, writing, and reflection in 2009–10. My first presentations of this research were at the museum, in two informal seminars and in the public Shapiro lecture, delivered in February 2010. My conversations during those months with Sara Horowitz, Brett Kaplan, Jürgen Matthaus, and other Fellows and researchers at the Center proved invaluable for my thinking; the enthusiastic support of my friend and colleague Sonya Michel convinced me that there could be broad interest in this book. At the other end of the process, the semester I spent as a Faculty Fellow at the Texas A&M University Institute for Advanced Study in spring 2016 allowed me to put the finishing touches to the manuscript and present parts of the book in public lectures and class visits. I thank the colleagues and students at "Aggieland" for their warm welcome.

As my many references to him make clear, my personal and professional debt to Olivier Philipponnat is immense. His work on Némirovsky is indispensable to anyone writing about her, and he has shared with me many hard-to-find documents and discoveries of his own, rare acts of generosity among researchers. I am truly grateful to him for his generous friendship.

I deeply regret that Denise Epstein-Dauplé did not live long enough for me to thank her in person for her warmth and helpfulness over several years and for her ongoing interest in this work. Her son Nicolas Dauplé has taken on the job of representing the family, and I am grateful to him for his support and friendship. Other family members and friends of Denise and of Elisabeth Gille have provided unique personal reminiscences in my interviews with them; I thank them all for their invaluable help. I am also very grateful to the people I met in Issy-l'Évêque who had a connection to this story and who kindly showed me around: Madeleine and Denise Jobert, Elisabeth Kulik, and Renée Michaud as well as the mayor M. Nivot and the secretary of the *mairie*, M. Granger. And I thank Nicolas Weill for putting me in touch with his mother, Denise Weill, who remembered seeing Némirovsky's books on her family's bookshelves in the 1930s and shared other memories dating to the war years.

In the course of my research, librarians and archivists at the U.S. Holocaust Memorial Museum in Washington, the Institut Mémoires de l'Édition Contemporaine outside Caen, the Archives Départementales in Mâcon, and the Cercil-Musée des Enfants du Vél-d'Hiv in Orléans were unfailingly helpful. I want especially to thank Hélène Mouchard-Zay, a founder and president of the Cercil, for guiding me around the camp site of Pithiviers and for sharing her memories of her father, Jean Zay. Margot Adler, the great-granddaughter of Raïssa Adler, kindly helped me look for traces (alas, not there) of Michel Epstein and Irène Némirovsky in her family archives. The young historian Daniel Lee shared his enthusiasm over archival research and provided precious suggestions at an important moment, as this book was nearing completion.

I thank my faithful and efficient research assistant, Violeta Banica, for her important help in collecting materials and hard-to-find publications; she also drew up the family tree that figures in chapter 7. My research assistant in Texas, Jonathan Bibeau, did an outstanding job in preparing the index. Earlier, I had the excellent research help of Laura Connor, especially in tracking down essential newspaper and journal articles. John d'Amico sent me books from the library during the summer when I was away, writing.

A number of people have read parts of the manuscript in progress and provided valuable comments and suggestions or just plain encouragement: Murray Baumgarten helped me rethink the chapter on Némirovsky's Jewish protagonists, and Annette Wieviorka shared her vast knowledge as a historian of the Holocaust for the chapter on Némirovsky's choices during the war. Sharon Bryan, Nicolas Dauplé, Laura Davulis, Fabrice Gille, Sheila Malovany-Chevallier, Joan Nathan, Olivier Philipponnat, Allen Reiner, Daniel Suleiman, and Michael Suleiman read individual chapters. Alan Riding read the whole manuscript in its next-to-last incarnation with his expert editorial eye. Joe Golsan and I have been discussing Némirovsky, very productively for me, for many years, in public and in private; the same holds true for Alice Kaplan, whose books on French literary figures of the 1930s and 1940s are an inspiration, and Sandra Smith, whose translations of Némirovsky's works have contributed to their worldwide success. Other friends who have been prized interlocutors for me on this project include Constance Borde, Jeanette Demesteere, Marianne Hirsch, Andreas Huyssen, Maurice Samuels, Leo Spitzer, and Judith Vichniac. In the very early stages of this work I benefited from discussions with my late and much-regretted friend and colleague Svetlana Boym, Helen Epstein, Dan Jacobs, Anna and Paul Ornstein, Sue Quinn, and Steve Zipperstein. My agent, Charlotte Sheedy, has been exemplary in her patience and encouragement. My first editor at Yale, Steve Wasserman, read the manuscript in record time and made important suggestions about style. I am grateful to his successor, Sarah Miller, for her responsiveness and support. Eva Skewes has been a model of efficiency in shepherding the manuscript into production, as has Jeffrey Schier. Lawrence Kenney's superb copyediting has made me rethink many a word and rework many a sentence. I thank Pierre-Emmanuel Dauzat, who is translating the book into French, for his careful going-over of the English text.

My family, as always, has been a source of emotional support and of much-needed diversion over the course of writing this book—as have my good friends Wini Breines, Marcia Folsom, Ruth Perry, and (last but not least) Allen Reiner. I have dedicated the book to my grandchildren, who are an unalloyed joy to me and a hope for the future.

Index